AF184322

PRINTING AND THE BOOK TRADE IN THE WEST INDIES

PRINTING AND THE BOOK TRADE IN THE WEST INDIES

RODERICK CAVE

The Pindar Press

London 1987

Published by The Pindar Press
66 Lyncroft Gardens
London NW6 1JY

British Library Cataloguing in Publication Data

Cave, Roderick
Printing and the book trade in the West Indies. – (Studies in the history of printing: 5)
1. Printing–West Indies–History
I. Title
II. Series
686.2′09729 Z213.W46

ISBN 0 907132 35 9

Printed in Great Britain by Woolnough Bookbinding
Church Street, Irthlingborough, Northants

CONTENTS

BERMUDA
SCOTLAND
ENGLAND
0 200 400 kilometres
New Orleans
Mobile
St. Augustine
Nassau
BAHAMAS
TURKS & CAICOS
Havana
CUBA
Merida
CAYMAN IS
Montego Bay
Falmouth
Savanna la Mar
Kingston
JAMAICA
Le Cap
Puerto Plata
ST. DOMINGUE
St. Marc
Port-au-Prince
Aux Cayes
Santo Domingo
PUERTO RICO
San Juan
ST. THOMAS
ST. CROIX
ANGUILLA
ST. BARTHOLEMEW
ST. EUSTATIUS
ST. KITTS
NEVIS
ANTIGUA
MONTSERRAT
GUADELOUPE
DOMINICA
MARTINIQUE
ST. LUCIA
BARBADOS
ST. VINCENT
GRENADA
TOBAGO
Port of Spain
TRINIDAD
San Fernando
CURAÇAO
Caracas
Belize
BELIZE
BAY ISLANDS
Guatemala
MOSQUITO COAST
Cartagena
Panama
SPANISH MAIN
Georgetown
New Amsterdam
Paramaribo
Cayenne
THE GUIANAS
Bogota
0 200 400 600
kilometres
R.B.M.

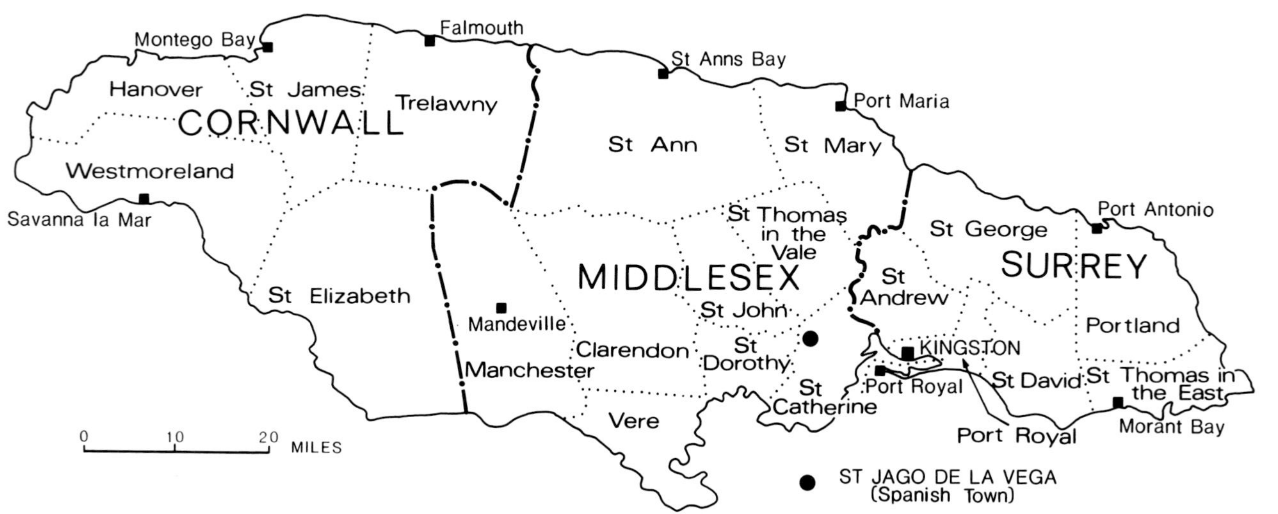

JAMAICA – SHOWING COUNTIES AND OLD PARISHES

PREFACE

An interest in printing in the Caribbean area was first aroused some twenty-five years ago during a period I spent working as a librarian in Jamaica and Trinidad. It would no doubt have remained entirely a passive interest had I not had the opportunity to return to the islands on a UNESCO assignment in 1972, to help set up new training programmes for librarians in Commonwealth Caribbean countries. In devising these programmes I believed it important that they should include an historical component, that there should be a course on 'The History of the Book' comparable with those given in British or American schools of librarianship, so that the West Indian librarians being trained had some appreciation of the importance of the older materials which would be under their care.

Very properly, the University of the West Indies in approving my proposals stipulated that the course on historical bibliography should have Caribbean content. The difficulty that was then presented was the dearth of suitable student texts which dealt at all with the West Indian book trade. Apart from Bradford F. Swan's useful but limited survey of *The Caribbean Area* prepared for the 'Spread of Printing' series edited by Colin Clair (Amsterdam, 1970) there was precious little available and in print. Among out-of-print material there were surveys of early printing in Jamaica by Frank Cundall, and in Guyana by James Rodway (both originally prepared at the instance of the American Antiquarian Society more than half a century earlier) and there were useful papers on Barbados by E. M. Shilstone, but for most territories there was nothing.

It was therefore initially in an attempt to provide suitable course material that I undertook the research represented by the selection of papers in this volume, many of which were first issued as interim 'Working Papers on West Indian Printing' by the University of the West Indies. The work was pleasurable in several ways. First, I was lucky enough to strike a vein of rich ore very early in my quarrying into the records held at the Jamaica Archives: the inventories of Thomas Craddock's books (no. 11) and of the island's first printer Robert Baldwin (no. 10) immediately provided substantial and important additions to the information gathered by Frank Cundall, who had not had access to these records. The richness of these records is indicated by the digest prepared of printers' wills and inventories (no. 9); enough came to light to sustain me through the long hours of searching. My investigations coincided with the increased study of provincial printing in Britain, with which many parallels could be drawn; D. F. McKenzie's work on Stationers Company apprentices also provided many useful clues on the men who had left Britain to work in the Antilles. As time went on the influence of the work towards the *Eighteenth Century Short Title Catalogue* provided additional stimulus. I should like to record the help Robin Alston and the ESTC team in the British Library gave, not only by bringing many West Indian imprints to my notice but also in other ways so many working on eighteenth century topics have shared.

Being based in Jamaica, most of my work originally was concentrated on the book trade of that island, which though in some respects untypical was by far the most substantial printing and publishing centre in the islands. Initially I used the resources of the West India Reference Library, Institute of Jamaica (now the National Library), the University of the West Indies Library, and the Jamaica Archives. Short periods spent working in the National Library, Belize, and in the Trinidad Archives and the Trinidad Public Library enabled me to undertake some work on early printing in those territories also.

A great difficulty in studying the book trade in the Caribbean colonies – as for other colonies, or indeed many provincial printing centres – is that many of their publications have not survived locally, but are to be found only in the copies taken or sent to Europe and North America. As well as having the *National Union Catalog* and other finding aids, and the chance to obtain xerox and microfilm copies which were not available to earlier writers, I have been fortunate to be able to spend some time working in the West Indian collections of several libraries in the United States. Of these, the American Antiquarian Society (to which I am indebted for a Fred Harris Daniels Fellowship in 1976), the New York Public Library, Library of Congress, Library Company of Philadelphia, John Carter Brown Library, Houghton Library (Harvard) and the New York and Massachusetts Historical Societies' libraries have proved most useful. In Britain, as well as using the Public Record Office, the British Library Reference Division, Bristol Reference Library, the Bodleian and Rhodes House Library (to name only some of the most important holdings) through the generous provision of a research grant by the British Academy I was able to explore some of the West Indian materials held in local record offices. Without the generous assistance unstintingly given by librarians and archivists in so many institutions, the essays here published could not have been prepared. As well as my thanks to them, I must also acknowledge the hospitality of the journal editors who published them, and have given permission for them to be reprinted here.

The arrangement adopted in this volume has been to give first place to papers dealing with aspects of the West Indian book trade in general (nos. 1–3) followed by those articles dealing with individual territories, arranged alphabetically. For those islands on which several papers are included, an approximately chronological sub-arrangement has been used (Jamaica, nos. 8–19; Trinidad, nos. 21–23). Because the early printing history of Barbados and Guyana has already been treated by Shilstone, Rodway and others, no attempt has been made to investigate these countries' bibliographical record. It will be evident that the total picture of the West Indian book trade is still very far from complete: apart from some discussion of the Danish island of St Croix in no. 3, and of the Swedish colony of St Bartholomew in no. 20, there is very little account in these essays of printing except in the British islands. Much work remains to be done on the very interesting printing history of such islands as Dominica, Grenada and St Lucia. (A survey article, indicating some of the available resources and desiderata was published on 'West Indian Printing' in the *Encyclopedia of Library and Information Science*, volume 33, pp. 25–38, New York 1982).

In this volume, I have where possible taken the opportunity to correct or augment the information given in the original papers. As the offset-litho reprint form does not allow for more than very modest change to the original text, some repetition of background information appears in several of the articles. For some, published before only as 'Working Papers on West Indian Printing' (nos. 15, 21, 23) the need for resetting has allowed more substantial revision, as has also been done for no. 3, originally presented at a conference held at the American Antiquarian Society in 1980. The papers on the Bahamas (no. 4), Grenada (no. 7), on the hydrographer Bernard Romans (no. 15) and on proposals for papermaking in Jamaica (no. 19) have not previously been published.

I hope that together these papers show that the book trade in the West Indies in the eighteenth and early nineteenth centuries was of much more importance than has generally been recognised – an importance not just as part of these islands' individual histories, but as an aspect of European expansion in general – and that the selection given here will be of use to others who work on the book trade and cultural history of the former colonies.

RODERICK CAVE
WELLINGTON, NEW ZEALAND

GENERAL ASPECTS OF PRINTING IN THE WEST INDIES

I

EARLY PRINTING AND THE BOOK TRADE IN THE WEST INDIES [1]

This paper considers developments in printing prior to 1865 in the British colonies in the Caribbean plus those Dutch, Danish, French, and Swedish colonial possessions which were influenced by the British islands. The reasons for the establishment of presses in these West Indian colonies are examined. Official printing, newspapers, periodicals, and ephemera formed the mainstay of the West Indian printer's business. Though there was some literary publication at the end of the eighteenth century, accompanied by the start of subscription libraries, the decline of the planter class and the weakening of the sugar colonies' economic position prevented indigenous publishing from developing successfully.

At the time of the independence of the not far distant American colonies, the West Indian islands were established and rich colonies, in several of which printing had long been exercised. Kingston, Jamaica, was preceded only by Boston in the publication of a regular weekly newspaper. Barbados had printing before South Carolina, Antigua and St. Christopher (better known as St. Kitts) before North Carolina and New Jersey [1, pp. 59–60]. Although by the time the thirteen American colonies became independent printing had not been introduced into all the West Indian islands — and was not to reach some of them for a remarkably long time[2] — there were sufficient centers and enough work being produced for us to consider the West Indian printer as distinct from the American colonial printer and to make a study of early printing and the book trade in the Caribbean of some interest.

There are, of course, many difficulties in an attempt of this kind. The

1. The research for this paper was in part made possible by a Daniels Fellowship at the American Antiquarian Society, to which my thanks are due as to the other libraries on whose holdings I have drawn. The paper was originally delivered at a meeting of the Liverpool Bibliographical Society in May 1977.

2. Printing was not introduced into the Turks Islands until the mid-1840s or the Dutch island of Aruba until the beginning of this century. In the Cayman Islands there was no press until after World War II.

geographical limits of the "West Indies" are imprecise, and the patterns of political control constantly changed until the end of the Napoleonic Wars. Bibliographical history is but one minor aspect of cultural history, and one can no more account for printing developments in many of the islands, except against the backdrop of their constant transfer back and forth between France and England, than one could disregard the War of Independence in considering Massachusetts printing in the 1770s. Even for those colonies, like Jamaica and Barbados, which remained securely British, the economic and social effects of the political kaleidoscope had a distinct effect. The "West Indies" in fact is not a unit; each island had its distinctive political and cultural history, just as it had its own racial and religious mix.

English administrators in the early nineteenth century often found it extremely difficult to cope with this complexity—that St. Lucia was governed under prerevolutionary French law, Trinidad by Spanish law, or Demerara according to the regulations of the Dutch West India Company. So difficult was it that, in at least one instance, advice had to be sought from the previous colonizing power.[3] These local differences had their bibliographical effect, notably in control of the periodical press.

A further difficulty in the study of early printing and the book trade in the area arises from the dearth of material on the book trade in the West Indies. With a handful of exceptions—Isaiah Thomas, Douglas McMurtrie, Bradford Swan—historians of typography have ignored it. There have been no regional studies, and the accounts of printing on individual islands have been written in most cases by local historians (often amateur) without special interest in bibliographical niceties and without access to a wide range of material, for the documents printed in the Indies which must form the basis for such accounts are excessively rare. With the exception of a handful of Caribbean libraries with respectable collections of local printing, "West Indiana" is not to be found in the islands at all. Instead, it is in the archives of the colonizing powers and in some of the research libraries of Europe and North America, such as the Royal Library, Stockholm, or John Carter Brown or the Bodleian.[4]

3. In the mid-1820s, the British Foreign Office had to seek explanation and elucidation from The Hague to clarify the role of the Court of Policy in the government of Demerara [2, pp. 588–89]. Similar problems had been encountered earlier with Spanish law in Trindad by Governors Picton and Hislop [3].

4. Jerome Handler's *Guide to Source Materials for the Study of Barbados History, 1627-1834* (Carbondale, Ill.: Southern Illinois University Press, 1971) is the only adequate guide to resources of the kind needed for a definitive study; Lowell Ragatz's seminal *Guide for the Study of British Caribbean History, 1763–1834* (Washington, D.C.: Carnegie Corp., 1932) is fatally flawed for this purpose by the lack of locations for works cited.

The present study, limited originally to those West Indian territories which are part of the British Commonwealth, has been extended to include those other Caribbean territories which had a formal British presence or British influence long enough to have bibliographical implications. In fact, this definition let in all the territories of all the other European colonial powers with the exception of Spain. The Spanish colonies' bibliographical history is so different from that of the other powers (Denmark, France, Holland, and Sweden) that it seemed more helpful to leave it out of consideration, save in the case of Trinidad, which was not taken from the Spanish by Britain until 1797. On the other hand, those British, Dutch, and French colonies in Central and South America whose cultural and economic (and bibliographical) ties were with the Caribbean colonies were included. For the purposes of this study, therefore, "West Indies" includes Bermuda, the Bahamas, Belize (British Honduras), and the Guianas but excludes Cuba and Puerto Rico.

The cutoff point for the study is 1865. As the date of the Morant Bay rebellion in Jamaica and almost exactly a century and a half from the introduction of printing, it is a particularly appropriate terminal point for the study of that island. For the British islands of the eastern Caribbean, 1876 would have been more meaningful, but for the area as a whole any date is arbitrary. However, the sixties or early seventies were in most cases the nadir of the islands' cultural and economic success and provide a reasonable dividing point between the period in which printing catered to the planter class and that of the emergence of new nationalist movements. In purely typographic terms, also, these decades mark the break between old hand production and the mechanized methods which assumed a more important place in the last third of the nineteenth century.

The Early West Indian Book Trade

Between the discovery of the West Indies by Columbus in the 1490s and the introduction of printing into the islands, there was a period of over two centuries of European colonization. It was, of course, slow: for nearly a century after Columbus the settlement was limited to the Spanish. But from the early seventeenth century on there was effective settlement by the British, Dutch, and French, and rather later by the Danes. Of course, the pattern of settlement was uneven: St. Vincent remained largely under Carib control until the second half of the eighteenth century, for instance. By 1700, there were substantial numbers of Englishmen in St. Kitts, Barbados, and Jamaica; of Frenchmen in

Martinique, Guadeloupe, and St. Domingue;[5] and of Dutchmen in Curaçao and the Guianas. However primitive these early settlers' societies may have been, they had a need for books, which were imported from the mother countries. What books these were (beyond the obvious devotional works) there is little surviving evidence to show. The inventory of the Port Royal merchant Thomas Craddock [4], who may have been the first Jamaican bookseller, is the only informative seventeenth-century record that has been traced.

By the early eighteenth century, there were facilities for bookbinding in Jamaica [5, pp. 9–10] and no doubt in other islands. In 1702, the British West Indian colonies were placed under the ecclesiastical control of the bishops of London. An inquiry addressed to his clergy by the bishop in 1725 reveals that there had been a good parish library in Port Royal some years earlier. However, the rector, Calvin Galpin, stated in his reply to the bishop that most of the books had been lost before his arrival in July 1721 and the rest since destroyed in a hurricane [6, fols. 215–16].[6]

The Anglican church was also responsible for at least one other parish library set up in Jamaica at this time. Records survive which list the "books sent 1st April 1724 wth Mr. Barrett Missionary to Jamaica towards a Catechetical Library . . . in the Parish to w[ch] he shall be appointed" [6, fols. 175–80]. Barrett was a recent convert from Roman Catholicism, and the books were in part intended to keep him personally steadfast in the Protestant faith, but they were also supposed to be used in catechizing the children of Negro slaves. Whether such titles as *Dr. Clarkes Practical Essays on Baptism, . . . Bp̄ Gibson on the Sacrament of the Lords Supper, Bp̄ Fleetwoods Reasonable Communicant,* [and] . . . *Mr. Kettlewells Death Made Comfortable or the Way to Dye Well* were an ideal selection for this purpose is open to question; what is interesting is that at this early period, and through the established church (commonly thought not to be interested in slaves), attempts at religious education were made through libraries of this kind.

The Introduction of Printing

Before presses were set up in the islands, material of local interest was produced elsewhere, either in the mother country or in the North American colonies. In 1703, for instance, a sermon preached in Kingston by William Corbin on June 7 (the anniversary of the great

5. That is, the French colony in the western part of Hispaniola now known as Haiti.
6. Probably in the great hurricane of August 28, 1722.

earthquake which devastated Fort Royal in 1692) was printed by William Bradford in New York [5, p. 1]. Similarly, when the Barbados Assembly passed a bill about privateers in 1698, it prayed the governor and council that the bill should be sent to New England to be printed—and printed it was, also by William Bradford in New York [7, p. 19].

To use the resources of one colony to fill the needs of another was a commonplace device of the old empire. It was one which was to continue in the West Indies for many years after the introduction of the first presses. Thus, Jamaican printers were employed to print material for the British settlements in the Bay of Honduras [8] and in the Cayman Islands. Antiguan printers supplied the wants of the British Virgin Islands; Nevis was served from St. Kitts. Political changes in the eighteenth century often imposed other temporary patterns of trade in which, for example, French royalist printers in Dominica printed material for circulation in Martinique, or St. Kitts printers moved for safety to the Dutch island of St. Eustatius. Most of such patterns are easily explained in terms of trade or shipping routes or the political and administrative structure. [7]

But some intercolonial trade in printing is much harder to understand. Why did the Abbé Roland have his *Mercure des Antilles*, which was intended for circulation in St. Domingue, printed with great trouble in Jamaica [9]? How did the printers of the *Bridgetown Ledger* in 1887 secure the position of printers to the constabulary in (British) Honduras, almost 2,000 miles distant from Barbados? In some cases, there is no doubt that the tiny local market on any one island was an influential factor, at any rate in the eastern Caribbean. [8] For instance, when in 1795 Henry Thornhill wrote *A Narrative of the Insurrection and Rebellion in the island of Grenada* immediately after the rebellion was crushed, he was unable to get it printed on the island, as the one local printer had already undertaken publication of Thomas Turner Wise's *Review of the events, which happened in Grenada* (St. George's, 1795). Even when, in 1797, Thornhill moved to Barbados he found the publisher of the *Barbados Mercury* equally unwilling. Only when a new printing house set up in business the following year was he able to have "recourse to the proprietor thereof, who was pleased to undertake and print the following sheets" [8, pp. 29–31].

The circumstances under which printers were introduced to the colonies follow several patterns.

7. Both the Bay settlements and the Caymans came within the area administered by the governors of Jamaica, for example.
8. For distribution of locally printed books, see below, "Publications of the West Indian Printers."

A government-controlled press, introduced at the wish of the local population and authorities.—In the case of the first press in the Antilles (that of Robert Baldwin in Jamaica, 1718), the council of the island and the governor-designate, Sir Nicolas Lawes, obtained permission from London for the introduction of a press. To persuade the commissioners for trade and plantations, however, Sir Nicolas suggested that "there should be but one, and that licensed to the Govr. for the time being," and for the first year or two each issue of the *Weekly Jamaica Courant* carried an imprimatur [10, p. 13]. In Belize, the first press was a public press [11]. In the Dutch colony of Demerara, a similar situation obtained for the press of J. C. de la Coste, in support of whose wish to start a paper the Court of Policy applied to the Hague for approval [12, pp. 3–8].

Presses for which a privilege had been granted by the metropolitan power.—This was the pattern in the French islands and an unsuccessful one. A *brevet d'imprimeur* was granted to a bookseller from Metz named Joseph Payen for the "Isles sous le vent" in April 1723. However, when the unfortunate printer arrived in St. Domingue, Governor de la Rochelard prevented him from establishing his printing office and had him imprisoned for selling obscene books. On his release, still circumvented by the governor, Payen was unwise enough to print the text of his letters patent at Léogane, with the false statement that it was "par ordre de M. le Chevalier de Rochelard," for which he was again imprisoned. This time he got the message and left for France as soon as released. The next printer did not set up office until 1764 [13, pp. 4—6]. It appears that the authorities in Martinque were no more welcoming than in St. Domingue: though a *brevet d'imprimeur* was granted in 1729, it was not until the 1760s that a printer set up in the island [14, p. 41]. A *brevet d'imprimeur* for Guadeloupe was granted by Louis XV to Jean Bénard in June 1764, and he established himself in Basse Terre the following spring [15, pp. 1, 23–25].

In only one instance does metropolitan planning seem to have envisaged sending out a press as a part of first settlement of a new colony—though "planning" may be the wrong word for the crack-brained Scottish schemes in Darien. Nevertheless, William Simpson, printer of Edinburgh, was contracted to perform the printing needed by the Scottish settlers at forty shillings per month, and had the venture succeeded Darien would have been the first Caribbean colony with its own press [16, p. 104].

Presses established as entrepreneurial ventures.—The press set up in Barbados by Benjamin Franklin's old colleague David Harry in 1730 and the

Antigua press which Franklin set up in 1748 under his employee Thomas Smith (and, after Smith's death, Franklin's own nephew Benjamin Mecom) appear to have been normal business ventures undertaken by shrewd businessmen [7, 17]. Later in the century, J. Stockdale's establishment of a press in Bermuda followed the same commercial instincts [18], while in many instances the establishment of second or subsequent printing houses in a colony came from the expectation (often disappointed) that the local society could support several printers.

Presses established as a result of conquest or occupation.—In many instances, English-language papers, issued from presses run by British subjects, rapidly followed the pattern of conquest. Joseph Berrow, in St. Lucia in the early 1780s, and Matthew Gallagher, in Trinidad (from 1799), are instances of the printing trade following the flag. Other British printers were active in Curaçao [19, pp. 39–40] and in the Danish Virgin Islands during the British occupation in the Napoleonic Wars. Similarly, there was a press with the British expeditionary force in St. Domingue (1793–98), while during Napoleon's abortive attempts to reconquer the island there was also a French press in the city of Santo Domingo itself. In other instances, after conquest, printers already established in a colony merely trimmed their sails to the wind: George Burnett was *imprimeur du roi* in Tobago during the French occupation in the late 1780s, while in Guadeloupe, one Ginet was official printer during the British occupation, 1810–14 [15, pp. 27–30].

Presses established as an escape from war.—On several islands, printing was introduced as a result of wars elsewhere. Save in Nassau, to which John Wells, printer of the *East Florida Gazette*, moved (when St. Augustine was evacuated by the British) in 1784, the Loyalists were not responsible for the spread of printing. [9] However, there seems little doubt that the introduction of printing into the Dutch island of St. Eustatius (Statia) in the late 1780s and into the Swedish colony of St. Bartholomew in the early years of the nineteenth century resulted from the unsettled state of the neighboring islands [19, pp. 37–39].

9. Several Loyalists were of importance in the colonial book trade in Jamaica, however: William Aikman from Annapolis and his brother Alexander Aikman, who had worked in Charleston, S.C., for Robert Wells (father of John Wells of Nassau) and was to become king's printer and a very wealthy man.

Presses established through colonial pride.—In Belize, though the first press was publicly owned, its introduction may be taken as an instance of local pride [11, pp. 21–22]. It may possibly have been a misguided entrepreneurial instinct which led Samuel Nelmes to set up shop in Grand Turk in 1845, but the separatist movement which three years later succeeded in having the Turks Islands removed from control of Nassau and made into a separate colony was also influential [20]. As no copies of the *Carriacou Observer* seem to survive, it is not possible to say why Alexander Murray set up there in the mid-1840s, unless the independent spirit of the inhabitants of this tiny island in the Grenadines (a chain of islets between St. Vincent and Grenada) was an influential factor: it seems an improbable choice for a purely commercial venture.

Presses set up with official support to counter prevailing attitudes.—In several instances, when the editorial tone of an existing colonial paper aroused official displeasure, other printers were invited to set up in competition. Thus in Bermuda, when the printers of the *Bermuda Gazette* had published some libelous attacks on Governor Hodgson, he invited Edmund Ward from Halifax to become king's printer [18, pp. 5–6]. The recalcitrant attitude of the planters and their newspapers in the period immediately before and after the emancipation of the slaves in 1834 led to the establishment of papers in both Jamaica and Trinidad which propounded the home government's colonial policies [21, vol. 2, pp. 264–67].

Presses set up for special political or religious reasons.—In the nineteenth century, as the number of presses increased, some were set up deliberately to further the interests of particular groups. In general, the older, established papers reflected the interests of the planters and merchants. In both Jamaica and Barbados, papers of a liberal cast which were aimed at the colored population appeared from the 1830s on. In other cases, Catholic papers were produced. In Guyana, the gold rush of the 1850s led to the production of such special interest papers as the *Nugget* and the *Gold Mining Gazette*. In the same colony, the 1870s saw the publication of *A Voz Portuguez, A Liberdade,* and other Portuguese papers catering to the Madeiran element in the population.

Though some unusual features appear in these different categories, no doubt, there is considerable resemblance to the expansion of printing in other parts of the world. It is worth remembering, though, that the West Indies were more dangerous and presented more difficulties to the intending printer than is apparent from this dry account. Losses at sea were not uncommon;[10] earthquakes and hurricanes took a regular toll.

In one instance, a printer's adventures had a Hollywood epic quality. Donald McPhee Lee, having gone from Bermuda to Halifax to obtain types for his new paper, the *Royal Gazette*, reembarked for Bermuda in the sloop *Sally Ann* in October 1827. The master of the sloop had no chronometer and little knowledge of navigation, and for two months the vessel drifted around the Gulf Stream until provisions had run out and the vessel was dismasted in a storm. A Spanish privateer was persuaded not to blow them out of the water but to replenish their supplies. With Lee navigating the sloop—the captain having gone blind—they made landfall in Bermuda on the seventy-seventh day out. So carefully had Lee guarded his heavy boxes that the crew were convinced they contained gold. One can imagine their surprise when—having carried them ashore through the surf—the boxes were opened to reveal not gold but printing type [22, pp. 204–5].

The Printers

What sort of men were the early West Indian printers, and where did they come from? This is an interesting question to which a partial answer is possible. Of particular interest is the role of the Sephardic Jews. Apparently responsible for the first press in Curaçao[11] and certainly active in early printing in Surinam [24], members of this small group were of great importance in nineteenth-century Jamaica, where the *Daily Gleaner*—the oldest of West Indian newspapers still appearing—remained under the control of the De Cordova family for many years [25].

In many instances, it is possible to identify the printers who came to the islands with some precision. Whether Jamaica's first printer, Robert Baldwin, is to be identified with the Stationers' Company apprentice freed by patrimony on February 6, 1716, is uncertain,[12] but in many instances it is possible to trace the printers' earlier careers, however sketchily. The records preserved in the Jamaica Archives are rich in the

10. For example, Michael Ryan, proprietor of the *Barbados Globe* and printer to the Assembly, set sail from Newfoundland to Bridgetown in 1828 in a vessel which disappeared without a trace.
11. The inventory of the estate of Jeosuah Guidon Mendes, who died in Curaçao in 1797, included a small printing press [23]. I am indebted to Eugene S. Richardson, Jr., for this reference.
12. He may have been connected with the Baldwins who were active in the London book trade, but no certain evidence has come to hand.

wills and inventories of the estates of those in the book trade. One can learn much about many of these men.[13] Robert Sherlock, a printer at Spanish Town and the first to exercise the art at Montego Bay, for example, was the son of Robert Sherlock, printer in the Strand, London. He was apprenticed to William [Mc]Faden in 1752 and when he died, in 1779, left an estate of some £3,000, most of which, apart from provision for his "housekeeper" and bequests to friends, was left to his younger brother Thomas, a printer in London. No detailed study of these records has yet been made,[14] but they offer many interesting sidelights on the lives of the Jamaican printers. Most, like Sherlock, had colored mistresses; only the most well-to-do printers seem to have been married to white women, and even then their wills often include bequests to various side children.[15] The wills reveal the riches that could be gained by the successful—James Fannin, of Montego Bay, was worth nearly £12,000 on his death in 1809 and Alexander Aikman some £13,600 in 1838—and the relative poverty of others like Alexander Davidson, whose work on the *Jamaica Gazette* in 1759 resulted in an estate of no more than £164 in value.[16] These were, of course, master printers. Their employees seldom had estates worth making an inventory; indeed, often the only record of their existence that I have been able to trace is in the obituary columns in the Jamaican press.

For a few of the more prosperous Jamaican printers, it is possible to establish family trees which illustrate the ramifications of their business concerns. Alexander Aikman and his son of the same name controlled official printing in Jamaica for many years and operated some successful bookselling and stationery ventures, as well as the prosperous *Royal Gazette*. Another family, the Lunans, controlled the *St. Jago de la Vega Gazette* and the *Kingston Chronicle* and various bookselling concerns for a long period. The Strupars had the *Jamaica Courant* and other papers under their control for nearly fifty years, from the 1780s onward. For

13. I am indebted to Donald McKenzie for assistance in identifying many West Indian printers in the records of the Stationers' Company.
14. A preliminary list, "A Digest of the Wills and Inventories of Members of the Jamaican Book Trade," has been published in *Working Papers on West Indian Printing*, no. 18 (1976).
15. West Indian attitudes to racial origins were ambivalent and different from those in the United States. Most housekeeper/mistresses were described as "mulattoes" or "free women of color" and were apparently free women of mixed blood rather than slaves or of pure African origin. Doubtless some of the white women, like the printers they married, were of mixed blood but were sufficiently high in the social scale for this to be forgotten.
16. Jamaican currency; in sterling, the sums quoted would be reduced by one-third.

such families, printing and bookselling were but a part of their activities. All these families owned extensive lands: the Aikmans the properties of Wallenfield, Dunsinane, and Birnamwood, the Strupars the coffee plantation of Bellevue in the Port Royal Mountains. They had made it into the ranks of the plantocracy.

It is also possible to reconstruct many details of the lives of such men from secondary sources. Yet only one printer in Jamaica, as far as I can trace, has left a firsthand account of his affairs. A series of autobiographical letters written by Curtis Brett (1720-84) to his son gives an excellent account of the way in which an industrious and lucky printer could make his fortune in the Caribbean. Apprenticed to a Dublin bookseller/printer who failed in business, he moved to London, where from 1743 to 1748 he worked for William Strahan. In 1748, he was tempted by a gentleman going to Jamaica to join him as a storekeeper and to invest his own small savings in a cargo of goods on his own account. In Jamaica, he set up in partnership with another merchant, lost everything, and was reduced to working as a plantation overseer. His fortunes gradually rose: having become partner in an ironmonger's business in Spanish Town (the Jamaican capital), his background as a printer became known to various members of the assembly who wanted a press set up in that town as a counter to the Kingston press. With support from them, he returned to London (where he arranged the printing of an edition of the *Laws of Jamaica* by his old master) to purchase equipment and on his return commenced publication of the *St. Jago Intelligencer* on May 8, 1756. "From that time to this," he observed with some complacency, "I have never . . . been in want of money." He was a capable printer and a hardworking one. Within five years he had amassed a fortune of some £5,000 and "having had the marrow of the printing business . . . thought it proper to quit and turn merchant" [26, 27].

Few other islands have such rich records, and it is particularly hard to gather such detail for them. The earliest printers were often English, sometimes Scots or Irish. By the beginning of the nineteenth century, Scots printers predominated, and the lack of centralized Scottish records comparable to those of the Stationers' Company make it difficult to trace their history before they went to the Indies. In the French colonies, the early printers came from France, as those in Surinam were of Dutch origin. But in the Danish Virgin Islands and in the Netherlands Antilles, most of the early printers seem to have been of British birth or descent. In the Swedish island of St. Bartholomew, the first printer was Swedish, but the press soon passed into English hands.

At what stage creole printers took over from the expatriates is difficult to judge. The colonial printers took creole apprentices, and by the early nineteenth century many printing businesses were owned by local men with local training, but there was a steady, if diminishing, flow of craftsmen to the islands until the last days of colonial rule, at any rate at the more senior levels.

The mobility of many of the printers who worked in the West Indies was reminiscent of fifteenth-century Europe. Jean Cassan had printed in Grenada before moving to (Spanish) Trinidad. Matthew Gallagher, the first printer in Trinidad under British rule, had worked previously in Dominica and Grenada and was later to spend some time in Caracas setting up the subsidiary firm of Gallagher y Lamb. Sextius Buffardin, originally from Aix, worked in both Dominica and Guadeloupe and Joseph Berrow in Dominica, then St. Lucia, and finally St. Vincent, where he was the first printer. Sometimes their moves came as a result of political changes, sometimes because they saw economic advantage in moving to a fresh territory. Alexander Holmes, for example, who had served his apprenticeship in Edinburgh, started the *Bermudian* in St. George's as a rival to the long established *Bermuda Gazette* in 1819. After some initial success, he ran afoul of the governor and had to leave Bermuda in 1823 [18, 22]. For a while he worked in a subordinate capacity in Falmouth, Jamaica, eventually in 1828 managing to buy the plant and copyright of the old, established *Cornwall Chronicle* in Montego Bay. Despite his editorial espousal of the planters' cause in the controversy over emancipation (an economic necessity with his early readership, and in any case his was a less fanatical advocacy than that of some other Jamaican papers), he successfully conducted the paper until his death in 1862, being remembered as "a genial old Scotchman" [28].

Other expatriates were less fortunate than Holmes. As suggested above, the risk of death from disease was not inconsiderable. As late as 1870 Otto Wenkstern, a Prussian who was proprietor of the *Trinidad Chronicle*, fell a victim in the last great yellow fever epidemic to strike Trinidad. Others who did not succumb were often shattered in health and had to sell their businesses (or leave them in the hands of managers) and return to temperate climes. It was not only expatriates who suffered, of course. Creole printers died young or had their health wrecked in the same way. In one instance, in the Cable family's business in St. Kitts, Robert Cable (who died from burns in 1829 through having set his bed hangings on fire) had been running the business since the age of fifteen in consequence of his father's early death. Several other West Indian printers had to assume editorial/managerial responsibilities while still underage for similar reasons.

Although the change of ownership of some West Indian printing houses was rapid, in other cases there were long dynasties. In little St. Kitts, the Howes and Cables ran rival concerns (and papers) for well over a century.

Very little evidence survives on the conditions of employment of those working for the master printers. There is occasional evidence of strikes[17] and occasional illustration of the regard in which a master printer was held.[18] Instances of the employment of slaves have been noted for the British islands [29]; slave labor was also used by the Dutch in Surinam. But of the wage rates and working conditions of free labor hardly any information has been found. The wages of personnel in the Government Printing Office at Scarboro' (Tobago) in 1899 show that the foreman received fifty pounds per year, the two compositors fifteen and twelve pounds, respectively, and the apprentice but ten shillings a month. This was at a time when the economic state of Tobago was at its worst, and it would be unwise to draw general conclusions from these pay scales.

The Places of Printing

Many West Indian islands are too small for printing to have been worth attempting outside the capital. The needs of Barbados, for instance, could very easily be served from Bridgetown. Only in a few colonies, therefore, did printing spread outside the capital. Admittedly, Guadeloupe had printers in both Basseterre and in Point-à-Pitre and Martinique in St. Pierre and Fort-de-France; and in Trinidad a printer set up in San Fernando as early as 1850. But in the eighteenth century, only two islands had several centers of printing. Both Jamaica and the French colony of St. Domingue were large enough for there to be commercial centers too remote from the capitals for easy communication and large enough to provide printers with a local market for a local paper. In St. Domingue, the two chief centers of printing were Cap Français and Port-au-Prince, but at times presses operated from St. Marc, Léogane, and Aux Cayes also; during the reign of Emperor Christophe in independent Haiti a royal printing office was also set up in his palace Sans Souci [30]. In the Spanish part of the island—the Dominican Republic—it is worth noting that, as well as the purely Dominican papers issued in Santo Domingo, there was a weekly *Journal*

17. For example, a compositors' strike at the Montego Bay *Jamaica Standard* in January 1837. There was a printers' general strike in Jamaica in 1908, broken by the *Daily Gleaner* by installing linotypes imported from New York. The luckless compositors, most of whom came from Barbados and Trinidad, were forced to return to their native islands to seek employment.
18. In Antigua in February 1850, when Frederick S. Jewett retired from the direction of the *Antigua Observer*, a letter of regret signed by all the printing house staff—the foreman, four journeymen, plus five occasional workmen—was published in the paper. Such tributes are rare.

of Commerce issued by a Bahamian printer in the north coast town of Puerto Plata in the late 1870s.

In Jamaica, printing spread from Kingston and Spanish Town to Montego Bay in 1771 and to Savanna-la-Mar in 1788. Though this last venture soon failed, the introduction of printing into the north coast town of Falmouth in 1791 was much more successful, despite its proximity to Montego Bay. Printing spread slowly to other towns in Jamaica—to Old Harbour in 1843, to Port Maria about 1862, and to Port Antonio later in the nineteenth century.[19] With improved internal communications in the island, only Kingston and Montego Bay remain of significance as printing centers today.

To locate the whereabouts of the printing houses in these various towns is not always easy. Although most of the colonial towns were laid out on a grid, many were far too small to make it necessary for the printers' imprints to specify their location, and when they did it was often in terms which, retrospectively, are valueless—"close by the Courthouse," "on the Parade," "in the house formerly occupied by Dr. Baker." In the cases of Port of Spain and Kingston (the most important printing centers by the mid-nineteenth century), the information gleaned suggests that there was no special center for the printing trade in the first, whereas in Kingston, Harbour Street had become the normal place for a printer to set up, with the bookshops and subscription libraries in King Street, the fashionable shopping area. Not until the suburban dispersal of Kingston after World War II did Harbour Street lose its special position in the trade.

Printers' Equipment

Until the late eighteenth century, printing facilities in the West Indies were limited to letterpress printing. When copperplate printing was required—for example, for various engraved views of planters' houses or for maps—local advertising always emphasized that the plates would be printed in Europe. The inventory of Robert Baldwin's business [32] was not untypical, nor was it very different from similar inventories of printers in North America or the English provinces. Paper was occasionally obtained from the American colonies in the early days,[20] but after 1776 importation direct from Europe was universal. In the late

19. Since this paper is concerned with the printing *trade*, I have left out reference to St. Ann's Bay, in which the Reverend George Wilson Bridges had a private press in the 1820s [31].
20. William Daniell of Kingston purchased paper from Benjamin Franklin in 1754 [33, pp. 51–52, 72]. Franklin also supplied printers in Antigua and Barbados.

eighteenth century, of course, Caslon's types were to be found in most printing houses in the British islands,[21] usually in a rather limited range. Several Jamaican printers had small Hebrew fonts, but in 1783 the Abbé Roland could find only one Kingston printer with the accented sorts needed for printing in French [8].

By the end of the eighteenth century, other types appear more often—from the Wilson foundry, for instance. When printers set up shop or reequipped, they often included advertisements for their supplies. In the 1840s the *Guiana Times* obtained its types from V. & J. Figgins. Woods & Sharwoods Austin Letter Foundry was responsible for equipping the *St. Lucia Palladium* in 1844 and the *Bermuda Royal Gazette* in 1850. By 1850, however, the European founders were being challenged. An advertisement from George Bruce & Co. of New York appeared in the *Antigua Weekly Register*, September 11, 1849, and Bruce's skillful advertising succeeded in placing his types in other West Indian printing houses very rapidly.

Other suppliers' advertisements are informative. William Gibbs, successor to Paas & Co. of High Holborn, advertised in the *St. Lucia Palladium* in March 1847 that he cut heads of newspapers, coats of arms, etc. We learn that the *Grenada Free Press* had a demy jobbing press by Ruthven and a royal press by Anderson in 1842. These were the only presses owned by this firm; few West Indian printers had more.[22] Wooden presses, of course, deteriorated rapidly in West Indian conditions, and one suspects that all were replaced by iron presses rather quickly. The fact that all surviving early iron hand presses in the islands are Columbians[23] suggests that these may have been the commonest, though in the second half of the nineteenth century treadle presses were widely used.

At what date rolling presses for copperplate printing were introduced is uncertain. Joshua Peterkin's *Treatise on Planting,* printed in St. Kitts in 1790, has a curious engraved frontispiece produced locally. There was at least one copperplate printer active in Kingston about the same time, while by the 1830s these presses were to be found also in Trinidad, Grenada, and, no doubt, other islands.

Lithographic printing in a primitive form had reached Bermuda by 1821. The circumstances were rather amusing: Governor Lumley,

21. The *Barbados Gazette*, January 30, 1788, and advertisements for the *New Jamaica Almanack*, 1790, both draw attention to their elegant new type cast by Caslon.
22. Alexander Aikman, Jr., had three wooden and three iron presses listed in his inventory of March 1832, but his was the largest printing house on the island.
23. One in Georgetown (Guyana), one in Port of Spain, and one still in use in Montego Bay [34].

having quarreled with the printers of both the colony's papers, tried to bypass them by having official proclamations produced on a little lithographic press imported for the purpose and published them in the old way of posting them as handbills about the streets of Hamilton. The newspapers' editorial comment, as can be imagined, did little to reconcile the governor to them [23, pp. 152–54]. There was some amateur lithographic work in St. Ann's Bay, Jamaica, later in the 1820s [31]. By the 1830s, Isaac Mendes Belisario of Kingston was producing some very accomplished work, notably in his splendid *Sketches of Character . . . of the Negro Population in the Island of Jamaica,* which was issued in three parts, 1837–38. Public support for Belisario's work, however, was disappointing.

Some primitive wood-engraved work was produced in Kingston in the 1840s to illustrate various agricultural works, but little sophisticated wood engraving seems to have been executed in the islands. One notable exception was in Port of Spain, where in 1884 the short-lived satirical magazine *Pixy* contained some vigorous and competently engraved cartoons. (*Pixy*'s advertising, incidentally, included telephone numbers — remarkably early for the Caribbean.)

The standards of workmanship of the West Indian printers varied widely. In general, the bookwork of the eighteenth century was of very good quality, and some of the more prestigious items such as Peter Pindar's *Persian love elegies* (Kingston: Joseph Thompson & Co., 1773), or Alexander Dirom's *Thoughts on the State of the Militia of Jamaica* (Spanish Town: Douglass & Aikman, 1783) are very attractively produced. Some of the more ephemeral items—the almanacs produced by printers in the French islands or, in St. Kitts, several of the newspapers—show the hands of accomplished craftsmen of some taste. Others show deplorable composition and presswork: the Aikmans, for example, were extremely slovenly in the production of their *Royal Gazette*, although their almanacs and bookwork were well done. In general, the declining economic position of the West Indian colonies in the second half of the nineteenth century was reflected in the printing: worn-out types badly set and printed without skill on defective presses by uncaring printers—this is to overstate the position, since competent work continued to appear, but one can produce many examples of such slovenliness. Perhaps the worst was the *Trinidad Recorder*, whose final issue of June 18, 1884, was of strange appearance: "The publishers of the 'Recorder' beg to be excused for issuing the paper without the first and fourth pages. Upon going to press the forme burst, and both pages went to pi. They also take this opportunity of thanking their many friends for past patronage, and to inform them that it being impossible to continue, under existing circumstance, the present issue closes the career of the 'Trinidad Recorder.' "

The Publications of the West Indian Printers

Newspapers

Almost without exception, printers in the West Indian colonies depended for their survival upon the production of a regular newspaper. The earliest were weeklies; in the more populous colonies, papers appearing twice or thrice weekly, or daily, had emerged before the end of the eighteenth century, though in the smaller settlements it was a struggle to keep even a weekly paper alive. The typical paper (before the mid-nineteenth century, when machine-made papers and powered presses led to a larger format) was a demy folio[24] with three or four columns to the page. Page 1 would contain proclamations and other official advertisements, plus world news culled from European and North American papers,[25] which generally spilled over onto page 2. Page 3 would contain local news, plus matter lifted from other West Indian papers and often a substantial number of advertisements, which usually occupied the whole of the fourth page.

If their matter stretched beyond a single sheet, many of the proprietors issued regular supplements with their papers. The Aikmans' *Royal Gazette* of 8 quarto pages, for example, usually had another 8 pages of *Supplement* and 8 pages of *Postscript*, while a further 4 or 8 pages of *Additional Postscript* were not uncommon. This was to accommodate the hosts of official advertisements required by Jamaican law—of pound sales, of runaway slaves lodged in the parish workhouses, and so forth—which made printing such a lucrative business for those running the semiofficial papers. Few other papers were quite as prolific in their provision of addenda, but most published occasional supplements or extraordinary issues from time to time—to report the British victory at Waterloo or the results of a British parliamentary election and so forth. In several instances, when the departure of the mail vessels from a particular island did not coincide with regular publication, a special "packet edition" of the paper was published.

Most newspaper proprietors aimed at the production of a long-lived paper, of course. Very occasionally, in response to local political stimuli, however, papers sprang up to play their part in the discussion of that single issue and then died. The "Federation Riots" of 1876 in Barbados, which marked a stormy episode in the tumultuous colonial career of John Pope Hennessy [35, pp. 156–82], were accompanied by a host of

24. Some proprietors, like the Aikmans with their *Royal Gazette*, preferred a quarto format.
25. Sometimes from further afield, for example, India, though I suspect most was taken at second hand from English papers and not directly from the Indian press.

short-lived papers whose owners evidently felt that the established press of the colony was unfair to the governor.

In earlier days, the prices quoted for the papers was the price to regular subscribers. Not until Victoria's reign did the newspaper proprietors recognize in print that purchases of single copies were an important source of income. The price to subscribers for the different colonies' papers is difficult to compare because of the fluctuations in colonial currency. In 1840, Jamaican dailies cost one doubloon,[26] the papers of Barbados, the Leewards and Windwards, some six to eight dollars; those of Trinidad twelve dollars per year [36].

These prices were not low (the era of the cheap West Indian paper was yet to come) and had been rising steadily from the 1780s until about 1820, when they leveled off or were lowered. In Jamaica, only subscribers in Kingston, Spanish Town, and Port Royal had their papers delivered (or could collect them from the printers). In the other parishes, they were sent by post, for which a substantial extra payment was due to the postmasters in each parish, who acted as subscription agents for the papers.[27]

The printed terms to subscribers always called for at least partial payment in advance—a vain hope. From Samuel Keimer's "Sorrowful Lamentation" in the *Barbados Gazette* of May 4, 1734, which he addressed to "those wou'd-be thought gentleman, who have long taken his paper, and never paid for it, and seem never to design to pay for it," onward, the West Indian papers are filled with a chorus of polite requests, jocular reminders, desperate pleas, or threats of immediate legal action against subscribers who were one—or two, or three—years in arrears. More than a few printers were placed in very difficult straits by this load of almost uncollectable debt; several newspapers were suspended or ceased publication completely for this reason.[28] Deliveries to subscribers were a constant headache. The *Antigua Free Press* of October 7, 1829, illustrates vividly the tribulations of the colonial printer:

> We have frequently, at different times, had complaints from some of our country subscribers, that persons who are not authorised, take the liberty of sending for the paper in their names. The practice is mean and paltry; it subjects us to some loss, and much inconvenience. Persons may, if they please, take the paper in shares of 8ths and 16ths, but we can only recognise one subscriber to each paper.

26. That is, £5 6s. 8d. in colonial currency. The semiweekly Spanish Town paper was little cheaper, but the semiweekly *Cornwall Chronicle* of Montego Bay cost only 12s. 6d. per quarter in 1841, though two years earlier it had cost £4 per annum.
27. In 1776, subscribers to the *Cornwall Chronicle* paid £1 10s. a year if they collected their papers or £2 10s. when they were sent by post. By 1803, this had risen to £3 5s. called for or £4 when "sent off the Bay."
28. For example, the *Trinidad Examiner* in 1854 and the *San Fernando Gazette* in 1877, to name only two instances from a single colony.

All persons are cautioned against purchasing papers of the lad (Frederick) who usually delivers them to the town subscribers. There is reason to believe that papers are frequently purchased in this way at a reduced price: the practice is dishonourable in the extreme: those who would thus encourage a young lad in a dishonest act, deserve the severest punishment of the law, as they must know he is not authorised to dispose of them, and they may rest assured that if once detected, a proper example will be made of them.

How many copies of the papers circulated is very hard to judge, as information on this is seldom to be found. The *Jamaica Despatch*, whose success was regarded with awe by other newspaper proprietors in the 1830s, was said to circulate some 1,400 copies in 1836. Thirty years earlier, the *Barbados Mercury* had some 616 subscribers, probably much nearer the normal circulation figure for a successful paper in a prosperous and populous colony. But in the smaller islands the situation was very different. The *Report of St. Bartholomew* had forty-three subscribers in 1814. The *Grenada Weekly Record* estimated in 1854 that not one of the three Bahamian newspapers had as many as 100 subscribers. When the *Tobago Chronicle* ceased publication in August 1871, the editor referred to his twenty-five or thirty subscribers[29]—not all of whom were paid up! When one reads in the *St. Christopher Advertiser* in September 1858 that the intending promoters of a newspaper in Tortola (in the British Virgin Islands) had abandoned the project for lack of support, one wonders whether their tentative subscription list had even reached double figures.

Periodicals

In several colonies, attempts were made from time to time to issue monthly or quarterly magazines. In Jamaica, in particular, there were several such attempts from the 1780s onward. Some, like the *Cornwall Magazine, or Temple of Pleasure*, issued from Savanna-la-Mar by Monk & Leyburn in 1788, were doomed from the start; but others, like William Smart's *Columbia Magazine or Monthly Miscellany* (Kingston, 1796–1800) or the *Jamaica Magazine* (Kingston, 1812–13), were competently produced and edited and contain much interesting and important matter.[30] But they, like the magazines which appeared in Grenada and Barbados, failed for lack of support. Henry Breen's comments on the (Barbados) *West India Magazine* sum up the typical expatriate's attitude: "The scant support given to the *West India Magazine* . . . has been referred to as

29. Out of a total population of some 17,000 in the colony, in which there was no rival paper—some indication of the parlous state of the island's economy.
30. *Characteristic Traits of the Creolian & African Negroes in Jamaica &c. &c. (1797)* edited by Barry Higman (Mona: Caldwell Press, 1976) reprints some valuable material from the *Columbian Magazine*.

evidence of a want of disposition to encourage a taste for polite literature. Upon the whole, however, it would hardly be fair to admit this test. The Magazine possessed the natural advantage of local interest on many colonial topics; but independently of the inartistic style in which it was got up, it gave very little promise in a literary point of view; its pages being generally characterised by bombast, triviality, 'bad grammar' (as the Editor used to term it) and worse taste . . . " [37, pp. 273–74].

Official Printing

Equally important as their newspapers for many West Indian printers were the contracts to be gained for official printing. Proclamations, editions of a colony's laws, votes of the Houses of Assembly—this was the kind of work which could put a printer into easy circumstances. Much official work could, of course, be published through the medium of a newspaper. From time to time, individual colonies attempted to force their contractors to issue an official gazette distinct from their own newspaper, but such attempts seldom lasted long. In Jamaica, all official advertisements had to appear in the three county papers—the *Royal Gazette* (Kingston), the *St. Jago de la Vega Gazette* (Spanish Town), and the *Cornwall Chronicle* (Montego Bay), at any rate until the 1830s. Other printers secured contractual positions as printer to the Corporation of Kingston or even as printer to the Parish of Hanover—such was the competition for official contract business in the colony. In other islands, official work was generally farmed out to a single printer for the whole island, and there was much jobbery to secure the position. Frequently, newspapers which did not have these contracts nevertheless included much official matter to improve the usefulness of their paper to subscribers and in the hope of securing official approval against the day their rivals fell from favor.

Ephemera

So little ephemera from West Indian printers survives and is easily accessible that it is easy to forget the enormous importance its production had for the colonial printer.[31] But from Robert Baldwin onward, all West Indian printers advertised a range of blank pro formas—attorneys' blanks, bills of lading, seamen's articles, articles of administration, muster rolls for the militia, letters of marque for privateers, and so forth. In addition, of course, there were innumerable official forms—certificates that vessels had checked with the appropriate port authorities, blanks for letters of administration, etc.—the production of

31. Bradford S. Swan identified some Antiguan ephemera in the Rhode Island archives [38], and much must survive in other record repositories.

which must have afforded the printers a substantial part of their living. Under the heading of ephemera also must be included the handbills for livestock and slave sales and theatrical performances (and the theater tickets), auction catalogs and catalogs of circulating libraries, and at times other matter which has disappeared from view almost completely.[32]

Almanacs

From the earliest days of West Indian printing, the publication of an annual almanac formed a normal part of the activities of most businesses. Sheet almanacs appeared regularly from 1719 onward in Jamaica. The first book almanac did not appear on that island until the publication by William Daniell of *The Merchant's Pocket Companion* for 1751. The subtitle of Daniell's venture gives a pretty good conspectus of the contents of this genre:

> An Almanack . . . fitted to this Meridian containing, the different Courts of Quarter Sessions, Common Pleas &c. for Port Royal and Kingston throughout the year, the last Day of summoning for ditto and Grand Court. The Jews Hollidays throughout the Year. A list of such Goods as are liable to pay Duty in the Receiver General's Office and the sums that are to be paid. A complete list of the Council and Assembly of this island. The Public Offices and Officers, Names of the Custos's, Judges of the Gr. Court, Chancery Office and Officers, Admiralty Office and Officers, King's Officers, Provost Marshall and his Deputies. Days for chusing vestrymen, &c. &c. To which is added, A Discourse upon Meteors.

Other almanacs would replace the discourse upon meteors with other improving essays (sometimes of great value, like those which appear in the *Honduras Almanacks* [11] on the lumber industry) and would include other material likely to be of value, such as the lists of officers in the militia. Many almanacs also had considerable information on the mother country: a court calendar, list of Members of Parliament, and so forth. In a few West Indian islands, whose printers obviously hoped for a wider Antillean circulation for their work, the almanacs included much useful information on sister colonies. Thus, J.-B. Thounens' *Almanach Historique . . . pour l'année 1789*, printed in Castries, is a valuable source of information on all the French colonies, as well as St. Lucia. The almanacs published in St. Kitts by Thomas Howe and Robert Cable deal with Nevis, Montserrat, and Tortola and to a lesser degree the Danish Virgin Islands and (Dutch) St. Eustatius, as well as St. Kitts itself.

In a good many colonies, there were several rival almanacs produced by the different printers, each one praising the accuracy and superior detail of his own work. Only in Jamaica, however, does the demand seem

32. In 1780 in St. Lucia, for example, masters of arriving vessels were required to have an inventory of their cargoes printed.

to have been great enough for printers regularly to produce two editions of a particular year's almanac: the first in mid-December of the previous year, the second in February or March after the elections of vestrymen, etc., had produced changes in the local information.

In general, the production standards of the West Indian book almanacs of the eighteenth and early nineteenth centuries were very high, both in internal design and execution (those of St. Kitts being particularly well done) and in their binding. Some were simply stitched in Dutch gilt or marbled papers, others full-bound in straight-grained morocco (green or red or, more occasionally, blue) with competent gold tooling.

During the nineteenth century, however, more and more of these almanacs were produced in Britain.[33] This had, strangely, always been the commoner pattern in Barbados where, for example, the long series of almanacs (1829?–58) calculated by Tobias Phillips was printed for him in Liverpool by Thomas Kaye [39].

Bookwork

To leave the mention of book printing until last may seem topsy turvy, but, in relation to its importance to the life of the printing trade, it is not. Unlike the settlers of New England, the West Indian planters preferred to have their substantial books published in London. Very little of the work of the Jamaican historian Bryan Edwards, for instance, was first published in Jamaica. Relatively few examples of "the literature of power" were printed in the islands, and those which were, were usually rather lightweight—such as the very handsome quarto *The Sable Venus; An Ode inscribed to Bryan Edwards Esq.* (Kingston: Bennett & Woolhead, 1765), which paints vividly the attractions of an African mistress.

For a short period, it must be confessed, it did appear as though colonial society had reached a point at which the idea of local literary publication was being consolidated. The theater was very popular in the islands, and several editions of the plays performed were printed—*The New Comic Opera of The Duenna* (Kingston: W. Aikman, 1779); *A School for Soldiers, or the Deserter* (Kingston [?], 1784); *The Patriot, a tragedy, altered from the Italian of Metastasio* (Montego Bay: Fannin, 1785). There were other local editions which point to a more cultivated market than one might have anticipated:

Montego Bay, May 21, 1785. This day is published, at the Printing Office, The Sorrows of Werther: a novel from the German of Mr. Goethè, first translated into French, then into English, and now reprinted from the London Edition, at

33. At any rate in part, although the local information might be printed in the islands to be bound up with sheets imported from Europe.

the particular desire of a number of Ladies and Gentlemen *** A few spare *copies* for sale.

Such enterprise on Fannin's part was, however, but a flash in the pan. The decline in the planter class, from the Napoleonic Wars onward, almost wiped out ventures of this kind, which became increasingly rare as the nineteenth century wore on.[34]

There were, of course, plenty of examples of "the literature of knowledge." Manuals on tropical diseases, on the care of horses, on improved methods of distillation, on botany, and on methods of planting formed the backbone of local book production, while in the first third of the nineteenth century the controversy over the slave trade gave birth to many pamphlets.

Sometimes the subscription proposals and other advertising and the subscription lists which were included in the more substantial of these books tell us a good deal about the publication history of the book or even the trading pattern of the printer/publisher concerned. Thus, we can learn that there were insufficient subscribers to John Lunan's *Hortus Jamaicensis* to permit publication in volume form, and we can follow the book's issue in parts with some accuracy. We will learn to beware of printed subscription lists, since the Jamaican agents for Cobbett's *Works* lost the additional list of subscribers not printed in the volume and had to advertise for the subscribers to call [40]. On the other hand, from the subscription list included in Peterkin's *Treatise on Planting* (St. Kitts, 1790) we get a very interesting distribution pattern for the edition of about 550 copies: St. Kitts, approximately 150 copies; Nevis, 40; Montserrat, 24; Antigua, 100; Tortola, 51;[35] St. Vincent, 1; Dominica, 2; Anguilla, 3; St. Eustatius, 5; St. Croix, 125; St. Martin, 45; Puerto Rico, 2;[36] and St. Thomas, 1. Few books enjoyed as wide a circulation as this.

Peterkin's work gives some indication of the cooperation between printers on the different islands who would advertise and act as subscription agents for one another. Because the receipt of foreign news was always slow and often a chancy business during the periods of war, even for neutral islands,[37] the colonial papers depended very much on being able to pick up from one another items of foreign as well as local news. Masters of arriving vessels were solicited for any papers they might

34. Trinidad is a partial exception in the mid-nineteenth century.

35. There were only two subscribers, but one was for 50 copies.

36. Both were men with Irish names. This is the only trade connection with the Spanish colonies that I have traced.

37. Mails for St. Bartholomew came via St. Kitts, so when the French intercepted the mails to the British islands, as they did frequently before Trafalgar, the Swedish colonists might be without direct news from Europe for two or three months at a stretch.

have with them and subscribers asked to let the editors have a view of any newspapers they received. Newspapers from the European and New England and Nova Scotian ports trading with the Caribbean were most frequently quoted, of course, but the array of papers occasionally quoted is very wide, with such unexpected bylines as the *Elgin Courier* and the *Cherokee Phoenix*. In the mid-nineteenth century, Australian papers were often quoted in the Jamaican and St. Kitts press;[38] the Sierra Leone *New Era* had a subscription agent in St. Vincent.[39]

By the middle years of the nineteenth century, the exchange of papers among the West Indian islands had become automatic and formalized, with most editors sending out perhaps 30 copies of their papers on a regular basis. In the case of the Turks Islands, as the cost of interisland postage was a burden on the editor of the *Royal Standard*, the islands' legislative council in 1861 voted a sum of ten shillings a month to relieve him of this charge.

By the 1840s, also, communications with Britain had improved considerably. The *European Times*, published by Willmer & Smith of Liverpool, had become a standard source for European news. Copies of West Indian papers were filed in the newsroom run by Peter Lund Simmonds.[40] Rather later, the London offices of Holloway's Pills (which were advertised very extensively in the West Indian press) were another place in which the colonial papers could easily be consulted.

The Control of the Press

Preceding sections of this paper have indicated some of the ways in which the islands' printers could be kept at heel. Both the stick and the carrot were used—the stick in the form of imprisonment or fines (or both) for contempt of the Privileges of the Houses of Assembly, the Judiciary, or the Executive. The carrot was usually in the form of the

38. There was a small migration of Jamaicans to the Australian goldfields in the 1850s; the St. Kitts interest is explained by the fact that the Howe family of printers in New South Wales and Tasmania was originally from St. Kitts.
39. Another family connection: William Drape of the *New Era* being a member of the Drape family who published the St. Vincent *Royal Gazette*.
40. Peter Lund Simmonds (1814–97) was a sugar planter in Jamaica shortly before the emancipation of the slaves in 1834. In the late 1830s and early 1840s he ran a newspaper room, subscription library, and colonial subscription agency, at first in Chichester and later in London. Many of the West Indian papers of 1839–41 now in the British Library (often the only known copies) are those sent to him when he was preparing his study of the newspaper press [36]. His interesting later career as a journalist of the use of tropical products merits a modern study.

award of government contracts but could at times be more subtle.[41] It would scarcely be an exaggeration to say that all printers in the West Indies suffered to some extent. Some would eat humble pie:

Whereas we, Woolhead, Gadd and Bennett, Printers did in the *Kingston Journal* . . . insert . . . a Paragraph scandalously reflecting on the Justice and Equity of the Judges of his Majesty's Courts of Admiralty in the American Colonies, and more particularly aspersing the Proceedings of His Majesty's Court of Vice Admiralty in this Island: And whereas the Judge of the said Court hath (upon our Entreaty) consented to withdraw the just Prosecution . . . provided we should make a Public Declaration acknowledging our sincere Regret for the offence we have committed: Conscious therefore of the malevolence and Injustice of the Defamation, we do in this public Manner, declare . . . ourselves heartily sorry . . . and we do hereby promise, that we will never again suffer this Paper to be prostituted to the servile and iniquitious Purpose of calling Abuse and Obloquy on Men in public Characters, or of questionning the Justice of any of His Majesty's Tribunals. [*Kingston Journal* October 24, 1761]

Others were more defiant, if less prudent. When the editor of the *Jamaica Standard* was arraigned for contempt in December 1839, he printed the following in his paper:

To the Usher of the Black Rod, and others whom it may concern, Greeting. Whereas it has come to our knowledge that a second Warrant is now against our Editorial Person, at the instance of their Honours of the Council, and whereas the state of our health and other circumstances do not second this apparent urgency on the part of that honourable Board, THIS IS TO GIVE NOTICE, that we have considered it expedient to retire for a while to Country quarters. . . .

How long the *Standard* editor managed to elude arrest I have yet to establish. Others were less fortunate. Charles Wells of the *St. Lucia Palladium* spent over four years in a debtor's prison for refusing to pay the fine imposed in another contempt case.

The subject of official control of the press in the Caribbean is too large for detailed consideration here. It will suffice to say that the control was always stricter in the French, Dutch, and Danish colonies than in the British possessions and that in British colonies the worst repression came as a rule from the local legislative bodies and from the judiciary, many of whose members played a contemptible part in attempts at muzzling the press in the 1830s and 1840s. The attitude of the islands' governors was usually more enlightened,[42] while appeal to Britain produced a much

41. An example is William Dyer of Falmouth, Jamaica, one of the bitterest and most vituperative opponents of the work of the Baptist missionaries on the north coast, who was given a gift of plate by admirers of his editorial stance in the *Cornwall Courier* in December 1839.

42. Governor Eyre in Jamaica was a significant exception to this general rule at the time of the Morant Bay rebellion.

more liberal response. That the printer of 1870 was less liable to harassment than the printer of thirty years earlier was almost entirely due to metropolitan influence and direction.

Bookselling and the Growth of Subscription Libraries

For the nineteenth-century colonial printer, the exchange of publications referred to above was not merely a convenience in obtaining news at little cost, it was a source of income. J. W. Irwin, proprietor of the *Trinidad Guardian*, for instance, in September 1826, advertised the opening of his St. Vincent Street reading room, in which for eight pounds a year subscribers would have access to files of some 10 British, 3 American, 3 French, and 24 West Indian papers, most of which he received on exchange. As soon as there were sufficient subscribers, Irwin stated, he would add a range of monthly and quarterly periodicals and would start a circulating library. Many other printers in other islands adopted a similar policy. There were attempts by persons in other fields of business to start similar ventures. In 1790, for instance, one Ebenezer Edie advertised that he had built a coffeehouse in Kingston at great cost, and among its many attractions would be a Subscribers' Room "furnished with all Newspapers and Prices Current, for the entertainment and information of the Subscribers"—but newspaper proprietors had an obvious economic advantage in such enterprises.

Importations of books into the West Indian colonies were very considerable. Giles Barber's invaluable analysis of the Customs House records [41] shows that in the period from 1700 to 1780 British exports of books to the West Indian colonies represented about a quarter of total exports to the New World and exceeded those to the East Indies. Importations to Jamaica were little less than to New York, Barbadians bought nearly as much as settlers in the Carolinas, and Antigua accounted for more than Nova Scotia and Canada, while the importations to the West Indies as a whole exceeded those into New England. Of the West Indian colonies separately listed, Jamaica took 43 percent and Barbados 30 percent, followed by Antigua with 10 percent, St. Kitts with 6½ percent, and Bermuda with 2 percent of the total.[43] In the nineteenth century Trinidad was to move into third (perhaps second) place, but the pattern of importation of the majority of reading material from Britain was to remain much the same. In the 1850s, to be sure,

43. The islands of the Leewards were mostly still under French control, Trinidad was Spanish, and the Guianas Dutch at this time.

American piracies of English periodicals were to be advertised in several colonies. At the end of the nineteenth century, the Trinidad blue books record the importation of some printed matter from Germany (whether this was of Tauchnitz's cheap paperbound reprints of standard English authors, of music, or of other matter I have been unable to learn). But in general substantial foreign (and particularly American) entry into the West Indian market was not to come until very recently.

From the inventories of the late eighteenth-century Jamaican booksellers and from the advertisements one finds in the West Indian papers of the early nineteenth century, one can reconstruct the stock of the bookseller in King Street, Kingston, or on the Parade in St. John's, Antigua. There would be a substantial stock of stationery—paper of all sizes, gilt-edged cards, ink, quills, standishes, sealing wax, files, memorandum and account books of various kinds. Pencils, brushes, and artists' colors, ruled music, packs of cards, chessboards and backgammon sets, fiddle strings and fishing tackle and the hundred and one other things one finds in a stationer's store would fill the shelves on one side of the room. There would be tobacco, silk purses, balls of blacking, satin ribbons, shoes, hats, and haberdashery, garden seeds, and patent cures for the gout—the extent of the merchant's trade in these other lines varying a great deal. The stock of books would consist of some standard schoolbooks, a range of medical and law books, history, biography, and political treatises for the man of affairs, charts and pilots for the mariner. In general, Sir John Shore's comment in 1772 that the libraries taken to the East Indies for sale "though very voluminous, consist mostly of novels, and such books as are termed, by the London shopkeepers 'light summer reading' " [41, p. 201] seems not to have been altogether true of the West Indies at the time he wrote, although by the end of the eighteenth century the stock advertised in the various circulating libraries had more than a leavening of poetry, magazines, gothic novels, and such frivolities. A study of the reading tastes of West Indian society is a desideratum and will contain some surprises—the demand in St. Vincent for Armstrong's *Gaelic Dictionary* in 1826, for example.

As the planter class left the islands, the market for polite literature declined. There were some outstanding exceptions to the general rule that by the mid-nineteenth century the West Indians were buying fewer books, and then books of a utilitarian nature, often in cheap reprints like Bohn's various series. Such men as the Jamaican naturalist Richard Hill, to give but one instance, remained closely in touch with advances in learning, but such men were exceptional and more often to be found in the rising class of men of color than in the dwindling ranks of the planters.

The history of circulating libraries in the islands is illustrative of this decline. Though there were subscription libraries in Kingston and

Montego Bay in the early 1790s, both failed for lack of subscribers. The circulating libraries set up with high hopes by printers in Port of Spain, St. George's (Grenada), and other towns in the 1820s and 1830s seldom lasted more than a year or two before their proprietors gave up the struggle to make them pay. However, several of the missionary and church groups in various colonies persevered with the provision of libraries for their own special purposes.

Conclusion

To compare West Indian printing of the late eighteenth and early nineteenth centuries with that emanating from the British colonial press in Canada, India, Africa, or the Far East is instructive but reopens once more the question, Was there a distinctive West Indian printer? At a cursory glance, the similarities between the work undertaken—and the way it was undertaken—in Kingston or Calcutta, Grenada or the Gold Coast, are very great indeed. Similarities between West Indian and West African printing are not surprising, since West Indian printers were often active in the early West African press. Nor are the other similarities, as the printers concerned were (at any rate in the first generation or two) Englishmen printing for other Englishmen. The fact that they were doing so in minor outposts of empire made little difference.

As the printers to client cultures in client states, the West Indian printers had (as well as their similarities to colonial printers elsewhere) many common areas of interest. Slavery, sugar, immigration: these were persistent themes in British, Dutch, French, and Danish possessions. The nature of the plantation economy was to impose a more uniform pattern than might be expected.

Although the West Indian colonies were not to maintain their importance as centers of printing that the early introduction of the art might have indicated or to produce material of lasting significance in the world of letters,[44] their bibliographical history is by no means insignificant. The inclusion of their output in the eighteenth-century *Short Title Catalogue*, or the recording of nineteenth-century West Indian imprints will be difficult tasks for thc bibliographer. When such work has been undertaken, a full assessment of West Indian printing and its part in the formation of contemporary Caribbean society will be possible.

44. West Indian literary work, whether of a Naipaul or a Cèsaire, has almost without exception been published outside the West Indies, despite the valiant efforts of such little magazines as *Bim* or *Savacou* to redress the balance.

REFERENCES

1. Wroth, L. C. *The Colonial Printer*. 2d ed. Charlottesville: University Press of Virginia, 1938.
2. Rousseau, I. J. "The Making of a Cape Governor—Sir Benjamin D'Urban." *South African Journal of Science* 28 (November 1931): 584–93.
3. Naipaul, V. S. *The Loss of El Dorado*. Rev. ed. Harmondsworth, Middx.: Penguin Books, 1972.
4. Cave, Roderick. "Thomas Craddock's Books: A West India Merchant's Stock." *Book Collector* 25 (Winter 1976): 481–90.
5. Cundall, Frank. *A History of Printing in Jamaica from 1717 to 1834*. Kingston: Institute of Jamaica, 1935.
6. Fulham Papers, v.XVII, Lambeth Palace.
7. Shilstone, E. M. "Some Notes on Early Presses and Newspapers in Barbados." *Journal of the Barbados Museum and Historical Society* 26 (November 1958): 19–33.
8. *Annual Report, John Carter Brown Library, 1960*. Providence, R. I.: John Carter Brown Library, 1962.
9. Debien, G. "Un Abbé maitre de pension à Saint Domingue pais journaliste à la Jamaique." *Notes d'histoire colonial* 43 (1953): 1–43.
10. Cave, Roderick. "Printing comes to Jamaica." *Jamaica Journal* 9 (Summer 1975): 11–17.
11. Cave, Roderick. "Printing in Nineteenth Century Belize." *Library Quarterly* 46 (January 1976): 20–37.
12. Rodway, James. *The Press in British Guiana*. Worcester, Mass.: American Antiquarian Society, 1918.
13. Cabon, Fr. Adolphe. "Un Siècle et demi de journalisme en Haiti." *Petite revue hebdomadaire*, 1919; reprinted as *Cabon's History of Haiti Journalism*, with an introduction and notes by Clarence S. Brigham (Worcester, Mass.: American Antiquarian Society, 1940). (Page references are to Brigham's edition.)
14. Bibliothèque Nationale. *Le Livre (catalogue d'un exposition)*. Paris: Bibliothèque Nationale, 1972.
15. Blanche, Lenis. *Contribution á l'histoire de la presse à la Guadeloupe.* Point-à-Pitre: Gouvernement de Guadeloupe, 1935.
16. Prebble, John. *The Darien Disaster*. London: Secker & Warburg, 1968.
17. Eames, Wilberforce. *The Antigua Press and Benjamin Mecom*. Worcester, Mass.: American Antiquarian Society, 1929.
18. Lincoln, Waldo. *History of Bermuda Newspapers*. Worcester, Mass.: American Antiquarian Society, 1925.
19. Swan, Bradford. *The Spread of Printing: The Caribbean Area*. Amsterdam: VanGendt, 1970.
20. Cave, Roderick. "The Early Printers of Grand Turk." *Papers of the Bibliographical Society of America* 70 (Winter 1976): 519–28.
21. Fraser, Lionel Mordaunt. *History of Trinidad*. Port of Spain: Government Printing Office, 1891–96.
22. Kennedy, Jean de Chantal. *Biography of a Colonial Town: Hamilton, Bermuda, 1790–1897*. Hamilton: Bermuda Bookstore, 1962.
23. Emmanuel, Isaac S., and Emmanuel, Susan A. *History of the Netherlands Antilles*. Cincinnati: American Jewish Archives, 1970.
24. Seeligmann, S. "David Nassy of Surinam." *Publications of the American Jewish Historical Society* 22 (1914): 25–38.
25. De Cordova, Joshua. "Early Enterprise." *Gleaner*, centenary no. (September 13, 1934), pp. 2–5.

26. Kingston. Institute of Jamaica. Curtis Brett letters, MST.10.
27. Cave, Roderick. "Two Jamaican Printers." *Amphora*, in press.
28. Judah, George F. "The Newspaper History of Jamaica." *Jamaica Times* (January 14, 1899), p. 4.
29. Cave, Roderick. "The Use of Slave Labour in West Indian Printing Houses." *Library*, 5th ser. 30 (September 1975): 241–43.
30. Esterquest, Ralph T. "L'Imprimerie Royale d'Hayti (1817–1819): A Little Known Royal Press of the Western Hemisphere." *Papers of the Bibliographical Society of America* 34 (1940): 171–84.
31. Cave, Roderick. "The First Jamaican Private Press." *Private Library*, 2d ser. 8 (Autumn 1975): 115–19.
32. Cave, Roderick. "An Inventory of the First Jamaican Printing House." *Papers of the Bibliographical Society of America* 69 (Winter 1975): 560–65.
33. Eddy, George S. *Account Books Kept by Benjamin Franklin, Ledger 'D'*. New York: Columbia University Press, 1929.
34. Cave, Roderick. "The St. James' Printery, Montego Bay." *Jamaica Library Association Bulletin* (1976): 7–8.
35. Pope-Hennessy, James. *Verandah: Some Episodes in the Crown Colonies, 1867–1889*. London: Allen & Unwin, 1964.
36. Simmonds, Peter Lund. "Statistics of Newspapers in Various Countries." *Journal of the Statistical Society* 4 (1841): 111–36.
37. Breen, Henry. *St. Lucia: Historical, Statistical and Descriptive*. London: Longmans, 1844.
38. Swan, Bradford S. "Checklist of Early Printing on the Island of Antigua." *Papers of the Bibliographical Society of America* 50 (1956): 285–92.
39. Shilstone, E. M. "Book and Pocket Almanacs." *Journal of the Barbados Museum and Historical Society* 28 (1960): 78–84.
40. Cave, Roderick. "The Plantocracy's Passion for Porcupine." *Library*, in press.
41. Barber, Giles. "Books from the Old World and for the New: The British International Trade in Books in the Eighteenth Century." *Studies on Voltaire and the Eighteenth Century* 151–55 (1976): 185–224.

II

THE USE OF SLAVE LABOUR IN WEST INDIAN PRINTING HOUSES

IN his volume on *The Caribbean area* in 'The Spread of Printing' series (Amsterdam 1970) Bradford F. Swan commented (p. 42) that

> though there is evidence that Negroes were sometimes used in printing houses in colonies on the American mainland, we suspect that the practice was even more common in the West Indies, Cundall in his monograph on early Jamaican printing[1] cites a specific instance. In 1794, he noted, when Alexander Aikman was printing for the Jamaica House of Assembly 200 copies of its minutes he notified a committee of the house that he planned to go to England and that while he was there, in order to 'give the impression all the beauty and elegance of which it is susceptible' he would 'secure a white pressman for its superintendance, that part of the business being executed here by Negroes'.

[1] Frank Cundall, *The press and printers of Jamaica prior to 1820*, Worcester, Mass. 1916.

The present writer has been investigating the inventories of Jamaican printers of the eighteenth and early nineteenth centuries which survive in the Jamaica Archives in the island's old capital, Spanish Town. Such inventories were required by law to be made within six months of a person's death. Not all those made have survived, and those which are extant vary considerably in the amount of detail they give on the deceased's property, but a few *inter alia* throw some light on the extent to which slaves were used in Jamaican printing houses.

In most instances, though the slaves were listed in the inventory together with other property, there is no indication of the slave's function. Some slaves listed were undoubtedly house servants and the like (sometimes being specified as 'laundress' etc.). Because most of the Jamaican printers combined their printing with other activities such as bookbinding, stationery, or in some instances planting, it is dangerous to assume that a printer's slaves were employed in the printing house without specific evidence of it, though one may hazard the guess that their duties would have included work connected with the printing business.

In the case of Jamaica's first printer Robert Baldwin (d. 1722) for example, the evidence of his inventory[2] that he possessed two women and two boys suggests that slaves were not used as pressmen. However, in 1730 Baldwin's widow Mary, by whom the business was continued, advertised for the return of an absconded slave

> a Negro man named *Apollo*, who did deliver the News Papers at *Kingston* and *Spanish Town*. Whoever brings him to his Mistress aforesaid shall be well rewarded.[3]

The first direct evidence for the use of slaves as pressmen comes in the inventory of Ann Woolhead[4] dated 29 November 1783, in which 'The apparatus belonging to the printing Business with the pressmen Bacchus Cannon Jack John and Primus' was valued at £800 (Jamaican currency).

A second list occurs in the inventory of George Eberall,[5] 12 October 1789, in which the list of printing equipment belonging to the copartnership of Lewis and Eberall names five slaves, Johnny, Horace, and Caesar valued at £90 each, and Brentford and London valued at £65 each.

The inventory of Thomas Strupar[6] 9 August 1797, names two pressmen, Chelsea £20 and Tom £90. That of William Dobie[7] in 1820 names 'James and Jamaica attached to the Printing Office' at the exceptionally high valuation of £500, substantially more than that set on Dobie's other slaves, most of whom were valued at £180 or less.

It is possible that the very high valuation set on Dobie's two slaves was because they were more than just pressmen. Alexander Aikman's statement

[2] Jamaica Archives, Inventories Liber 12, fols. 131^v–132^v.
[3] *Weekly Jamaica courant*, no. 675, 25 March 1730, p. 1.
[4] Jamaica Archives, Inventories Liber 66, fol. 146^r.
[5] Jamaica Archives, Inventories Liber 74, fols. 116^v–117^v.
[6] Jamaica Archives, Inventories Liber 87, fol. 54^r.
[7] Jamaica Archives, Inventories Liber 133, fol. 132^r.

suggests that only the presswork was entrusted to negroes. However, in at least one instance there is direct evidence that West Indian printers used their slaves as compositors also. This evidence comes not from Jamaica but from Antigua, where the Will of William Collins[8] dated 10 June 1819 includes the following bequest:

> And whereas it has long been my intention to establish a printing Office of my own in this Island and I have for that purpose long since caused three young negro men named Tom, Charles and Cato belonging to me to be properly taught to read, write and spell and have placed them in the Gazette Office where they have for several years been working as Compositors and are now good Workmen, and have for that purpose also placed three Negro Boys named Robert, George and Elyas, also belonging to me, at school to be instructed in the same manner as the former, the eldest of whom, Robert aged between thirteen and fourteen, is now nearly fit to be taken into the Office and whereas I have within the last three years purchased a new Printing Press of the best materials, together with a fount of Printing Types, weighing six hundred pounds weight, and upwards, and have also purchased a new standing Press and a New Cutting Press, and have also procured several new Stands and many pairs of new cases, with Stools, Iron Chases, Brass rules and various other Implements for carrying on the Trade or Business of a Printer, now I do hereby Give, Devise and Bequeath the three young Negro men above mentioned named Tom, Charles and Cato and the three boys above mentioned named Robert, George and Elyas, being all of them sons of my late Negro Woman Kate together with the said Printing Press, Standing Press, Cutting Press, Types, Stands, Cases, Chases, and all singular the materials in the said Office belonging to me, and which I have from time to time purchased, . . . unto my two Nephews, George and William Collins the only male children of my said Brother, the Reverend George Collins, and to their Heirs Executors, Adminstrators and Assign as Tennants in Common and not as joint Tennants, and I recommend it to my said Brother to cause his said sons to be properly educated to qualify them for conducting a Printing Office, unless anything should occur as a more eligible provision for them, . . .

The 'Appraisement of Wm. Collins dec^{d},' dated 23 November 1824, valued these workmen as follows:

Tom, printer, can read & write	£127	10	0
Charles ,, ,, ,,	106		
Cato ,, ,, ,,	87		
Robert (sick)	43	12	0
George, a boy	58		
Elyas	52		

As a footnote to this account of the connection between slavery and the printing trade and as a slight counterbalance to its unpleasant overtones, it should be recorded that Collins's bequests included £20 to Tom, £10 each to Charles and Cato, and £5 each for the three boys.

[8] Antigua, Book of Wills 1822–8, p. 39. I am grateful to Dr. Barry Higman of the University of the West Indies for drawing my attention to Collins, and to Miss Marjorie Gonsalves of Antigua for procuring a copy of Collins's will for me.

III

THE WEST INDIAN PLANTER AND HIS READING [1]

'A Taste for Literature does by no means prevail in this Country' complained Mary Ricketts when writing home to her sister in England in May 1759.[2] Mrs Ricketts, wife of a Jamaican planter, had some cause for complaint: in selling up their effects prior to a return to Britain they had disposed easily enough of their furniture, but there was so little demand for their library that she could foresee having to ship many of the books home.

It comes as no surprise to read this; it merely confirms the general impression gained of planter society [3] in the sugar islands of the Caribbean—whether through hazy memories of *Tom Cringle's Log* or more purposeful reading of such writers as Edward Long, Bryan Edwards or Lady Nugent—which is emphatically not one of a society with much taste for intellectual pursuits. In Britain, the popular idea of the intellectual level of the islands was nicely summarised in Samuel Foote's *The Author*, first performed at Drury Lane in February 1757:

Cape [the writer]	You have no further commands, Mr Vamp?
Vamp [bookseller]	Not at present; about the Spring I'll deal with you, if we can agree for a couple of volumes in octavo.
Sprightly	Upon what subject?
Vamp	I leave that to him; master Cape knows what will do, though novels are a pretty light summer reading, and do well at Tunbridge, Bristol, and the other watering places: *no bad commodity for the West-India trade neither*; let 'em be novels, master Cape.[4]

Yet there *were* those of a bookish turn in the West Indies, however exceptional; even the most unbookish of merchants and planters (for whom books meant account books) had some need for printed matter. The purpose of this paper is to examine some of the evidence for the circulation of reading matter in the West Indian colonies during their period of greatest prosperity, the period when for Britain to have kept Canada and returned Guadeloupe to France (rather than vice-versa) seemed to many the height of folly.

To speak of the West Indies as though they formed a coherent whole is of course incorrect. Even in the eighteenth century, before the post-emancipation influx of immigrants from Madeira, China, Java and India was to change the individual racial composition of the islands' population, each island had its own special flavour derived from its history, climate and strategic importance in the struggles between France, Spain and Britain. Only the British islands are considered here, as having more in common with the United States, with concentration on Jamaica whose records I have studied most fully, and for which more evidence is available than for most of the islands of the eastern Caribbean.

Jamaica was not typical. It was the largest, most prosperous and most populous British colony, with about 300,000 slaves, 20–30,000 white and twice the number of free coloured people by 1800. Furthermore, despite recurrent scares about

French invasion, it was securely in British hands from 1655 onwards. For these reasons, there was more chance that a book trade would develop early and flourish there than in any other colony. Even Barbados which was its closest rival—and perhaps in cultural terms its superior—lacked the population base for similar development. Thus in Jamaica printing was introduced to Kingston in 1718, spreading to St Jago de la Vega (Spanish Town) in 1756, to Montego Bay in 1773 and to another two centres before the end of the eighteenth century[5] whereas in Barbados it was not until David Harry arrived from Philadelphia in 1730 that printing was introduced,[6] and printing never spread beyond the capital Bridgetown. What material was available and read in Jamaica, therefore, presents a greater range than was available in the smaller islands, but in character was probably very similar.

In only one respect is Jamaica certainly likely to be different from the other British colonies. There was considerable inter-island trading in the eastern Caribbean, with one island's newspapers, almanacs and other publications circulating to its neighbours. The columns of a newspaper such as the *St George's Chronicle and New Grenada Gazette*, for instance, include advertisements from St Vincent and Tobago; and papers from Antigua, Barbados, Dominica, Jamaica, Martinique, St Kitts, St Thomas and St Vincent are quoted in its columns. Books printed in one island circulated widely in others. In contrast, Jamaican newspapers seldom quoted from their eastern Caribbean contemporaries, and books printed in those colonies do not seem to have enjoyed a Jamaican circulation.[7] Exceptionally, work originating in the eastern Caribbean was republished in Jamaica, but this seems to have been the result of unusual enterprise by the Jamaican printer rather than a normal event.[8] Some books produced and read in those islands will not therefore figure in this account.

The West Indian colonies were an important export market for the British book trade in the eighteenth century. As Giles Barber has shown in his analysis of the Customs House records[9] in the period from 1700 to 1780 shipments of books to the Caribbean colonies represented about a quarter of total exports to the New World, and exceeded those to the East Indies. As a whole, the West Indies took more from Britain in this period than did New England; Jamaica almost as much as New York. Naturally, the volume of exports were affected markedly by the periods of war between Britain and France, during which the numbers of books taken to the colonies show a decline—though local disasters in the islands (such as earthquake or hurricanes) do not seem to have had a discernable effect on the trade. Events in North America were not much less devastating in the islands in the early years of the American war in reducing the importation of books from Britain.

The Customs House records do not, of course, provide information on anything except the West Indies' importations from Britain. We know that throughout the early part of the eighteenth century a good deal of material produced in North America circulated in the islands, and that before printing was introduced to the islands (and even afterwards) North American as well as English printers produced the work of West Indian authors. Benjamin Franklin's connections with Antigua, Barbados and Jamaica are well known. In the early 1770s, discontent was little less marked among the planter societies of the islands than it was in the thirteen colonies. The circulation of 'inflammatory' works was a cause of worry to British officialdom; in reporting his concern to Whitehall on 27 March 1776, Sir Basil Keith (Governor of Jamaica) enclosed a copy of the Bradfords' Philadelphia edition of *Common Sense* which was said to have a wide local circulation.[10]

Although the planters' sympathy with the North American cause was considerable, any circulation of North American material (other than loyalist work) was surreptitious and slight after 1776. We may suspect that as far as the Jamaican book trade was concerned, it would not have been regarded with any more favour than it would in official circles, since the trade soon became dominated by the Aikman family: men whose aggressive loyalism was certainly profitable. The Aikmans and other members of the local booktrade are discussed below.

For the first three quarters of the century (the period covered by the Customs House records) there is very little evidence of which books circulated in Jamaica. There was a weekly newspaper published in Kingston from 1718 onwards, and by the later 1750s at least three papers were appearing regularly, but the handful of surviving copies contain little precise information either in their advertisements or editorial matter.

Nor are the other available records in Jamaica itself very enlightening. The Jamaica Archives contain (in their remarkably complete run of the Inventories required to be made of deceased persons' estates) much useful information on the local booktrade, such as it was. We have, for example, a valuable account of the stock and equipment of Robert Baldwin, the island's first printer,[11] and quite extraordinarily full lists of the different types of account books and other stationery supplies available from several of these men.[12] But for that part of their stock-in-trade which consisted of books, such detail is, alas, all too rare. We know, for example, how many Dutch Quills, Hudson's Bay Quills best quality and so forth that were held by William Aikman, but for his bookstock, that of the best bookshop in Jamaica (and probably the whole Caribbean), the inventories tell us little more than that there were 1819 'books various'.[13] Between the Inventory prepared in 1684 for the estate of Thomas Craddock (who *may* have been Jamaica's first bookseller)[14] and that made in 1798 of the effects of the Spanish Town bookseller David Dickson[15] the Inventories are less helpful a source than one would wish.

The booktrade inventories are not of course the only inventories to include information on books; a systematic search through the whole file held by the Jamaica Archives remains a *desideratum*. Some limited investigations on the reading of individuals in Jamaica is possible; on such men as Thomas Thistlewood[16] and Nathaniel Phillips,[17] for example.

Analysis of subscription lists in eighteenth century British and American books to identify purchasers from the West Indies remains an avenue as yet very little explored. The amazing demand in Jamaica for Cobbett's *Porcupine's Works* revealed by the subscription lists was no doubt thoroughly untypical,[18] but there may well have been other books with a strong West Indian market which will be revealed by such analysis.

Subscription lists appear in a very small number of books published in the island.[19] As one would expect, the lists usually reflect the civil, military and naval official establishment, members of the House of Assembly and so forth. Thomas Dancer's *A Short Dissertation on the Jamaica Bath Waters* (Kingston, Douglass & Aikman, 1784) is fairly typical in this respect, though (unremarkably enough in view of its medical content) it also includes the names of 56 doctors among its 327 subscribers. Of the 327, only two were outside Jamaica: Major Lawrie, Superintendent of the Mosquito Shore, and J. Murray Esq. of Philiphaugh, Scotland, taking a copy each.

In one instance the subscription list is very different from this normal pattern. In Joshua Hezekia de Cordova's *Reason and faith, or philisophical absurdities . . . by one of the Sons of Abraham to his brethren* (Kingston, 1788) the printers Strupar and Preston specified in their imprint that the book was printed 'at the cost and for the use of his subscribers'. Only thirty-four subscribers were named, all members of Jamaica's long-established Jewish community. No other work produced specifically for this community in the eighteenth century is known, but in the nineteenth century members of the De Cordova family were to assume an important position in the Jamaican booktrade, and as well as their general printing, produced some publications for the use of the Jewish group. Interestingly *Reason and Faith* was one of the rather few Jamaican works to be re-issued in the United States, an edition being produced in Philadelphia by F. Bailey in 1791, and another printed by John Dixon at Richmond in 1804.[20] In the 1820s members of the Jamaican De Cordova family had moved to the United States, and it is probable that they, like other members of the Jewish community, had family links with North America at a much earlier date.

Though it was very unusual, *Reason and Faith* was one publication of the Jamaican press at a time when genuine local literary production seemed to be emerging.[21] It did not in fact develop, but the last twenty years or so of the eighteenth and the first decade of the nineteenth century seem something of a high point for the book in Jamaica. The Customs House records of exports of books from Britain are not available, but other evidence would appear to indicate that the volume of books coming into the island reached and perhaps surpassed the numbers for the years before the American war.

By contrast with the first three quarters of the century, from the late 1770s onwards, there is a much more ample record on the circulation of books in Jamaica. Although the files of Jamaican newspapers are still pitifully incomplete for this period, enough copies of the island's three semi-official papers (the *Royal Gazette*, the *St Jago de la Vega Gazette* and the *Cornwall Chronicle*) survive and are augmented by short runs of some of the other Kingston journals to furnish us with a good deal of information to flesh out the meagre record of the Inventories. Jamaican printers of the time were like their contemporaries in provincial England, and to their trade as printers usually added bookbinding, stationery and bookselling, and often a whole range of other mercantile enterprises, from musical instruments through haberdashery to other less obviously appropriate lines. It was natural enough that they should use the columns of their papers for extensive advertisements detailing their new stock received from London. A summary note of these advertisements is given as Appendix II.

In addition to the booksellers' announcements of new stock available in their shops, there is clear indication that the more enterprising businessmen were willing to obtain books on demand from Britain. Thus in 1792 Edward Lewis, bookseller and stationer in the capital St Jago de la Vega (Spanish Town) included a note in an advertisement that he had received the *London Catalogue of Books*, last edition. In 1804 Munds & McIntosh, who at that time[22] were managing the bookselling business attached to His Majesty's Printing Office (Alexander Aikman senior and junior) announced that the file of Bent's Monthly List of New Publications for 1803 was available for consultation.

Sales of books were not limited to these regular members of the booktrade. Eighteenth century Jamaica was not a healthy place, and the structure of the planting economy could and did cause economic stresses. Both death and bankruptcy were among the reasons for a fair number of auction sales of books which were held in Kingston during this period. Details of auctions and private sales noted are summarised in Appendix III. Undoubtedly there were many other such sales of which I am not aware because of the *lacunae* in the newspaper files.

Although the books offered at most of these sales can only be guessed at, Donald Campbell's advertisement for one sale in the *Jamaica Courant* 28 May 1806 listed them in some detail; the range and composition was very much that of the contemporary booksellers' lists. One would dearly like to know something of the prices realised at these sales – as indeed it would be good to be able to compare the prices charged by Jamaican booksellers with those obtaining in London at the time. Henry Lemoine's article on 'Printing and Bookselling in America' in the November 1796 issue of the *Gentleman's Magazine* [23] suggested that in the West Indies the capital of each island would have

> one person who calls himself a bookseller . . . keeps a few books, such as he judges are most in demand, which he sells at an advance of 70L. and 100L. *per cent.*

No doubt this was true of the smaller islands of the eastern Caribbean, but whether the more advanced booktrade and element of competition in Jamaica resulted in a lower mark-up cannot be established.

Planters and merchants (and their wives) could at this time not only buy a fair selection of books in Jamaica, they could also borrow them. Very early in the century there had been a parochial library in Port Royal, which had already fallen on evil days before being destroyed by hurricane in 1722. No doubt another parochial library sent out in 1724 had also disappeared completely fifty years later and I have found no Jamaican references to it.[24] What seems to have been the first circulating library in the island, that started by William Aikman in 1779, was discontinued for lack of support in 1781. Several other attempts also failed for the same reason, but the Circulating Library established in 1788/9 by Thomas Stevenson (who had been manager of Aikman's shop, and succeeded to his business) lasted until at least 1838 and probably longer. As I have discussed Jamaican Circulating Libraries (and Kingston's one Coffee House provision) elsewhere[25] this important aspect of reading in Jamaica is not considered further here.

There are other ways of investigating Jamaican reading tastes. The appendices to this paper summarise some of the evidence from the advertising columns in the island's press. Their editorial matter is also interesting, and the newspapers often contained poetry in their columns. A certain amount of this may be original, but much was probably reprinted from non-Jamaican sources. The verses of 'Peter Pindar' for example were not seldom quoted: natural enough because of the writer's connection with Jamaica,[26] but analysis of other poetry (and prose extracts) would be instructive. Similarly the contents of the various magazines produced in the island from the 1780s onwards deserve study. In the unique set of the *Savanna-la-Mar Gazette* held by the American Antiquarian Society there are tantalising references to another paper also published in Savanna-la-Mar by Monk & Leyburn in 1788: *The Cornwall Magazine or Temple of Pleasure*

> 'each number to contain 16pp. 8vo Demy of letterpress, to be printed on [sic] a beautiful new type of FRY'S, and on the best paper.'

At least twelve numbers of this non-political, non-scandalous paper were published; from the description of the contents of number II ('Instructions for Fine Ladies', 'Attraction and Repulsion, a fable' etc.) it seems as if the paper was aimed at the planters' wives as much as the planters themselves. No copies are now known of this ill-fated venture.[27] Other magazines of the period lasted longer, though none received the number of regular subscriptions hoped for: study of those which survive will reveal more on what their editors hoped the planter class would wish to read than what they actually read.

There is one further Jamaican publication which deserves study for the evidence it contains on another facet of the plantocracy's recreation. In the British Library is a copy[28] of *Wilsone's St Cecilia, being a choice collection of those celebrated British, Scottish and Irish songs, which have been so much esteemed in this island . . .* (St Jago, Printed for 'C. Wilsone' 1785). An advertisement for this very rare book in the *Cornwall Chronicle*, dated from Spanish Town 15 December 1785, listed the sources of some of the songs, which had been taken from *Rosina, The Duenna, The Maid of the Mill, Thomas and Sally* and other plays which

> the editor has most carefully inserted; and whatever would tend to suppress virtue he has most attentively excluded.

The theatre enjoyed considerable popularity in Jamaica, where David Douglass had brought the American Company of Players through the hard years of the revolutionary war. Some of the local publications reflect this interest. As well as drama, music enjoyed considerable support, though it was not until the 1830s that there was to be any local music publication, and that mostly of a rather light and frivolous nature: the St Mary's ShaSha, the Sligo quadrille and so forth. To indicate local musical taste, an advertisement by John McIntosh & Co. from 1809 is given as Appendix IV.

More important than these, perhaps, are some of the records held by H. M.

Customs & Excise in London. For the early nineteenth century Jamaica was an obvious battleground in the trade and copyright conflicts between Britain and the United States, and the Customs House reports of seizures of American publications (including some piracies of English editions) will provide valuable supplementary information on local reading tastes.[29]

The present writer has conflated those lists of books included in inventories and advertisements of the period 1790–1810, to try to identify in an impressionistic way which subjects, and which titles, were conspicuous by their inclusion or absence. To be sure, this is only a very crude guide to Jamaican reading and book buying. A good many categories of books were so extensively imported and used that the booksellers had no need to itemise them in this way. R. Loosely's *Jamaica Gazette* advertisement of 4 October 1788, for example, concluded the lengthy listing of authors and titles with a blanket reference to

> New song books, newest acting farces, a variety of loose plays, school and children's books.

These, together with dictionaries, cookery books, periodicals and reviews were seldom specified in more detail – though fortunately there is one advertisement included by Stevenson, Aikman and Smith [30] in their *Diary and Kingston Daily Advertiser* of 16 July 1802 which itemises these as well as the more serious contributions to literature which normally figure in such lists.

Most bookseller's advertisements were miscellaneous lists. It is interesting to compare three of the rather uncommon classified lists:

Lewis, Lunan & Jones (St Jago) January 1801		*Lewis, Lunan & Jones* (St Jago) October 1801		*Stevenson, Aikman & Smith* (Kingston) July 1802	
Law	22 titles	Law	8 titles	Law	17 titles
Medicine	6 titles	Medicine	5 titles	Medicine	27 titles
Poetry	26 titles	Poetry	30 titles	Poetry	32 titles
Novels	23 titles	Novels	25 titles	Novels	16 titles
Military	4 titles	Military	2 titles	–	
Miscellaneous	107 titles	Miscellaneous	114 titles	Miscellaneous	51 titles
(incl. History, biography, dictionaries)				Plays	26 titles
				Song & Jest books	26 titles
				Children's books	40 titles
				School books, etc.	45 titles
				French, Spanish	9 titles
Total	*188 titles*	Total	*204 titles*	Total	*322 titles*

As most of the island's administrative and legal business was transacted in the capital St Jago, one would have expected rather more legal works to be imported by the St Jago firm, but this was not the case, and the proportions are very similar for both firms.

The similarity of range, and of actual titles imported by these and other booksellers suggests that we can discount one potential defect of my conflated list as a gauge of Jamaica reading tastes. That a particular bookseller imported and advertised a certain book is of course no evidence that he sold it. Repeated advertisements for one book from one firm over a period of time may be negative rather than positive evidence[31] – showing that the dealer was trying to dispose of unsold stock, and not importing additional copies to meet demand – but the broad similarity of the lists is reassuring. To some extent, of course, books were sent to Jamaica on consignment and might be returned unsold,[32] and there is little to guide us on the numbers sold of particular titles.

We cannot do more than guess at the extent to which the Jamaican booksellers' stock reflected local demand, or how far they were limited by selections made for them by wholesale suppliers in London. It is clear how far English provincial booksellers were restricted in their service by their London agents[33] and one can presume that the colonial bookseller had still less chance of getting entirely appropriate material shipped to him. On the other hand, partners in the more substantial Jamaican firms (or members of their immediate families) spent substantial periods of time in Britain – or were even more or less permanently resident there – and with their special knowledge of local conditions and tastes would have been able to select the right stock for their own clientele.

Most previous writers on Jamaica have emphasised the philistine nature of planter society. In an early paper by the great Jamaican bibliographer Frank Cundall we read that

> In the 'great house' of an estate in the so-called palmy days, it was quite the exception to find either a book-case or pictures . . . Men of letters who have visited and written in and of Jamaica . . . have had no influence in forming a taste for literature on the island.[34]

Cundall went on to quote an earlier writer, J. Stewart, whose *Account of Jamaica and its inhabitants* (London, 1808) stated that

> Literature is very little cultivated in Jamaica; nor is reading a very general favorite amusement. There is a circulating library in Kingston, and in one or two other places a paltry attempt at such a thing, these collections of books not being of that choice and miscellaneous native which they ought to be, but usually composed of a few good novels, mixed with a much larger proportion of those ephemeral ones which are daily springing up, and which are a disgrace to literature and an insult to common-sense.

There is a very familiar ring about this; upright men of some literary taste fulminated often enough about circulating libraries, and particularly about the gothic novels which were so popular with the circulating libraries' clientele.[35] No doubt Stevenson's Circulating Library contained *The Mysterious Freebooter, The Spirit of the Elbe* and others of the same class, just as he sold them in his shop, but my list (far too lengthy to print here) shows that there was a much more substantial and worthwhile side to Jamaican reading than Stewart (or following him, Cundall) allows to have been the case.

The books bought and used by the settlers fall into a number of reasonably well-defined categories. For the efficient management of the planters' business were needed the various manuals on agriculture and planting, the production of sugar and molasses and the distillation of rum. Such books as Labourie's *Coffee Planter of St Domingo* were of considerable importance at a time when the Blue Mountains were being planted on a large scale. Not only was Labourie's book imported, the publishers of the *New Jamaica Magazine* also found it worthwhile to serialise the work.[36] For the pen-keepers, work on sheep and cattle was appropriate. Interest in agricultural works clearly extended beyond those specifically for the West Indian market. The advertisements are for such books as those by Bartle, Reeve and Taplin on farriery, Culley on livestock, Moseley's *Treatise on Sugar*, Kennedy on planting, Lord Dundonald's *Treatise on Agriculture and Chemistry*, and Kames's *Gentleman Farmer.*

No doubt some of the manuals on book-keeping included in advertisements were for use in the mercantile houses, but for the planter attempting to keep his accounts straight these works were no less necessary. The very sizeable proportion of medical works though no doubt directed to a large extent towards the naval and military surgeons, and those in private practice, also enjoyed a circulation going beyond this small group.[37] The health of his slaves was a matter of vital interest to the planter and to the merchant, and a good deal of amateur doctoring was undertaken for purely economic (and perhaps also for humane) reasons. Every 'Great House', we can safely assume, would have had its selection of books for this purpose: Dancer's *Medical Assistant* (which was locally published, in several editions); Buchan's *Domestic Medicine*, Granger on West Indian diseases, Chisholm on fevers. Such works would be supplemented by other more specialised texts: the progressive planter had his slaves innoculated against smallpox, and had an obvious interest in works on this; while no doubt several of the planters whose amours were too freely conducted had a personal interest in the treatises on venereal complaints by Jesse Foot and others.

Not only would the planters and merchants wish to preserve the health of themselves and their slaves, there was their livestock. As already suggested, veterinary texts and manuals on farriery enjoyed a wide sale. There was some local production of such work to supplement or compete with such standard sellers as Taplin's *Farriery*; in 1803 'An entirely new treatise on the symptoms and treatment of various diseases incident to horses, by a veterinary surgeon now in the island' was published,[38] while outside our period the Montego Bay printer Alexander Holmes took a leaf from the Aikman's book and produced a piracy of Francis Clater's *Every man his own farrier.*[39]

For the planter's domestic comfort, or for the convenience of his wife or housekeeper,[40] the Jamaican booksellers carried a good number of cookery books and works on domestic economy. It was a surprisingly good range, from the old established favourites like Mrs Glasse to the newer works like Mrs Rundell's *New System of Domestic Cookery* (1808) which no less than Byron's work was to set the finances of John Murray on a firm footing.

A good many of the large number of law books figuring in the booksellers' advertisements were intended for the legal profession. As most legal business was transacted in the capital St Jago de la Vega, it was natural that such works should form a considerable proportion of the St Jago firms' stock. Most of such works were intended for those in practice – and one of the early essays in commercial library provision was directed at the legal profession [41] – but not all were of direct practical usefulness. The treatises on conveyancing, the manuals on pleading, the digests of English law, and English law reports were of undoubted value. But though English law was relevant, Scots law was not, and the occasional Scottish text is probably a tribute to the heavy Scottish input to colonial life at the end of the century.

Some of the legal works were intended, no doubt, for the legislators in the House of Assembly, who spent large sums of public money on an edition of Jamaican laws published by the Aikmans. One of the 'lost' books of Jamaican bibliography is *The Justice of the Peace's pocket companion* (Kingston, Daniell, 1754) and a good many of the imported works would have been required by the various magistrates charged with the administration of law around the island.

Jamaica's geographical isolation and the various naval wars of the period account for a number of the texts. The Court of Vice Admiralty was important; works on prize law of direct relevance. For the merchants of Kingston, an understanding of mercantile and shipping law, of bills of exchange, and alas of bankruptcy was a necessity.

Some of the works of military interest were probably imported in the expectation that there would be sales to the officers of the British troops which garrisoned the island. But this garrison was small, and Jamaica lived in constant dread of slave revolts, or wars with the Maroons living in the mountainous interior,[42] and in some fear of Spanish or French invasion. All able-bodied white men were required to serve in the militia. [43] By all accounts they were a thoroughly inept and unwarlike body of men but nevertheless the militia required drill manuals and the like. Some of these were produced by the local printers (also responsible for producing the roll books and other ephemera needed by the military machine) but among the importations such works as Reid's *Infantry Officer*, the *Little Bombardier* or Adye on courts-martial were intended for these amateur soldiers.

In the stock of the booksellers of Montego Bay and of Kingston, though obviously not those of inland St Jago, were to be found manuals aimed at the sailor – Moore's *Navigation*, Haselden's *Seaman's Daily Assistant, Nautical almanacs* – and a range of charts and pilots (some perhaps locally produced) [44] to ease his problems in navigating in the Caribbean.

Last among the 'useful' books represented in the stocks of the Jamaican book-trade came the school books and the range of dictionaries and similar reference books. The lists of educational texts seem to an inexpert eye to be (like the cookery books) fairly well representative of those published in Britain at the time. The same is true of the dictionaries, with a sufficient showing of those dealing with French and Spanish as well as English. Later than the period of this survey, the very strong Scottish element in the population was to give ample support to Armstrong's *Gaelic Dictionary*. The classical tongues were perhaps under-represented: certainly the planters seem to have been men of little Greek, though with enough Latin to appreciate the attacks which Thomas Dancer levelled[45] against the style as well as the content of Jamaica's sole publication in Latin, David Grant's *Tractatus de febre flava* (Regioduni [Doddington], 1805).

Among the works of less immediate practical usefulness, books on travel and topography and history form a large proportion. Some clearly reflect the home-sickness of the expatriate Scot or Englishman, though others illustrate a more general interest in the world at large. That Bligh's narrative of the Bounty should have local appeal is not surprising, since Bligh was responsible for bringing the breadfruit among other introductions from the east. Botanical works attracted fair interest, and there was some worthwhile local production in this field, though John Lunan was compelled to issue his *Hortus Jamaicensis* in parts for lack of support for his earlier subscription proposals.[46]

In the other sciences, and in philosophy, religion, politics and government the range of work is less impressive. Some works, such as Sibbit on luxury, had some special local interest as the author was an island clergyman. The obvious, basic English texts are there, but there are significant gaps. The French writers of the Enlightenment hardly appear (Diderot is represented by *The Nun* and *Jacques the Fatalist*, Voltaire by *Candide*!) and one can conclude that the intell-ectual tone of the island, unsurprisingly, was that of the *Britannica* and not of the *Encyclopedie*. Writers of the revolutionary period who were widely read in the United States – such as St Just – do not appear at all.

It is however in the field of aesthetics, and the fine arts, that the lists seem most deficient. At the turn of the centuries, if Jamaica merely represented in little what was being published, read and discussed in Britain, one might have expected to find Repton, Payne Knight or Sir Uvedale Price on the picturesque. One does not, and in fact it is hard to find anything beyond a few basic manuals (Alston's *Hints . . . in landscape painting*, for instance) in the field of the arts at all. Cundall was clearly in error when he mentioned the lack of books in the 'great house', but his reference to lack of pictures is perhaps supported by the dearth of books on the arts. Delightful though Bewick's *Quadrupeds* is, it scarcely represents all that was available from Britain, and very little else was advertised.

The novels, poetry and plays, on the other hand, are a truer reflection of con-temporary British tastes. Once more, one can discern some special local interests here and there. The Dallas family were planters in the Port Royal mountains, which accounts for the prominence often given to R. C. Dallas's work in the local press.

To turn briefly from Jamaica to two other West Indian islands of a very different kind will illustrate the strength of the local book trade, and the relative ease with which Jamaican society could obtain a good range of reading.

For the first, St Croix in the Danish Virgin Islands, there is a twofold advantage in such comparison. Printing was introduced into Christianstaed by Daniel Thibou from St Kitts in 1769, and the good file of his paper, the *Royal Danish American Gazette* which survives in the Royal Library Copenhagen for 1770–75 and 1789–92 permits reasonable comparison with the Jamaican press of the time. More importantly, as a Danish colony there was not the same trade isolation from North America, nor from the eastern Caribbean colonies: this is amply shown by the bylines on news reports which were taken from the *New York Journal, Newport Mercury, Pennsylvania Journal, Massachusetts Spy, Dominica Gazette, Hague Courant, St Christopher Advertiser, Martinique Gazette, American Mercury* and several others.

From the columns of Thibou's paper we learn much about the local theatre, where the Leeward Islands Company of Comedians had an ample and typical repertoire – The Beaux Stratagem, Mock Doctor, The Recruiting Officer, The Wonder of an honest Yorkshireman, Richard III, The King and the Miller of Mansfield, A Bold Stroke for a Wife, The Citizen, The London Merchant or the history of George Barnwell, and Flora or the Hob in the Well were all played in July 1770, the first month of the paper's publication.

Unusually, the printer did not combine his printing business with book-selling and stationery in the normal way (although he advertised the usual blanks) [47] but instead with saddlery, scabbards, harness-making and the supply of chaises and chariots. Stationery and account-book advertisements appear from a few merchants. There are a very few advertisements and subscription proposals for local publications: *A Table of Money from One Ryal to 1000 Pieces of Eight* (11 August 1770), *An Abridgement of the English and Prussian Military Exercise for the Foot* (proposals 13 April, published 1 June 1771), and from 1773 the *St Croix Almanack*. There are a few advertisements or subscription proposals from outside: the *St Christopher Almanack*, the American reprint of Blackstone's *Commentaries* (12 August 1772), Peterkin's *Treatise on Planting*. [48]

There are isolated announcements of books for sale (*Miscellaneous Poems from the German* 'a work lately published', 15 August 1772) or lost (*Adventures of a Guinea*, vol. 2, 7 January 1775) but the overall impression one gains from scanning the papers is that St Croix was almost a bibliographical desert. But with one oasis, in the improbable figure of Hugh Knox,[49] who combined his duties as Presbyterian Pastor with those of Physician, Merchant and ultimately Attorney for the printer Thibou and proprietor of a circulating library.

Knox first appears in the columns of the *Royal Danish American Gazette* as author, [50] with an advertisement for various discourses and sermons (26 Sept 1772). On 8 July 1775 he advised his subscribers that copies of his essays, *The Moral and Religious Miscellany* had been received from Hodge & Shober, the printers in New York. Fourteen years later he was transmuted into bookseller:

> Just imported from London, and to be sold by Hugh Knox (for cash) a choice collection of the latest novels, and only such as have met with the approbation and recommendation of the Monthly Reviews, a catalogue of which, with the prices, may be seen at my house, and at my shop on the King's Wharf; also School Bibles, New Testaments, and spelling-books; Guthrie's Geographical

Grammar and Buchan's Domestic Medicine, latest editions; An abridgement of Cooke's Voyages, with the Cuts &c. Orders will be duly attended to.
St. Croix, Christianstaed, May 30th, 1789.

The contents of this choice collection can be gathered from another advertisement of 5 August 1789 in which Knox announced that he would 'let out for reading' these 'new and entertaining novels':

Memoirs of the Bellmoor Family 4 vols
Zoreada 3 vols
Mrs Bellamy 5 vols
Oswald Castle 2 vols
Air Balloon 2 vols
Diversities of Fortune 3 vols
Francis the Philanthropist 3 vols
Clarenden 2 vols
Vale of Glendor 2 vols
Tales of the Castle 5 vols
Pompey the Little 1 vol
Victim of Fancy 4 vols
Eleanor 2 vols
Excessive Sensibility 2 vols
Nabob 2 vols
Liberal American 2 vols
Matilda 2 vols
Caroline of Litchfield 3 vols
Werbeck 2 vols
Fitzosborne 3 vols
Belford and Woodvill 3 vols
Adelaide and Theodore 3 vols
Vale of Martindale 2 vols

Knox allowed his readers only two days for each volume, and charged 2 bitts for each. Whether the venture enjoyed much success is uncertain, but there are no other advertisements for this rudimentary library before his death on 9 October 1790. His executors auctioned his house, stock-in-trade and library on 26/27th October, and thereafter the columns of the *Royal Danish American Gazette* are even more empty than before of references to books.

A second comparison is possible with Grenada. The southernmost of the Windward islands, it changed hands several times between the French and English in the eighteenth century: a large proportion of the 3,500 white population when it passed to Britain in 1763 were French settlers, and one might anticipate some French element in any reference to books and reading – just as the island's papers were (in the eighteenth century) largely bilingual.

Grenada's interesting typographical history remains to be written. Though William Wayland started the *Royal Grenada Gazette* in 1765, too few copies of any before the 1790s survive to furnish any information, but the sets of the *St George's Chronicle* in the American Antiquarian Society and in the National Library of Scotland [51] permit comparisons with Jamaica for the turn of the century.

As with the St Croix paper, and in contrast with the Jamaican press, there is little to be found. On 5 April 1799 John Waugh, Vendue-Master, announced the forthcoming auction of the law library of the late K. F. McKenzie, Attorney-General. There were the usual advertisements for almanacs, and for a few other local pamphlet publications and for stationery. The columns of the *Gazette* are annually enlivened by fiercely patriotic doggerel commendatory verses from the Printer's Devil; even by a verse advertisement from a general merchant, offering

Snuff-boxes shaped like Ladies shoes,
And pocket-books with nice *quelques choses*,
Gold seals, watch keys and also hooks
With German Flutes and Music books . . .
The best of needles e'er imported,
And Reeve's water-colours sorted, . . .
Paper and Cards of Old King Harry,
and every sort of Stationery . . . [52]

– but apart from this mention of Music books, I have found no other reference to books until the *Chronicle* passed into the proprietorship of John Spahn in July 1808. Like William Aikman or Knox before him, Spahn was to set up a circulating library, which by December 1811 numbered some 2,500 volumes, though it appears not to have started operations before 1810. In later years, circulating libraries were to assume some importance in the cultural life of Grenada (and also to be conducted by Scotsmen), but the evidence of the *St George's Chronicle*, like that of the St Croix paper, suggests that in the eighteenth century and at the start of the nineteenth, the planters in the smaller islands had significantly less chance of obtaining reading matter locally than their contemporaries in Jamaica.

In examining the evidence for reading in the sugar islands, one fact shows itself very clearly. The entrepreneurs were Scotsmen, just as their customers were also very largely of Scottish origin. Even if born in the islands, they retained a fierce attachment to what they considered their homeland. Two remarkable letters written to Sir Walter Scott by Alexander Aikman junior[53] in 1830 illustrate this well. In the first Aikman wrote of his schooldays at Edinburgh High School in the 1790's, and attributes his improved editorial style to reading the Waverley novels. He goes on to say

> I have a beautiful and elegant library, and moreover, it is most valuable, for the books have cost me upwards of 5,000 currency.[54]

In the second, Aikman asked Scott to persuade the Lord Provost and Council of Edinburgh to send him the Foulis edition of Virgil, 'embellished with the City Arms', as part of a prize from the High School Aikman had earned in 1791! Whether Aikman ever received it is doubtful, but his wish illustrates the high regard in which the Scottish West Indian colonists held the book.

NOTES

1. My thanks are due to the American Antiquarian Society for a Fred Harris Daniels Fellowship, and to the British Academy for a research grant making the preparation of this paper possible. Acknowledgements are due also to the staff of the many libraries and record repositories whose holdings of West Indiana I consulted.
2. BL Add. MSS 30001.f.12; quoted in K. E. Ingram, *Sources of Jamaican History* 1655–1838. Zug, Switzerland, Inter-Documentation Co., 1976, p. 72.
3. In this study 'planter' is interpreted in its widest sense to include not only those engaged directly in the planting business but also the other elements of colonial society: officials of government, military and naval personnel based at the Jamaica station, professional men (doctors, lawyers, clergy), merchants, shopmen and artisans. As well as the expatriate and white creole population, it certainly includes free persons of colour; although as the most liberal estimates judge that only 2½% of the slave population could read in the 1830s, the slave population can probably be left out of account.
4. *The Dramatic Works of Samuel Foote* (London, W. Lowndes, 1809) v. 1. *The Author*, p. 15. The italics are mine.
5. Roderick Cave, 'Printing in eighteenth century Jamaica', *The Library* 5th series, v. 33 no. 3 (1978) pp. 187–206 [reprinted here, pp. 105–124].
6. E. M. Shilstone, 'Some notes on early presses and newspapers in Barbados', *Journal of the Barbados Museum and Historical Society*, v. 26 (1968) pp. 19–33; Douglas McMurtrie, *Early Printing in Barbados*, London, privately printed, 1933.
7. Two examples based on analysis of subscription lists: Peterkin's *Treatise on planting* (St Kitts, 1790) which was a book of obvious practical value printed in an edition of about 550 copies, had subscribers in St Kitts (150) Nevis (40) Montserrat (24) Antigua (100) Tortola (51) Dominica (2) St Vincent (1) Anguilla (3); Danish St Croix (125) and St Thomas (1); Dutch St Martin (45) and St Eustatius (5); and Spanish Puerto Rico (2). Much later, Charles Shepherd's *Historical account of St Vincent* (London, 1831) had 212 subscribers based in St Vincent (125) Britain (44) Trinidad (18) Montserrat (12) Barbados (3) and Dominica (3); with single copies going to Antigua, Bermuda, Demarara, Grenada and as far afield as France and Ceylon. Neither seems to have been advertised or to have circulated in Jamaica.
8. Alexander Aikman senior in 1780 published William Belgrove's *A Treatise on the Planting Business containing the work for the whole twelve months . . .* 'by J. Bellgrove [sic] Planter of Barbados'; apparently a disguised reprint of the work originally published at Boston, 1755. Among several editions pirating work published in Britain he included a reprint of the London edition of Samuel Martin's *Essay on Plantership* (Antigua, 1750) in 1802. A 'fourth edition' of Martin's *Essay* was published by John Lunan from the office of the St Jago de la Vega Gazette in 1821.

closely.

38. Subscription proposals, *St Jago de la Vega Gazette* 8 January 1803; 'this day is published' 13 August 1803. No copy has been traced.
39. 'Twenty-eighth edition' Montego Bay, Holmes, 1829 (Copy in the Institute of Jamaica). Clater's book was very successful, NUC listing 32 English editions, as well as American, French, German and Spanish – including one from Havana, 1834.
40. Regular marriages there were in planter society, of course, but among the poorer planters and tradesmen to have a coloured 'housekeeper' was no less common. Many of these common-law marriages were as long-lasting (and no doubt as happy) as regular unions.
41. Cave, 'Early circulating libraries' *loc. cit.*, pp. 58–9 [reprinted here, pp. 232–3].
42. There were Maroon Wars in the 1730s and again in 1795.
43. Save for a few favoured individuals: the Aikmans succeeded in having this obligation waived for those employed in His Majesty's Printing Office.
44. Bernard Roman's work figures in several advertisements. In a prolix and interesting announcement 'to the Public' which Romans issued from Montego Bay, 27 March 1784, he stated that he planned republishing his large hydrographic surveys from Hispaniola to the Mississippi in Europe, and referred to a number of inadequate and spurious editions: 'even Mrs Woodhead's press in Kingston brought forth an essay of this kind . . . ' (*Cornwall Chronicle*, 10 April 1784).
45. In the *Jamaica Courant*, 18 June 1806 continuing an entertaining pamphlet war with Grant's *The Critic criticised or strictures on Thomas Dancer's 'Jamaica Practice of Physic'* (1805), Dancer's *The Exposer exposed, an answer to Dr Grant's libellous invective* (1805) and other equally choleric works.
46. The twenty-four parts appeared between October 1809 and April 1814.
47. e.g. 'Danish, English and Dutch Bills of Lading, English Bills of Exchange and Powers of Attorney &c. All kinds of blanks printed at the said office with the greatest dispatch' *R. Danish Amer. Gazette* 11 July 1770.
48. See above, note 6. Advertising in St Croix obviously paid.
49. Knox, born in Ireland about 1727, emigrated to America in 1751, and became a student at Princeton in the class of 1754, being ordained in 1755. He subsequently served as presbyterian minister on Saba, 1755–72, and from then until his death in 1790 at St Croix. There is a lengthy account of his career in James McLachlan, *Princetonians 1748–1768; a biographical dictionary* (Princeton, 1976) pp. 101–105.
50. The range of imprints on his work listed in *NUC* is impressive: New York, London, St Kitts, St Croix, Glasgow and Hartford (Me) in his lifetime; Gettysburg, Harrisburg, New Ipswich, Brunswick (Me) and New York subsequently.
51. A.A.S. has July 1790–January 1791; February 1798–December 1801; January–June 1810 within our period; National Library of Scotland scattered issues for 1799 and 1800 and a reasonably complete set from June 1801 to April 1813.
52. David Napier's advertisement, 19 November 1790.
53. National Library of Scotland, MS 3914 ff. 8–12 and f. 161.
54. The valuation of £500 currency placed on Aikman's library by his Inventorists

is suggestive of the slighter value in which Jamaican Society as a whole placed on the written word.

Appendix I

List of Books Shipped by Nathaniel Phillips to Jamaica, 1775.
(National Library of Wales, Slebech 9402)

Tull's Husbandry
Martin's Philosophy
Critical Reviews
Sermon on American Affairs
Pliny's Letters 2 vol.
Ash's Dictionary 2 vol. 12/-
Nugent's French & Eng. Diction.[y] 3/6
Ash's Grammar 1/-
2 Court Kalendars
Map of London
Do. Roads, Book of Do.
Treatise on Whist 1/-
Martin's Treatise 3/6
English Grammar

. . .

Hist[y] of Jamaica 3 vol. 2 L Cy.
Chesterfield's Letters 4 vol.
Grand Tour 4 vol.
Ludlow's Memoirs 3 vol.
French treatise on refining Sugar
Span: Grammar
2 Eng. Do.
Tour thro' France

E. Burke's Speech. Appeal to Gt Britain
Notes of Congress. McAuley's Address
Sr J. Dalrymple's address to America
Donaldson on Agriculture
Essay on Plantership
Glovers Speech on West Indian Affairs
Tour thro' Holland
Robsone's [?] Catalogue of Books
Atlas 42/- Jacob's Law Dictionary,
fol: 40/-
Lyttleton's Works 4to 30/-
Kent's Agriculture 5/-
Mortimer's Do. 2 vol: 8/-
Sheridan's Art of Reading
Do. on Education
Blackstone's Comment. 4 vol: 30/-
Sterne's Letters 2/-
Burn's Justice 4 vol: 24/-
Bielfeld's Erudition 3 vol: 18/-
Stillingfleet's Tracts 6/-
Mawe's Gardener 5/-
French Grammar

. . .

Appendix II

Some Booksellers' Advertisements

1. *St. Jago Intelligencer* 16 April 1768: books, legal blanks, bookbinding, by Lowry and Sherlock, St. Jago de la Vega.
2. *Cornwall Chronicle* 1 March 1788: long list of books offered for sale by David McHardie, Montego Bay.
3. *Cornwall Chronicle* 29 March 1788: ditto.
4. *Jamaica Gazette* 4 October 1788: long list of books for sale by R. Loosely, Kingston.
5. *Daily Advertiser* 31 May 1790: maps, charts, books advertised by Thomas Stevenson & Co., Kingston.
6. *Daily Advertiser* 12 August 1790: advertisement by Loosely & Linwood, Kingston; stationery and some books.
7. *Daily Advertiser* 29 November 1790: includes list of books for sale by Thomas Stevenson & Co.
8. *Daily Advertiser* 1 June 1791: further stock imported by Stevenson & Aikman and for sale at their Stationery Store and Circulating Library.
9. *Daily Advertiser* 9 August 1791: ditto.
10. *St. Jago de la Vega Gazette* 5 January 1792: stationery and books for sale by Edward Lewis, St. Jago.
11. *Royal Gazette* 8 March 1794: further importations by Edward Lewis, St. Jago.
12. *Royal Gazette* 12 July 1794: stationery and some books for sale by W. Linwood, Kingston.
13. *Royal Gazette* 2 August 1794: list of new (and some second-hand) stock by Edward Lewis, St. Jago.
14. *Royal Gazette* 15 October 1794: detailed list of about 90 new books imported by Edward Lewis, St. Jago.
15. *Diary and Kingston Daily Advertiser* 20 April 1795: general advertisement for new stock imported by H. Meyer, Kingston.
16. *Diary and Kingston Daily Advertiser* 6 July 1795: stationery, books etc. advertised by J. Dingwall, Kingston.
17. *Diary and Kingston Daily Advertiser* 7 June 1976: dry goods and books advertised by Linwood & Nicoll, Kingston.
18. *Diary and Kingston Daily Advertiser* 8 June 1796: Thomas Stevenson advertising new importation of about 60 books.
19. *Diary and Kingston Daily Advertiser* 28 September 1796: advertisement by H. Meyer (Kingston) of new importation of books and stationery.
20. *Diary and Kingston Daily Advertiser* 30 September 1796: Thomas Stevenson advertising further additions to his stock from London.

21. *Jamaica Mercury and Trelawny Advertiser* 29 March 1797: stationery, charts, spelling books &c. offered by James K. Kelly, Falmouth.
22. *Diary and Kingston Daily Advertiser* 14 February 1799: Meyer & Schutze advertise new importation of about 50 books from London.
23. *Diary and Kingston Daily Advertiser* 15 March 1799: Stevenson Aikman & Smith offer about 50 new books imported from London
24. *Diary and Kingston Daily Advertiser* 18 June 1799: new stock imported from London advertised by Stevenson, Aikman & Smith.
25. *St Jago de la Vega Gazette* 3 January 1801: detailed list of new stock for sale by Lewis, Lunan & Jones, St Jago.
26. *Royal Gazette* 24 January 1801: 60–70 books plus stationery advertised for by John Whetcombe, Kingston.
27. *Royal Gazette* 30 May 1801: books and paper for sale by Meyer & Schutze, Kingston.
28. *Kingston Mercantile Advertiser* 3 July 1801: books &c. for sale by Meyer & Schutze, Kingston.
29. *Kingston Mercantile Advertiser* 7 September 1801: new stock advertised by Meyer & Schutze, Kingston.
30. *St Jago de la Vega Gazette* 17 October 1801: further importations by Lewis, Lunan & Jones, St Jago.
31. *Royal Gazette* 27 February 1802: a small consignment of books just imported, for sale by John Munds at H. M. Printing Office.
32. *Diary and Kingston Daily Advertiser* 16 July 1802: books newly imported by Stevenson, Aikman & Smith, Kingston.
33. *Royal Gazette* 12 February 1803: fresh importation of books by Munds & McIntosh at H. M. Printing Office.
34. *Jamaica Courant* 6 January 1806: fresh importations by H. Meyer, Kingston.
35. *Jamaica Courant* 28 June 1806: new stock imported by Stevenson & Smith, Kingston.
36. *Royal Gazette* 2 June 1809: new importation of stock for sale by John McIntosh & Co., Kingston.
37. *Royal Gazette* 10 October 1809: further importations by John McIntosh & Co., Kingston.
38. *St Jago de la Vega Gazette* 20 January 1810: new books imported by John McIntosh & Co., Kingston.
39. *St Jago de la Vega Gazette* 3 October 1810: new importations, and stock remaining from previous importations, for sale [by John Lunan] at the Printing Office, St Jago.

Appendix III

Advertisements of Auctions and General Sales

1. *Jamaica Mercury* 16 October 1779: Book auction, 'including a variety of the most approved Law Books' to be held 19 October; printed catalogues to be had at William Aikman's store. [Sale, postponed to 26/28 October, continued into early November.]
2. *Jamaica Gazette* 20 November 1779: A collection of books, most of them elegantly bound, for auction by G. Hughes at the *Gazette* office, 23 & 24 Nov.
3. *Royal Gazette* October 1781: Disposal of stock of William Aikman's Circulating Library by auction, 6 & 7 Nov.
4. *Cornwall Chronicle* 4 June 1785: Disposal of stock of St James's Circulating Library (Montego Bay); sale from 14 June.
5. *Daily Advertiser* 14 March 1791: Disposal of Kingston Circulating Library and other book stock owned by David Bower, by auction at McCormack's Vendue Store from 21 March.
6. *Daily Advertiser* 30 May 1791: Sale by public vendue of contents of Dr. James Skene's house; furniture, plate, china, horses, carriages, medical and other books . . . from 5 July.
7. *Cornwall Chronicle* 9 July 1791: A small collection of books and four horses to be sold at auction by John Anderson (Montego Bay).
8. *Royal Gazette* 26 January 1793: 'To be sold, a very elegant secretary and Bookcase, with the library of books therein contained, consisting of between two and three hundred volumes, of the most esteemed authors, as good as new, and most of them very elegantly bound. For particulars enquire at His Majesty's Printing Office.'
9. *Royal Gazette* 10 May 1793: Sale by raffle of a collection of books previously advertised for sale on 9 February.
10. *Royal Gazette* 19 July 1793: Auction of property of late William Fortescue Harris, from 30 July; his 'elegant and well-chosen library' to be sold from 1 August; printed catalogues available from William McMurdo, Vendue Master.
11. *Royal Gazette* 1 March 1794: 'For public sale, on Monday evening next . . . a large and elegant collection of new books, just imported, consisting of history , travels, voyages, novels &c. &c. catalogues of which will be delivered previous to the sale. John Douglas.'
12. *Royal Gazette* 16 May 1795: 'For sale by auction, at the subscriber's vendue-store, . . . A large and elegant Collection of Books, Catalogues of which may be had by applying to John Douglas.'
13. *Diary and Kingston Daily Advertiser* 3 June 1795: 'For peremptory sale on Friday morning . . . A large and choice collection of books. Catalogues may be had on application to William McMurdo . . .'

14. *Diary and Kingston Daily Advertiser* 13 July 1795: 'To be sold, an elegant bookcase, with glass doors, containing the undermentioned books . . . with other books. Apply for further particulars to Robert Hibbert Esq. or Mrs Fuhr.'
15. *Diary and Kingston Daily Advertiser* 25 November 1796: About a thousand second-hand books offered for sale by Robertson & McNeill: 'history, geography, biography, divinity, voyages, travels, agriculture, horticulture, plays, novels, romances, &c. &c.'
16. *Royal Gazette* 21 January 1797: 'A small neat collection of books' offered for private sale by William Younger.
17. *Royal Gazette* 19 May 1804: Announcement of raffle of a set of the *Encyclopaedia Britannica* plus supplement, 20 vols; to be drawn as soon as there are twenty subscribers at a doubloon apiece.
18. *Royal Gazette* 24 November 1804: 'To be sold, the valuable and extensive library, lately belonging to the Hon. Henry Shirley, consisting of Books in various languages, and in the different departments of literature. The proprietor wishes to dispose of it in one lot, and to any person taking it so it will be sold a bargain. It would form an excellent groundwork for the establishment of a public library: it is therefore submitted to the Gentlemen of Kingston or Spanish Town,whether a plan might not be formed for purchasing it by subscription, with that view. A Catalogue, with the valuation may be seen on application at His Majesty's Printing Office.'
19. *Jamaica Courant* 28 May 1806: 'For public sale on Friday morning at the Vendue Store of the subscriber the following books . . . Donald Campbell.'

Appendix IV

Music advertised by John McIntosh & Co. in the *Royal Gazette* (Kingston) August 1809

Pianoforte Music

Giornovichi's Sonatas
  Ditto's Concertos
Attwood's Airs
Mazi's Waltzes
  Ditto's Variations to the Maid of Lodi
Clementi's Op. 2
  Ditto's Op. 7
  Ditto's Op. 15
  Ditto's La Chasse
La Croix's Waltzes
Pleyel's Sonatas
  Ditto's Concertante
  Ditto's, by Cramer
Battle of Prague
Battle of Trafalgar
Siege of Valenciennes
Haydn's Op. 14
  Ditto's Op. 17
Ditters's Concerto
Dussek's Op. 1
  Ditto's Op. 5
  Ditto's Op. 15
  Ditto's Op. 25
Pleyel's Concerto
Viotti's ditto
Stamitz's ditto
Haydn's La Chasse
  Ditto's Reine de France
  Ditto's Symphony
  Ditto's Overture
Overture in Lodoiska
Barbara and Allen
Bach's Sonatas

A variety of the most popular Airs, with variations, and an extensive Collection of the most esteemed Songs

Harp Music

Krumpholtz's Op. 5
  Ditto's Andante
  Ditto's Concerto
  Ditto's Op. 8
Marin's Op. 6
  Ditto's Op. 15

Misler's Melody
Ditto's Sonatinas
Ditto's Musette de la Nina
Overture in Blue Beard
Les Follies d'Espagne
Air "Vous l'ordonnez"
Ditto "Avec Jeux dans Village"
Air "On ne saurait trop embellir"
Ditto dans le Verger de Cythere
Welch Airs
Irish Airs
Fiorilio's Exercises, just published
Newbourg's new Method of Teaching the Harp agreeably to the principles of the best Parisian Masters
Ditto, in French

Violin Music

Quartets

Giornovichi's Op. 1
Haydn's Op. 1
Ditto's Op. 57
Ditto's Op. 61
Devienne's Op. 2
Hoffmeister's Op. 2
Ditto's Op. 16
Boccherini's Op. 32
Ditto's Op. 33
Pleyel's Op. 1
Ditto's Op. 2
Ditto's Op. 3
Ditto's Op. 6

Quintets

Pleyel's Op. 8
Giornovichi's Waltzes; for two horns, violoncello, and bass.

Concertos

Pleyel's 1st Concertante
Ditto's 3rd ditto
Giornovichi's Concertante, 12, 13, 15

Dances

Anderson's 1st Book
Ditto's 2nd ditto
Gow's 1st, 2d, 3d, and 4th Set of Reels
Challoner's Dances
Broderip and Wilkinson's ditto
Claget's Airs
Mozart's Waltzes
Beethoven's ditto
McGlashan's Dances
Gow's Repository
Steibelt's ditto
Cramer's ditto

Flute and Clarinet Music:

Blane's Duetts
Cambini's Airs
Devienne's Op. 1
Ditto's Op. 57
Ditto's Op. 58
Ditto's Op. 68
Hooke's Duettinos
Schetky's Duetts
Lidarti's Sonatas
Mancinelli's Op. 3
Stumpff's Op. 17
Ditto's Airs
Pleyel's Duetts
Ditto's Sonatinas
Ditto's Op. 32, 55
Krasinsky's Op. 39
Haydn's Duetts
Hoffmeister's Concerto
Le Brun's Concerto, 1 and 3
Ditto ditto 4
Ditto ditto 6 and 7
Overture in Lodoiska
Pleyel's Concerto (Flute)
Ditto ditto (Clarinet)
Michel's Op. 6 (ditto)
Opera of the Woodman
Do. Midnight Wanderers
Do. Blue Beard
Do. Travellers
Do. Zorinsky
Do. Tekeli
Do. Rosina
Wragg's Flute Instructor
Common ditto

PRINTING IN THE BAHAMAS

IV

AN ADVERTISEMENT BY JOHN WELLS, 1785

Although the products of the early Bahamian press survive (in Nassau Public Library, the American Antiquarian Society, the Public Record Office and elsewhere) in greater numbers than those of most Commonwealth Caribbean countries, no study of the local printing trade or of Bahamian newspapers has been made. In the course of a preliminary examination of the files of The Bahama Gazette *the writer found the advertisement reprinted below; an advertisement which reflects unusually well the stock of an enterprising tradesman in the early years of Nassau's development.*

John Wells, who started *The Bahama Gazette* on 7 August 1784 and conducted it until his death in Nassau on 29 October 1799, was the eldest son of Robert Wells, a printer from Dumfries who settled at Charleston, South Carolina, in 1753. According to Isaiah Thomas,[1] John Wells took over publication of his father's newspaper, the *South-Carolina and America General Gazette* in 1775, running it in the patriotic interest until Charleston fell to the British forces in 1780. To save the property, Wells changed sides and printed a *Royal Gazette* thereafter until December 1782 – thereby making Charleston too dangerous for him to remain after the end of the war. The tag from Horace, *Nullius addictus jurare in verba magistri*, which Wells senior had adopted for his paper continued to grace all the newspapers produced by his son.[2]

From Charleston John Wells apparently went to Britain, then early in 1784 recrossed the Atlantic to St Augustine where he took over direction of Florida's first paper, the *East-Florida Gazette*, from his younger brother Dr Robert Wells.[3] By that time, evacuation of the loyalists from Florida was under way, and John Wells was among those who went to the Bahamas in the next months.[4] He took the printing plant with him (the cut of the royal arms used at the head of the *East-Florida Gazette* is identical with that he used on his Nassau paper) and from the start his new paper was one of the most competently printed and edited newspapers produced in any of the West Indian colonies. He did not have a complete monopoly of the local printing trade[5] but his own connections gave him some distinct advantages. In the twenty-third issue of the *Bahama Gazette*, 1 January 1785, he listed five subscription agents in the United States (three in Charleston, one each in Savannah and Baltimore) and for Kingston Jamaica his agents were Douglass & Aikman, the King's Printers. This last was more than just a business connection: Alexander Aikman (who succeeded to his elder brother William's title as King's Printer on the latter's death in 1784) had worked for Robert Wells senior in Charleston, and in 1782 had married his old master's daughter Louisa Susannah. John Wells was therefore brother-in-law to the most substantial and prosperous printer and bookseller in the Caribbean.[6]

Booksellers and printers in the West Indies, like those in North America or in provincial towns in Britain, not infrequently branched into other fields of trade in their shops. Musical instruments, medicines, even some haberdashery and hardware were relatively common as additions to the normal lines of books and stationery. Sometimes the need to accept payment in kind forced printers to turn to more general merchandising. Nevertheless, Well's advertisement in the *Bahama Gazette* of 30 July 1785 [7] remains the only one I have ever seen which shows a printer moving into the grocery business as well.

Was it, I wonder, intended merely as a shot across the bows of Peter Dean & Company, hardware, haberdashery and provision merchants of Nassau, whose advertisements in the *Gazette* of this period show that they had started to import books into the Bahamas? We shall never know, but it is noticeable that after 1785 Wells's advertisements were for books and stationery alone, and Peter Dean & Co. never again advertised stock which impinged on Wells's business interests.

The original advertisement in Wells's folio paper filled a little more than two columns (of the three per page), each column of the advertisement being set double. For convenience, it has also been set double below; obvious typographical errors have been corrected but it is otherwise unedited.

JUST IMPORTED
In the Ship SALLY, Captain CROSSKILL, from
LONDON,
AND NOW OPENING FOR SALE,
BY JOHN WELLS,
At his SHOP on the BAY

Books, Stationery, Charts, &c.

Bibles
Testaments
Prayer Books, elegantly
  bound and gilt
Church Primmers
Dilworth's and Dyche's
  Spelling Books
Royal Battledores
Children's Books
Spelling Dictionaries
Lowth's Grammar
Ashe's Introduction to do.
Dilworth's Assistant
----- Bookkeeping
Croxall's Æsop
Enfield's Speaker
Hill's, Tenning's, Fisher's
  Cocker's and Mair's
  Arithmetic
Mair's Book-keeping
Johnston's, Bailey's, Dyche's
  & Fenning's English
  Dictionaries
Chambaud's French Exercises,
  Grammar & Dictionary
Boyer's French Grammar
  and Dictionary
French Pocket Dictionary
Porney's French Grammar
Murdoch's French Vocabulary
Ruddiman's Latin
  Rudiments and Grammar
Lilly's Accidence & Grammar
Clark's Introduction, Cordery,
  Erasmus, Caesar & Ovid
Mair's Introduction
Ainsworth's, Young's and
  Entick's Latin Dictionaries
Guthrie's Geography
Salmon's Gazetteer
Elegant Extracts
Spectator, 8 vols
Rambler, 4 vols
Mirror, 3 vols
Lady's Library, 3 vols
Oeconomy of Human Life
Death of Abel
Dryden's Virgil, 3 vols
---- Poems, 1 vol
---- Fables, 2 vols
Pope's Homer, 7 vols
---- Works, 6 vols
---- Poems, 4 vols
Hudibras, 4 vols

Mason's Poems, 2 vols
Milton's Poetical Works, 4 vols
Thomson's Poems, 3 vols
----- Seasons
Selected Poems, 4 vols
Poetical Works of Richardson, Addison, Lyttleton, Gray, Denham, Shenstone, and Garth
Tom Jones, 3 vols
Sir C. Grandison, 7 vols
Man of Feeling
Man of the World, 2 vols
Julia de Roubigne, 2 vols
Cecelia, 3 vols
Evelina, 3 vols
Chrysal, 4 vols
Marmontel's Tales, 3 vols
Sterne's Works, 10 vols
History of the Devil
Gil Blas, 4 vols
Cyrus's Travels
Don Quixote, 4 vols
Peregrine Pickle, 4 vols
Roderic Random, 2 vols
Julia Mandeville, 2 vols
Sidney Biddulph, 2 vols
Arabian Nights Entertainment, 4 vols
Rousseau's Eloisa, 4 vols
---- Confessions
Fool of Quality, 4 vols
Robinson Cruso, 2 vols
Joseph Andrews, 2 vols
Wolf's Adventures
Shakespeares Works, 8 vols
English Theatre, 2 vols
Victor's Theatre, 2 vols
Colman's Works, 4 vols
Lord Chesterfield's Letters, 4 vols
Hume's History of England, 8 vols
----- Essays, 2 vols
Smollet's History of England, 7 vols
Goldsmith's Roman History
Ferguson's History of the Roman Republic, 3 vols 4to
Gibbon's History of the Roman Emperors, 6 vols
Smith's Wealth of Nations, 3 vols
Watson's Philip II, 3 vols
Rollin's Ancient History, 8 vols
Elements of Criticism, 2 vols
Ossians's Poems, 2 vols
Hool's Ariosto, 5 vols
Jones's Hoyle's Games
Preston's Illustration of Masonry
Campbell's Lives of the British Admirals, 4 vols
Wraxell's Tours, 2 vols
Brydone's Tour, 2 vols
Anson's Voyage
Junius's Letters, 2 vols
Every Man his own Lawyer
Complete Juryman
Burn's Justice, 4 vols
Blackstone's Commentaries, 4 vols
Ruffhead's Statutes, 14 vol
Wiskett's Insurance
Jacob's Law Dictionary
Trials for Adultery, 2 vols
Simson's Euclid
Cunn's Euclid
Sherwin's Tables
Thomson's and Hayes's Tables of Interest
Ferguson's Mechanics
------ Astronomy
------ Exercises
------ Electricity
Moore's, Wilson's. Crosby's, Atkinson's, and Nicholson's Navigation
Seaman's Assistant
Mariner's Compass
----- Kalendar
Buchan's Domestic Medicine
Quincy's Dispensatory
Glasse's, Raffald's, & Farley's Cookery
Atlas and Elephant Drawing Paper
Imperial, Super Royal,

Royal Medium, Demi-Royal thick & thin, Folio Post, Gilt, plain & black edged 4to Post, gilt and plain Foolscap, and Post Writing Paper
Cartridge, Blotting and Wrapping Paper
Milliner's Pasteboard
Gilt and plain Message and Name Cards
Mogul, Henry VIII, and Merry Andrew Playing Cards
Red and Black Ink Powder
Patent ink cakes
Best Dutch Quills and Office Pens
Sevigny's Penknives and Scrapers
Mahogany Portable Writing Desks
Black Leather Travelling Cases
Crown, Half Crown and Common sized wafers
Red & Black Sealing Wax
Writing Vellum & Parchment
Slates and Slate Pencils
Asses Skin Memorandum Books
Etwees and Pocket Books
Pewter and Japanned Ink Stands
Spare Glasses for ditto
Red Tape
Middleton's Black Lead Pencils
Sliding ditto
Camel Hair Pencils
Boxes of Water Colours
Shell Paint
China Ink
Drawing Books
Copy Books
Slip Copies
Ivory Paper Knives
Rulers
Quire Books, ruled and plain
Indexes
Bills of Lading Books
Receipt Books
Pocket Ledgers
Blank Books of various sizes, ruled and plain
Cases of Mathematical Instruments
Pocket Compasses
Ship ditto
Circumferentors
2 & 4 pole chains
Magnets
Dividers
4 foot Guaging Rods
Gunter's Scales
Hadley's Quadrants
Pocket and Long Telescopes
Temple Spectacles
Thermometers in fish skin and mahogany cases
Sun dials for this latitude
Portraits, Views, Sea Pictures, &c. printed on glass and framed
Humorous and Political Prints
Optical Pillar Machine
Coloured perspective view for ditto
Watch Prints
Counting House Files
Port Folio

CHARTS, viz.

English Channel
St George's Channel
S. W. Coast of Ireland
Coast of Holland
Atlantic Ocean
North American Pilot, 2 Parts
Bishop's Draughts, with

Directions
Roman's Gulf & Windward
Passage, with Directions
- - - - - Gulf passage
Bay of Chesapeake
Delaware Bay and River
General Charts of the West Indies
&c. &c. &c.

Musical Instruments, &c.

A long 3 stop Piano Forte
Barrel Organs
Guitars
Guitar Strings in sets
Violins of different prices
Violin bows, and hair
for ditto
Violin Cases, Bridges
and Pegs
Best Roman Violin Strings
Rosin Boxes
German and common flutes
B. and C. Fifes
Drum Heads and Snares
Pipes and Tabors
Instructions for the Violin,
Harpsichord, Guitar,
Flute and Fife
A Collection of Music,
Single Songs &c.
Newest Song Books
Scotch Songs
Musical Miscellany
&c. &c. &c.

Jewellery & Hardware

Paste Shoe and Knee Buckles
Pleated, yellow metal and mourning
Shoe, Knee and Stock Buckles
Breast Pins
Silver Watches
Silver and Steel Pencil Cases
Plated Spurs
Gilt and brass Watch Keys
Gilt Watch Chains
Silk & Hair Watch Strings
Glass Lockets
Ground Watch Chrystals
Brass barrelled Pistols
Fencing Foils
Ladies Steel Collars
Cypher and Fancy Seals
Book Backgammon Tables
Spare Dice
Billiard Balls, Maces,
and Ques [Cues]
Cricket Batts and Balls
Cribbage Boards
Sportsmen's Pocket Knives
Boxes of Marking Types
Wax Tapers and Brass
Stands
Smoaking Pans

Perfumery, &c.

Marechall's and plain
Hair Powder
Hard and soft Pomatum
Essence of Bergamot,
Lemon and Lavendar
Mahogany and Japanned
Dressing Cases of various
sorts
Tortoise Shell, Ivory and
Horn Combs
Shaving Boxes
Powder Masks
Servigny's best Cast Steel
Razors
Homer's Dentifrice and
Tooth Powder

Fillers
Wash Balls
Cloth Powder
Smelling Bottles
Teeth Instruments
Toupes & Pinching Irons
Powder Machines & Puffs
&c. &c. &c.

Medicines, &c.

Boxes of Medicines
 for Plantations
Epsom and Glauber Salts
Anderson's Pills
Godfrey's Cordial
James's Powder
Daffy's Elixir
Keyser's Pills
Magnesia
Tartar Emetic
Powdered [Cinchona] Bark
 in Pint Bottles
Hannay's Specific
 for Adventurers
Ivory Syringes
&c. &c. &c.

Haberdashery, Linen Drapery, Hosiery, &c.

Gentlemen's fashionable
 cocked Hats
Ditto brown fashionable
 Sporting Beavers
Ditto brown broad
 Riding ditto
Ditto Black ditto, with
 bands and buckles
Ditto brown and green do.
Ladies Riding Hats of the
 newest fashion, with
 elegant trimmings
White and black Chip
 Hats
Ladies Habit and
 Dress Gloves
Men's Silk, Thread, Kid
 and Doeskin Gloves
Ladies Italian Cross
 Bone Stays
Fashionable Ticking ditto
Paper and Pound Pins
An assortment of Ribbons
Lisle Thread
Irish Linens
Cambricks
Osnaburgs
Children's Red Morocco
 Shoes
Ladies and Girls Calli-
 manco Shoes
Ladies Morocco Slippers
Ladies Silk and Sattin
 Dress Shoes
Gentlemen's Dress Shoes
Cordovan Boots
Men's Thread and Silk
 Stockings
Saddles with furniture
 compleat
Bridles
Silver Capt Twigs
Green Silk Umbrellas
Red Leather Trunks

Grocery, &c.

Hyson Tea, purchased at
 the last India sales
Double refined Loaf Sugar
North Wiltshire, Double

Gloucester and Cheshire
cheeses
Yorkshire Hams
Ox tongues in small
kegs
Split pease in stone jugs
Pickled Walnuts, Onions
Gherkins and India
Mangoes
Karr's bottled Porter:
cases of 6 dozen
London bottled Port Wine
Pigtail tobacco
Rogers's Oronoke & ... Smoaking ditto
Scotch snuff
&c. &c. &c.

NOTES

1. Isaiah Thomas, *The History of Printing in America . . .*, ed. by Marcus McCorison from the second edition (New York, 1977) pp. 569–70, 577–82, 609–10.
2. As indeed it is still retained today on the *Nassau Daily Tribune.*
3. Wilbur H. Siebert, *Loyalists in East Florida 1774 to 1785* (Deland, 1929) p. 135; Louisa Susannah Wells, *The Journal of a Voyage from Charleston, S. C., to London undertaken during the American Revolution* (New York, 1906), p. 99.
4. Siebert, op. cit., p. 189.
5. There are references to Alexander Cameron's *Lucayan Herald* in the columns of the *Bahama Gazette* of 22 August 1789 and 1 January 1790, and an advertisement by the administrator of Cameron's estate dated 10 October 1789. No copies have been traced, and the existence of this rival newspaper was not previously recorded.
6. A comparison of his stock of stationery with that revealed in the inventory of William Aikman (pp. 137–146 of this volume) is instructive. One may guess that Aikman's bookstock, though considerably more extensive, was broadly similar to that of Wells's advertisement.
7. It was repeated intermittently, and in modified form, until 17 December 1785. In those days before cold storage, one would prefer not to think about the condition of some of the foodstuffs still being offered.

PRINTING IN BELIZE

V

PRINTING IN NINETEENTH-CENTURY BELIZE

After an initial period in which the printing needs of the British settlements in Central America were met from Jamaica, printing was introduced into Belize in 1825. The settlement's first press was unusual in being bought with public funds and controlled by the magistrates. Subsequent printing developments in Belize were closer to the norm for British colonies in the West Indies, with government contractual printing and newspaper publishing forming the mainstay of most printers' businesses in the nineteenth century. Printing for two other former British areas, the Bay Islands and the Mosquito Coast, is also discussed. The article is based on a variety of sources, principally the Belize Archives and the sets of Belize papers preserved in the British Library. Handlists of Belize printers and of Belizean newspapers published in the nineteenth century are included as appendices.

Although the spread of printing in the British settlements of North America has been thoroughly chronicled, as to a lesser extent has that in the "sugar islands" of the West Indies, the origins and early development of printing in the English-speaking areas of Central America have remained shrouded in obscurity.

Of these areas, the only one remaining in the Commonwealth is Belize (officially called British Honduras until 1973). Still a British colony, Belize is a subtropical country bounded on the north by Mexico, on the west and south by Guatemala, and on the east by the Caribbean Sea, dotted with many islets and cays. About twice the size of Jamaica, its small but rapidly growing population (119,645 at the 1970 census) is composed of many different racial and cultural groups. In the early nineteenth century these were Mayan Indians, Caribs, European settlers and their Negro slaves, plus a free Creole element. The troubled state of the Central American republics and, from the late 1840s, the caste wars of Yucatan led to a considerable influx of

1. Thanks are due to Mrs. Narda Dobson, the staff of the National Library Service, Belize (and particularly Miss A. Gibson and Miss T. Fairweather), Ms. Irene Moran, Bancroft Library, F. E. Leese, Rhodes House Library, D. H. Simpson, Royal Commonwealth Society, and Clinton Black, Jamaica Archives. Without their help this paper would have been much more tentative in nature.

Spanish-speaking peoples, particularly in the northern part of the country. After 1865 there was also some immigration from the defeated Confederate States [1, pp. 243–58].

Though there were considerable settlements of "Baymen," the British logwood and mahogany woodcutters and their Negro slaves, by the end of the seventeenth century the constitutional position of the British on the Spanish Main was by no means clear. Indeed, the problems of sovereignty over British Honduras—which was described in a Parliamentary Act of 1817 as "a settlement, for certain purposes, in the possession and under the protection of His Majesty, but not within the territory and dominion of His Majesty"—have always been very complex. The settlement was regarded in London as being a place where British subjects had the right to cut timber but which nevertheless was under Spanish sovereignty, however fitfully and ineffectually that was exercised through the captains-general of Yucatan. Not until 1786 was the first superintendent in the Bay of Honduras appointed as Crown representative by the British governor in Jamaica; not until 1862 did Britain officially create British Honduras a colony [1, pp. 79–92, 179–213]. The principal barrier to the country's independence today stems from this old constitutional problem, Guatemala claiming (by the doctrine of *uti possidetis*) that she inherited Spanish sovereignty over the area and that "Belice" is a department of the Republic of Guatemala [1, pp. 229–42].

In the late eighteenth and early nineteenth centuries control over the affairs of the settlement was divided between the superintendent and the local settlers. The superintendent's powers were not great, and his authority could not be increased while the authorities in Whitehall persisted in denying that the British had anything more than usufructuary rights in the Bay. As late as 1838 a Colonial Office memorandum described the superintendent as "not much more than a Looker-on, and who supplies the want of authority by dexterity and address in acquiring and using influence over the general meeting and the Magistracy." Real power in the settlement was vested in the Public Meeting of the settlers. The qualifications for membership varied at different periods, but it is roughly true to say that it represented the monied section of the community, including free men of color, and was a lot closer to Athenian ideas of democracy than most other modern governments. For most practical purposes the power of the Public Meeting was delegated to the seven magistrates who were elected from its members [1, pp. 95–120].

In the very small British settlement at the town of Belize, there was little call for printing at an early stage. The government and the trade of the Bay settlements came through Jamaica, and one may safely assume that if standard printed proformas for such things as laborers' agreements and bills of lading were required in the settlement they would have been provided from Jamaica. As late as 1824, when a number of the more powerful settlers in Belize were incensed by a report to Parliament by Colonel Arthur, an ex-superintendent who had criticized their position over slavery, they had to have their *Defence of the Settlers of Honduras against the Unjust and Undefended Representations of Colonel George Arthur* printed for them by Alexander Aikman, Jr., in Kingston, Jamaica, for subsequent distribution to members of Parliament in London.

It may be speculated that it was as a result of this special order for printing from Jamaica, with the difficulties and expense caused by having the work done at such a distance, that the need for a press in Belize was felt to be urgent. In Colonel Arthur's evidence to the House of Commons the settlement had been described as "the most detestable spot on the face of the globe" [1, p. 159]. This was not the best publicity for a territory anxious to encourage immigration, and the early productions of the Belize press were certainly designed to show that the settlement was better than Arthur had suggested.

In the West Indian islands under British rule printing was introduced in a number of different ways in the eighteenth century. In Jamaica, where Robert Baldwin started printing in 1718, the impetus seems to have come partly from the House of Assembly but above all from the governor, Sir Nicholas Lawes, who was of the opinion that a press there would be "a publick convenience and advantage to commerce." Baldwin was induced to come, not only as a printer licensed to the governor to undertake official printing on a contractual basis, but also as able to undertake private ventures on his own behalf as well [2]. In Barbados, on the other hand, David Harry set up office as a printer in 1731 as a normal commercial venture [3], and this was to be the more common pattern in most of the larger and more prosperous island colonies, although in some—like Tobago in 1799—it was only the inducement of public support which made the introduction of printing a reasonable venture to undertake [4].

In Belize the situation was closer to that in Jamaica a century earlier, with printing starting not because a printer arrived but because local pressure caused a printer to be sent for. No doubt the guarantee of official support was necessary to persuade a printer to come to Belize at all, for in 1835 (ten years after the first introduction of printing) the total population of the settlement, including slaves, was under 4,000 [1, p. 243], and the commercial prospects for a printer were not very promising.

Local pressure came from some of the magistrates of the settlement who had begun to plan for the new press in Belize by the fall of 1825. On December 6, 1825, at a meeting of the magistrates, it was ordered that a "printing apparatus" should be procured without delay so that the records and laws of the settlement could be printed [5, p. 288].

No records survive to show what kind of "printing apparatus" was thus procured with public funds. There seems little doubt that for letterpress work it was an iron press of the Stanhope/Columbian/Albion variety imported from Britain. The presswork of the earliest productions is excellent, bearing comparison with good English provincial work of the period and in general far superior to that prevailing in Belize later in the century. The choice of types was such as would have been made by an English newspaper-cum-jobbing printer of the period: Scotch romans for the text faces, plus a range of fat-faced romans, black letter, grotesques, and shaded types in display sizes. Some of these appear to have come from the typefoundry of Vincent Figgins in London. To the types were added a number of printers' flowers and typefounders' stockblocks of wood engravings of a sub-Bewickian character. Equipped with this material, the first Belize press was able to produce publications of more than merely competent design in the self-assured Regency manner.

In addition to the letterpress equipment, there is some indication that the "printing apparatus" included an engravers' rolling press, since early volumes of the *Honduras Almanack* include a number of engraved plates. By 1829 some lithographic plates of good quality had also been printed for inclusion in local publications, and (though no later lithographic work from Belize has been traced) it is probable that these were printed locally rather than imported. Lithography was already practiced in Jamaica in the 1820s and a small iron lithographic press like those marketed in Britain by Taylor and Martineau, or Ruthven [6] no doubt formed part of the equipment imported by the magistrates of Belize.

The first substantial piece of work to be printed in the settlement, and the earliest to have survived, was the *Honduras Almanack for the Year of Our Lord 1827, Calculated to the Meridian of Belize*, which was published "by authority of the Magistrates" on March 9, 1826. The compilers of this first almanac were not named in it. No doubt in so small a society it was felt to be superfluous. The printer was James Cruickshank, apparently a Scot like so many of the printers and other craftsmen who moved to the West Indian colonies in the early nineteenth century. By the middle of 1826 Cruickshank was sufficiently well settled in the printing office—the precise location of which is never given, again a superfluity in a very small town—for his sponsors to embark on a weekly paper, the *Honduras Gazette and Commercial Advertiser.*

According to a manuscript note by Thomas Philip Pickstock at the end of the first volume of his set,[2] the *Honduras Gazette* was, from "1 July 1826 to no. 38 in [*sic*] 17 March 1827, Edited by the Magistrates; and from that period, until the 5th November 1827, vol. 2 no. 88 conducted by the Printer: when, on that day, the Legislative Assembly at their Meeting, in their Wisdom, took it out of his hands, by reason of his intemperence, and very properly appointed a Committee, for its better Government." Pickstock was one of the Belize magistrates at this time and, as will be shown below, was very closely involved in the editorial direction of this first Belize press.

The Honduras Almanacks

The 1826 *Almanack*[3] is a small octavo volume of 92 + 4 + 21 pages, well printed, with an engraved title leaf and two other copper plates. Its contents

2. Now in Rhodes House Library, Oxford.
3. Copies in the British Library and in Rhodes House Library.

are characteristic of such compilations: a historical account of the settlement, calendar, list of superintendents, of sovereigns of Europe, of the civil and military establishment in Belize, conversion tables, directions for mariners navigating to the coast of Honduras, and so forth. The last 21-page section deals with the Honduras Society for the Propogation of Christian Knowledge which had been established in 1825; and I suspect that it was also issued separately from the *Almanack*, its production costs being underwritten by another source. The plates are an unsigned chart of the "Private Signals of the Merchants of Belize" and a "View of St John's Church." This and the engraved title were both signed *A & S sc.* The paper is an unwatermarked wove; the text types typical Scotch romans of the period and evidently new.

As early as December 16, 1825 the secretary of state for the colonies had requested that two copies of the *Almanack* be forwarded to him each year [7]. The superintendent's letter of transmittal was dated March 1, 1826 [8], eight days before the date of publication named in subsequent issues of the *Almanack*.

The 1827 *Almanack*[4] was also printed by Cruickshank, and advertised by him for sale on February 17, 1827 at $3.00, copies of the 1826 volume being offered at half price. The same engraved title leaf, suitably corrected in the plate, was used. There was also a fresh folding plate of the merchants' private signals and, as frontispiece, a further copper engraving of the "Manner of Trucking Mahogany in Honduras" signed *A. Bayntun del.* The text, of 188 + iv + [iv] pages, shows considerable change from the previous issue (including a long and useful account of the methods used in the timber trade). There was also an editorial request that addenda and corrigenda should be notified to the Office of the Keeper of the Records or to the residences of John Waldron Wright or Thomas Pickstock. Some 78 subscribers to the volume are listed.

Andrew Bayntun, keeper of the records, was a public notary and assistant to the clerk of the courts. Both Wright and Pickstock were merchants and magistrates. Together with William Walsh, the public treasurer, it seems almost certain that they formed the editorial body to which the Public Meeting of March 5, 1827 expressed appreciation, according to the account given in the *Honduras Gazette* of March 17, 1827: "Resolved unanimously, That the thanks of this Meeting, be given to the Gentlemen, who have hitherto conducted the compilation, and publication, of the HONDURAS ALMANACK; and they are hereby requested to accept the same accordingly,—and should the subscription not be adequate to the expence, that this PUBLIC should make good the deficiency."

I have not seen a copy of the 1828 *Almanack*. The only copy traced lacks title leaf and prelims but has one plate, an unsigned lithograph of the Courthouse of Belize.[5]

4. Copy in the British Library.
5. In the Royal Commonwealth Society, London.

The volume for 1829, like its predecessors, is a substantial octavo volume.[6] Like the 1828 issue, it contains some lithographic plates: Andrew Bayntun drew "A View in Belize" which was used as frontispiece; there are "A View of Fort George" and "The Honduras Lighthouse," both signed *Pickstock del.*, and a freshly drawn but unsigned plate of the merchants' signals. At the end is a folding map of Belize City "by William Maskell, Surveyor." Some copies contain an engraved title leaf, apparently an adaptation of that signed *A & S sc.* in earlier issues. There is no indication of the printer. The list of subscribers totals 85.

The *Almanack* for 1830[7] is in the same typographical dress as its forerunners and shows yet further variety in its illustrations. It contains an aquatint frontispiece by Bayntun of the "Interior of the Courts of British Honduras" (rather crudely hand colored in the copies I have handled), a fresh "View in Belize" also by Bayntun and reproduced by lithography, and a redrawn and amended version of Maskell's map of the city, also lithographed. For the first time the list of public departments and officers in the settlement which is given in the text includes the "Printing Department" with Henry Whitney named as head printer and John Lindo as his assistant. There were 84 subscribers.

The only other *Honduras Almanack* I traced is that for the year 1839,[8] which is a much thinner and althogether inferior work to the volumes already described. Like the 1830 issue it was printed by Henry Whitney: it is therefore possible that the series continued throughout the 1830s, although (if this were the case) it is surprising that none of these issues for 1831–38 has survived in any of the usual repositories.

The Honduras Gazette

The *Honduras Gazette and Commercial Advertiser* which commenced publication on July 1, 1826 was, by Pickstock's account, edited at first by the magistrates, although in practice the work probably devolved upon the same smaller group responsible for the content of the *Almanacks*. The first issue contains an address "To the Public" similar to those in many new colonial papers: "In offering this GAZETTE to the notice of the public, we solicit that due allowance be made for the imperfections which like all new undertakings we are sensible it must contain. It is our intention to be strictly careful of its improvement, so as to render it useful, convenient, and amusing to the community. Its establishment has been projected under the idea of benefiting the settlement,

6. Copies in the British Library, the Royal Commonwealth Society, and the Bancroft Library, Berkeley.
7. Copies in the British Library, Rhodes House Library, the Institute of Jamaica and the National Library Service, Belize.
8. Copy in Rhodes House Library; there is also one with the U.S. consular dispatches from Kingston, Jamaica, in the National Archives, Washington.

9. Giles Barber, 'Books from the old world and for the new: the British international trade in books in the eighteenth century'. *Studies on Voltaire and the eighteenth century,* v. CLI–CLV, 1976, pp. 185–224. It should be noted that the arithmetic in the Customs House Records is not altogether reliable, but Mr Barber advises me (personal communication) that the individual annual figures should usually be trustworthy.
10. Public Record Office, C. O. 137/71.
11. Roderick Cave, 'An inventory of the first Jamaican printing house', *Papers of the Bibliographical Society of America*, v. 69, 1975, pp. 560–565 [reprinted here, pp. 175–180].
12. Roderick Cave, *A digest of the Wills and Inventories of the Jamaican Book Trade*, pp. 125–174 of this volume.
13. Jamaica Archives Inventories liber 69 ff. 9–22; summarised in *Digest of the Wills* (n. 12 above).
14. Roderick Cave, 'Thomas Craddock's books: a West India Merchant's stock', *Book Collector*, v. 25, 1976, pp. 481–490 [reprinted here, pp. 181–190].
15. *Digest of the Wills* (n. 12 above).
16. Thistlewood was an overseer in Jamaica for over thirty years, and left a full account of his reading and book buying, which is currently being researched by Dr John Ward of the Department of Economic History, Edinburgh University, based on the Thistlewood Papers in Jamaica and in Lincolnshire Record Office.
17. Phillips was a Kingston merchant who turned planter about 1761, eventually retiring to Wales in 1789. His Diaries include a list of books taken by him from England to Jamaica in 1775; the list is included below as Appendix I. I am grateful to the National Library of Wales for providing xerox copies from the Phillips Papers (Slebech 9402).
18. Roderick Cave, 'The Plantocracy's passion for *Porcupine*', *The Library*, 5th series, v. 33, 1978, pp. 233–235 [reprinted here, pp. 219–221].
19. The only lists I have seen for 18th century Jamaican publications are those in Peter Pindar's *Persian Love Elegies* (1773), Dancer's *Bath Waters* (1784) and *Reason and Faith* (1788). Though occasional Jamaican books include subscription lists as late as 1855, very few of those for which subscriptions were sought included a list of the subscribers' names.
20. Cf. Aron Freimann, *A Gazeteer of Hebrew Printing*, New York Public Library, 1946.
21. Roderick Cave, 'Printing in eighteenth century Jamaica', *The Library*, 5th series, v. 33, no. 3 (1978) pp. 196–8 [reprinted here, pp. 114–116].
22. Soon afterwards the partnership broke up, Munds continuing independently as a dealer in music and musical instruments, while McIntosh continued to direct the Aikman's business for a short period until he too set up shop as stationer and bookseller.
23. It was based largely (and without acknowledgement) on Thomas Rede's 'Introductory Discourse' to his *Bibliotheca America* (London, 1789).
24. Roderick Cave, 'Early printing and the book trade in the West Indies', *Library Quarterly*, v. 48 no. 2, 1978, p. 166 [reprinted here, pp. 1–30].
25. Roderick Cave, 'Early Circulating Libraries in Jamaica', *Libri* v. 30 no. 1, 1980, pp. 53–65 [reprinted here, pp. 227–239].

26. His first book, *Persian Love Elegies, to which is added The Nymph of Tauris* had been published in Kingston from the Press of Joseph Thompson & Co. in 1773.
27. Neither the *Gazette* nor the *Magazine* was profitable, and Monk & Leyburn abandoned their business at Savanna-la-Mar in May, 1789, begging 'leave to tender their sincere acknowledgements to those *few* whose endeavours have been so earnest on their behalf' (*Cornwall Chronicle*, 6 June 1789). Their subsequent attempt to establish a paper in Kingston, *The Centinel and Kingston Daily Advertiser*, was little more successful.
28. Pressmark 11621. aa. 42.
29. *Customs* 34/433/481; 34/434/498; 34/439/12; 34/444/J.1 (Reference from Ingram, *Sources of Jamaican History*, p. 869).
30. After the death of William Aikman, his business was divided: Alexander Aikman senior succeeding to the business as King's Printer; Stevenson and a younger Aikman brother taking over the bookselling and stationery side. Both businesses subsequently encroached on the other's territory: Stevenson & Aikman moving into newspaper printing, the King's Printers into bookselling (Munds & McIntosh) but the rivalry between the two remained muted until the original Stevenson-Aikman partnership passed into other hands at a slightly later period.
31. Most of the advertisements are phrased in a form of words such as 'Lately imported from London in the *Charming Sukey* the following assortment of books'. To take this at face value is no safer than relying on the 'This day is published' formula.
32. Edinburgh University Library, La. III. 353, a letter from Jacques, Laing & Ewing, Jamaica to Messrs. C. Stewart & Co., Edinburgh, 15 July 1797, deals with such an unsaleable consignment: 'The few books which we have been able to sell – and they are but very few – consist chiefly of the British Poets, Scottish Register and Brutus' Letter'. Ingram, *op. cit.*, p. 912.
33. As James Lackington put it, 'Thousands of books are yearly written for to London that are never sent; and in these cases plausible reasons are assigned for such omissions – As, "The book is too dear" or "it is out of print", "the work is not worth your purchasing, such a one wrote better on the subject".' The question is discussed, with suggestions no less illuminating for the colonial than the provincial book trade in Graham Pollard's Sandars Lectures, 1959; now printed as 'The English Market for Printed Books', *Publishing History*, no. 4, 1978, pp. 7–48.
34. Frank Cundall, 'Library Work in Jamaica', in *Transactions and Proceedings of the Second International Library Conference* (London, 1897), pp. 173–8.
35. Cf. W. F. Gallaway, 'The conservative attitude towards fiction, 1700–1830', *PMLA*, 55, Dec. 1940, pp. 1041–59, and John T. Taylor, *Early opposition to the English novel* (New York, 1943).
36. It may be coincidence only, but the Bodleian set of the *Magazine* (Hope Adds. 296–8) covers the serialisation of Labourie perfectly.
37. The 56 medical men subscribing to Dancer's *Dissertation on the Jamaica Bath Waters* (Kingston, 1784) probably represented the vast majority of local practitioners. The range of books imported for their use is impressive; not surprisingly it reflects the contributions of the Edinburgh school very

and nothing shall be left undone on our part to accomplish the object."

The editors continued by enlarging on the advantages of a newspaper, stressing their intention to be impartial. After a request that their venture should be patronized, they went on:

We feel satisfied that our present endeavour, humble as it may be, will raise us in the scale of the BRITISH COLONIES. It will preserve our rights, encrease our Commerce, and improve our rising generation. Let us, therefore, ever remember, that the LIBERTY OF THE PRESS, is the PALLADIUM of all the rights—Civil, Religious and Political—which Nations, or Communities enjoy.

THE HONDURAS GAZETTE will be published weekly, at eight dollars, per annum, payable in advance, or 1s.8d. [Belizean currency][9] each number. Subscribers residing in the Interior may have it delivered to their AGENTS in town.

The paper will be issued every Saturday morning; advertisements or other matter intended for insertion, can only be introduced, if sent on or before the preceding Thursday.

Advertisements will be inserted ONCE, at the rate of FIFTEEN shillings for twelve lines or less, and for greater lengths in proportion.

Payment of the first year's subscription will be received during the present week by WILLIAM WALSH ESQ.

The content of the paper (the "normal" issues of which were of 4 pages approximately 12 1/4 x 9 5/8 inches, each of 2 columns) was very similar to that of most West Indian papers of the period: shipping intelligence, overseas news culled from the English, American, and West Indian papers brought by the latest vessels to call at the settlement, merchants' advertisements, government proclamations, some literary matter, and local news. Because of the very close interest the Baymen took in the decidedly unsettled affairs of the neighboring Central American republics, considerable attention was devoted by the *Gazette* to reports received from Guatemala, El Salvador, and Honduras. This was to be a continuing pattern for Belize papers.

On several occasions subscribers received, free of charge, supplements to the regular paper. Usually these contained proclamations and other government matter plus additional advertisements squeezed out of the regular edition, but on occasion the supplement was of foreign news, just received in the settlement. That for August 26, 1826, for instance, contained a list of candidates in the forthcoming parliamentary election in Britain.

At the rather high price charged for the *Honduras Gazette* its circulation in the settlement cannot have been very large, but with a substantial income derived from advertising it probably paid its way.[10] Some copies no doubt

9. The sum of £1 Belize equaled 13*s* sterling. Unless otherwise stated all references are to Belize currency which, until stabilized in 1894, was liable to fluctuate considerably as did the mongrel currency common to the other Central American states which also circulated in Belize.

10. Because of local currency fluctuations it is very difficult to compare with other colonial papers, but writing in 1841 Simmonds [9] quoted subscription rates of $6.00–$8.00 for weeklies in the eastern Caribbean; £5 6*s* 8*d* for Jamaican dailies. In Jamaica (a high-cost colony)

circulated to the British settlements in the Bay Islands and on the Mosquito Coast. That there was a demand for the paper is shown by the fact that in the issue for March 3, 1827 Cruickshank was offering 50¢ each for copies of some 11 different issues he needed to complete sets for subscribers in England and the United States.

Undoubtedly from the earliest days of the *Honduras Gazette* Cruickshank had some part in its editorial production, but he was quick to take refuge behind authority when it suited him, as on July 8, 1826: "To correspondents. 'Paul Pry' who informs us he should just like *to pop in and take a 'peep'* at our Printing Office, is informed that by doing so he would greatly 'intrude', as no person whatever can be admitted to *the interior*, except on special business, *without an order*, in writing, *from the Magistrates.*"

Government by committee is bad enough; editorship by committee an abomination, and particularly so in a small community where the editors can be made accountable by those who dislike their editorial direction. In the report of the Public Meeting of March 5, 1827, given in the issue for March 17, 1827, Cruickshank recorded that

> Mr Coffin . . . desired Mr Westby to read the notice of his motion in regard to the Printing Establishment, which enables us to supply the Public with the information, and in consequence of the proceedings that followed, we are *not sorry* to say, is no longer a *Public* but a *Private* Establishment; but we shall be most happy at all times to employ it in the manner which may be most conducive to the Public weal, . . .
> 'Resolved, that the Public will not from this time be liable to any further charge of, or expense arising from, the Printing Establishment of this Settlement (except the contracts already entered into) but that the present Printer shall be allowed the use of the Printing Press during the pleasure of the Public. The motion was seconded by Mr Maskall, and carried unanimously.'

The first period of Belizean journalism, with what was in effect a state-controlled newspaper, was over. The settlement seemed to be moving closer to the pattern of the West Indian islands, with a printer/proprietor in sole charge of a paper's direction. Interference with the liberty of the press was of course common enough in the other colonies: in some printers could be chased out of the colony for criticizing the governor too freely,[11] in others printers were harassed by the House of Assembly for breach of privilege[12] or by overfree recourse to libel actions. More subtly papers could be killed or brought to heel by the withholding of government advertising.[13] Cruick-

advertisements "of moderate length" cost 5*s* per week, or 15*s* for a month's insertions in the weekly papers; in the Turks Islands a similar rate was charged in the 1840s. The charge in Belize therefore seems distinctly high.

11. As happened to two Bermuda printers, Edmund Ward (dismissed by Governor Cockburn in 1812) and Charles Beach (ousted by Governor Lumley in 1824) [10, pp. 107, 189].
12. The fate of several Jamaican printers [11, pp. 37–38].
13. In St. Lucia the press was stifled for nearly five years, 1831–36, by these means [12, pp. 265–67], while in the Turks Islands in the 1850s both papers were at different times disciplined by this method [13].

shank, who was allowed the use of the Belize press "during the pleasure of the Public," was in a peculiarly vulnerable position and, as Pickstock records, did not enjoy this right very long. The intemperence to which Pickstock referred was not of course drunkenness (few officials would have lasted long in the West Indies, one gathers, had this been regarded as serious) but rather an outspokenness which was found objectionable by enough members of the Public Meeting to have him removed from office after the issue of the *Honduras Gazette* of November 3, 1827. The new series of the paper at first bore the imprint "Printed and published at the Honduras Gazette Office for the Editor"; later this became "Printed and published by Henry Whitney." Pickstock's set of the newspaper ceases with the issue of June 27, 1829, which may have been the last issue published.

Cruickshank's Other Work

As well as printing the *Almanack* and the *Gazette*, Cruickshank was a jobbing printer, from time to time advertising the usual range of blank proformas for bills of lading, powers of attorney, manifests, laborers' agreements and the like. He also published *A Comprehensive Interest Table* (advertised on November 25, 1826 for publication "on Saturday next," price 10*d*). The *Gazette* of February 10, 1827 contained an advertisement for "two responsible lads" as apprentices. It is tempting to see his successors at the printing establishment, Whitney and Lindo, in these apprentices.

Like most printers in pioneering areas, Cruickshank's business interests were diversified. He was a binder, a stationer, and a bookseller (advertising stock in both English and Spanish) who attempted to attack the feminine market by importing the *Ladies Magazine* and other suitable reading. He had an interest in a hotel and in the running of the Olympic Theatre. On April 27, 1827 he advertised that he intended "opening a *well-supplied* Newspaper and General Reading Room, on *Liberal Terms*, provided he receives adequate encouragement. Gentlemen therefore wishing to patronize it, will oblige him by sending in their names." There is no evidence surviving as to the success of this venture, which would no doubt have been the first subscription library in Belize. Nor, after his loss of favor later that year, is there any evidence for Cruickshank's later career.

Later Printers in Belize

As in all the West Indian colonies, the printers of British Honduras for a long time were dependent upon the production of a newspaper to provide a backbone for their business. Apart from newspaper printing and contract work for the government, there was little chance of great commercial success in the declining state of the colony in the second half of the century. Even then it was a meager living, and many of the later newspaper proprietors were also merchants or hotel keepers. From files of Belizean papers which have survived it is possible to create a reasonably complete list of the printers of the settlement, given as appendix I.

Henry Whitney, Cruickshank's successor in producing the *Honduras Gazette*, seems to have enjoyed a monopoly of printing in the settlement throughout the 1830s. On September 29, 1838 he commenced publication of the *Belize Advertiser*, a weekly paper which Peter L. Simmonds (who had a good knowledge of the West Indian press) described as "likely to last" in a paper on newspaper printing which he read to the Statistical Society of London in 1841 [9]. But at the time Simmonds delivered his paper there was already a rival paper being published in the settlement, the *Honduras Observer*, which had started publication on November 25, 1840. "There can hardly be room for two papers here" was Simmonds's observation, and a correct one. Some time in 1841 the *Belize Advertiser* ceased publication, and Whitney went out of business. It may have been succeeded by the *Belize Gazette*, a weekly published by E. Cramond, which started soon after the *Honduras Observer*.

John M. Daly, the printer of the *Observer*, was the longest-lasting of Belize printers in the nineteenth century, though like many of his contemporaries elsewhere he was associated with several different papers at different times. As early as November 1841 Daly had fallen foul of the superintendent by attacking the local government in the columns of the *Observer*. Superintendents had much less power than governors of colonies, and Superintendent McDonald was unsure what action he could take against the paper. "In the absence of everything in the shape of a law authority here," he wrote rather plaintively to the secretary of state for the colonies asking advice on how to deal with these attacks and enclosed copies of the offending paper and also of the *Belize Gazette* [5, vol. 3, p. 52]. The reply, when it came eighteen months later, reflected a more liberal approach to criticism than many colonial governors would have liked:

> 17 April 1843. Jamaican Governor to Superintendent.
> I entirely concur with Sir Charles Metcalfe in recommending a disregard of false attacks in the Newspapers unless they be so serious as to render legal Proceedings unavoidable. However annoying it may be to faithful Public Servants to find their actions and motives misinterpreted and however considerable the temporary inconvenience which the Public Service may sustain from such false attacks I am of opinion that a recurrence to forcible measures of repression has a tendency to produce evils of greater magnitude. Nor can I doubt that Justice will ultimately be done to those who exhibit forbearance, and maintain a calm and dignified demeanour under such inflictions. [Ibid.]

Only the first few volumes of the *Honduras Observer* were both printed and published by Daly. In March 1844 Henry Gunter became the paper's proprietor with Daly continuing to print it as before. But by November of the same year its direction and production were in other hands. Daly continued as a printer, doing some contract work for the government and again attempting newspaper publishing on his own account with the *Packet Intelligencer* in 1854 and *Daly's Advertising Sheet* in 1867. Subsequently, his equipment passed into the possession of Edward C. Garnett at the "New Era Printing Office," which was active in the early 1870s.

Daly's successor as printer of the *Honduras Observer* was William E. Fitzgibbon, an American citizen, who in 1845 absorbed his paper's old rival. Henceforth his own was named the *Honduras Observer and Belize Gazette.* Early in 1848 Fitzgibbon ran into trouble with the legal authorities of the settlement for printing the text of a letter purporting to have been written by the chief justice, a memorial signed by various jurors protesting at the contents of this letter, the text of a resolution of the Public Meeting, and a couple of other documents relating to the chief justice's letter. On the chief justice's orders Fitzgibbon was arrested by the provost marshal and taken before the chief justice, who fined him £100 (local currency) and sentenced him to six months' imprisonment for contempt of court [5, vol. 3, p. 103].

West Indian law officers were often much more willing to interfere with the freedom of the press than was the executive branch of government. There was the case of Matthew Gallagher in Trinidad in 1810, who was imprisoned by George Smith, the one-man Royal Audiencia, despite the protests of Governor Hislop [14, p. 293], or the trumped-up libel action brought by the only two lawyers practicing in the Supreme Court of Grand Turk against the printer of the *Royal Standard of the Turks and Caicos Islands* in 1854 [13], which will serve to illustrate the response of the West Indian legal mind to criticism or even comment. In Fitzgibbon's case, Superintendent Fancourt was sufficiently troubled by the chief justice's action to request the advice of the Colonial Office in London. In June 1848 he received their recommendation that Fitzgibbon be released from jail and his fine remitted [5, vol. 3, p. 107].

The previous year Fitzgibbon had experienced another difficulty not infrequently encountered by West Indian printers: that of collecting payment for official printing. In January 1847 he had submitted a tender for printing government documents and inserting public advertisements in his paper, for £100 (local currency) per annum. The superintendent had authorized this for a four-month period, but a subsequent Public Meeting had rejected the tender. He was paid $100 for the four months, but by the time the Public Meeting rejected his tender he had completed eight months' work. It took him a great deal of trouble before the Public Meeting of February 1, 1848, in considering his petition for payment, agreed in view of the "peculiar circumstances" to disburse a further £33 6*s* 8*d* [15]. With this difficulty in collecting payment, exacerbated by his fine and imprisonment the following year, Fitzgibbon may well have decided to seek new pastures. I have found no trace of printing by him after 1848.

Other government printing on a contractual basis was undertaken in the 1850s by Daly and also by Edward L. Rhys, later the publisher of the *Colonist* newspaper. On Rhys's death in November 1866 his plant was bought for $900 by one John Jex, who worked in collaboration with Middleton and Company, publishers of the *British Honduras Colonist and Belize Advertiser*, and whose imprint appears on several government publications of the late sixties.

The Government Printing Office

The first press in the settlement had been bought with public funds for public printing. There appears to have survived no evidence as to the eventual fate of this equipment, and by the 1840s official printing was being farmed out among the various printers in Belize. There are several references to public printing in the National Archives in Belize City from which it is clear that all the printers named above were engaged at one time or another on government work. Permission for the purchase of a press was given at the meeting of the council on April 10, 1871, after some consideration of comparative printing costs, and it appears that the establishment of the Government Printing Office dates from this decision. Regular printing of the *Government Gazette* had started in 1865. At some stage, perhaps as early as 1889 and certainly by 1904, a press and other equipment were set up in the prison. Some routine printing of government forms, etc., was farmed out by the Government Printing Office to the Prisons Department, printing and binding being two of the trades taught the prisoners.[14]

Printing in the Bay Islands and on the Mosquito Coast

The colony now called Belize was only one of several areas on the Caribbean coast of Central America to be occupied from time to time by groups of British logwood cutters. In most cases these settlements were purely temporary, without even the equivocal status of the Baymen in Belize itself. But there were two other areas in which more permanent settlements were established. These were the Bay Islands (Ruatan, Bonacca, Utilla) a few miles off the coast of Honduras, and the Mosquito Coast, the Caribbean seaboard of Nicaragua from Cape Gracios a Dios (or even further north into Honduran territory) down to the mouth of the San Juan River. The British had long enjoyed cordial relations with the Mosquito Indians, with some of the Mosquito kings being educated in Jamaica, etc. A protectorate over Mosquitia was proclaimed in 1847.

The clash between British and American expansionism in Central America

14. The Government Printing Office is scheduled to be moved in the near future from Belize City to the new capital of Belize at Belmopan. I was able to visit it in April 1974. Apart from a ruling press, a couple of platen jobbers, and a disused Monotype caster of early date (which may date back to the original installation of Monotypes in the printing office in 1921), there was little to detain the printing historian since all the equipment was modern and, as elsewhere, with letterpress being ousted fairly rapidly by lithography.

in the mid-nineteenth century and the confusion of treaties to resolve it are fortunately none of our conern here. There is no evidence in the Archives of Belize or those of the short-lived Bay Islands Colony[15] (1852–59) to suggest that printing was carried on there before the islands were ceded by Britain to Honduras in 1859. Similarly I have found no evidence for a press in Bluefields or elsewhere on the Mosquito Coast before the Anglo-Nicaraguan treaty of 1860 brought the separate existence of Mosquitia to an end.

It seems clear that just as before 1826 Belize's printing needs were met from Jamaica, so Belize later provided whatever printing was required for these territories. One of the most interesting pieces of early Belize printing to have survived is the Order of Service for the Coronation of George Augustus Frederick, King of the Mosquito Nation,[16] which was printed by William E. Fitzgibbon in Belize in 1845.

"Mosquitiana" is today excessively rare. Apart from Fitzgibbon's coronation service I have been able to trace only some printed proformas for Mosquito land grants [16]. Another document in the library of the Royal Commonwealth Society, appointing Leonard Cox "Receiver General of the Mosquito Nation" in 1840, has been ably described by D. H. Simpson [17]. Like the coronation service, these documents were probably printed in Belize as a part of the contract printing for the government of the settlement by the printers discussed above.

APPENDIX I

A LIST OF PRINTERS IN BELIZE IN THE NINETEENTH CENTURY

A list of Belize printers in the nineteenth century includes:

1. James Cruickshank: active 1825–28?; printer of the *Honduras Gazette*, *Honduras Almanacks*.
2. Henry Whitney: active 1828–41?; printer of the *Honduras Gazette, Honduras Almanacks, Belize Advertiser* 1838–41.
3. John M. Daly: active 1841–67?; printer of the *Honduras Observer* 1840–44, *Packet Intelligencer* 1854, *Daly's Advertising Sheet* 1867; Acts of British Honduras 1861–66. His equipment later passed into the possession of the New Era Printing Office.
4. E. Cramond: publisher of the *Belize Gazette* in 1842; otherwise no references found.
5. William E. Fitzgibbon: active 1844–48?; printer of the *Honduras Observer* from November 1844; absorbed the *Belize Gazette* 1845. Contractor for government printing.

15. Now housed in the Jamaica Archives, Spanish Town.
16. In the National Library Service, Belize City.

6. Edward L. Rhys: active 1850–66; contractor for various government printing contracts and printer of the *Colonist.* On his death in November 1866 his plant was purchased for $900 by John Jex, who was associated with Middleton and Co. (see below, no. 8).

7. The *Colonist* Office, publishers of the *Colonist* newspaper before it was taken over by Rhys in November 1864. It advertised that it had a job-printing department. I have been unable to discover the names of its proprietors.

8. Middleton and Co.: active 1867–69?; contractors for government printing and printers of the *British Honduras Colonist.*

9. W. J. S. Scobell: publisher of the *Commercial Advertiser* in 1867.

10. Edward C. Garnett: proprietor of the New Era Printing Office and successor to Daly (see above, no. 3). Printer of the *New Era* and contractor for government printing in the early 1870s.

11. J. Robert Caines: active 1882–86; at first at the Colonial Press Association, Ltd. as printer of the *Colonial Guardian* and later printer of the *Observer.*

12. Claude L. Goodrich: active from 1881 as printer of the *Belize Advertiser* at C. T. Hunter's Printing Office and from 1888 associated with George Banham in the firm of Banham and Goodrich, publishers of the *Belize Independent.* There was a firm of jobbing printers, V. Goodrich, active in Belize in 1925, which may have been a continuation of the firm.

13. George S. Banham: active from 1887 as publisher of the *Belize Advertiser and British Honduras Gazette,* new series; later a partner in the firm of Banham and Goodrich.

14. George Mitchell: publisher of the *Belize Advertiser* 1888–89.

15. W. A. Burn: active 1894–96 as publisher of the *Times of Central America.*

16. Philip Stanley Woods: proprietor of the *Clarion* from 1897 until after 1925.

17. The Angelus Press: a firm of Roman Catholic booksellers, stationers, binders, and jobbing printers; started in 1885 and still in existence.

APPENDIX II

A HANDLIST OF BELIZE NEWSPAPERS PUBLISHED BEFORE 1900

In common with many West Indian colonies, nineteenth-century Belize saw the production of many newspapers. Most of them were short lived and seldom had a large circulation. As late as 1925 the two weekly papers then being published in the colony, the *Clarion* and the *Belize Independent,* had circulations of only 800 and 1,000 copies, respectively, and these were both long lived and successful ventures. Circulation of the papers outside the colony was very limited, and their survival rate has been poor.

Because of the situation of Belize, its press has been ill-served by bibliographers. As it is in Central America and not the West Indies, it was not included in Ragatz [18]. As it is a British colony, it has been excluded from bibliographies and union lists concerned with Latin America.

The handlist which follows is based upon the holdings of the British Library Reference Division (and particularly the contents of the Newspaper Room, Colindale); the National Library Service, Belize; the Jamaica Archives; the West India Reference Library of the Institute of Jamaica; the Royal Commonwealth Society, London; Rhodes House Library, Oxford; and the Bancroft Library at Berkeley; with reference to other locations as traced.

The contents of the Belize papers of the second half of the nineteenth century have been well discussed by Clegern [19], whose work was largely based on the Bancroft Library's microfilm copies of the British Library's holdings at Colindale.

1. *Honduras Gazette and Commercial Advertiser*; weekly July 1, 1826–June 27, 1829 or later. Edited by the magistrates, and for a period by its first printer, James Cruickshank. Rhodes House Library has set for period given above; British Library has volume 1 (July 1826–June 1827).

2. *Belize Advertiser*; printed and published weekly by Henry Whitney from September 29, 1838 until some time in 1841. The British Library has numbers 40–68 (June 29, 1839–January 11, 1840).

3. *Honduras Observer*; weekly from November 25, 1840 until 1848 or later. At first printed and published by John M. Daly, in March 1844 Henry Gunter became proprietor and in November 1844 it passed into the hands of William E. Fitzgibbon, absorbing the *Belize Gazette* (see below, no. 4) the following year. A copy of number 16 (March 10, 1841) is with U.S. consular dispatches from Jamaica in the National Archives, Washington; the Royal Commonwealth Society has issues for May 12, 1841, May 19, 1841, June 9, 1841, and February 15, 1844; the National Library Service in Belize owns an incomplete run from January 1844–November 1847.

4. *Belize Gazette*; published weekly by E. Cramond, started publication on December 12, 1840. Absorbed by the *Honduras Observer* 1845. A copy of the issue for June 18, 1842 was included with U.S. consular dispatches from Kingston, Jamaica, and is in the National Archives, Washington.

5. *Packet Intelligencer*; weekly, published by John M. Daly from June 10, 1854. The Bancroft Library, Berkeley, has a copy of the second issue for June 17.

6. *Colonist*; published weekly from the Colonist Office, Regent Street, Belize, from December 31, 1864. In the issue for November 4, 1865, Edward L. Rhys announced that the paper had changed its conduct for the third time and was now under his direction. At the end of that year Rhys announced that the paper would no longer be issued in its present form; that the income from the paper was $2,000, of which staffing costs absorbed at least $1,200, and paper, type, etc. another $500, leaving the editor $300. Public and jobbing printing, he concluded, could be done without a newspaper for a quarter of the outlay. Nevertheless he continued with a new series of the paper in a more economical format in 1866. The British Library's set runs from December 31, 1864 to October 13, 1866.

7. *Daly's Advertising Sheet.* The only copy traced, for December 17, 1867, was included in U.S. consular dispatches from Belize and is now in the National Archives, Washington.

8. *British Honduras Colonist and Belize Advertiser*; published weekly by Middleton and Co. and sold also by John Jex who had purchased Rhys's plant. The

British Library's set runs from July 20, 1867 to November 28, 1868 (nos. 1–72).

9. *Commercial Advertiser*; published weekly by W. J. S. Scobell, proprietor, from July 3, 1867. The British Library's holdings cease with number 9 (August 28, 1867); there is no indication in the paper that it was ceasing publication.

10. *New Era, and British Honduras Chronicle*; weekly, printed and published by Edward C. Garnett, who had taken over John Daly's plant, from January 7, 1871. The British Library's set runs from February 11, 1871 to May 18, 1872; there is no internal evidence in the paper that it was ceasing publication.

11. *Central American Telegraph*; published twice monthly from March 12, 1873 under the editorship of Dr. F. Gahné (see also below, no. 15), Colonel John Tracy, Rafael Padilla, and General E. Viada. There is no indication of the printer. A pioneering attempt at a paper in Spanish and English, evidently intended to circulate in Honduras as well as Belize, it attracted few subscribers and ceased publication after the first quarter. The British Library has numbers 2–6 (March 26–May 26, 1873).

12. *Belize Advertiser*; published weekly from the Printing Office of C. T. Hunter, North Front Street, Belize, from May 21, 1881 and printed at first by Claude L. Goodrich. Its first proprietor, C. T. Hunter, was a controversial figure in Belizean affairs [19, pp. 76–77, 80–91]. On November 26, 1881 Hunter was replaced by A. R. Gibbs as proprietor. The British Library's holdings are incomplete (vol. 1–vol. 4, no. 1 [May 21, 1881–October 25, 1884]; n. s. nos. 1–2 [December 25, 1886–January 1, 1887]), but it is clear from these that the paper was running into financial difficulties.

13. *Belize Advertiser and British Honduras Gazette*, "New Series," which commenced weekly publication on February 26, 1887, purports to be a continuation, under the direction of George S. Banham, of number 12 (and is so treated in the British Library's cataloging), but in fact is a distinct journal, with a different editorial standpoint. The British Library's holdings cease with volume 2, number 20 (May 19, 1888), and I suspect that Banham was bought out or persuaded by other means to cease by those allied to C. T. Hunter's interests.

14. *Belize Advertiser*, new series; printed and published weekly by George Mitchell at North Front Street, Belize (the original *Advertiser* office). The British Library has a set from volume 1, number 1 to volume 2, number 16 (July 28, 1888–November 9, 1889).

15. *Colonial Guardian*; printed weekly at the office of the Colonial Press Association, Ltd., Albert Street, Belize, initially by J. Robert Caines. The paper, which first appeared on January 7, 1882, was throughout its life edited by Dr. Frederick Gahné, the most important of all Belizean editors [19, pp. 193–94]. It ceased publication in 1913 (set in the British Library).

16. *Observer*; printed and published weekly by John Robert Caines at the Observer Printing Office, Water Lane, Belize, after Caines had severed his connection with the *Colonial Guardian*. It was evidently not a success and ceased publication after one year with the issue for February 13, 1886 (set in the British Library). The last few issues of the paper advertise the Observer

office (with the opportunity to continue the paper) for lease or sale. The offer included the types, a Novelty Press which was worked by a boy and used to print the paper, and a self-inking Excelsior Press which was used for jobbing work.[17] If the plant were not disposed of before the publication of the last issue of the paper, the firm was going to continue with jobbing printing only. I have not been able to trace the subsequent history of this plant.

17. *Belize Independent*; edited by George S. Banham and published weekly by Banham and Goodrich from October 11, 1888 as a sort of continuation of Banham's previous venture (see above, no. 13) and as a rival to the *Belize Advertiser*, new series (see above, no. 14). More successful than most other Belizean papers, it continued publication until near the end of World War II (set in the British Library).

18. *Times of Central America*; printed and published weekly from July 6, 1894 by Walter Adam Burn, barrister-at-law, from his printing office in the Hunter Building, North Front Street, Belize—from which address one presumes a connection with the *Belize Advertiser* and the interests of C. T. Hunter. One of the worst-printed of Belizean papers, publication was suspended from December 31, 1896. The British Library has a set from number 9 (August 31, 1894) onward.

19. *Clarion*; printed and published weekly by Philip Stanley Woods of Foresters' Hall, Regent Street, at the Clarion Office, Hunter's Buildings, North Front Street, Belize, from November 19, 1897. In the first issue of the paper it was emphasized that the journal and the press, types, and other accessories were the sole property of the proprietor, and that the paper was "not called into existence for the sole purpose of puffing the enterprises of Mr C. T. Hunter." Despite an inauspicious start (publication of the first issue being delayed because the press had broken down) this was to be the most successful of all Belizean papers, remaining under Woods's editorial direction for well over a quarter of a century. It was transformed into a daily paper in 1935, eventually ceasing publication in 1961.

REFERENCES

1. Dobson, Narda. *A History of Belize*. Port-of-Spain: Longmans Caribbean, 1973.
2. Cave, Roderick. "Printing Comes to Jamaica: The Work of Robert and Mary Baldwin." *Jamaica Journal* (in press).
3. Shilstone, E. M. "Some Notes on Early Presses and Newspapers in Barbados." *Journal of the Barbados Museum and Historical Society* 26 (November 1958): 19–33.
4. McMurtrie, Douglas. *The First Printing on the Island of Tobago*. Fort Worth, Tex.: National Association for Printing Education, 1943.
5. Burdon, Sir John, ed. *The Archives of British Honduras*. London: Sifton Praed, 1931–35.

17. The Novelty Press was a lightweight treadle platen of simple clamshell design, marketed by B. O. Woods of Boston; several different firms marketed presses with the name excelsior; this may have been the very small card and job press developed by William Kelsey which is substantially the same as that still being marketed for amateur use by the Kelsey Company of Meriden, Connecticut [20; 21, pp. 241–42].

6. Twyman, Michael. "The Lithographic Handpress 1796–1850." *Journal of the Printing Historical Society* 3 (1967): 3–50.
7. Belize Archives, R 5 a, p. 122.
8. Belize Archives, R 6 a, p. 13.
9. Simmonds, Peter L. "Statistics of Newpapers in Various Countries." *Journal of the Statistical Society of London* 4 (1841): 111–36.
10. Kennedy, Jean de Chantal. *Biography of a Colonial Town: Hamilton, Bermuda 1790–1897*. Hamilton: Bermuda Book Stores, [1962].
11. Cundall, Frank. *The Press and Printers of Jamaica prior to 1820*. Worcester, Mass.: American Antiquarian Society, 1916.
12. Breen, Henry H. *St Lucia: Historical, Statistical and Descriptive*. London: Longmans, 1844.
13. Cave, Roderick. "The Early Printers of Grand Turk." *Papers of the Bibliographical Society of America* (in press).
14. Naipaul, V. S. *The Loss of El Dorado*. New York: Alfred A. Knopf, 1970.
15. Belize Archives, R 20, pp. 62–65.
16. Institute.of Jamaica, MSS 1260 and 1374.
17. Simpson, D. H. "A Document of the Mosquito Nation." *Royal Commonwealth Society Library Notes*, n.s. 57 (September 1961): 2–4.
18. Ragatz, Lowell J. *A Guide for the Study of British Caribbean History 1763–1834*. Washington, D.C.: Government Printing Office, 1932.
19. Clegern, Wayne M. *British Honduras: Colonial Dead End 1859–1900*. Baton Rouge: Louisiana State University Press, 1967.
20. Green, Ralph. *A History of the Platen Jobber*. Chicago: Printing Office of Philip Reed, 1953.
21. Moran, James. *Printing Presses: History and Development from the Fifteenth Century to Modern Times*. London: Faber & Faber, 1973.

VI
THE PRINTING OF *THE HONDURAS ALMANACK*

The British colony of Belize, or British Honduras as it was called until 1973, is an English-speaking enclave on the Spanish Main, tucked between the Mexican territory of Quintana Roo to the north and Guatemala to the south and west. The Baymen (as the English mahogany cutters and their Negro slaves were known) were governed via Jamaica until 1862, and it was natural that the printing needs of the Bay were met by Jamaican printers for a considerable time.

Belize itself was almost the last of the various British colonial territories in the Caribbean into which printing was introduced. In the first study of printing in the settlement[1] I concluded that the first printer in British Honduras, James Cruickshank, was responsible for the production of *The Honduras Almanack* for 1826 which was published in March of that year. The evidence to be found in the National Archives of Belize tended to support this conclusion, which was strengthened by the similarity of the types used in the *Almanack* and by Cruickshank in his semiofficial paper *The Honduras Gazette.*

Examination of the copies of *The Honduras Almanacks* for 1826, 1827, 1828, and 1830 in the American Antiquarian Society[2] shows conclusively, however, that they were *not* printed in the settlement at all, but were produced in Boston, Massachusetts.

The AAS copies of the 1826 and 1827 *Almanacks* are bound

[1] Roderick Cave, 'Printing in Nineteenth-Century Belize,' *Library Quarterly* 46 (1976):20–37.

[2] This research was made possible through a Fred Harris Daniels Fellowship at the Society, July–August 1976.

together. They had[3] three receipted bills loosely tucked into the volume, and these are very clear on the printing of the *Almanacks*.

The bills, addressed to Messrs. Brown & Ellis, Boston, are as follows:

[1. From Annin & Smith]

1826 Feb.	To engraving a view of Honduras Church including the drawing		$35.00
—	Engraving the arms of the settlement of Honduras, including the drawing		25.00
—	Engraving the Private Signals of the merchants of Honduras		8.00
—	Copper for the whole, 84 inches @ 4 cts.		3.36
—	Printing 333 impressions of the Church @ 6/		3.33
	Printing 333 impressions of the Arms @ 80¢		2.67
—	Printing 333 impressions of the Signals @ 80¢		2.66
—	8 2/16th French Plate Paper (for the whole @ 50¢		4.06
			$84.08
March 10	Eng. bill of lading, T. Pickstock	$50.00	
	Printing 700 inc. paper & pressing	11.50	61.50
		61.50	145.58
	Received payment Annin & Smith		

[2. From Annin & Smith]

1826 Sept. 23	To engraving a Plate of Private signals for the merchants of Belize including Copper	$11.00	
Oct. 7	To printing 300 impressions from signal plates	2.25	
	Paper for same	.81	14.06

[3] They have now been transferred to the Book Trades Collection, Department of Manuscripts.

〃	Engraving a plate representing the manner of trucking Mahogany in Honduras	50.00	
	Reducing the drawing for the same	8.00	58.00
〃	Printing 300 impressions from the manner of trucking Mahogany in Honduras	3.00	
〃	Printing 300 impressions of the plate of Arms	2.40	
〃	3 10/16th French Plate Paper @ 3/	1.81	
	Altering the plate of Arms	2.00	9.21
			$81.21

Received payment Annin & Smith

[3. From Edgar W. Davies]

1827 Nov. 17	306 copies Honduras Almanack 288 pages @ 7/	$336.00
	Discount 5 per cent	16.80
		$319.20
	Binding of Honduras Almanack & 2 reams Letter Paper for interleaving	35.00
	Binding 12 copies elegant-morocco, gilt, lettered &c	18.00
	1 ream Letter Paper for interleaving of Honduras Almanack throughout	3.50
	Box & Packing	1.00
		$376.70

Received Payment, by Note
Edgar W. Davies

William B. Annin (1791?–1839) and George G. Smith were partners in an engraving business in Boston as Annin & Smith from 1820 to 1831. The items for which they were charging Brown & Ellis in February 1826 were the copper engraving plates used in the 1826 *Almanack*, the Arms appearing on the title page. Thomas Pickstock, for whose Bill of Lading a total of $61.50 was charged on March 10, was a Belize merchant and one of the seven magistrates to whom the Public Meeting of Baymen deputed the government of the settlement. He was very much involved in the editorial compilation of the *Almanacks*[4] and with *The Honduras Gazette*. Clearly he acted as the agent in Belize through whom the commission for printing these plates was passed (via Brown & Ellis) to Annin & Smith.

The second invoice from Annin & Smith refers to the plates in the 1827 *Almanack*: the title leaf suitably amended, a fresh plate of signals plus the drawing of mahogany-hauling by Andrew Baynton, public notary, assistant to the clerk of the courts, and keeper of the records in Belize.

The invoice from Edgar W. Davies[5] for printing and binding refers to this same 1827 *Almanack*. The binding on the AAS copy is, one presumes, identical with that of the 'elegant-morocco' copies, and bears the name 'Charles Brown' blocked in gold in the center of the front board. The 1830 volume is similarly blocked; that for 1828, though unblocked, bears the signature of Nathaniel Brown on the endleaf. 'Nathaniel Brown of Boston' appears in the subscription list for 1828, 'Brown & Ellis, Boston' among the subscribers to the 1830 volume.

Although the invoices refer only to the 1826 and 1827 *Almanacks*, the very close similarity in paper and typographic dress of the 1828, 1829, and 1830 volumes to these earlier issues suggests that Pickstock probably arranged through Brown & Ellis to have these also printed in Boston. Annin & Smith may have been involved in the production, since the 1829 volume contains an engraved title leaf apparently modified from their plate. The other illustrations are all litho-

[4] And with its physical production also. The 1829 volume contains lithographs after drawings by Pickstock of 'A View of Fort George' and of 'The Honduras Lighthouse.'

[5] I have not been able to trace Davies otherwise.

graphs, save for one plate by Baynton in the 1830 volume, which is a rather crude aquatint.

The high technical quality of the plates and variety of processes used in the *Honduras Almanacks* would have been very surprising had they been printed in the settlement, rather than in Boston, since they were produced at a level of technical accomplishment far higher than that possessed by printers elsewhere in the British Caribbean at that time, or by Belize printers later in the 1830s. In the period before 1776 it had not been uncommon for the West Indian colonies to have work printed in New England, and by the late 1840s the American domination of the West Indian printing trade was beginning to show,[6] but U.S. commissions were very unusual in the period around 1830. In this, as in so many aspects of its history, Belize was different from the sugar colonies.

[6] Note, for example, the inclusion of the Bruce Typefoundry's advertisements in the *San Fernando Gazette* (Trinidad) of May 1851 and in the *Antigua Weekly Register*, September 1849.

PRINTING IN GRENADA

VII

COMMENDATORY VERSE FROM THE PRINTER'S DEVIL

Most West Indian newspaper proprietors, on completion of a volume of their newspapers, contented themselves with a simple announcement to their readers that another year's subscription was due – sometimes adding to this a plaintive reminder that subscriptions were supposed to be paid *in advance*, and that unpleasant measures would be taken against those whose payments were seriously in arrears.

It was no doubt in an attempt to engage their subscribers' sympathies that a few attempted a lighter approach, by sending their apprentices and newsboys to the subscribers, bearing not only their account but also some doggerel verses on the events of the past year. I have seen several such from the *St George's Chronicle and Grenada Gazette* [1] for the 1790s, and from the *Bahama Gazette* as late as 1814. [2]

There seems to have been something of a taste for such things in Grenada in the late eighteenth century. The merchant David Napier in 1790 [3] made his miscellaneous stock seem more interesting by the way he listed the goods

> Spy-glasses, Mirrors, leather straps,
> And buckles with best patent chapes,
> Enamell'd hat-pins, sliding rules,
> And chests complete of Joiners tools . . .

reminding his customers that

> . . . well you know that none sells cheaper
> Than Yours, &c. David Napier.

The splendidly patriotic verses used in the *St George's Chronicle* of 1 January 1799 were less than tactful in view of Grenada's sizable number of French settlers. But they probably did not subscribe to the *Chronicle*, and in any case the attitude of the British officials and merchants in the island was by no means conciliatory. The *Address* will serve as a characteristic example of the genre. Whether James Finlay, who was then the printer of the paper, or his former partner William Park (who had been killed in Fédon's insurrection of 1795) [4] was responsible for introducing the custom, surviving files of the newspaper are too incomplete for us to judge. Whoever it was, though scarcely increasing the wealth of English poetry, made colonial life a little more entertaining. And a few more subscribers may have been persuaded to settle their accounts, and to give a tip to the Devil . . .

Address to the Subscribers to the St George's Chronicle from the Printer's Devil. January 1st 1799

Now *99*'s arrived, I would relate
The Wonders of the glorious *98* !
My *Devilish* rhime, no doubt, you will excuse
An Angel could not bring you better News;
Some I have got. I know will make you smile
The very latest from *the Deep Mouth'd Nile.*
"In Egypt now the French will fight no more,
"Turn'd Mussulmen who Atheists were before !
"Their Chief 'tis said (I do not mean to hum ye)
"Has been embalmed, and makes a noble mummy !"–
Masters, I fear my head is not quite right,
I dream of gallant Nelson every night.
I hear the thunder, and I see the Fight !
IO TRIUMPHE ! (in my Sleep I cry),
They burn, they strike – *Ours is the Victory* !
Here, you all know we all for joy got tipsy,
To tell the truth, your Devil was *non se ipse*;
Then *Warren*'s glorious Victory following close–
This was another very pleasant dose !
Huzza the *Irish* bus'ness then was o'er !
And so we all got tipsy as before.
But to my task, the Printer bids me say,
"Masters, remember this is *New Year's Day*;"
With his warm wishes, thanks by me he sends
To all his gen'rous customers and friends;
Hopes, tho' his Paper has some times been dull,
Of late it made you reparations full;
And boasts, with pride he boasts, its little columns
Contain much more than many weighty volumes !
He thinks *next century* may bring us peace;
If not, he prays our victories may increase –
Now for myself, I likewise beg to say,
"Masters remember this is New Year's Day,*"
And your poor Devil shall forever pray.

* A modest kind of dun both from the Printer and the Devil.

NOTES

1. Copies in the American Antiquarian Society and the New York Historical Society libraries.
2. *Bahama Gazette* 1 January 1814 (Copy in Nassau Public Library).
3. *St. George's Chronicle* 19 November 1790 (Copy in the American Antiquarian Society Library).
4. Raymund Devas, *Conception Island* (London, 1932) p. 103. Fédon's insurrection, which was put down only with great difficulty and with help from the Spanish in Trinidad, had received much local support from the non-British population in Grenada.

PRINTING IN JAMAICA

VIII
PRINTING IN EIGHTEENTH-CENTURY JAMAICA

Although the settlers of Barbados (and perhaps even those of St. Christopher) would have disputed it, there is little doubt that within twenty years of its conquest from the Spanish in 1655, Jamaica had become the chief English colony in the Caribbean area. It was therefore appropriate that it was the first centre of printing in the West Indies. Compared with the Spanish settlements on the Main, of course, Jamaica was at first of little importance except as a strategic base, though Sir Henry Morgan and the other buccaneers were to ensure that the Spaniards were well aware of that fact. In the eighteenth century the development of the island as a producer of sugar and of coffee by means of slave labour was to secure for it an economic importance it has never regained. Though perhaps outdistanced in economic terms by the French colony in St. Domingue, the heyday of the planter class in Jamaica produced a society little less brilliant than that of Port-au-Prince and Cap François. Unlike the French colony, whose brilliance was to be extinguished by Toussaint L'Ouverture and the Haitian revolution, the planter class in Jamaica was to fade away relatively slowly, from the Napoleonic wars onwards. Jamaica's strategic position, moreover, was to ensure that it was the administrative *and printing* centre for the British in the Western Caribbean in general; not only for the regular Jamaican dependencies of the Mosquito Coast, the Honduras Bay settlements and the Cayman Islands, but also for British military adventures at Mobile[1] and in St. Domingue.[2]

Planter society may have been brilliant, but the brilliance did not come from its intellectual life. There is some evidence for book collecting and bookselling at Port Royal in the 1680s,[3] and some evidence for the creation

[1] Douglas MacMurtie, *A broadside issued at Mobile . . . in 1763, but printed on the island of Jamaica*, Washington 1939.

[2] The British army in St. Domingue (1793–8) was accompanied by a printer equipped with Fry's Baskerville types. At least one piece of this work (which has not been studied) survived in the Institute of Jamaica. It is worth noting also that Jamaican printers were employed by the Abbé Roland to print the monthly *Mercure des Antilles*. Cf. Gabriel Debien, 'Un abbé maitre de pension à Saint Domingue puis journaliste à la Jamaïque (1781–1783)', *Notes d'histoire coloniale*, 43.

[3] Roderick Cave, 'Thomas Craddock's books: a West India merchant's stock', *Book collector*, 25 (1976), 481–90.

of parish libraries[4] in the early eighteenth century, but the general impression one gains is not that of a book-loving society. Thus Mrs. Mary Ricketts, the wife of a Jamaican planter who was leaving the island, wrote to her sister in England on 6 May 1759:

> Our Furniture is all Disposed of except the Books, a good many of these I Doubt we shall carry back as a taste for literature Does by no Means Prevail in this country.[5]

Similarly, the depressing picture given of the island by Lady Nugent in her well-known *Journal* of her residence in the island in the Napoleonic wars—of the vapid, foolish creole ladies and their lumpish husbands who 'really eat like cormorants and drink like porpoises'—is remarkable for the absence of any suggestion of intellectual life.[6]

It is no doubt partly the impression gained from such sources that West Indian printing would be a stony and unprofitable ground to till that has dissuaded British typographic historians from a study of Jamaican printing. Apart from Isaiah Thomas,[7] or in this century Douglas McMurtrie[8] and Bradford Swan,[9] the only studies of Jamaican printing have been produced in Jamaica.[10] The pioneering work of Frank Cundall, Secretary and Librarian of the Institute of Jamaica and responsible for building up the Institute's splendid West India Reference Library, effectively laid the foundations for the island's bibliographical history. For a man whose interests were not primarily typographical, and working before microfilm and xerox, before the reorganization of the Jamaica Archives had made many records accessible, and before the publication of several important guides,[11] it is remarkable how full and accurate a picture of the first century of Jamaican printing Cundall could produce.[12]

Printing in Kingston

The introduction of printing into Kingston in 1718 and the work of the first printer Robert Baldwin, his wife Mary, and their sons, has been

[4] The Fulham papers in Lambeth Palace reveal that there had been a parish library at Port Royal, destroyed or dispersed by 1721 (Fulham Papers, xvii, ff. 215–16) and that another collection towards a catechetical library was sent with Mr. Barrett missionary to Jamaica in 1724 (Fulham Papers xvii, ff, 175–79).

[5] B.M. Add. MSS. 30001.f.12.

[6] Maria Nugent, *Lady Nugent's journal of her residence in Jamaica from 1801 to 1805*, new rev. edn. by Philip Wright, Kingston 1966, p. 81.

[7] In his *A history of printing in America*, Worcester, Mass., 1810.

[8] In his *The first printing on the island of Jamaica*, Metuchen, N.J., 1934; and in the more important *The first printing in Jamaica*, Evanston, Illinois, 1942, which includes a facsimile of the earliest extant Jamaican imprint.

[9] In his volume on *The Caribbean region* in the 'Spread of Printing' series edited by Colin Clair (Amsterdam, 1970).

[10] e.g. George F. Judah, 'The newspaper history of Jamaica', *Jamaica times*, 14 Jan. 1899, p. 4, and 21 Jan. 1899, p. 5; H. P. Jacobs, 'The Jamaican press 1789–1865', *Jamaica journal*, Sept. 1972, 2–6, as well as the books by Cundall cited below.

[11] Such as Lowell Ragatz, *Guide for the study of British Caribbean history 1763–1834*, Washington, 1932 (flawed by the lack of locations for items cited) and K. E. Ingram's invaluable *Sources of Jamaican history 1655–1838; a bibliographical survey with particular reference to manuscript sources.* Zug, Switzerland, 1976.

[12] In his *The press and printers of Jamaica prior to 1820*, Worcester, Mass., 1916, which was supplemented but not entirely superseded by his *A history of printing in Jamaica from 1717* [sic] *to 1834*, Kingston, 1935.

described too thoroughly elsewhere[13] for more than a brief summary of their work to be necessary here. With encouragement from Sir Nicholas Lawes, the island's governor to whom Baldwin's press was licensed, Baldwin set up shop in Church Street, Kingston early in 1718. The bread and butter of his *printing* business was the production of the *Weekly Jamaica courant*, supplemented by printing the *Votes of the Assembly* and various other official and semi-official pieces, such as the *Tryal of Captain John Rackham, and other pirates* (1721) and private ventures including a sheet almanac. Book-binding was an important aspect of his business, and he seems also to have had a virtual monopoly of the island's stationery trade. After his death, in 1722, his wife Mary continued the business (apparently with considerable financial success) until some time after 1734; by 1740 it was in the hands of their sons Robert and Peter Baldwin. In 1745 they were publishing a second weekly newspaper, *The Jamaica gazette*, and seem to have extended their business interests to include insurance and estate agency as well as printing and binding and selling stationery. After February 1746 the Baldwins disappear from view; Peter Baldwin was dead, and his brother Robert had either died earlier or left the island.

Production of *The Jamaica gazette* passed into the hands of Alexander Davidson, whose estate was valued at £164. 8s. 9d. in an inventory drawn up in September 1759.[14] I have not traced any of his surviving work, though *The Jamaica gazette* itself continued as a weekly and later bi-weekly until the 1780s or possibly later; in 1765 being produced by the firm of Weatherby, Allen & McCann, and in 1788 by Thomas Strupar[15] and Joseph Preston.

The profitable contract for printing the *Votes of the Assembly*, however, was not passed on by the Baldwins to their successors with the *Gazette*. Instead William Daniell,[16] of Harbour Street, Kingston, who had commenced publication of his rival newspaper *The Jamaica courant* in October 1748, became Printer to the Assembly, retaining the office until his death in the summer of 1755, after which for a year the post was held by his widow, and then for a further year by Charles Woodham, who had presumably either purchased the business from Mary Daniell, or was running it on her behalf.

Daniell was an enterprising man. As well as his printing of the *Votes* (originally as a speculation, but with a subsidy from the Assembly, when it proved unprofitable), he commenced publication of a book almanac, *The merchant's pocket companion*, in 1751. In 1750 he issued John William's *Essay on the bilious, or yellow fever of Jamaica*, plus *An enquiry into the late essay* by Parker Bennett[17] and probably several of the other pamphlets resulting from

[13] Roderick Cave, 'Printing comes to Jamaica', *Jamaica journal*, 1975, 11–17; 'The first printers in Jamaica', *Amphora*, 27 (1977), 22–36; 'An inventory of the first Jamaican printing house', *PBSA*, 69 (1975), 560–5.

[14] Jamaica Archives, *Inventories*, liber 38, f. 169v.

[15] Son of George Worral Strupar, printer of Red Lion Street, Clerkenwell, to whom he was apprenticed on 8 June 1773.

[16] Probably to be identified with the William Daniel, son of Richard Daniel, farmer of Padworth, Berks., who was apprenticed to Abel Roper, bookseller, of Westminster for the usual seven years on 2 July 1723.

[17] The only known copy is in the American Antiquarian Society's library in Worcester, Mass.

this war of medical men. Another publication was the useful-sounding *Justice of the Peace's pocket companion*[18] in 1754. In other ways also Daniell showed considerable enterprise, calling on the resources of Benjamin Franklin in Philadelphia to ease his problems in obtaining paper.[19]

It is clear that by the time Daniell died there were at least two printing offices active in Kingston, and there continued to be at least two newspapers published there from the 1750s on. Daniell's *Courant* disappeared, but was probably absorbed into *The Kingston journal*, which Thomas Woolhead started in 1756. This paper was subsequently printed by the co-partnership of Woolhead, Gadd,[20] and Bennett; in 1776 by Joseph Thompson & Co., and by 1788 was being produced by Bennett & Dickson.

The permutations of Kingston printers' partnerships are too complex for further discussion to be appropriate here. By the last decade of the eighteenth century there were sufficient printers at work in the town to permit production of at least two daily papers (perhaps three) and one very substantial weekly newspaper in addition to the other printing business carried on. But by that time printing had also spread to four other towns in the island.

Most West Indian colonies were small enough for a single printing centre to be perfectly adequate for the island's needs, and that printing centre was normally the colony's administrative capital. In the French colony of St. Domingue, however, and only to a slightly lesser degree in Jamaica, the size of the colony and the difficult terrain (which made communication by land a slow and painful business before the coming of railways or the motor vehicle), created a situation in which other substantial towns with their own hinterlands, might serve as bases for a sound printing business.

Printing in Spanish Town and Montego Bay

Jamaica was unusual in that its administrative capital, St. Jago de la Vega (or Spanish Town as it is called today), was not the island's chief port nor indeed on the coast at all. By setting up his press in Kingston in 1718 Robert Baldwin had made a sensible economic decision: it was the mercantile centre of the island and he could circulate his newspaper in St. Jago and Port Royal, as well as in Kingston, far more easily than if he had settled in either of those towns. In the early 1750s there was considerable controversy over the future of St. Jago as the island's capital. Masters of vessels arriving at Port Royal or the Kingston wharves, the Kingston merchants, and the planters to windward, all resented the need to make the tedious journey across the St. Catherine plains to conduct their legal and administrative business in St. Jago. Under Governor Knowles an Act for the removal of

[18] No copy is known to survive.

[19] Cf. George S. Eddy, *Account books kept by Benjamin Franklin, Ledger 'D' 1737–1747*, New York, 1929, pp. 51–2 and 72; and *The papers of Benjamin Franklin*, ed. by Leonard Labaree *et al.*, vol. 5, New Haven, 1962.

[20] William Gadd is to be identified as the son of William Ged the stereotyper, but tantalizingly little information is available on his career in Jamaica. When he made his will in December 1766 he described himself as planter, and he seems only to have been a sleeping partner in the printing business.

the capital and of various public offices to Kingston passed the Assembly. Bitterly opposed by the St. Jago lobby, this Act was eventually disallowed by London, but while the matter was in dispute St. Jago's advocates felt hampered by the fact that all the island's printers were in Kingston, and naturally supported the Kingston move in their papers. This fact was to make the fortune of a young Irishman who was then working in the counting house of Archibald Sinclair in St. Jago.

Curtis Brett is the only West Indian printer of the eighteenth century who left any account of his career, in a series of autobiographical letters written to his young son towards the end of his life.[21] Born in Dublin in 1720, the youngest son of a clothier, he was apprenticed to a Dublin bookseller who had a small printing business. His master failing in his affairs, Curtis's indentures were given up to him though he was still under age. Like many another young Irishman he went to London to seek his fortune.

Hearing that Mr. Gardner, a printer near Temple Bar, wanted a compositor, I ventured to offer him my services, with fear and trembling from a conscious deficiency in the art. Finding upon enquiry, I had not run away (which my young looks might well raise some suspicion of) he humanely employed me and gave me opportunity of improvement, of which I made good use, that in a little time I bought a new watch and had a convenient little purse. I was now ambitious of appearing well and keeping good company, which proved of great service to me as it made me carefully avoid all shabby, lazy, idle, disorderly fellows, and this recommended me to the notice of many persons of credit. I found myself in as happy a situation as anyone in my station of life.

From Thomas Gardner, Brett moved in 1743 into the employment of William Strahan in Wine Office Court. Five years later he was tempted by a gentleman going to Jamaica (no doubt one of the 'persons of credit' to whom Brett recommended himself) into joining him as a storekeeper.

With Brett's first impressions of the island, and his account of his early life there, we cannot be concerned. Having lost all his savings in some unlucky business ventures, he had tried work as an overseer on a sugar plantation and employment in a Kingston ironmonger's before moving to St. Jago at precisely the right time. Learning of his background as a printer, Sir Charles Price, Judge Askew, and several other Spanish Town gentlemen suggested he should set up as a printer there. They hit on a simple scheme to enable him to acquire the necessary capital and equipment, through the production of a new edition of *The laws of Jamaica.*

Subscription proposals for this were published in Daniell's *Courant* on 29 June 1754. Priced at four pistoles (two on subscription, two on delivery)[22] the work was to be put to press as soon as two hundred subscriptions were received. Sir Charles Price personally guaranteed the return of subscriptions

[21] In private hands; a summary is now in the Institute of Jamaica, MST10 (Curtis Brett letters). For a fuller account of Brett's career in Jamaica, see my article 'Two Jamaican printers', *Amphora* 30 (1977), 20–32.

[22] One pistole was worth £1. 5*s*. Jamaican currency; £1 Jamaican was approximately 13*s*. 4*d*. sterling. Unless otherwise stated, all sums quoted are in Jamaican currency.

should the work be abandoned, but he ensured that this would not be necessary by persuading Governor, Council, and Assembly to support it. For Brett, placed in charge of production, a profitable return for his labour was guaranteed.

In June 1755 Brett took ship for London, taking the copy for the *Laws* with him, and using his time on board to get it ready for the press. On arrival in London, he passed the work over to his old employer Strahan to be printed and bound. While this was being done, Brett busied himself in buying equipment for a printing office and in seeking out capable journeymen willing to work in Jamaica.

Early in March 1756 Brett returned to the island taking with him the bound copies of the new edition of *The laws of Jamaica*, his printing-office equipment, and presumably compositors and pressmen, since within a week and a day of the vessel's arrival at Port Royal on 30 April he issued the first number of his own newspaper.

> *The St. Jago Intelligencer* . . . was received with very good general applause and immediately a good number of gentlemen subscribed to it . . . so that our paper answered very well. Our volume of Laws went off pretty fast at a doubloon each . . . and from that time to this, I have never, thanks to the Almighty, been in want of money.

As only one issue of the *Intelligencer* is known to survive,[23] one cannot discuss its editorial policies. That issue, for 15 May 1757 (after Brett had succeeded C.S. Woodham as Printer to the Assembly) is a well-printed post folio in three columns. From its columns we learn that advertisements 'of a moderate length' cost 5*s*., or 15*s*. for a month's insertion, and that Brett had appointed the bookseller, James Forsyth, as advertisement agent in Kingston. Subscriptions were 30*s*. per annum in Spanish Town, and two pistoles to country subscribers.

Apart from the *Intelligencer*, almost certainly Curtis Brett printed his own book almanac, distributed by James Forsyth. One imperfect copy of his *Votes of the Assembly* is known.[24] Of his private ventures *An enquiry concerning the trade, commerce and policy of Jamaica relative to the scarcity of money . . . to which is added a scheme for establishing a public book* (1757) survives.[25]

That so little of his work is still to be found is not an indication that Curtis Brett was unsuccessful. Far from it. In 1761, 'finding myself worth about £5000, and having had the marrow of the printing business', he decided to quit his old trade and once more turn merchant. His letters, though they contain a fascinating account of his subsequent career in Jamaica, New York, and London before he retired to Chester, contain no further references to printing, nor any indication of how he disposed of his printing office at Spanish Town. One can presume that he was bought out by his partner Charles White, who was named Printer to the Assembly in Brett's place. A creole, White was not a trained printer, and no doubt the direction of the

23 In the Institute of Jamaica.
24 Now in the Massachusetts Historical Society.
25 There are copies in the Institute of Jamaica and in Bodley (23262.d.1).

printing business was put into the care of Matthew Moss with whom White worked in partnership until 1769.

In 1769 two new printers in St. Jago were named printers to the Assembly: John Lowry and Robert Sherlock,[26] both of them men for whose careers the Jamaica Archives furnish some information to eke out the scant detail of their printing, while Sherlock is also of special interest for the start of printing at Montego Bay. It would seem that until 1773 Lowry and Sherlock merely leased the printing office from Charles White. Between 1769 and 1771 they printed a two-volume edition of the *Acts of the Assembly . . . to 1769*, their own book almanac for 1771 and no doubt other works. From 1771 until 1775 the Spanish Town business seems to have been run by Lowry, but after his death early in September that year Sherlock took over control of the printing house and ran it until he sold or leased it in 1778.

Lowry's will,[27] proved 14 September 1775, made provision for an inventory of his printing equipment and stock in trade, which unfortunately appears not to have survived. Most of his estate (of £819. 16*s*. 6*d*.) was settled for life on his mistress, Lydia Long, 'a free negro woman', and afterwards on his natural daughter Mary Lowry. Sherlock was his Executor, and two other printers James Fannin[28] and George Eberall[29] legatee and witness respectively.

When Sherlock moved from Spanish Town to Montego Bay is uncertain. His printing office there was certainly established by 29 May 1773, the date which Isaiah Thomas tells us he started publication of *The Cornwall chronicle*, an important newspaper that was to last until the 1860s, although none printed by Sherlock is now known. When Sherlock returned to Spanish Town he left the Montego Bay business in the care of James Fannin, who had given bonds for £500 to Lowry for a partnership, and was to remain as printer of the paper till his death in 1808.

Sherlock's own will (proved 27 January 1780, two years after he had retired from active work)[30] reveals that like his old partner he had a liaison with a local girl, a free mulatto woman named Ann Witter. Considerably more prosperous than Lowry (his estate totalled nearly £3,000) he left his mistress a comfortable competence—£200, two horses, four slaves, and some furniture; to James Fannin, his half-share in the Montego Bay printing office; but the bulk of his estate 'to my brother Thomas Sherlock of the City of London in the Kingdom of Great Britain printer'. Subsequent documentation in 1783 shows that Thomas Sherlock had come out to Jamaica to wind up Robert's affairs. (The Sherlocks who turn up later in Jamaican printing history—Jonathan Nevett Sherlock, who worked for Alexander Aikman and died in October 1802, or Robert Aird Sherlock, who printed the

26 Son of Robert Sherlock printer of The Strand; apprenticed on 7 July 1752 to William [Mc]Faden of Wine Office Court.

27 Jamaica Archives, *Wills*, liber 42, f. 178ᵛ.

28 Perhaps the son of Pierce Fannen, tailor; apprenticed to Christopher Pigeon, printer of Fleet Street on 5 May 1767.

29 Son of Thomas Eberall, tailor; apprenticed to Josiah Millidge printer of Maiden Lane on 6 Nov. 1770.

30 Jamaica Archives, *Wills*, liber 46, f. 55ᵛ

Jamaica Almanacs in 1839 and 1840—were presumably descendants of one or other of the brothers, but my research has not yet clarified the relationships.)

The printers who took over from Robert Sherlock in Spanish Town were loyalists from the North American colonies. Loyalists, but not impoverished exiles, they came to Jamaica before the American revolution was properly under way.

William Aikman, eldest son of Andrew Aikman of Linlithgow in Scotland, had been a bookseller and binder[31] in Annapolis in 1773–5. In October 1775 he moved to Jamaica where he joined forces with David Douglass, a fellow Scot, who the previous year had brought the American Company of Comedians (which he had started in New York in 1758) from Charleston, S.C. (The acquisition of this theatre company was to liven up the dreary years of planter life during the American war very successfully.) Together Douglass and Aikman set up as booksellers and stationers with shops in both Spanish Town and Kingston. They leased the printing house in Spanish Town from Robert Sherlock, later adding another printing office in Kingston to their empire. They were extraordinarily good businessmen, acquired the office of 'Printers to the King's Most Excellent Majesty' and in their paper, *The Jamaica mercury and Kingston weekly advertiser* (from 1780 renamed *The royal gazette*), established what was quickly accepted as the prime outlet for official advertising and announcements.

Of quarto rather than folio format (as most Jamaican papers were) the *Royal gazette* was to flourish, and its printers to grow rich from the very extensive official advertising it contained at a time when Jamaican bureaucracy was burgeoning, and the island was prosperous enough to bear the costs. Not only official announcements ordered by the island government, but extensive lists of runaway slaves housed in the various parish gaols and poorhouses, of pound sales, etc., ordered by the parish vestries all appeared in the columns of the newspaper. So much was there, indeed, that the eight pages of each issue were normally followed by eight pages of *Supplement* and eight pages of *Postscript*, while a further eight pages of *Additional postscript* were sometimes necessary.

About this time, or a little after, the convention grew up in the Jamaican Council and Assembly that all their advertisements should be published in the three 'county' papers, i.e. the Kingston *Royal gazette*, the *St. Jago gazette*, and Fannin's *Cornwall chronicle*. Parish vestries might advertise only in their own county newspaper, but the convention was obviously worth a good deal to the proprietors of these three newspapers. As may be imagined, it was bitterly unpopular with other Jamaican printers, but nevertheless survived until the change in the island's political climate in the 1830s.

William Aikman took charge of the Kingston business, and David Douglass of that in Spanish Town. But a busy actor-manager clearly had little time for the day-to-day supervision of the St. Jago printing business, and for this they were joined about 1779 by William Aikman's younger

[31] One of his bindings is illustrated in the Pierpoint Morgan Library's catalogue *Early American bookbindings from the collection of Michael Papantonio*, New York, 1972, pl. 11.

brother Alexander who had been working for Robert Wells in Charleston, S.C. In Charleston, one of his workmates had been Isaiah Thomas, later to jeer at Aikman for his profitable royalist principles. John Wells, younger son of Robert was later to be the first printer in Nassau in the Bahamas, and became Aikman's brother-in-law when Aikman married his sister Louisa Susanna (who had also worked in her father's shop).

Alexander Aikman, his brother, and David Douglass bought Robert Sherlock's business for £1,507, and on this plant Alexander Aikman (by 1781 Printer to the Council and Assembly) printed the weekly Spanish Town paper, now retitled *The gazette of St. Jago de la Vega.*

In November 1784 William Aikman died, having amassed a fortune of over £22,000. In his will,[32] the most substantial bequests were to his father, to a married sister in Scotland, and to Thomas Stevenson, manager of his bookshop in Kingston. Smaller bequests were made to Douglass's daughter, to various cousins living with him in Kingston, and to his under-age brother John Aikman by whom (with Stevenson) the bookselling business was to be continued. Alexander Aikman received only £100. Whether this was because it had already been arranged that he should take over direction of the *Royal gazette* and His Majesty's Printing Office in Kingston, or whether it marks a rift in the Aikman family one cannot tell, but it is worth noting that the firm of Stevenson and [John] Aikman was to operate in business rivalry with that of Alexander Aikman, both firms, for example, producing their own book almanacs.

When David Douglass died in November 1789, his printing business was continued on his widow's and children's behalf by Alexander MacKenzie, but subsequently passed into the control of David Dickson. By 1800 it was under the direction of John Lunan by whom the *St. Jago de la Vega gazette* was continued into the 1830s.

Printing in Savanna-la-Mar

Before William Aikman's death and Alexander Aikman's move to Kingston, an attempt was made to introduce printing into the Parish of Westmoreland. As those unfashionable enough to enjoy De Quincey know, God smote Savanna-la-Mar in 1748 and again in 1780, destroying the principal town at the south-western end of the island even more thoroughly than the 1692 earthquake had wrecked Port Royal. In September 1782, when the town was largely rebuilt and its prosperity seemed assured, subscription proposals for a newspaper to be called the *Cornwall mercury and Savanna-la-Mar weekly advertiser* were issued by David McHardie, who was employed by James Fannin at Montego Bay. Evidently too few potential subscribers came forward, and McHardie's plans for his own newspaper were abandoned.

By 1788, however, the Parish of Westmoreland had its own weekly newspaper in the *Savanna-la-Mar gazette* for which subscription proposals were advertised in the *Cornwall chronicle*, 1 December 1787. The American

[32] Jamaica Archives, *Wills*, liber 50, f. 180v.

Antiquarian Society has a short run of this from no. 29 of 15 July to no. 40 of 30 September 1788. Printed by Monk & Leyburn, it was not a bad paper but attracted too little local support (particularly advertising) for the printers to continue, and by June 1789 they had abandoned its publication and were back in Kingston with proposals for a new paper, *The centinel and Kingston daily advertiser*, which they were to issue on 1 August 1789. Monk & Leyburn were not unskilled printers, nor unenterprising; as well as their *Gazette* they had published at least twelve numbers of *The Cornwall magazine, or temple of pleasure*, a weekly magazine apparently aimed at the planters' wives; no copies are known to have survived.

No further printing at Savanna-la-Mar in the eighteenth century is known, but it seems certain that there was some. When John Lewis (who had worked for Ann Woolhead before 1781 and was in 1787 in partnership with George Eberall in publishing the *Kingston morning post*), made his will[33] on 17 August 1791, he described himself as 'of the Parish of Westmoreland printer' and his Inventory of 12 October 1791 (given below as Appendix I) gives an interesting account of the equipment he had at Savanna-la-Mar. A letter to the editor of the *Cornwall chronicle* of 6 October 1790 mentions *The Westmoreland gazette*, and no doubt this was Lewis's newspaper. No further printing at Savanna-la-Mar is known until the second half of the nineteenth century.

Printing at Falmouth

In 1770 a new parish named Trelawny was created on the north coast to the east from Montego Bay, and in 1790 a new town called Falmouth was laid out as the parish capital some eighteen miles east of Montego Bay, which by 1793 had more than 150 houses. By that time it had a weekly newspaper for two years, for in 1791 David McHardie had at last managed to start as printer on his own behalf with *The Jamaican mercury and Trelawny advertiser*. McHardie had died by 3 June 1794, leaving an estate valued at £3,013 of which 'the types, presses and printing materials as they stand in the office' accounted for £251.[34] The printing business was then purchased from his widow Emilia by one James Killi Kelly who had previously been a saddler and harness-maker in Montego Bay, and under whose direction the paper was continued until his death in 1814.

The Output of the Jamaican Press

In the kind of work produced, the Jamaican printers were at least superficially typical of those in the other West Indian colonies, though more frequently printing and publishing for internal consumption only than was normal in the eastern Caribbean islands. Newspapers were the bread-and-butter of every printer's business, while almanacs and legal blanks and ephemera of one kind or another—auction catalogues, handbills for slave sales and so forth—were of very considerable importance. For the lucky

[33] Jamaica Archives, Wills, liber 56 f. 87^{v}.
[34] Jamaica Archives, *Inventories*, liber 81 f. 128^{r}.

few, official printing was a source of rapid enrichment; for a few of the more enterprising printers at the end of the century, the publication of a monthly or quarterly magazine of literary pretensions was a source of loss, worry, and disappointment.[35] Publications produced in the colony were usually useful works in the fields of botany, agriculture, medicine, or slavery, like David Bryce's translation of Fr. Labat's *Treatise on the cultivation and manufacture of the tobacco plant* (Fannin, Montego Bay, 1779) J. P. Sator's *Treatise on Planting* (Sherlock, McLeran & Co., Kingston, 1786), Benjamin Dancer's *Short dissertation on the Jamaican bath waters* (Douglass & Aikman, Kingston, 1784) and Richard Chamberlaine's *A light to the planters* (A. Aikman?, Kingston?, 1799).

Nevertheless, some other works of much more literary interest were produced. Original works include 'Peter Pindar's *Persian love elegies*, (Joseph Thompson, Kingston, 1773) and the fairly well-known poem *The sable venus* (Bennett & Woolhead, Kingston, 1765), and two editions of *The elements of free-masonry delineated* (Douglass & Aikman, Kingston, 1781) by Brother William Moore, who was one of the American Company of Comedians. Plays certainly published in Jamaica include *The new comic opera of the duenna* (W. Aikman, Kingston, 1779), John Henry's *School for soldiers, or the deserter* (1783 according to Deschamps; a second edition was advertised as 'in the press' in the *Cornwall chronicle* in May 1784), and *The patriot, a tragedy, altered from . . . Metastasio* (Fannin, Montego Bay, 1785), though there were subscription proposals for others which may have achieved publication. Verse was seldom of high quality, but *The providential Deliverance, or the triumph of fortitude*; [a] *poem illustrative of the unparalleled rescue of a youth from the jaws of an alligator* . . . (to be had at H. Meyer, James Dingwall, and Elias Levy, Kingston, 1795) sounds splendid stuff.

It is difficult to generalize about the size of Jamaican editions, since so few Jamaican books of the eighteenth century included subscription lists. *Persian love elegies* in 1773 had some 282 copies subscribed for; Dancer's *Dissertation on the Jamaican bath waters* ten years later included a list accounting for 327 copies—but both these were works to appeal to fashionable planter society. At the other extreme, a pamphlet by one of the Jewish population in Jamaica, *Reason and faith or philosophical absurdities* by one of the sons of Abraham to his brethren (Strupar & Preston, Kingston, 1788) had only thirty-four subscribers' names included, all of them Jewish. On the other hand, Jamaica brought 170 copies of the London edition of *Porcupine's works* in 1801.[36]

For a very brief period in the mid 1780s it seemed as if local literary publishing might be at take-off point. A collection of songs, *Wilsone's St. Cecilia* was published at Spanish Town in 1785, and the same year saw the production by James Fannin in Montego Bay of *The sorrows of Werther* . . .

[35] These included *The Jamaica magazine* (1781), the Abbé Roland's *Mercure des Antilles* (1783), *The bon ésprit magazine* (1793), *The new Jamaica magazine* (1798–9), and *The Columbian magazine* (1796–1800).

[36] Roderick Cave, 'The Plantocracy's passion for *Porcupine*', also in this issue of *The Library*.

now reprinted from the London edition and in the following year *Letters between Yorick and Eliza, reprinted from the London edition of 1775*. We know of these because a good file of Fannin's *Cornwall chronicle* survives in Bristol Public Library, and these editions are there advertised. Perhaps the work for the eighteenth century *Short Title Catalogue* will turn up similar unexpected publications by other Jamaican printers.

In 1813, William Sheldon of Worcester, Massachusetts, inquired of George Lawrence of Montego Bay about printing there. Lawrence was able to tell him about the early history of the *Cornwall chronicle*, and to provide some biographical information about Fannin, and mentioned 'some few works' had been published at Montego Bay, but was unable to furnish any details about them.[37] In a tropical climate literary memories are short . . . .[38]

Loughborough

APPENDIX I

John Lewis's Equipment at Savanna-la-Mar, 12 October 1791 as given in his Inventory (*see p. 10*)

3	pair new Roman Bougiois [*sic*] cases		
1	Do	Italic	Do
3	Do	Old Roman	
1	small Pica Roman		
2	English Roman & Italick		
1	great Primmer		
1	double Pica		
1	two line English		
1	old flow case		
6	Stands		
1	Press		
6	Composing sticks		
11	Chases		
5	Galleys		
3	Phisketts		
4	Candlesticks		
2	Card Borders		
1	Improving Stone		
1	laying up board		
1	pair bellows		

[37] The letter from Lawrence is now in the Isaiah Thomas papers, American Antiquarian Society.

[38] Nevertheless, the author remembers vividly the kindness and help received from Clinton Black, Government Archivist, K. E. Ingram, Universities Librarian, and the staff of the West India Reference Library in Jamaica, and would like to thank them for their assistance with the research for this paper. Similar thanks are due to the American Antiquarian Society, John Carter Brown Library, Houghton Library, Massachusetts Historical Society and the New York Public Library, and to the Bodleian, Bristol Public Library, British Library Reference Division, Public Record Office, Rhodes House, and the Royal Commonwealth Society. To Donald MacKenzie I am particularly indebted for assistance in tracing Jamaican printers' apprenticeships.

1 pair ballstocks
1 mallett & plainer
2 watter jares
4 cuts
13 ships

This equipment was valued by George Woodbine and John MacLachan the inventorists (who were evidently familiar with printers' jargon) at £160 currency. Source: Jamaica Archives, *Inventories*, liber 77, f. 77r.

APPENDIX 2

A Handlist of Eighteenth-century Jamaican Subscription Proposals and Publications not in Cundall or Ingram

Notes: Information about the individual laws of Jamaica which were ordered to be printed can be obtained from the records of the House of Assembly. This list does *not* note editions advertised in the Jamaican press of the period, but merely records surviving copies of laws not noted by Cundall or Ingram.

No attempt is made to record issues of sheet or book almanacs; a supplement to the list in Ingram, Appendix G would be too complex for useful inclusion here, and would consist very largely of entries for almanacs of which no copies are now known.

The list contains entries culled from contemporary Jamaican newspapers as well as modern bibliographies, library catalogues, etc. Since the surviving files of Jamaican newspapers are too imperfect to be entirely reliable guides, and as a better indication of the intellectual tone of Jamaican society, subscription proposals are included in the list even when there is no certainty (or even probability) that the work was published. Subscription proposals are indicated by the section (§) before the entry. Other advertising formulae are indicated in a similar way: 'This day is published' by an asterisk (*) and such phrases as 'In the Press' or 'Speedily will be published', or 'In preparation', or 'On Monday next will be published', by a dagger (†).

Locations are given when possible, but no systematic attempt has been made to search for copies of the books listed. The writer will be very glad to hear of locations for any items on the list, or other early Jamaica imprints which should be added to it.

1. *Books and Pamphlets*

1718 A sermon [Deus nobiscum, a narrative of a great deliverance at sea] by the Rev. William Johnston. Kingston [R. Baldwin]. 4°.
Title from Deschamps, quoting Cotton. No copy traced.

1720 The speech of His Excellency Sir Nicholas Lawes, Kt. On Tuesday October 4, 1720. Kingston, R. Baldwin, 2720 [*sic*]. f°.
PRO (C.O. 137/13 f. 294)

1720 The speech of his excellency Sir Nicholas Lawes, Kt. On Tuesday October 25, 1720. Kingston, R. Baldwin. f°.
PRO (C.O. 137/13 f. 295)

1721 The humble address and representation of the Assembly of Jamaica to His Majesty, and some messages in relation thereto . . . Kingston, R. Baldwin. f°.
Bodley (Pamph. 368 (13)). *Cundall records only the second edition* (*PRO* (C.O. 137/14 f. 65)).

1721 An act to encourage the settling of the north-east part of this island. Kingston, R. Baldwin. Pp. 7 f°.
B. L. (1471. d.2(8)).

1723 The speech of his grace Henry Duke of Portland . . . On Tuesday the first of October. Kingston, M. Baldwin. f°.
PRO (C.O. 137/14 f. 256).

1724 His grace's speech to the Assembly. The seventh of January, 172¾. [Kingston, M. Baldwin]. f°.
PRO (C.O. 137/14 f. 287).

1725 Jamaica ss. To his grace Henry Duke of Portland . . . The humble address of the Assembly [16 Sept. 1725] with his grace's answer. [Kingston, M. Baldwin]. f°.
PRO (C.O. 137/16 f. 137).

1725 The humble address of the Council [16 Sept. 1725]. His grace's answer. [Kingston, M. Baldwin]. f°.
PRO (C.O. 137/16 f. 138).

1729 The speech of his excellency Robert Hunter . . . to the Council and Assembly of Jamaica. July 24, 1729. [Kingston, M. Baldwin]. f°.
PRO (C.O. 137/18 f. 38).

1735 Jamaica ss. His honor the President, John Gregory . . . His speech to the Council and gentlemen of the Assembly, March 9, 1735. [Kingston, M. Baldwin?]. f°.
PRO (C.O. 137/22 ff. 74–5).

[1741?] These are to certify the Honorable the Commissioners of the Navy . . . [that a vessel arriving at Port Royal was taken into the Navy]. [Kingston, P. &. R. Baldwin?] Broadside *JCB* (bDB.G7861.1741.1)

1747 An act for the more effectual execution of an act intitled, an act for the amendment of an act intitled, an act for the better discovery of his majesty's quit rents . . . Kingston, James Forsyth and James Alves. f°.
PRO (C.O. 137/24 ff. 237–8).

1750 An enquiry into the late essay on the bilious fever. By Parker Bennett M.D. 2nd edn. Kingston, Daniell. 4°.
Harvard (*EC7.B4392.750eb).

[*c.* 1751] These are to certify that . . . [a vessel arriving at Port Royal has cleared with the Port Authorities] [Kingston, Daniell?]. Broadside. *JCB* (Cataloguing).

1753 [Votes of the Assembly] session 18 Sept. 1753–25 Nov. 1753. Kingston, Daniell. f°.
Mass. Hist. Soc.

1753 A bill for the better peopling of the island of Jamaica with white inhabitants; for encouraging the cultivation of lands at present uncultivated . . . and making a proper distribution of such lands. [Kingston], Daniell. f°.
NYPL (*KD+1753).

1754 †The Justice of the Peace's pocket-companion: or the office and duty of a Justice epitomized . . . to which is added, the office and duty of a Coroner . . . with a compleat appendix; containing lists of the fees taken in the several public offices in this island. [Kingston, Daniell.] *7s. 6d.*

Jamaica Courant, 29 June 1754. No copy traced.

1755 [Votes of the Assembly] Session 8 Apr. 1755–19 May 1755. Kingston, Daniell. f°.

Mass. Hist. Soc.

1756 [Votes of the Assembly] Session 23 Sept. 1755–7 Feb. 1756. Kingston, Mary Daniell and Charles S. Woodham. f°.

Mass. Hist. Soc.

1757 [Votes of the Assembly] Session . . . 22 Sept. 1757. St. Jago, Curtis Brett & Co. f°.

Mass. Hist. Soc.

1757 *Articles of war. [St. Jago, Curtis Brett & Co.]

St. Jago Intelligencer, 14 May 1757. No copy traced.

1758 An act for dividing the island of Jamaica into three countries, and for appointing justices of the assize . . . St. Jago de la Vega, Curtis Brett & Co.

Harvard (fe C 75. J 2205 L. 758a).

[1765] A letter concerning the privileges of the Assembly of Jamaica. Kingston, Weatherby, Allen & McCann. 4°.

JCB; *LC*(JL580. J7).

—— —— [2nd edn.]

Lib. Co. Philadelphia.

[1765] Kingston. July 13th, 1765. For London or Bristol, the brigantine Rebecca, Arthur Dunn, commander. Kingston, Bennett & Woolhead. Broadside.

Boston P. L.

1765 A vindication of the proceedings of the House of Assembly of Jamaica. On a late occasion, by an impartial hand. [Kingston?] 4°.

Lib. Co. Philadelphia.

1775 An essay on the art of making muscovado sugar, wherein a new process is proposed . . . [by J. P. Baker]. Kingston, Joseph Weatherby.

L.C.(RC 206. W7).

1778 [Tobacco broadside. Printed announcement of auction at Kingston 16 Apr. 1778. The schooner Charming Sukey, plus her cargo of 50 hogsheads of tobacco to be sold . . .] Kingston, Ann Woolhead. Broadside.

Swann Galleries sale 392 (11 Nov. 1954) no. 109. Details from NYPL Imprint Catalogue.

1779 A treatise on the cultivation and manufacture of the tobacco plant, translated from the French of the R. P. Labat. By David Bryce. Montego Bay, James Fannin.

NYPL Arents Collection (816A).

[1779?] An act to oblige the several inhabitants of this island, to provide themselves with a sufficient number of white men, white women or white children . . . [St. Jago? Douglass & Aikman]. 4°.

Sabin 35613; *NYPL Ford collection* (*KD1779).

[*c.* 1780] The narrative of Captain Samuel Mackay, commandant of a

provincial regiment in North America . . . Kingston, Douglass & Aikman. Pp. 18, 4°.
Boston PL (*XH. 89A. 20).

1780 A treatise on the planting business, containing the work for the whole twelve months from January to December; the method of claying sugar, and the art of making rum. By J. Bellgrove, planter of Barbados. [St. Jago? A. Aikman?] 5*s*.
Gazette of St. Jago de la Vega 21 Sept. 1780. No copy traced. Presumably a new edition of the work by J. Belgrave [sic] *printed at Boston, 1753.*

1780 §Supplement to Acts of the Assembly 1769–1780. *£3 in law binding; 2 pistoles in boards; to be ready 1 July 1780.*
Jamaica Mercury, 11 Dec. 1779.

1781 A short letter to a member of the Assembly . . . Kingston, 1781.
In J. Grant (Edinburgh) Cat. Feb. 1934, no. 1624. Details from NYPL Imprint Catalogue.

[1781] The elements of freemasonry delineated. [Printed by Brother Moore, at the Office of Douglass & Aikman? 1781?]
The proposals for the second edition of 1782, published in the Cornwall Chronicle, 8 Dec. 1781, and in a follow-up advertisement 23 Feb. 1782, refer to a printing the previous year in an edition of 1000 copies.

1782 *Reflections occasioned by the late additional imposts on muscovado sugar . . . by John Gardner Kemeys . . . [Sold by J. T. W. Bennett & Alex Aikman.] $2.
Royal Gazette 21 Dec. 1782. No copy traced.

1783 A school for soldiers, or, the deserter, a play by John Henry. Kingston [Douglass & Aikman]. 8°.
Listed in Deschamps. An advertisement in the Royal gazette, 4 July 1783, states that the 200 copies Henry had had printed in London had been destroyed by a fire in his lodgings, and it was being reprinted by Douglass & Aikman.

1783? †A treatise on the Phthisis pulmonalis, or consumption of the lungs, with some remarks on the diseases of children, particularly those arising from worms. By Thomas Langley, M.D.
Royal Gazette, 12 July 1783.

1784? §A treatise on the nature and effects of heat and cold (considered as auxiliaries to medicine) by John McLaughlin B.A. £1. 12*s*. 6*d*.
Cornwall Chronicle, 13 Dec. 1783, 28 Feb. 1784 etc.

1784? To the King's . . . Majesty in Council. The humble memorial and Petition of the Council and Assembly . . . [11 Dec. 1784].
[St. Jago?] 4°.
B.L. (6605.f.19(2)).

1784 †A school for soldiers, or the deserter. 2nd edn. prepared by Mr. Henry.
Cornwall Chronicle, 8 May 1784. No copy traced.

1784 [Catalogue of the St. James's Circulating Library. Montego Bay, Fannin.]
Cornwall Chronicle, 19 June 1784. No copy traced.

1784 Some remarks and observations respecting a certain species of population, peculiar to this island; and the tendency of certain privileges, granted by law to these people . . . Kingston, Walker & Strupar.
'Title from early ms. note prepared for Sabin's Dict. 86733.' Details from NYPL imprint catalogue.

1785 *The patriot, a tragedy; altered from the Italian of Metastasio, by Charles Hamilton Esq. [Montego Bay, Fannin.] 5*s*.

Cornwall Chronicle, 25 Jan. 1785. No copy traced. Presumably reprinted from the London edition, 1784.

1785 *An address to Bryan Edwards Esq., containing remarks on his pamphlet entitled 'Thoughts on the late Proceedings of Government . . .' also, Observations on some parts of a pamphlet lately published by the West India Planters and Merchants, entitled 'Considerations on the present state of the intercourse between H. M. sugar colonies and the dominions of the U.S.A.' By John Stevenson . . . [Montego Bay, Fannin.] 6*s*. 8*d*.

Cornwall Chronicle, 26 Feb. 1785. No copy traced. A reprint of the London edition, 1784.

1785 *The sorrows of Werther; a novel from the German of Mr. Goethè, first trans. into French then into English, and now reprinted from the London edition. [Montego Bay, Fannin.]

Cornwall Chronicle, 21 May 1785. No copy traced.

1785 *Proceedings of a court of enquiry, held at the Court House, Montego Bay, on Tuesday the 22nd day of March 1785, upon the conduct of Edward Peter Sergeant Esq., Lieut. Col. of the St. Elizabeth Regiment of Militia. [Montego Bay, Fannin.] 5*s*.

Cornwall Chronicle, 17 June 1785. No copy traced.

1785 Wilsone's St. Cecilia, being a choice collection of those celebrated English, Scottish and Irish songs, which have been so much esteemed in this island . . . St. Jago. Printed for C. Wilsone. 12mo.

B.L. (11621.aa.42).

1786 *Letters between Yorick and Eliza; reprinted from the London edition of 1775. [Montego Bay, Fannin] $2 calf; 10*s*. sewed.

Cornwall Chronicle, 11 March 1786. No copy traced.

1786 §Fifty receipts for the cure of most disorders incident to the climate of Jamaica . . . selected from the *ms*. of Dr. Barham [Kingston].

Cornwall Chronicle, 24 June 1786.

1786 *A treatise on planting, from the origin of the semen to ebullation, with a correct mode of distillation . . . by J. P. Sator. Kingston, Sherlock, McLeran & Co. 20*s*. to subscribers; 25*s*. to others.

Cornwall Chronicle, 22 Sept. 1786. No copy traced.

1788 *An answer to Observations, occasioned by the attempts made in England to effect the abolition of the slave trade [by G. Franklyn]. By a sugar planter of the island of Jamaica . . .

Jamaica Gazette, 11 Oct. 1788. No copy traced.

1788 †The passage of twenty four hours, a poem. Printed for the author.

Jamaica Gazette, 22 Oct. 1788.

1788 §The contrast, a comedy; written by Major Tyler and performed at the theatres of New York and Maryland with approbation . . . $1.

Cornwall Chronicle, 8 Nov. 1788.

1789 †The rape of Amaryllis, or the aged libertine. A ludicrous poem, in 3 cantos . . . by C. Tissell. [Montego Bay, Fannin.] $1 stitched in blue paper.

Cornwall Chronicle, 2 Jan. 1789.

1790 §The case of John Gardner Kemeys Esq., a freeholder of Jamaica; who

has suffered a cruel and lawless imprisonment since the 6th Feb. 1785 . . . One doubloon
Cornwall Chronicle, 29 May 1790.

1791 *Orders and regulations for the St. James's Regiment of Foot Militia . . . Thomas Reid Esq., Colonel. [Montego Bay, Fannin.] 6*s.* 8*d.*
Cornwall Chronicle, 2 Apr. 1791. No copy traced.

[1791] Two funeral sermons: the first occasioned by the death of . . . Katherine, Countess of Effingham . . . the other . . . by the death of . . . the late Earl . . . by Thomas Warren . . . [St. Jago, printed by David Dickson.]
Sabin 101490. L.C. (Theol. Pamphs. v. 35 no. 4)

1792 Form of prayer for 7th June.
St. Jago Gazette, 9 Aug. 1792.

1792 Form of prayer for 28th August.
St. Jago Gazette, 9 August 1792.
[*Both these were regularly advertised, and no doubt frequently reprinted.*]

1792 Proceedings of the . . . Assembly on the sugar and slave trade, in a session which began the 23rd Oct. 1792 . . . St. Jago, A. Aikman. 4°.
B.L. (Add. Mss. 12432(4)); *NYPL* (*KD1792); *JCB.*

1792 §Duelling explained from philanthropic motives . . . by Lieut. Samuel Stanton late 97th Regt. $2; for delivery 4 June 1792.
St. Jago Gazette, 12 Apr. 1792. Presumably a new edition of the work published by T. Hookham, London, 1790.

1792 §The guide through life, suitable for all ages and capacities . . . by Samuel Stanton. $2; for delivery 1 Sept. 1792.
St. Jago Gazette, 12 Apr. 1792.

1792 §Evolution and manoeuvres . . . adapted to the use of the Horse Militia of Jamaica . . . by the Sergeant Major of H.M. 20th Regt. of Light Dragoons. 6*s.* 8*d.*
Royal Gazette, 28 July 1792.

1793 §Treatise on Planting and distillation, by James Keith. Falmouth, McHardie. 20*s.*
Royal Gazette 5 Feb. 1793.

1793 §The twelfth of April; a comic opera of three acts, written in this parish by W. W. . . . 10*s*; subs. to Stupar Bennett & Doddington.
Cornwall Chronicle, 4 May 1793.

[1794?] A short account of the origin, symptoms, and most approved method of treating the putrid bilious fever, vulgarly called the black vomit . . . As practised by Mr. John Holliday . . . Falmouth, William Brander.
The Wellcome Institute for the History of Medicine has a copy of this work with the imprint London: reprinted for J. Johnson . . . 1795. *Almost certainly the original edition was printed in Falmouth, Jamaica, though Brander is otherwise unknown.*

1795 †The providential deliverance, or the triumph of fortitude; [a] poem illustrative of the unparallelled rescue of a youth from the jaws of an alligator . . . $0.50 sewed; sold by H. Meyer, James Dingwall and Elias Elias Levy.
Cornwall Chronicle and Royal Gazette, 14 Nov. 1795.

1795 §A series of letters to the trustees of Wolmer's Free School, originally addressed to the Annual Trustees of a free school in Surrey. [8vo edn.

at $1, or $1.50 half-bound; 4 to edn. in leather, with engravings; £1.1s., intended to be printed in England.]
Royal Gazette, 23 Jan. 1795.

1795 §Two systems of the laws of England, with the laws of this island added thereto . . . by Thomas Beath . . . [To be printed in form of two charts, mounted on linen, at 2 doubloons.]
Royal Gazette, 1 May 1795.

1796 *An essay upon pen-keeping and plantership. [Kingston? Aikman?] 10*s.*
Royal Gazette, 31 Oct. 1796. No copy traced.

1799 *A light to the planters, or cursory observations on the importation of savage cannibals and other worthless negroes into this island . . . by Richard Chamberlain . . . 6*s.* 8*d.*
Advertised as forthcoming 23 Sept. 1799; published with a toned-down sub-title 4 Nov. 1799. (*Royal Gazette*). *No copy traced.*

[1800?] The immortals, or the heroes of the eighteenth century. [Kingston]. Printed by W. Smart for the author.
Political satire in verse. L.C. (PR 329.A1I5). *Details from NYPL Imprint Catalogue*

1800 Report from the Committee of the . . . Assembly appointed to enquire into the state of the colony as to trade navigation, and culture &c. &c. since the report made to the House on 23 Nov. 1792. St. Jago, A. Aikman, 1800.

2. *Serial publications*

1783 *Le Mercure des Antilles*
Printed for the Abbé Roland by Lewis & Eberall, only the first number (dated Dec. 1783, but published 8 Jan. 1784) seems to have been issued. According to the subscription proposals (*Royal Gazette*, 20 Dec. 1783) it was to cost £5. 10*s.* p. a. The only known copy (according to Debien, *vide supra* note 2) is in the Bibliothèque Moreau de St. Mery.

1786 *Jamaican Magazine and Literary Miscellany*
Subscription proposals, and a specimen issue, were advertised in the *Cornwall Chronicle* from 4 Nov. 1786 into 1787. No copies are known, and it is probable that only the specimen issue was published.

1788 *The Cornwall Magazine, or temple of pleasure*
Printed by Mark & Leyburn at Savanna-la-Mar for 3 July 1788. Priced at two bitts per weekly number, at least twelve issues were published. No copies are known.

1789 *The Centinel, and Kingston Daily Advertiser*
A preliminary advertisement by Monk & Leyburn (in the *Cornwall Chronicle*, 6 June 1789) was followed in July by another stating publication would definitely start on 1 August. Subscriptions were 40*s.* in Kingston, Port Royal and Spanish Town; 50*s.* elsewhere. No copies are known, and the *Kingston Daily Advertiser* of 1790 is a different paper from different printers.

1790 *The Phoenix of Jamaica and Kingston Evening Herald*
A first attempt at a (thrice weekly) evening paper, which started publication 2 April 1790 (advert. in *Cornwall Chronicle*, 24 April 1790) under the imprint of Herrdeng and Learned. Subscriptions were 35s.

in Kingston, £3 elsewhere. No copies are known, nor is any other printing from this partnership, though from 1 Sept. 1804 John Learned entered a partnership with James Fannin and Henry Shergold at Montego Bay.

1790 *The Westmorland Gazette*

Mentioned in a letter in the *Cornwall Chronicle*, 6 Oct. 1790; probably published by John Lewis at Savanna-la-Mar. No copies are known.

IX
WILLS AND INVENTORIES OF MEMBERS OF THE JAMAICAN BOOK TRADE

A Digest

Introduction

The records available for studying the lives and business activities of printers, booksellers, bookbinders and others who worked in related trades in the West Indies are scanty. In many instances, the only record that a particular man was at work in the islands is to be found in the imprint of a newspaper he printed, on the ticket of a book he bound, in an advertisement he inserted in one of the local newspapers which has by chance survived--even in a two-line notice of his death inserted in one of these papers. Sometimes one can find a little more, for instance in reports of lawsuits in which a printer was involved, or in the financial records of a House of Assembly for which he had undertaken official work. In other instances it may be entirely a matter of chance: only because Benjamin Franklin's papers have been preserved by the American Philosophical Society do we have the record of the business dealings which the Kingston printer William Daniell had with him. Only because the letters were to Sir Walter Scott can we find (in the National Library of Scotland) the text of two curious letters written to him by Alexander Aikman, letters which enlarge our knowledge of Aikman and of printing in early nineteenth century Jamaica.

In preparing his study of the pre-1820 Jamaican book trade for the American Antiquarian Society in 1916, and in revising it and carrying the story forward to 1834 for the centenary issue of *The Gleaner* in 1934, the late Frank Cundall made excellent use of all the resources he could command in Kingston. Despite their age, and some inadequacies of treatment, Cundall's studies remain the basis for any further work on Jamaican printing.

Almost the only sources in Jamaica which were not used by Cundall are to be found in some of the various kinds of records surviving at Spanish Town, the island's old capital. In Cundall's day Jamaican archives were not as easy of access nor as well cared for as they are today, and one can well understand why he did not use them. In any case, though such books as Henry Plomer's *Abstracts from the Wills of English Printers and Stationers 1492-1630* (London, 1903) had been published earlier, the special value of such records for the history of the book trade was by no means as well understood by bibliographers as it is today.

Having by happy chance found rich ore in a preliminary search in some of the records in the Jamaica Archives, in the period 1974-76 the present writer made as systematic and exhaustive a study of these as he was able, using as the basis for searching the lists of printers appended to Cundall's *Printing in Jamaica 1717-1834* (Kingston, 1935), supplemented by such other names as had come to notice. The digest below summarises those matters of interest which were found in this search at Spanish Town. The principal records examined were the *Wills* (housed in the Island Record Office) and the *Inventories* (in the Jamaica Archives). In appropriate instances other associated categories of records such as *Letters of Administration* were also consulted.

For a good many of the printers named by Cundall no information was found in the records. In some instances this was clearly because the persons concerned had already severed all connection with Jamaica before the events--usually their deaths--which would trigger entries in these records. Curtis Brett is one such. In other cases I suspect that I failed to identify an individual correctly either because he had already severed his connection with the book trade, or because the information contained in the Will or Inventory did not reveal the connection to me. To give one example: for the firm of booksellers 'Munds & MacIntosh' which was of some importance at the beginning of the nineteenth century although I eventually found a (disappointingly uninformative) entry for John Munds, among the many wills and inventories examined for men with the much commoner surname of MacIntosh I failed to find anything to make it certain that a particular record was for John Munds's partner in the firm.

The usefulness of the Wills, in revealing how a particular tradesman's business interests were disposed among various legatees, and in indicating various business relationships, needs no stressing. In several cases it is only through the information that the Wills contain that we learn the names of other tradesmen or apprentices, and the details of partnerships.

Under Jamaican law, Inventories were required to be made within six months of a death. The Inventories are often very useful indeed, some of them having been prepared in such minute detail that we can gain from them a very precise picture of a man's home and his business. Unfortunately, those prepared from the end of the eighteenth century onwards are frequently much less informative, especially for the property of persons in partnership, when the Inventory would often give a simple cash valuation for their share in the business rather than the detailed analysis of plant and stock which we would prefer to find--but there are still some Inventories so rich in detail that we can gain much information from them. From about 1840 onwards the number of Inventories made, and the information contained in those which were made, decreased steadily until they ceased altogether about 1880. As my digest was prepared on the basis of names found in Cundall in the first instance--that is, of men active in the trade by 1834--I have no doubt missed records for some of the Victorian tradesmen, but as the late Inventories are relatively so uninformative the loss is not great.

The records at Spanish Town are in general in very good condition, and their coverage is remarkably good, many fewer having perished than one might have expected. Nevertheless, it is clear that some records have perished. In the case of Peter Baldwin in the 1740s for instance, an Inventory was ordered to be made but no trace of it is to be found.

In the Digest which follows I have listed in full those items in Wills and Inventories which relate directly to a man's involvement in the book trade, but have omitted (or mentioned only very briefly) those which lack any overt trade connection. Of course it is interesting and often useful to have enough information to be able to gauge a man's wealth or social standing--to know if he kept a carriage and horses, had substantial quantities of plate, owned a coffee plantation, had gangs of field-slaves for hire--but to have included all such information would have bulked the digest beyond reasonable bounds. The brief notes given should suffice to guide those interested to those Inventories and Wills which are rich in such extra detail.

In general, the notes do not record the names of all those who drew up the Inventories, nor those of Executors or Administrators of Estates unless there is a book trade connection. To know, for example, that Peter Baldwin's estate was being administered by 'a practitioner in physick' rather than a member of the Baldwin family was regarded as useful information, because it suggests that the other Baldwins were no longer in the island and that the business was more likely to be sold than continued. Similarly to know that the printer Alexander Aikman was one of the inventorists of the estate of J. T. W. Bennett seemed worth noting, since it gives some assurance that the valuation was based on expert knowledge. It was not always possible to determine whether a particular inventorist or administrator had a connection with the book trade: early records often helpfully recorded occupations, but later records frequently append 'Gentleman' or 'Esquire' instead.

I have used the word 'mistress' to describe those legatees and others with whom it is clear there was such an intimate relationship. In the Wills they usually appear as 'housekeeper' or in some other similar guise. Some of them were in effect common-law wives, but some individuals who were married also had their 'housekeepers'. It was felt that the term 'mistress' was less ambiguous than the others.

It will be noted that although all the Inventories include valuations, the valuations vary wildly in detail and accuracy. Some gave a very precise indication of wholesale or retail values; some were little more than figures plucked out of the air by a lawyer's clerk anxious to be finished with the task. Inventorists' arithmetic could be faulty: I have made no attempt to correct it, nor generally to comment on the figures but simply to present them as given in the original records. Except where otherwise stated, all sums are in Jamaican currency: one pound currency was approximately 13s.4d. sterling.

For those members of the Jamaican book trade who can be identified with reasonable certainty as having served their apprenticeships in London, I have indicated the references to D. F. McKenzie's *Stationers Company Apprentices*. Most are from his volume covering the period 1701-1800, cited simply as 'McKenzie', those in the the earlier volume are cited as 'McKenzie 1641-1700'.

My thanks are due to John Aarons, Clinton Black, David Buisseret and D. F. McKenzie for their advice and assistance.

DIGEST OF THE WILLS AND INVENTORIES

1. THOMAS CRADDOCK

Port Royal Merchant, and perhaps Jamaica's first dealer in books, died 1684. Inventory undated, but prepared about January/February 1685, includes an extensive list of books. This has been separately published ('Thomas Craddock's Books: a West India Merchant's Stock' Book Collector, Winter 1976, pp.481-90) and is therefore omitted here. (Inventories, liber 2 folios 78-81)

2. THOMAS LANE

Bookbinder of Port Royal, died 1715. McKenzie no.5519?

Inventory dated 3 August 1715; total value £307 14s.3d., includes

25 Common prayer books 2 Bibles 1 Testament	£2	5	-
301 small books of divers sorts	10	-	-
a parcell of paper and past board		10	-
a parcell of bookbinders tools	15	-	-
65 quire of small white paper	5	-	-
A negro woman	60	-	-

(miscellaneous household items, clothing, gold, silver, rings, buckles, spurs &c.)

Administrator: George Flemming (Inventories, liber 10 folio 193^r)

3. ROBERT BALDWIN

First printer in Jamaica 1718-22; father of Robert Baldwin junior and of Peter Baldwin (no.7). McKenzie no.391?

Letters of Administration granted 13 April 1722 to widow, Mary Baldwin (Letters Admin.liber 2 folio 58).

Inventory dated 18 February 1722 [i.e. 1723] is useful and detailed; it has been printed in full in 'An Inventory of the First Jamaican Printing House' which see.

Administratrix: Mary Baldwin (Inventories, liber 12 folios 131^v-132^r).

4. JAMES FISHER

Robert Baldwin's agent in Port Royal for The Weekly Jamaica Courant, stationery etc.; died 1723.

Inventory dated 27 December 1723 shows him to have been a prosperous ship's chandler/hardware merchant; apart from 'a parcell of old books' it contains nothing of book trade interest. (Inventories liber 13 folio 46).

5. ISAAC TAYLOR

Innkeeper, Baldwin's agent in Spanish Town for the Courant, died 1725.

Inventory dated 4 June 1725 for an estate valued at £823 13s.9d. plus £342 11s.6d.

for debts due. Except for a 'Parcell of Old Books' at the high valuation of £15, there is nothing of book trade interest.

Executrix: Hannah Taylor (Inventories liber 13 folios 149^r-150^v).

JOHN LETTS

Printer in Kingston employed by the Baldwin family, fl.1734-1740. McKenzie 1641-1700 no.469.

No Will or Inventory traced.

PETER BALDWIN

Son of Mary and Robert Baldwin (no.3); printer in Kingston in partnership with his brother Robert by 1740; died 1746 or early 1747.

Letters of Administration granted 5 February 1746/7 to John Cochrane 'Practitioner in Physick and Chirurgery' of Kingston. No Inventory traced.

(Letters Admin. liber 7 folio 30).

. WILLIAM DANIELL

Printer in Kingston from about 1749; died 1755. McKenzie no.6995.

Inventory dated 1 September 1755, total value £761 16s.3d., excluding book debts. It included

In the Stable	
Printing Office Materials &c.	£11 15 -
Sundries in Back Store	2 - -
Book binding Materials	15 - -
In the Shop	
15 Ream of Printing Paper	6 - -
4 Boxes damaged Wafers	2 6
2 Mahogony Counters	1 15 -
One writing desk	1 3 9
One large Mahogony Bookcase	23 15 -
Sundry Books	25 - -
3 Ream Blue Paper	1 3 9

(Plus household goods and other property, including 8 male and 4 female slaves).

Administratrix: Mary Daniel, widow (Inventories liber 35 folio 204).

. ALEXANDER DAVIDSON

Printer in Kingston, fl.1752-6; died 1759.

Inventory dated 3 September 1859 total value £164 8s.9d. included

A Press	£ 2 10 -
16 Rheams Paper	4 - -
A Parcell of Old Books	1 10 -
A Counter	2 - -

To a Printing Press and Materials
sold at Public Vendue 42 10 -
(Plus household effects etc.)
Executor: Abraham Torres (Inventories liber 38 folio 169[v]).

10. CURTIS BRETT

First printer in Spanish Town, active 1757-61.
Brett,'having had the marrow of the printing business' left Jamaica and is not therefore represented in the Wills and Inventories at Spanish Town. A descendant h however deposited transcripts of a very interesting series of letters which Brett wrote to his son in which he gave an account of his career. Access to this transcript in the Jamaica Archives is restricted; another transcript (in part in summary)is available in the National Library of Jamaica (West India Reference Library MST 10).

11. CHARLES SOMERSET WOODHAM

Printer to the Assembly 1755-6; died 1766.
Woodham seems to have held this office without himself being a printer. Neither hi Will proved 2 October 1766, bequeathing his property to his sister, son and daughter) nor the extensive Inventory, value £5,986 8s.0$\frac{3}{4}$d., reveal any connectio with the printing trade. (Wills liber 36 folio 129).
Acting Executor: Langford Woodham (Inventories liber 47 folio 45[v]).

12. WILLIAM GADD

Son of William Ged the inventor of stereotyping; printer in Kingston in partnership with Bennett (no.14) and Woolhead (no.16) in the 1760s; died 1767.
Will proved 5 August 1767, left £100 to George son of his housekeeper (mistress?) Margaret Gooldin. There were small bequests to friends in Jamaica, but the bulk of his estate was to be sold and the proceeds paid 'to my loving sisters Ann Ged, Margaret Ged and Jean Ged" of Edinburgh. (Wills liber 36 folio 195).
Inventory dated 28 November 1767 describes him as a Planter late of the Parish of St James. Total value £8,527 11s.3$\frac{3}{4}$d., it consists almost entirely of a plante stock and effects including books valued at £15, but among debts due has

Woolhead, Gadd & Bennett £90 2 6
John Bennett Printer his Book Acco[t]. 92 11 3
(Inventories liber 47 folio 152[v]).

13. CHARLES WHITE

Printer to the Assembly 1763-9; died 1774. Like Woodham (no.11) White held the office without himself being a printer by trade.
Will dated 20December 1773 (to which John Lowry, no.15, was a witness) left his

property to his family; including his law books to his son William, his other books to his son Charles. (Wills liber 41 folio 199).

Inventory dated 8 October 1774 was extensive, but contained few book trade references. As well as 'a parcel of books given to his sons by will' valued at £30, the only references are among 'Bonds & other debts':

> Lowry & Sherlock & Robert Morgan their joint bond to Charles White dated 3rd April 1773 payable 3rd April 1775 on wch Judgment was obtained in November 1773 for the Principal sum of — £ 200
>
> Ditto Bond to Ditto as above of the same date & payable 3rd April 1776 for the Principal sum of — £ 84

(Inventories liber 55 folio 107^{r})

. JOHN BENNETT

Printer in Kingston, fl.1760-1772; sometime partner with Gadd (no.12) and Woolhead (no.16) and with Joseph Thompson. Related by marriage to Ann Woolhead (no.19); father of John Thomas William Bennett (no.30). Died intestate 1772.

Inventory dated 11 July 1772, total value £777 8s.$7\frac{1}{2}$d., is mostly of household effects but includes

> Joseph Thompson's Bond to Jno.Bennett for £150 principal payable the 5th April next to bear interest till the day of payment — £150
>
> John Bennett's share of the profits arising from the copartnership of Bennett Thompson & Co^{py} upon an Account calculation made to the 5th April 1773 after making all just and reasonable allowances — £300

Administratrix: Mary Bennett (Inventories liber 51 folio 136^{r}).

. JOHN LOWRY

Printer in Spanish Town, fl.1763-75; sometime partner with Robert Sherlock (no.17); died 1775.

Will proved 12 September 1775, to which George Eberall (no.21) was a witness, made provision for an Inventory of his printing equipment and stock-in-trade; this has not been traced. Small bequests were made to Robert Sherlock (Mourning suit, a silver-hilted sword, £5 for a mourning ring,) and to James Fannin, no.32 (£2 for a mourning ring). The bulk of his estate was settled for life on his mistress

Lydia Long 'a Free Negro Woman', and afterwards on Mary Lowry his natural daughter by her. Should Mary Lowry die first, his estate was to be divided between Lydia Long and Robert Sherlock. (Wills, liber 42 folio 178^{v}).
Inventory, dated 1 February 1776, valued Lowry's prpoerty at £819 16s.6d. It listed disappointingly little of relevance, save

Some old books	£0	10	-
Three bonds from James Fannin of the Parish of St James printer (bearing interest) for the principal sum of	500	-	-
A judgment against the Estate of Charles White Esq. dece^{d}. (doubtful)	53	6	6

Acting Executor: Robert Sherlock (Inventories liber 57 folio 35^{v}).

16. THOMAS WOOLHEAD

Printer in Kingston, fl.1756-77; sometime partner with Gadd (no.12) an Bennett (no.14), died 1778.
Will proved 30 April 1778 apart from minor bequests to his sisters Abigail and Judith left all his property to his wife Ann, daughter of John Matthew of Port Royal merchant deceased. (Wills liber 45 folio 49^{r}).
Inventory dated 17 October 1778 valued his total estate at £7,965 18s.10½d. (including £4,500 18s.10½d. for 'Book debts outstanding the Particulars unascertained deemed precarious'). It is extremely detailed on all his property--the contents of his dwelling-house in east Kingston, his coffee plantations in Upper St Andrew &c.--and includes

In the Shop			
5 Large Account Books at 25/	£ 6	5	-
34 Smaller ditto at 15/	25	10	-
10 Rheams and an ½ of Tea paper at 5/	2	12	6
14 Ditto of large French printing paper at 15/	10	10	-
17 Ditto of Cut and uncut Foolscap paper at 10/	8	10	-
2 Ditto and an ½ of Blotting paper at 5/		12	6
16 Quires of Cartridge paper at 2/6	2	-	-
16 Rheams of Q^{to} Post, thick, thin and black edged at 7/6	6	-	-
137 Boxes Wafers (Large and Small) at 7½d	4	5	7½
51 Black lead Pencils at 2½d	-	10	7½
1 Slate Book	-	-	7½
22 Ivory and Bone Folders at 10d.	-	18	4
37 Bundles of Red Sealing Wax at 1/3	-	15	-
16 Sticks of Red ditto at 7½d	-	10	-
16 Papers Red Ink Powder	1	-	-

Thomas Woolhead , continued

Some loose Red Ink Powder	-	2	6
151 Papers Black Ink Powder at $7\frac{1}{2}$d	4	14	$4\frac{1}{2}$
3 Boxes and 4 Papers of Pounce at 1/3	1	11	3
100 Cakes of Ink at 1/	5	-	-
1 Box of brass Seals	-	1	3
5 Quires of Thick Post paper at 1/3	-	6	3
101 Quires Books ruled and unruled at 1/3	6	6	3
22 Half Quire Ditto at $7\frac{1}{2}$d	-	13	9
16 Quires of Marble Paper at 1/3	1	-	-
4 Ditto of Embossed paper at 1/3	-	5	-
8 Red Bazils at 2/6	1	-	-
12 Calf Skins at 2/6	1	10	-
2 Pieces of Labels at 2/6	-	5	-
11 Ditto of Writing Vellum at 5/	2	15	-
4 Demy Paper Cases at 2/6	-	10	-
19 Quires of Imperial paper at 7/6	7	2	6
1 Rheam of Royal Paper	3	10	-
16 Quires of Medium at 2/6	2	-	-
16 Quires of Demy at $1/10\frac{1}{2}$	1	10	-
2 Quires of Thick Post	-	2	6
11 Tin Ruling Pens	-	5	-
33 Files with and without Laces	1	13	-
53 Large Copperplate Pieces for children at $2\frac{1}{2}$d	-	11	$\frac{1}{2}$
]28 Small Ditto at 2d	1	1	4
2 Ivory Pounce Boxes	-	2	6
5 Black Pocket books with clasps	-	12	6
8 Ditto with Tape	-	6	3
5 Cases with Asses Skin leaves	-	10	-
14 Ditto with Slate leaves	-	8	9
4 Black leather pockett cases	-	2	6
6 Red gilt pocket books with Clasps at 2/6	-	15	-
5 Ditto with tapes at 1/3	-	6	3
10 Quires of Thin post at $1/10\frac{1}{2}$	1	15	$7\frac{1}{2}$
7 Rheams of Pot papers at 20/	7	-	-
12 Quires of Ditto	-	12	-
24 Books bound in Calf and Marble of different sizes	9	-	-
2 TwoQuire Books bound in Marble at 3/9	-	7	6
2 Rheams of Shop Paper at 7/6	-	15	-
104 Pounce boxes wood and horn at $2\frac{1}{2}$d	1	1	8

Thomas Woolhead, continued

10 Bookbinding knives at 1/3	-	12	6
5 Bodkins at $7\frac{1}{2}$d	-	3	$1\frac{1}{2}$
2 Parcels of Glue	-	3	9
2 Pieces of Bookbinders buckram	-	10	-
78 Large Grammar copy books at $7\frac{1}{2}$d	2	8	9
85 Small ditto at $2\frac{1}{2}$d	-	17	$8\frac{1}{2}$
2 Ink Stands at 2/6	-	5	-
A parcel of paper Ink horns	-	2	6
4 Q^{to}. books bound in Vellum and buckram at 3/9	-	15	-
8 Childrens reading books	-	5	-
2 Psalters	-	2	6
67 Childrens Alphabets	-	5	-
138 Common memorandum books at 1d.	-	11	6
88 Ditto large and small at 1/	4	8	-
121 Alphabets large and small at 1/	7	11	3
6 Pocket books at 1/3	-	7	6
1 Pocket ledger	-	1	3
7 Receipt Books	1	-	-
69 Marble covered copy books at 10d.	2	17	6
38 Sand boxes at $7\frac{1}{2}$d	1	3	9
9 Writing books bound in vellum and buckram of different sizes at $3/1\frac{1}{2}$	1	5	$\frac{1}{2}$
5 Large Quire books at 2/6	1	-	-
1 Mat black Ebony Standish with Glasses	-	15	-
35 Small memorandum books with blotting paper at $7\frac{1}{2}$d	1	1	$10\frac{1}{2}$
7 Packs of Message Cards at $7\frac{1}{2}$d	-	4	$4\frac{1}{2}$
2 Ditto with borders at $7\frac{1}{2}$	-	1	3
1 Ditto of Compliments cards	-	1	3
2 Brass pens for ruling Music	-	5	-
1 Glazed tile	-	2	6
9 Penknives	-	10	-
7 Quires and an $\frac{1}{2}$ of lines for Music	-	15	-
Some Pearl Ash	-	7	6
About 2 Rheams of Blank forms	4	10	-
29 Skins of Parchments at 5/	7	5	-
2 Large boxes of Slate pencils	-	10	-
7 Slates	-	5	-
3 Neat Morocco cases at 5/	-	15	-
2 Ladies Pocket books with Instruments	1	5	-
A few volumes of reading books	10	-	-

Thomas Woolhead continued

In the Shop below stairs

3 Bookbinders Presses and Tools	1 - -

In the Printing Office

The Printing materials consisting of Presses, Cases, Types, Implements	500 - -

(Shop and house hold furniture and fittings, and most book debts are omitted as of no interest here, save for one bond:)

Joseph Thompson's bond dated 5th April 1770, ballance due for principal and interest to 13 December 1777 is	27 8 4

Of the 15 male , 5 female and 3 child slaves listed among Woolhead's property, only three can positively be identified as pressmen:

Jack	70 - -
Cannon	65 - -
Bacchus	50 - -

(Inventories, liber 60 folio 195^{v}).

7. ROBERT SHERLOCK

Printer in Spanish Town and Montego Bay, fl.1768-79, in partnerships with John Lowry (no.15) and James Fannin (no.31); died 1780. McKenzie no.2803.

Will (to which Alexander Aikman senior was a witness) proved 27 January 1780 included these bequests:

1. £200, some furniture, 2 horses and four slaves to his mistress Ann Witter, a free mulatto woman.
2. £500 to the daughter of his friend George Cocksedge.
3. 'To my friend James Fannin ... all my Right Claim and Estate in one Moiety in the Printing office at Montego Bay now occupied in co-partnership between us. Together with all my Household Furniture there, and my right to all debts and demands accruing ... '
4. 'To my brother Thomas Sherlock of the City of London in the Kingdom of Great Britain Printer' [McKenzie no.3165] the residue of his estate.

Executors: George Cocksedge, James Fannin (Wills liber 46 folio 55^{v}).

Inventory dated 27 July 1780, of Sherlock's Spanish Town property, valued it at £2,705 4s.2$\frac{1}{2}$d. The list includes

A parcell of Books	£2 10 -
Sundry newspapers Votes of Assembly and Journals of Council	3 - -
A bond of Alexander Aikmans to Robt Sherlock	39 15 2
The following joint bonds of Alexander Aikman, William Aikman and David Douglass	
1 payable 1 May 1780	157 - -

Robert Sherlock, continued

2 do.	[do.]	100 - -
3 do.	1781	312 10 -
4 do.	1782	312 10 -
5 do.	1783	312 10 -
6. do.	1784	312 10 -
		1507 - -

(Inventories, liber 61 folio 156^r).

A separate Inventory also dated 27 July 1780 was prepared for Sherlock's property in Montego Bay. Valued at £300 7s. 6d. it included

A Press for papers	5 - -
A bookbinder cutting press	2 - -
Printing Office and Materials	200 - -

(Inventories, liber 61 folio 164^v).

Following the death of George Cocksedge, the acting executor in Spanish Town, a fresh Inventory of the residue of Sherlock's estate was prepared in 1783. It reveal that the bonds of Aikman, Aikman and Douglass which had fallen due had been redeemed, and also that Thomas Sherlock had come out to Jamaica to settle his brother's affairs. (Inventories, liber 64 folio 135^r).

18. JOSEPH WEATHERBY

Printer in Kingston, fl. 1770-1775. Died 1782.

Will, proved 10 October 1782, left a small bequest to his God-daughter Frances Mass Strupar (wife or daughter to Thomas Strupar, no.28); the bulk of his estate to his two reputed sons John and Joseph Weatherby, both by Eleanor Plummer a free mulatto woman (Wills, liber 48 folio 207^r).

Inventory dated 20 January 1784 valued his property at £106 13s.9d., but 'the [account] books being in a confused situation renders it impossible to return a state of book debts' as the unfortunate inventorist put it. The only items of interest recorded were

122 books different sizes	10 - -
18 News paper books	1 - -

(Inventories, liber 65 folio 111^v).

19. ANN WOOLHEAD

Printer at Kingston, widow of Thomas Woolhead (no.16); died 1782.

Will (of which John Lewis, Thomas Reeves and George Caffey were witnesses) proved 5 December 1782 left £25 to her nephew and heir-at-law James Fleming Matthews of Port Royal, as settlement in full of any claims on her estate. Her dwelling-hous in east Kingston was left to her niece Ann Fleming Matthews. Two female slaves and their children were manumitted, and the remainder of her considerable estate bequeathed to [her nephew?] John Thomas William Bennett, son of John Bennett late of Kingston printer deceased.

Ann Woolhead continued

Executors: John Woolfrys, J. T. W. Bennett (Wills liber 49 folio 72^r).

Inventory dated 29 November 1783 included lists of furniture etc in the dwelling-house in High Holborn Street and in the printing office in Harbour Street which correspond very closely with those in Thomas Woolhead's Inventory. It does not however mention the stocks of stationery &c.; this side of the business had no doubt been sold before her death. Her property was valued at £5,905 4s.11d., and included 'at the House in Harbour Street'

The apparatus belonging to the Printing
Business with the pressmen Bacchus
Cannon Jack John and Primus £800 - -

Inventorists: Lawrence Mughan, Thomas Reeves (Inventories liber 66 folio 146^r).

WILLIAM AIKMAN

Stationer, bookbinder and printer, previously of Annapolis, Md.; in Kingston 1775-84. With David Douglass (no.22) and his younger brother Alexander Aikman (no.44) bought the Spanish Town business of Robert Sherlock (no.17). Died 1784.

Will proved 11 November 1784 included these bequests and instructions:

1. £ 2,000 sterling to his father Andrew Aikman of Bo'ness, Scotland.
2. £ 2,000 sterling to his married sister Mary Henderson of Falkirk, Scotland.
3. From 1785, his business was to be carried on jointly by Thomas Stevenson (its manager) and his younger brother John Aikman, giving their bonds to the executors for the stock-in-trade.
4. £ 2,000, some furniture and the slave boys Billy and Ned, to Thomas Stevenson.
5. £ 500 sterling to his cousin James Hunter then living with him.
6. £ 100 sterling to James Dingwall then living with him.
7. £ 700 currency to Mary, daughter of his friend David Douglass.
8. £ 200 to his nephew Alexander Aikman junior.
9. £ 100 to his brother Alexander Aikman.
10. Manumission, and 10s. per week for life to his slave woman [mistress?] Sally.
11. £ 500 and his wearing apparel to his brother John Aikman, then still a minor.

Executors: David Douglass, Thomas Stevenson (Wills, liber 50 folio 180^v).

Inventory dated 10 May 1785 for an estate valued at some £22,000 in all, was exceptionally full and detailed. The list of bonds, debts etc. includes many entries for Douglass & Aikman, Alexander Aikman, James Fannin, Walker & Strupar &c. among many others with no book trade connections. The transcript below is only of the stock of the shop in Kingston; I have silently omitted from it many entries for fishing tackle, seeds, toothbrushes , stockings &c. and for the furniture and fittings.

William Aikman continued

Note that part of the valuation is in sterling, not Jamaican currency.

Stock in trades

12	Rheams of	Imperiall Paper	76/	45 12 -	
$5\frac{2}{3}$	Do.	Superfine Royal	56/	15 17 4	
$4\frac{1}{2}$	Do.	Royal	42/	30 9 -	
$2\frac{2}{3}$	Do.	Medium	33/	4 8 -	
$29\frac{1}{2}$	Do.	Demy Royal	23/	33 18 6	
$13\frac{1}{3}$	Do.	Thick folio Post	19/	2 13 4	
					142 18 4
38	Do.	Thin Do.	15/	28 10 -	
$47\frac{1}{3}$	Do.	Extra large Thick Do	21/	49 14 -	
10	Do.	Am[o] [4to?] Demy Royal	7/	3 10 -	
15	Quire	thick Folio Post gilt	21/	- 18 -	
$5\frac{2}{3}$	Rhms	4[to] treasury Post	10/	2 16 3	
1	Do.	extra large Thin 4[to]	9/	9 - -	[sic]
					85 17 3
16	Do.	Thin 4[to] Post	8/	6 8 -	
$36\frac{1}{4}$	Do.	thick 4[to] Gilt	12/	21 15 -	
6	Do.	Thin Do.	10/6	3 3 -	
3	Do.	extra large 4[to] gilt	12/	1 16 -	
4	Do.	thick lined Folio	12/	2 8 -	
5	Do.	thin Do.	10/	2 10 -	
1	Do.	4[to] lined Post	5/	- 5 -	
					38 5 -
5	Do.	Genoa folio post	10/	2 10 -	
$2\frac{1}{4}$	Do.	$\frac{1}{4}$ Do.	5/	- 11 3	
190	Do.	best fools Cap	13/6	128 5 -	
$35\frac{2}{3}$	Do.	2nd Do.	12/6	22 5 10	
$23\frac{1}{2}$	Do.	3rd Do.	8/	9 8 -	
28	Do.	4th Do.	6/6	9 2 -	
51	Do.	best Pott Do.	10/	25 10 -	
					197 12 1
79	Do.	2nd Do.	7/	27 13 -	
23	Do.	3rd Do.	6/3	7 3 9	
25	Do.	Post fools Cap size	10/	12 10 -	
20	Do.	fine Crown	12/	12 - -	
40	Do.	2nd Do.	6/	12 - -	
$15\frac{1}{4}$	Do.	gilt fools cap	18/	13 15 -	
6	Do.	extra large thick Gilt 4[to]	11/	3 6 -	
					88 7 9

William Aikman continued

$56\frac{1}{4}$	Do.	extra thin folio Post	17/	47 16 3		
$7\frac{1}{2}$	Do.	thin Blue Demy	10/6	3 18 9		
$11\frac{1}{4}$	Do.	blossom Blotting paper	7/6	4 4 $4\frac{1}{2}$		
3	Do.	single copy 4[to]	6/	- 18 -		
33	Do.	Great Gun Cartridge	17/6	28 17 6		
28	Do.	Royal Hand	5/	7 - -		
					92 14 $10\frac{1}{2}$	
16	Do.	inferior Quality French	5/	4 - -		
19	Do.	Single Hand	3/	2 17 -		
61	Do.	dam[age]d thick f^{o}.post and demy bo^{t}.of R.Wells	2/6	7 12 6		
3	Do.	large brown sheathing	11/	1 13 -		
$\frac{5}{6}$	Do.	Medium Marble	50/	2 1 8		
$3\frac{1}{2}$	Do.	Demy Do.	40/	7 - -		
					25 4 2	
Brought forward						670 19 $3\frac{1}{2}$
$3\frac{1}{2}$	Rhms	fools Cap Marbled	35/	6 2 6		
2	--	small Brown	6/	- 12 -		
$19\frac{1}{2}$		folio Copy 2d. table	13/	12 13 6		
7		smallest brown	3/6	1 4 6		
137	Bunds.	printing Demy	25/	171 5 -		
4	Rhms	dam[age]d Crown		- 4 -		
					192 1 6	
26	Quires	Music paper	3/10	4 19 8		
2	Rhms	extra large Thick post dam^{d}.	10/6	1 1 -		
1	Do.	Thin D. Do.		- 8 6		
6	Do.	Thick folio do. do.	5/	1 10 -		
2	Do.	extra 4[to] Do.	2/	- 4 -		
					8 3 2	
8	Do.	Dutch fools Cap	7/	2 16 -		
2	Rhms.	Mourning 4[to] post	8/	- 16 -		
6	Do.	Dutch Do.	6/	1 16 -		
6,275		Dutch Quils	7/6	23 9 $4\frac{1}{2}$		
7,600		Hudson's bay Do.	5/6	20 18 -		
					49 15 $4\frac{1}{2}$	
1,300		red string Do. 2nd quality	4/6	29 5 -		
1,000		best pens red strings	6/	3 - -		

William Aikman continued

			£	s	d	£	s	d
2,600	Pens second quality	3/6	4	11	-			
13,600	Quills	3/	20	8	-			
500	Red Blue and Green	3/	-	15	-			
						57	19	-
350 Crow quills		1/6	-	5	9			
4,200	Quills inferior quality	1/	2	2	-			
8 lb.	red Carnation tape	8/	3	4	-			
						5	11	3
60 Boxes	marking Types no.1 2 3 4		25	8	6			
4	Ebony Quadrants	55/	11	-	-			
92	Small slates	4/6	1	13	6			
73	Large Do.	7/6	2	5	$7\frac{1}{2}$			
						[40	7	$7\frac{1}{2}$]
7 Gro[ss] & 5 Doz.	Millenar's paste boards	21/	7	17	-			
16 Doz.	pressing papers	1/	-	16	-			
68 Doz.	black Ink powder	3/4	11	6	8			
59 Doz.	patent Ink Cakes	4/9	14	1	3			
$6\frac{1}{2}$ Doz.	red Ink Powder	3/4	1	1	8			
12	Ebony Sand boxes	6/	-	6	-			
						35	7	7
$6\frac{1}{2}$ lb.	Dutch wax	8/6	2	15	3			
6 lb.	Damag'd Do.	2/	-	12	-			
2 Packs	large gilt Cards	1/	-	2	-			
8 Doz.	small Do.	9/	3	12	-			
4 Doz.	large black Edge Do.	9/	1	16	-			
$8\frac{1}{2}$ Doz.	small Do.	6/	2	11	-			
						11	8	3
11 Doz.	small bord^{d}. Message Do.	6/	3	6	-			
32 Doz.	small plain Do.	3/	4	16	-			
2 Packs	large Do.	6/	-	1	-			
15 Doz.	small Bord^{d}. Do.	6/	4	10	-			
						12	13	-
Brought forward						1,084	6	$-\frac{1}{2}$
2 Quarts	Tambour Ebony Stands cut glass, plated tops	24/	2	8	-			
2 lb.	Pounce	2/	-	4	-			
34	Ebony Ink Stands assorted	6/	10	4	-			
42	Fountain Glass Do.	2/	4	4	-			

William Aikman continued

77	Wedgwood	8d	2 11 4	
30	Glass	1d	- 2 6	
				19 3 10
2	large Dutch pewter Do.	5/	- 10 -	
16	middle D.	4/6	[3 12 -]	
2	smallest Do.	3/	- 6 -	
2	large Pewter Chest Do.	5/	- 10 -	
8	Middle Do.	3/	1 4 -	
13	large Loggerhead Do.	3/	1 19 -	
				8 1 -
17	middle Do.	2/	1 14 -	
21	small Do.	10d	- 17 6	
A basket of spare glass for loggerheads			1 10 -	
4 Boxes	white Phials	25/	5 - -	
1½ Gro[ss] of large Nests Chip Boxes				
	8 in a nest	63/	4 14 6	
				12 16 -
1 Gro[ss]	smaller wafers		1 1 -	
36 lb.	Shining Land	8d	1 4 -	
130 Dozen	Midleton's Pencils	5/	32 10 -	
3 Doz.	Plummetts	3/	- 9 -	
8 Savignies best 4 bladed penknives		5/	2 - -	
3½ Doz.	2 blades Do.	54/	9 9 -	
				46 13 -
9½ Doz.	1 Do. Do.	33/	15 13 6	
20 Doz.	Counting House	27/	27 - -	
4	Common Do.	1/	- 4 -	
6	Do. double bladed	1/	- 6 -	
11 Pr	large leaded featts [?]	2/	1 2 -	
18 P	small Do.	8d	- 12 -	
				44 17 6
30 Doz.	Pencils inferior quality	1/	1 10 -	
18 Skins	large Writing Vellum	7/	6 13 -	
101	Drum heads	2/6	12 12 6	
14 Skins	fine Writing Parchment	3/4	2 6 8	
3 doz.	skins very course parchment	6/	- 18 -	
3½ doz.	Gunter's Scales	19/	3 6 6	
1 plated Ink Stand bo[t] of P. H.			1 2 -	

William Aikman continued

43 skins	smallest Vellum	5/	10 15 -		
				39 3 8	
58	large Morocco pkt Books No 1 2 3 4		7 14 -		
51	Ass Skin Mem Books 1 2 3 4		6 8 -		
3 lb.	best Irish wafers	5/6	- 16 6		
13	long Rules	16d	- 17 4		
14	small Do.	12d	- 14 -		
				8 15 10	
21	long Ivory folders	18d	1 11 6		
17	small Do.		- 12 9		
28 Doz.	Gold Leaf	21/	29 8 -		
25	Ivory Pounce Boxes	2/	2 10 -		
9	D. Do. & Wood Do.	3/	- 9 -		
31	Common Wood Do.	3/	- 7 9		
8	Bone Do.	3/	- 2 -		
				35 1 -	
Brought forward					1,307 1 $10\frac{1}{2}$
$21\frac{1}{2}$ Quire	Bills of Exchange	2/3	2 8 4		
$16\frac{1}{2}$	Bills of Loading	2/3	1 17 1		
10	Power of Attorney	2/1	1 - 10		
36 Do.	Bonds	2/1	3 15 -		
$2\frac{1}{2}$ Do.	Wills	2/1	- 4 $9\frac{1}{2}$		
				9 6 -$\frac{1}{2}$	
9	Tin ruling pens	4d	- 3 -		
$2\frac{1}{3}$ Doz.	marking Ink	11	1 16 8		
19	large India Rubbers	$10\frac{1}{2}$	- 16 6		
4 small	Do.	$5\frac{1}{2}$	- 1 $10\frac{1}{2}$		
$3\frac{1}{2}$ dozen	silk purses	2/	4 2 -		
6 Dozen	blacking Balls	4/4	1 6 -		
9 Dozen	patent blacking	4/4	1 19 -		
				26 10 9	
22 Packet	Ink Pots	$9\frac{1}{2}$	- 17 5		
24	Do.	$11\frac{1}{2}$	1 3 -		
$3\frac{9}{12}$ Doz. Pr	brass Compasses	9/6	5 15 $7\frac{1}{2}$		
40 bdls.	Roman [violin] 1st strings	6/	12 - -		
14 Do.	2nd Do.	6/6	4 11 -		
9 Do.	3d. Do.	12/	5 8 -		
				25 15 -$\frac{1}{2}$	

William Aikman continued

78	Rings of silver 4	9/	2 18 6	
27 lbs	Pigtail Tobacco	18d.	2 - 6	
41 lbs	Saffron Cut	18	3 1 6	
26	Silver Cut Pencil Cases	2/2	2 16 4	
4 Pieces	black Sattin Ribband	10/	2 - -	
2 Ps	Black Silk	10/	1 - -	
				13 6 10
22 Boxes	Water Colours	5/	5 10 -	
12 Ps	Green Silk Ferret	5/	3 - -	
36 Bottles	Scotch Snuff	10/	1 8 4	
				9 18 4
5 large Boxes	Reeves Patent Colours		3 10 -	
3 small	Do.	7/	1 1 -	
18 Rulers		4/	- 6 -	
...				
Brought forward				1,416 17 11
12 boxes	weights & scales	11/	4 19 -	
23 ditto	inferior	10/6	6 6 -	
2 Gro[ss]	Camel hair pencils	4/6	5 3 6	
...				
$3\frac{1}{2}$ Dozen	China Ink	4/6	1 15 9	
20	Sheets of Carmin	5/	- 8 4	
3 Boxes	Chalk for Crayons	6d	- 1 6	
...				
25 Damaged Pocket Books		2	2 7	
...				
A Parcell Childrens Books			2 - -	
Material for 20 Galls. black Ink			1 16 -	
Do. 20 D. red Do.			2 10 -	
17 Dozen	skins	4/9	4 - 9	
2 Dozen	Seal Skins	66/	6 12 -	
				24 16 9
2	West India Atlas halfbound	65/	6 10 -	
6	Do. Pilot Do.	31/6	9 9 -	
4	Do. Do. Stitched	13/6	3 14 -	
4	Do. Do.of 34 Bays and Harbours in the West Indies	13/6	3 14 -	
7	Romans Charts of the Gulph and Passage	19/6	6 16 6	
				30 3 6

William Aikman continued

12	General Do. of the West Indies		2 8 -		
4	Charts of Coast of Nova Scotia	9/6	1 18 -		
2	Do. Coasts of New York & Maryland		- 15 -		
				5 1 -	
Brought forward					1,520 7 11
6	Charts Coast of New England	7/6	2 5 -		
4	Do. Coast of Carolina & Georgia	7/	1 8 -		
				8 14 -	
6 Do.	Chessapeak Bay	5/	1 10 -		
6 Do.	River St Lawrence	11/6	3 9 -		
4	Hudert's Survey St George's Channel		2 6 -		
3 Do.	Delawar Bay and River	2/6	- 7 6		
6 Do.	Charlston Bar & Harbour	1/9	- 10 6		
4 Do.	Musqueto Shore		- 7 -		
				8 10 -	
4 Do.	Bay Honduras		- 7 -		
2 Do.	N E Shore Gulph Mexico		- 5 -		
A parcel	French Charts		- 10 -		
				1 2 -	
19	French & Spanish Dictionaries			12 - 8	
47	Spanish Grammars & 1 Blackstone's Commts.			9 - 3	
209	Books various			16 15 7	
286	Do. Do.			12 6 1	
52	Do. Do.			5 14 6	
44	Do. Do.			10 13 9	
41	Do. Do.			5 3 2	
6	Do. Do.			5 13 6	
8	Do. Do.			4 12 2	
181	Do. Do.			24 9 9	
820	Do. Do.			24 6 10	
59	Do. Do.			8 - -	
17	Do. Do.			9 15 -	
			Sterling Amount		1,687 5 5
			Add 40 p.c^{t}.		674 18 2
			[Jamaica Currency]		2,362 3 7

Binding Materials Currency

$18\frac{1}{2}$ Doz.	rough Calf	56/	51 16 -
7 Doz.	red Turkey	168	58 16 -

William Aikman continued

2 Doz. & 2	blue Do.	140	15 3 4		
$2\frac{1}{2}$ Doz.	Green Do.	120	15 - -		
$14\frac{1}{2}$ Doz.	Smooth Calf	56	40 12 -		
$24\frac{1}{2}$ Doz.	Sheep Skins	28	34 6 -		
7 Doz. 8	red Bazils		14 7 6		
9 lb.	Sewing Thread		- 9 -		
44 lb.	Bookbinders twine	20/	3 13 3		
14 lb.	Glue		- 8 9		
				235 2 3	
					2,597 5 10
		Add 10 p ct Charges			259 14 6
Amount brought forward					2,807 0 4

Binding Utensils

1 Standing press with boards		15 - -		
2 Cutting Do. with Plow pins &c.		2 - -		
2 Sewing Benches		1 - -		
4 Doz. cutting boards dift. sizes		- 10 -		
1 Doz. small pressing boards		- 1 3		
10 Pressing Horns		- 3 4		
4 Setts Old Letters		1 10 -		
A Parcell Old Stamps		- 1 3		
12 Rolls		2 5 -		
2 Polishers		- 7 6		
15 Cutting knives		1 17 6		
1 Shaving Tub		- 5 -		
2 beating Hammers		- 10 -		
3 Tables in Work Shop		- 15 -		
7 cwt Milled Boards	26/3	9 3 9		
3 lb. Vermillion		1 2 1		
1 Grindstone		- 10 -		
			37 11 8	

Account Books

6 Imperiall 7 Sr Royal R Calf 28 Royal R Calf	80 1 3	
6 Setts Medium R Calf Wastebook 5 Ledgers	28 1 3	
21 Ledgers	14 1 3	
49 Books Demy R Calf	41 3 $6\frac{1}{2}$	
24 Do. Do.	19 15 -	
47 Do. Demy hf bound & 1 Sett fools Cap R Calf	21 12 11	
14 Do. Fools Cap R Calf	10 10 10	
36 Do. Do. Do.	15 11 3	

William Aikman continued

46 Do. half bound	12	5	-
34 Do. Course fooscap 1-- 4to Royal R Calf 6 Demy	8	12	1
42 Do. & 8 doz. Quire foolscap	13	14	$9\frac{1}{2}$
298 Books	14	2	7
87 Do.	14	16	$5\frac{1}{2}$
47 Pocket Ledgers	13	-	-
45 Damag'd Books	13	12	6
	321	-	$8\frac{1}{2}$

Inventorists: Thomas Sherwood, John Herbert Lloyd (Inventories liber 69 folio 9-22)

21. GEORGE EBERALL

Printer of Kingston, fl.1775-89; sometime partner with John Lewis (no.23); died 1789. McKenzie no.5481.

Will proved 27 April 1789 included £20 left to his former mistress Sarah Aldred a free mulatto woman of St Catherine; £50 plus 'a new negro' to George Aldred Eberall (his son by Sarah); the bulk of his estate went to Joseph Preston printer, James Bradley merchant and Catherine Leighton spinster as trustees for his two reputed children Sarah Manning Eberall and John Eberall, both under C.L.'s guardianship. £8 for a mourning coat was bequeathed to Charles Pringle of Kingston printer. (Wills, liber 54 folio 78).

Inventory, dated 12 October 1789, which valued his property at £2,573 16s. $4\frac{1}{2}$d., briefly lists household furniture etc., and then

One moiety of the following belonging to the co-partnership of Lewis & Eberall

Printing Office			
1000 lbs small letter			
1350 large Do.			
New printing press			
Old ditto			
Printing furniture, chases and frames	315	-	-
Stationery Desk &c. below stairs	45	-	-
Clock and 3 chairs	7	-	-
Stationery upstairs	44	18	9
12 doz. printing Ink	11	1	-
Slaves			
Johnny	90	-	-
Horace	90	-	-
Caesar	30	-	-

George Eberall continued

Brentford	65 - -
London	65 - -
Debts	
One moiety of outstanding debts due the Copartnership of Lewis & Eberall, as per the books of Account	4,000 - -
Total of Stock &c. belonging to the said copartnership	4,672 12 9
George Eberall's moiety	2,381 6 4½

Inventorists: Thomas Strupar, David Dickson (Inventories liber 74 folio 116^v).

22. DAVID DOUGLASS

Actor and impresario; printer and stationer in Spanish Town, in partnership with William Aikman (no.20); fl.1778-89. Died 1789.

Will dated 15 November 1788 was irregular and incomplete (with gaps left for executors' names etc.) and was not properly witnessed; but on Alexander Aikman's deposition that it was Douglass's Will it was upheld 17 November 1789. It bequeathed his house in Spanish Town to his son David; other property was divided equally between Douglass's widow Mary and their children David and Mary. It left instructions that an agreement was to be made with Alexander McKenzie, a printer employed in his office 'of whose probity and capacity I am fully assured' to continue the business for his widow and children on a profit-sharing basis. (Wills, liber 55 folio 2^v).

Inventory in part prepared by Alexander McKenzie, valued Douglass's total estate at £ 7,209 14s.7¼d. Of this, the record of the stationery and printing business formed a relatively small part

Printing Office			265 - -
20 packs	large Gilt Cards		1 13 4
2 Do.	Black Edged Do.		- 3 4
26 Do.	Small Do.		1 1 8
9 Do.	Do. Gilt Do.		- 14 2
15 Reams & 3 Quires	printing Demy	17/6	2 17 7½
14 Reams	printing pott 2nd table	10/	7 - -
4 Reams 7 quires	Foolscap 1st table	20/	4 6 8
19 Quires	quarto post Gilt		- 15 -
24 Quires	printing Crown		1 - -
6 Bundles	Brown Demy	20/	6 - -
14 Copies	3rd Vol. Laws Jamaica	10/	7 - -
17 Copies	votes of Assembly		- 10 -
727 quires and 30 sheets Blanks and 176 vestry forms			36 - -
11 Reams	quarto Draft paper	10/	5 10 -

David Douglass continued

12 Quires	thin Folio post		12	-	-
14 Sticks	Sealing wax		-	8	9
1,000	quils Green Strings		3	-	-
600	red Ditto		3	-	-
7	Ivory folders		-	10	-
11	Sand Boxes		-	7	6
26	Letter Files		-	2	6
7	Chest Inkstands		2	6	8
12	Loggerheads with tops		1	-	-
10	small Ditto		1	5	-
3	Ebony Inkstands with plated tops		1	-	-
3	Small Memorandum books red leather		-	1	$10\frac{1}{2}$
10 Bunches	Tape		-	4	2
6 Rolls	Ferreting	7/6	2	5	-
272	Black Edg'd 4to paper		-	2	6
6 Phials	Red Ink		-	2	6
130	Pasteboards		1	14	2
8 Boxes	marking instruments		3	-	-
12	Rulers different sizes		1	7	6
3 Reams	Blotting paper		1	10	-
26	Slates		1	12	6
14	Lead pressers		-	8	9
56	Slave Laws		-	5	-
65 Copies	Inveighing Act		-	5	-
42 Do.	Highway Act		-	5	-
1	Pound Law		-	-	$7\frac{1}{2}$
4	Process Laws		-	2	6
13	Wharfage & Storage Laws		-	5	-
127 Copies	house rent Laws		-	5	-
56 Do.	Emblements		-	5	-
20 Do.	Smuggling Laws		-	5	-
1 Do.	Election & I Maroon Town		-	-	$7\frac{1}{2}$
8	Paper cases Fine Sand & Pounce		1	10	-
1	Writing Desk		2	-	-
1	Small Counter with Drawers		2	-	-
5	Mahogony Presses		25	-	-
4	hair trunks		1	-	-
A parcel of Books			5	-	-
Debts appearing by the Books to be outstanding and unsettled			48	19	$1\frac{3}{4}$

Acting administrator: David Dickson (Inventories liber 76 folio 81[r]).

23. JOHN LEWIS

Printer of Kingston and Savanna-la-Mar, fl.1781-91; a sometime employee of Ann Woolhead (no.19) and partner of George Eberall (no.21). Died 179]. McKenzie no. 5712/8682?

Will proved 21 September 1791 directed that he was to be buried as a master mason. Apart from a gold ring valued at £10 left to his assistant Hugh Colvin, and a similar ring plus £20 for mourning clothes to his apprentice Thomas Brown, he simply directed that his property was to be sold for the benefit of his nieces and nephews in Westminster, England. (Wills, liber 56 folio 87^{v}).

Two separate Inventories were prepared. The first, made 12 October 1791 by George Woodbine and John MacLachlan, valued his property in Savanna-la-Mar at £429 14s.2d., including £165 5s. for his printing equipment. [This list has been separately printed as Appendix I to my 'Printing in Eighteenth Century Jamaica' which see]. The second Inventory, totalling £106 11s.3d., was prepared on 21 October 1791, and was evidently of the equipment remaining from the partnership of Lewis & Eberall. The list, prepared by James MacLehose and Thomas Bean, included

An old broken press	5	-	-
A printing press with types &c, which we suppose to be compleat and value at	60	-	-
A Silver Marker with the letters L & E	-	7	6
140 Quires of attornies blanks, damaged by Rain at 2/6 per quire	17	10	-
A few printed forms of prayer for the fast appointed by the Law of the Island	-	1	3
Two copies of the Laws of Jama. both damaged	3	-	-
11 copies of the Illustrations of the New Testament	-	10	-
Five ruled Paper Books & eight paste boards		2	6

(Inventories liber 77 folio 77^{r}).

24. DAVID McHARDIE

Printer at Falmouth, publisher of the Jamaica Mercury; earlier had (unsucessfully) tried to start the Cornwall Mercury and Savanna-la-Mar Weekly Advertiser. Died 1794.

Will proved 3 June 1794 left £200 for the education of his natural son, a free mulatto named David; 500 sterling to his wife Emilia and a number of other small bequests, the rest of his estate to go to his sisters Jacobine and Elizabeth McHardie of Leith, Scotland. (Wills, liber 61 folio 5^{r}).

Inventory dated 28 May 1794, valued his property at £3,013 5s.5d.--most of it in book debts, which include

Stevenson & Aikman	3	6	9
James Fannin	21	15	-
James K. Kelly	36	9	2

David McHardie continued

David Dickson 55 - -

The lists of household effects, rum, stock-in-trade &c. includes

3 Reams & one quire	Cartridge paper	at 3/	4	11	6
54 Sheets	pasteboard paper	5/	1	2	6
9 Quires	Bills Ex[chang]e	@ 6/3	2	16	3
7 Quires	Bills Lading	@ 3/9	1	13	9
4 doz.	coffee certificates	5s.	1	-	-
14	Vestry forms	5/	-	5	-
7 broken quire	summons	5/	-	5	-
5 doz.	su[b]poenas	$3/\frac{1}{4}$	-	18	9
16 Volumes	of the Edinburgh Magazine	7/6	6	-	-
2	Mason colections	3/9	-	7	6
5	Institutes	1/3	-	6	3
2 Volumes	Johnston's Dictionary	32/6	3	5	-
1 do.	Boyer's do.	32/6	1	12	6
1	Sermon		-	5	-
8	Old Books		-	10	-
Sundry	Old Quills		1	12	6
11	Ruled Music Books	1/	-	11	-
6	Black lead pencils		-	2	6
6	ruling pens		-	2	6
13	Blanks	2	1	12	6
16	Marble pressers		-	15	-
33 Packs	plain Cards	$7\frac{1}{2}$	1	-	$7\frac{1}{2}$
32	Log Books	2/6	4	-	-
5	India rubbers		-	7	6
3 Boxes	wafers		1	2	6
1 Box	Pounce		-	3	9
2 Papers	Red Ink		1	5	-
1 Do.	Black			10	-
9	Memorandum Books	1/3		11	3
$6\frac{1}{2}$ Quire	Marble Paper	10d		5	5
6 Do	Blue Do.	1/6		9	-
1 Box	Musick pens	1/3	1	6	3
21 lb.	Baked Flour	2/	2	2	-
4 Reams	2nd pott paper	15/	3	-	-
4 Do.	1st Do. Do.	15/	3	15	-
1 Do.17 Quire	quarto paste		1	17	6
4 Do.	folio paste	30/	6	-	-
10 Quires	Ruled Musick			5	-
$5\frac{1}{2}$ quire	quarto Gilt paste	at 1/8		9	2

David McHardie continued

$3\frac{1}{2}$ quire	imperial paper 5 per sheet		1 15 -
$4\frac{1}{2}$ quire	Royall		1 13 9
23	Past Board files	1/3	1 8 9
63	Manual Exercises	1/3	4 6 3
1	Mahogony Table		- 7 6
9	Alphabetts		- 11 3
58	Rules & Regulations		3 12 6
3	Old Desks 2 25/ 1 do.10/		1 15 -
One	bench		- 15 -
The whole of the types presses and printing materials as they stand in the office			251 - -

From the wording, and the valuations placed on some of the items, it seems that the inventorists were not familiar with the printing and stationery trade. (Inventories liber 81 folio 128^{r}).

(When searching for McHardie's Inventory, I chanced on that of his widow Emilia. She had remarried and had been widowed again by the time that she died in 185, worth £2,840. Inventories liber 125 folio 56).

25. JAMES LUNAN

'Gentleman' of Kingston, died 1794.

Like several of the other Jamaican families--the Aikmans, the Strupars, the DeCordovas --the Lunans had a long connection with the printing and book trade of the island. I have not worked out all the ramifications of this family and its members' interests in the different businesses controlled. According to his own Inventory (which is certainly incomplete) James Lunan's only property in Jamaica, apart from his clothing, was £4,000, still in the hands of the executor of John Lunan 'land surveyor of the parish of St George' who had died worth £6,348 18s.$\frac{1}{2}$d. in 1776 (Inventories liber 58 folio 8) with James Lunan as one of his residuary legatees (Inventories liber 82 folio 259). In his own Will proved 30 October 1794, James Lunan bequeathed

£25 sterling per annum for life to his mother Catharine Lunan of Scotland, widow;

£500 currency to his brother Andrew Lunan 'bookbinder of the City of London';

Residue of his estate to his brother John Lunan, printer of Kingston.

Executor: John Lunan (Wills, liber61 folio 44^{r}).

26. DAVID DICKSON

Printer and stationer in Spanish Town, fl. 1791-7. For some time ran the business of David Douglass (no.22) on behalf of his heirs; in partnerships with J. T. W. Bennett (no.29) and with Stevenson & Aikman. Died 1797.

David Dickson continued

Will dated 22 November 1796 made a number of small bequests to his five sisters and to Mary Daly, wife of Captain Hyacinth Daly; £10 each 'as a small acknowledgement of the friendship I have received from each of them' to Thomas Stevenson stationer, Andrew Aikman printer, and George Harrison merchant. £10 was left to Richard Aldred'now a clerk in my office' and £20 to James Robertson printer of St Catherine. The bulk of his estate was to go to his widow Ann, his young son David and any other children. Ann Dickson died in July 1797, and in a codicil dated 13 August 1797 Dickson revoked the bequest to James Robertson and named his mother-in-law Ann Ward 'late of Hampstead Middlesex' as guardian to his son. The will was proved 12 October 1797; executor Thomas Stevenson

(Wills liber 62 folio 166^{v}).

Inventory dated 13 February 1798 valued his estate (excluding 'a house in Spanish Town 100 acres of land in St Catherine [and] $\frac{1}{3}$ Diary office in Kingston from the 16th May 1695 to 16th September 1797') at £8,490 13s.5$\frac{1}{4}$d. Of this,'good' book debts made up £2,547 6s.8$\frac{1}{2}$d.; 'bad or doubtful' debts £1,021 2s.4$\frac{1}{2}$d. It is an exceptionally detailed record, not only of his household effects but also of his stocks of stationery, printing paper and so forth. As the lists of these are very similar to those of Woolhead (no.16) and William Aikman (no.20) I have not included these below, but have recorded only the list of his bookstock for which I have found no parallels among other eighteenth century inventories. The list is as given in the inventory; I suspect it was prepared by dictation from binders' titles. It includes

Stock in Trade ... Books &c. &c.

Conveyancers Assistant	-	16	3		
Pattersons Roads	-	5	-		
Adventure of Telemaque	-	2	6		
Treatise on Coffee	-	3	4		
A Prayer Book	-	15	-		
A 4to Bible	-	40	-		
			4	2	1
Russel on Conveyance	-	8	4		
Van Swietons Commentaries	-	6	8		
Essay on Punctuation	-	16	3		
Barhams Hortus Americanus	-	16	3		
Swintons Abridgement	-	15	-		
			3	2	6
Delanvilles Dictionary	-	7	6		
Bailey Dictionary	-	11	3		
Gentlemans Magazine	-	5	-		
2 Bibles in Calf	-	10	7$\frac{1}{2}$		

David Dickson continued

Magistrates Assistant	1 13 9	
		3 8 $1\frac{1}{2}$
Cooks Bankrupt Law	- 6 8	
Foots Works	- 15 -	
Kames Elucidations	- 11 3	
Fosters Voyage	2 10 -	
Office of Sheriff	- 13 4	
Delolmes English Constitution	- 21 3	
		5 18 4
History of the Ottoman Empire	- 7 6	
Sheridans Dictionary	1 7 6	
Buchans Medicine	- 15 -	
Guthries Geographical Grammar with Maps	1 15 -	
		4 5 -
Priestly on Electricity	- 10 -	
Boyers Dictionary	- 11 3	
Whittakers History of Queen Mary	- 32 6	
Pomfrets Poems	- 3 9	
Dictionary of Arts and Sciences	1 15 -	4 12 6
McBrides Essays	- 1 3	
Hills Reveiw	- 6 8	
Handmaid to the Arts	1 6 8	
Degrinos Spanish Grammar	- 13 4	
Elements of Geography	- 5 -	
Allans Synopses	- 5 -	
		2 17 11
Northcotes Anatomy	- 5 -	
2 Bibles	- 25 10	
6 Prayer Books	3 10 $7\frac{1}{2}$	
Eustrachus Anatomy	- 6 8	
Juids [?] Essays	- 3 9	
Meads Medical Works	- 3 9	
Balfour on Fevers	- 6 8	
		6 2 $3\frac{1}{2}$
Medical commentaries	2 16 3	
New Dispensatory	- 22 6	
Winslows Anatomy	- 4 $4\frac{1}{2}$	
Hamilton Midwifery	- 22 6	

David Dickson continued

Hamilton Letters on Do.	- 3 $1\frac{1}{2}$		
Treatise of Coffee	- 3 4		
		4 17 7	
Gentleman Farmer	- 8 9		
Modern Gazettere	- 5 -		
Buchans Medicine	- 15 -		
Poems	1 - -		
Consideration on Indian Affairs	- 4 $4\frac{1}{2}$		
Fontana on Poisons	- 7 6		
		3 - $7\frac{1}{2}$	
Barclays Appology	- 5 -		
Sherlocks Sermons	- 16 3		
Foot on the Veneral Complaints	- 18 9		
Physical Friend	- 3 4		
Rigbys Essays	- 8 9		
Bell on Ulcers	- 10 -		
		2 17 1	
Edinburgh Medical Essays	- 3 9		
Thompsons Art of Dissecting	- 3 $1\frac{1}{2}$		
23 Volumes of Old Medical Books	1 - -		
Buttersons Fevers	- 3 9		
Cullens Nosologee	- 5 -		
		1 15 $7\frac{1}{2}$	
Cleghorns Defence of Minorca	- 5 -		
Smellies Midwifery	- 12 6		
Chirurgical Tracts	- 6 8		
Medical Observations	- 35 -		
Medical Facts	- 13 4		
		3 12 6	
Franklins Antient Tragedy	- 2 6		
Cullen Institutions	- 3 $1\frac{1}{2}$		
Balfour on Fevers	- 7 6		
Gregorys Elements	- 3 9		
Huxham on Fevers	- 3 $1\frac{1}{2}$		
Journal of American Congress	- 13 9		
		1 13 9	
London Practice of Physic	- 12 6		
Duncans Medical Essays	- 6 8		
Sharps Surgery	- 7 6		
Elliots Chemistry	- 7 6		

David Dickson continued

Magazine of Magazines	1	10	-			
1 Bible	-	10	-			
				3	14	2
Entick Dictionary	-	5	-			
Elegant Epistles	1	8	9			
A Treatise on the Conversion of Slaves	-	6	8			
Biloes Miscellanies	1	-	-			
Merciers Fragments	1	7	6			
				4	7	11
Gardenstones Miscellanies	-	8	9			
Knights Marcus Flaminius	-	13	9			
5 Vols. of Songs	1	-	$7\frac{1}{2}$			
MacDonalds Travels	-	10	-			
Clarks Letters	-	6	3			
				2	19	$4\frac{1}{2}$
Mars Arethmetic	-	16	$10\frac{1}{2}$			
Questions to be Resolved	-	11	3			
Roscomons Poems	-	3	9			
Blairs Letters and Sermons	-	12	6			
Caesars Commentaries	-	7	6			
Shakespears Works	-	16	3			
				3	8	$1\frac{1}{2}$
Kames Elements of Criticism	-	15	-			
Wilds Address	-	10	-			
Johnsons Dictionary	-	15	-			
Laws of Jamaica	8	5	-			
2 Bibles	-	15	-			
Boyers French Grammar	-	7	6			
				11	7	6
Harrisons Letters	-	2	6			
1 Octavo Bible	-	16	3			
A Prayer Book	-	10	-			
Overys Life of Swift	-	6	8			
Stocks Observations	-	3	9			
Sayers Poems	-	3	$1\frac{1}{2}$			
A Prayer Book	-	12	6			
				2	14	$9\frac{1}{2}$
Pringle on Diseases of the Army	-	3	9			
1 large Bible	2	2	6			

David Dickson continued

1 Bible	-	10	-	
A prayer book	-	10	-	
Statistical Account of Scotland	14	5	-	
				17 11 3
Wilkie on Annuities	-	7	-	
Johnsons Dictionary 2 vols	1	7	6	
Buchans Medicine 2 copies	1	10	-	
49 Volumes of Old Books	2	15	-	
1 Quarto Bible	2	-	-	
1 Prayer Book	-	16	3	
				8 16 3
Boyers French and English Dictionary	1	2	6	
Deletanvilles Do.	-	7	6	
Ainsworths Latin ditto	-	17	6	
Cullens Practice of Physic	-	20	-	
Thesarus Medicus	-	15	-	
				4 2 6
Statistical Account of Scotland 2 vols	10	-	-	
Chancery Pleading	-	3	9	
Cruise on fines and recoveries	[-	5	-]	
Harrisons Chancery Practice	-	1	3	
Bayleys Dictionary	-	56	3	
				3 16 3
2 Boyers French Grammars	-	15	-	
Book of Maps	-	10	-	
Munro on deceases of the Army	-	10	-	
2 Treatises on Coffee	-	5	-	
2 Doz. & 9 Enticks Dictionaries	6	9	6	
				8 3 9
Gibbons Roman Empire	8	-	-	
Durnford & Easts Reports	8	6	8	
Principals of Equity	-	17	6	
Horsemans Conveyancer 2 vol	-	32	6	
Bridgemans Do.	-	5	-	
				19 16 8
Potts Chirurgical Works	-	10	-	
Hunter on Teeth	-	15	-	
Whist a Poem	-	3	9	

David Dickson continued

Cullens Materia Medica	8 5 -	
		9 13 9
4 Dillworth Spelling Books	- 5 -	
17 Prayer Books	- 80 -	
2 Prayer Books	1 5 -	
5 Ditto	1 13 4	
8 Ditto	2 - -	
23 Bibles	4 15 -	
Alphabets and Copy Books	1 15 $7\frac{1}{2}$	
1 Bible	- 20 $7\frac{1}{2}$	
Forms of Prayer	- 32 6	
Psalters	- 11 3	
3 Doz. & 9 Dillworth Assistant	- 65 $7\frac{1}{2}$	
16 Prayer Books	- 17 6	
7 do.	- 25 -	
a Parcel Childrens Books	1 - -	
3 Prayer Books	- 32 6	

(Inventories liber 88 folios 122-6).

27. THOMAS STRUPAR

Printer in Kingston fl.1780-96; sometime partner with J. T. W. Bennett (no.29) and -. Doddington; died 1797. McKenzie no.8043.

Strupar died intestate. His Inventory dated 9 August 1797 gave an incomplete valuation of his estate at £1,542 5s.)d. It did not include any specification of printing equipment etc., but had among 8 slaves named;

Chelsea	Pressman	20 - -
Tom	ditto	90 - -

Book debts as listed included

Bennett & Doddington 3 bonds	700 - -
$\frac{1}{3}$ outstanding debts due Strupar Bennett & Doddington the exact amount of which cannot be ascertained	

Administratrix: Frances Massey Strupar (Inventories liber 87 folio 54^r).

28. JONATHAN NEVETT SHERLOCK

Printer in Kingston employed by Alexander Aikman on the Royal Gazette 1801-2; died October 1802.

Inventory dated 20 March 1803 valued his propert at £662 12s.6d., mostly in slaves, a chaise and two horses, and household effects. As Sherlock was only manager of Aikman's printing office there are no references to printing equipment but the

Jonathan Nevett Sherlock continued

inventory does list a few books:

Beaumont & Fletcher 10 vols and plates	6	-	-
Spectator 8 vols	4	-	-
Porcupines Works 12 vols	4	-	-
Edwards Hist^y. 2 vols	3	5	-
A parcel of old Books	2	-	-

(Inventories liber 99 folio 111^r).

29. JOHN THOMAS WILLIAM BENNETT

Printer of Kingston, fl.1790-1806. Son of Mary and John Bennett (no.14); in partnerships with David Dickson (no.26), Thomas Strupar (no.27) and with -.Doddington. Died 1806.

Will made 23 March 1803 left all his property to his wife Eleanor Catherine Bennett, his child Ann Woolhead Bennett and to Mary Ann Bennett his natural daughter by Mary Clifford Davis. Should all die before marriage or reaching maturity, the Mayor and Corporation of Kingston were to inherit and set up a trust 'for indigent white Christian people' in the City. As residuary legatee of Ann Woolhead (no.19) he discharged all debts due to him before 31 December 1799. He hoped that the Daily Advertiser could be continued for the benefit of his heirs; if not it was to continue until the plant was sold. His widow Eleanor Catherine, Frances Massey Strupar (widow of no.27) and two merchants were named as executors. In a codicil dated 25 March 1805 Mrs Strupar was struck out of the list of executors, and a new daughter Mary Johnson Bennett was named as joint heiress with her mother and sisters. Proved 5 June 1806.

(Wills liber 77 folio 178^v).

Inventory prepared by John Gutzmer and Alexander Aikman valued Bennett's estate at £18,266 14s.9$\frac{3}{4}$d., of which the high proportion of £14, 832 15s.3d. was for book debts 'good, dubious and bad.' The lists included 17 slaves (with no apparent printing trade connection) and was mostly concerned with household effects etc. No printing plant was listed, but some equipment and stock was included:

Two Jars Pearl Ash 50 lbs. @ 1/3 p lb.	3	2	6
Two hundred and thirty six Rheams printing demy paper @ 30/	654	-	-
Two kegs Ink	15	-	-
Six boxes types as p Invoice 101 G lbs 11 oz	220	4	6
Twenty two and a half dozens of Blank Cards @ 30/	33	15	-
A parcel of Outside demy paper, every twenty quires 15/ (say 40 quires)	1	10	-

(Inventories liber 109 folio 21^r).

30. EDWARD LEWIS

Stationer and bookseller at Spanish Town, fl.1801-8; sometime partner with John Lunan (no.42) and William Jones. Died 1808.

Inventory dated 19 October 1808 was for an estate valued at over £6,700, but the entries are mostly concerned with household, plantation or pen-keeping matters. The only item relating to the book trade is

> A proportion in the Concerns of Lewis Lunan and Jones and Lewis & Lunan in the hands of the surviving Copartners subject to Debts neither of which fully ascertained 799 18 $1\frac{1}{2}$

(Inventories liber 112 folio 52^r).

31. JAMES FANNIN

Printer at Montego Bay, fl.1776-1807; sometime partner of Robert Sherlock (no.17); died 1809. McKenzie no.6358.

Will proved 2 February 1809 left an annuity of £350 sterling to his brother Francis Clifton of New Hall, Chelmsford, Essex; substantial bequests to his two godchildren in Jamaica and to his friend William Allen of Hanover, with Allen's mother and sisters as residuary legatees. (Wills liber 80 folio 117^v).

Inventory dated 22 April 1809 shows that Fannin had sold the plant and goodwill of his paper the Cornwall Chronicle to Shergold (no.37) and Guthrie in 1807. It lists nine bonds of Shergold & Guthrie, each dated 1 July 1807 and for £1,000, payable (with interest) annually from 1 July 1809 to 1 July 1817. Apart from a few minor Book Debts (e.g. Shergold & Guthrie £2 13s.9d.) it contains no further entries of book trade interest. Including the bonds, Fannin's estate was valued at £11.771 16s.3d. (Inventories liber 113 folio 124^r).

32. JAMES KILLI KELLY

Printer in Falmouth of the Jamaica Mercury. Died 1814.

Will, dated 24 November 1812, bequeathed to his two reputed sons John Kelly and James Kelly, free men of colour,

> All my printing presses with all the types papers artists materials and things thereunto attached or appertaining and used therewith provided [they] edit publish and conduct the paper ... called "The Jamaica Mercury."

Should they not do so, the plant was to be sold for their benefit. They were also to receive £100 each; John his father's library and James his wearing apparel. The residue of the estate was to go to Killi Kelly's daughter Marianna, wife of Daniel Stephenson master mariner. A codicil dated 9 May 1813 revoked the section on the newspaper; instead the two sons were to receive £600 each. Proved 21 March 1814. (Wills liber 88 folio 27).

James Killi Kelly continued

Inventory dated 5 April 1814 valued Killi Kell's property at £5,424 2s.8d. of which some £3,421 was in Book Debts collected or outstanding; those which were 'considered bad and irrecoverable' amounted to £1,114. Apart from these the inventory was concerned mainly with stocks of rum, household effects etc., plus

Types Presses and Printing Materials in Jamaica Mercury Office valued at	1,217 15 6

(Inventories liber 123 folio 200).

33. WILLIAM DOBIE

Printer of Falmouth, partner with Edward Hoole, fl.1817-19. Died 1820.
Will proved 13 January 1820 left all his property to his wife Ann living at 8 St George's Place, Walworth, London. Of the three executors named, Edward Hoole and William Dyer were printers. (Wills liber 97 folio 14r).
Inventory valued his total estate at the considerable sum of £11,882; largely in farm and plantation stock. Among the slaves named were

James and Jamaica attached to the Printing Office		500 - -
	one half is	250 - -

Also specified:

Outstanding debts due to Dobie & Hoole		2,254 10 -
	one half is	1,127 5 -

(Inventories liber 133 folio 132v).

34. JOHN MUNDS

Bookseller and Music Seller in Kingston in 1790; in partnership with John McIntosh by 1803; partnership dissolved 1810. It seems Munds & McIntosh were running the bookselling/stationery side of the business of Alexander Aikman (no.43); after the partnership was dissolved Munds seems to have set up on his own with greater concentration on music. Died 1821.

Inventory dated 4 July 1821 valued his total estate at £2,206 15s.3d.; of this £359 15s.5d. was for sundries in the store and showcases and a pianoforte.

(Inventories liber 134 folio 71r).

35. GEORGE WORRALL STRUPAR

Printer in Kingston; son of Thomas Strupar (no.27) to whose business he succeeded when he came of age. He seems to have disposed of his printing business before his death in 1826.
Will proved 19 October 1826 described him as 'formerly of Kingston ... but late of 14 Surry Street Strand', and included these bequests:

1. To his mistress Margaret Wolfreys free woman of colour, his household effects plus £100.
2. To his sister Elizabeth Walker Jackson (wife of his partner John Rawleigh Jackson) £500.
3. To John Rawleigh Jackson, his library both in England and Jamaica.

George Worral Strupar continued

4. To James Mitchell 'gent.of Kingston, many years in my employ' £300.
5. To his mother Frances Massey Strupar a life interest in all his rights as heir to Thomas Strupar printer deceased intestate, plus his rights as heir to his sister Frances Massey Strupar of Port Royal spinster deceased intestate, plus all moneys owed by his mother to the Jamaica Courant office.
6. To his two natural children by Margaret Wolfreys the residue of his estate in trust. Should both of them die before reaching maturity, the estate would revert to Elizabeth Walker Jackson.

Executors: Frances Massey Strupar, John R.Jackson. (Wills liber 107 folio 135^v).
Inventory dated 5 January 1828 was incomplete as Margaret Wolfreys refused the inventorists access to the books and furniture in her possession. As submitted the Inventory totalled £6,622 4s.$2\frac{3}{4}$d., very largely in Book Debts 'good bad & doubtful'. Among the slaves listed I strongly suspect that as Strupar owned only a moiety in two of them, Evans and Dublin, valued at £30 each, they were employed in the Courant office. (Inventories liber 144 folio 65^r).

36. HENRY SHERGOLD

Printer of Montego Bay, fl. 1807-27; sometime partner with James Guthrie and Daniel Duncan (no.37). Died 1827.
Will dated 8 May 1820, proved 3 November 1827, left his mistress Mary Trought the building in Montego Bay which contained the printing office, plus some furniture, household effects and £100. The rest of his estate was left to his four children by her: most to their sons Henry and James then at school in Scotland, but some to their daughters Sophia and Ann, with instructions that they were to be brought up as good housewives not as fine ladies. An undated codicil provided two slaves and the children to his daughters. (Wills liber 108 folio 75^v).
Inventory dated 8 May 1828 was for a total of £13,905 11s.9d. Inter alia it included 27 slaves (none having any clear connection with printing) and also

Daniel Duncan's Bonds	5,000	-	-
Moiety of Stationery	267	16	5
Moiety of Printing Press and Materials	225	-	-
Moiety of Outstanding Debts due to Shergold and Duncan	744	-	11
First Cost of the Types and new Printing Press £224 9 3 sterling	314	4	11

Executors: Alexander Rae, James Guthrie
Inventorists: William Ewart, George Cragg (Inventories liber 144 folio 163^r).

37. DANIEL DUNCAN

Printer of Montego Bay; in partnership with Henry Shergold (no.37). Died 1827.

Daniel Duncan continued

Will dated 5 December 1827 named James Guthrie, John Cameron and Alexander Wark his executors, and bequeathed all his property to his mistress Bessy Smith, a free woman of colour, and to Richard, Adam and Mary Daniel his children by her. All three executors refused the office on 7 December; the Will was eventually entered 22 December 1827 with Alexander Rae as Administrator. (Wills liber 108 folio 90

Inventory dated 27 May 1828 and prepared by the same men (Ewart and Cragg) as for Shergold's Inventory, shows that Duncan had sold his share in the copyright and goodwill of the Cornwall Chronicle:

William Miller and Alexander Holmes joint bonds payable 1st January 1829, 1830, 1831, 1832, and 1833 respectively with Interest after due further Copy Right of the Cornwall Chronicle	5,450 - -	

Other items of interest, in an estate valued at £8,298 19s.3d. overall were

Stationery as p. Sales	207 3 4	
Furniture as p. Sales	74 13 2	
A Small lot of Stationery unsold	12 10 -	
		294 6 4
Moiety of outstanding Book Debts due to Shergold & Duncan		744 - 11
The Printing Press and Materials		265 - -

(Inventories liber 144 folio

38. JAMES MITCHELL

Sometime employee of the Strupars (cf.no.35); partner in the Courant and Public Advertiser; died 1829.

Will, proved 15 September 1829, named him as proprietor of the Commercial Rooms, Kingston, and late co-partner in the Courant. All his bequests were to family or friends with no apparent book trade connection. (Wills liber 110 folio 160^{v}).

No Inventory was traced for Mitchell.

39. ALEXANDER AIKMAN junior

Nephew of William Aikman (no.20) and son of Alexander Aikman (no.43); printer of the Royal Gazette; died 1831.

Aiikman appears to have died intestate; no Will has been traced not Letters of Administration although his widow Mary was named as Administrator in his Invento

Inventory dated 31 March 1832 and prepared by Robert Smith and Francis Treadway valued his property at £10,523 2s.7d . It was very detailed on the contents of h home Friendship Park (including a library valued at the low figure of £450) and on his slaves, who were manumitted at his request. The list of Book Debts was very extensive and included many entries for small sums for members of the book trade; probably for purchase of single copies etc. The most substantial item in the list of Book Debts is

Public of Jamaica to 11th April [1832] for unfinished Laws Votes & other work for the public	987	1	3	

The other main items of interest are for the stock and equipment at his printing office:

A Collection of Books at Office		80	-	-	
46 Copies Militia Law		40	-	-	
40 Copies 13th volume Journals [of the Assembly]		100	-	-	
Jamaica Almanac (incomplete)		50	-	-	
I Bookbinders standing press		16	-	-	
1 Cutting Press & Shaving Tub		2	-	-	
1 Grindstone and frame		2	-	-	
Sundry Bookbinders Tools		5	-	-	
Sundry Binding Materials		40	-	-	
Sundries of old stock		25	-	-	
					364 - -
$4\frac{1}{2}$ Reams 4to Post	@ 20/	4	10	-	
30 Reams folio Post	@ 30/	45	-	-	
26 ditto foolscap	@ 25/	32	10	-	
147 ditto Demy very thin	@ 15	110	5	-	
1 ditto Black Edge Notepaper		-	10	-	
4 ditto Imperial Brown		6	13	4	
2 ditto Marble Paper	26/8	2	13	4	
$\frac{1}{2}$ ditto Cartridge		1	-	-	
60 Reams foolscap (Votes)	@ 25/	75	-	-	
47 ditto Medium (Laws)	@ 25/	58	5	-	
80 ditto Demy (Gazette)	@ 25/	100	-	-	
3 Iron and 3 Wood Presses		180	-	-	
News paper Types		200	-	-	
Laws Votes & other Types		300	-	-	
Cases frames & other apparatus		100	-	-	
140 copies 8th Volume Laws Incomplete		700	-	-	
					2,302 6 8

(Inventories liber 148 folios 189^{v}-92^{r}).

40. ANDREW LUNAN

Printer of Kingston, publisher of the Jamaica Journal and Kingston Chronicle; brother of James Lunan (no.25) and John Lunan (no.42); died 1831.

Andrew Lunan continued

Will proved 8 July 1831, left a life interest in his house, its furniture and som slaves to his widow Susannah and thereafter to his daughter Susannah. Small beque were left to his three sisters and to two friends. To his son James Lunan he left all Book Debts due to the printing office, plus 'all that my established Newspape and newspaper property ... called The Kingston Chronicle & City Advertiser' together with the printing equipment, copyright etc. provided that James Lunan undertook to pay annuities (£300 to his mother, £200 to a sister until her marriage, £60 to an aunt); should James Lunan decline this responsibility the exe were to sell the business and share the proceeds equally between his widow, daughter and son. Together with his widow and son, John Lunan, Francis Treadway, and Charles Satchell were named as executors. (Wills liber 112 folio 62^{r}).
I have been unable to trace an Inventory of Andrew Lunan's estate; the business was continued by James Lunan and not sold.

41. FRANCIS TREADWAY

Bookseller and printer in Kingston, fl.1819-30. Died 1835.
Will dated 2 November 1835 and entered 5 February 1836, left his property to be divided equally between his five children. His friend Charles Satchell and his nephew Ligonier Treadway (who had been running his business) were named as executors. (Wills liber 116 folio 162^{v}).
Inventory prepared 24 March 1836 valued his estate at £7,454 12s.8d. Apart from t single entry 'Stock in Trade for Valuation £718 7s.11d.' it does not include anything of book trade interest. (Inventories liber 151 folio 230^{r}).

42. JOHN LUNAN

Printer of Kingston, later of Spanish Town; brother of James Lunan (no.25) and Andrew Lunan (no.40); died 1838. McKenzie no 3104.
Will proved 6 January 1839 included these bequests:

1. To his son John Lunan, his property in Spanish Town including the St Jago de la Vega Gazette Office and printing equipment, plus £500.
2. To his nephew James Lunan, the house used as the Kingston Chronicle office, plus £500.
3. To his nieces Catherine and Susan Lunan, £4,000 each.
4. To his daughters Eliza wife of Peter Wilkie and Maria wife of Charles Barry, £10,000 invested in British government bonds.

A codicil dated 8 December 1838 added small bequests to his nurses in his final illness. Charles Satchell, Peter Wilkie and James Lunan were named as executors. (Wills liber 119 folio 39^{v}).
Inventory dated 27 January 1839 valued his property at £10,787 5s.10d., of which s £3,000 was for Book Debts. It was not very detailed, the book trade items being

John Lunan continued

simply summarised as

Books at Office in [Spanish] Town	80 13 4	
do. do. at the Pen	220 - -	
		300 13 4
Stock in Trade at Office in Town	322 - -	
do. do. at the Pen	53 6 8	375 6 8
Printing Press Types &c. &c.		700 - -

(Inventories liber 153 folio 208r).

43. ALEXANDER AIKMAN

Printer of Spanish Town and Kingston; brother of William Aikman (no.20), father of Alexander Aikman junior (no.39); active as printer in Jamaica from about 1779/80, withdrew from the business in favour of his son but took control again on the latter's death until it could be disposed of. Died 1838.

Will proved 13 July 1838 was long and complex, and concerned mainly with setting up trust funds and providing annuities for his many legitimate children and grandchildren. Small sums were also left in trust for his own and his son's natural children. The two houses in Water Lane and in Harbour Street which were used as printing houses, plus the unexpired period of apprenticeship of the (former slave)'Negro Pressman or Printer named John' were left to Aikman's daughter-in-law Mary (widow of Alexander junior) and to her son Alexander Wells Aikman as part of the provision for his grandchildren. (Wills liber 119 folio 3v).

Inventory dated 22 November 1838 for an estate valued at £13,616 11s.2½d., though very detailed contains very little of interest as Aikman's interests in the book trade had all been sold off earlier in the 1830s. There is however a reference to his own very fine library:

Library of Books about 3300 vols	500 - -

(Inventories liber 153 folio 192r).

44. JOHN LUNAN junior

Son of no.42, and inherited the St Jago Gazette office; died 1839.

John Lunan junior was a lawyer who leased the St Jago Gazette to others when he inherited it from his father in 1838. I have not traced his Will but John Thomas Pinnock and George West Wilkins were named as his executors in the Inventory dated 31 August 1839. Drawn up by Samuel Clarke of Spanish Town and William Smellie of Kingston it valued his estate at £874 2s.6d. Much more detailed than that of his father, its valuations show marked discrepancies from those of the previous inventory

29 bottles of ink	3 4 2
22 metal Inkstands	1 6 8
19 volumes New Weeks preparation	2 7 6
23 testaments	1 18 4

John Lunan junior continued

349 volumes of school books	14 3 4	
Brushes and Razor Strops	103 4	
		29 - 10
19 Packages of Cards	4 15 -	
2 Canisters Wafers & String	2 13 4	
80 Packages Ink Powder @ 3/4	13 6 8	
9 Ditto @ 40/	18 - -	
8 ditto red ink	1 - -	
98 Slates	4 1 8	
6 Portfolios	2 - -	
12 Pots Marking Ink	1 - -	
		44 16 8
17 half reams letter paper	6 - -	
8 empty instrument cases	1 6 8	
8 bottles blue ink	13 4	
2 Thermometers	13 4	
12 Pocket Ledgers	2 - -	
7 half Quires Imperial paper	1 15 -	
		12 8 4
a lot of attorneys forms	3 - -	
a ditto old newspapers	- 13 4	
10 half reams gilt edge notepaper	6 13 4	
80 reams assorted paper	53 6 8	
2 writing desks	5 6 8	
6 paint boxes	8 - -	
		77 - -
a lot (odd volumes) Bridges works	1 6 8	
3 umbrellas	2 - -	
14 rollers	- 6 8	
20 pairs of shoes and 2 trunks	7 6 8	
6 prayer Books	2 - -	
1 copy Valpys Shakespeare 15 vols	5 - -	
		18 - -
1 copy Southeys Cowper 15 vols	5 - -	
39 volumes of Books assorted	3 15 -	
a lot of small articles	6 - -	
a lot of old Magazines & Reviews	2 - -	
a keg of nails	2 - -	
		18 5 -

John Lunan junior continued

8 volumes of Ballantyne's Novelists Library	2	3	4			
5 shelves presses & counter	26	13	4			
Bookbinding Establishment including presses Tables Types &c.	30	-	-			
				79	6	8
a Miscellaneous lot of old Books & papers	20	-	-			
Law books 200 volumes or thereabout	60	-	-			
Printing Establishment						
3 presses £16 & £16 & £20	52	-	-			
Other implements including Types forms tables stones desks stands and cases	250	-	-			
				302	-	-

(Inventories liber 154 folio 52^r).

45. JOSHUA DE CORDOVA

Printer in Kingston; with his brother Jacob DeCordova founder of The Gleaner in 1834. Died 1843.

Will proved 9 October 1843 required that his (under-age) son Raphael continue to run the printing business for his mother Esther DeCordova. All profits, after living expenses had been deducted, were to be applied to discharge the debts of Joshua or of the late firm of Rivers & DeCordova. When Raphael came of age, he was to receive an equal share in the business with his mother. Esther DeCordova, her brother-in-law Aaron and Raphael Nunes were named as executors.

(Wills liber 122 folio 189^v).

Inventory dated 24 February 1844 was brief in the extreme:

Amount due to the above estate in good & doubtful debts	1,001	14	7
Amount due to same in debts decidedly bad	219	7	3
Amount of stock-in-trade consisting of Letter Foolscap & other paper Sundry types Printing Presses &c.	415	10	6
Amount in household furniture & wearing apparel	60	-	-
Total	£ 1,696	12	4

(Inventories liber 156 folio 86^r).

46. JOHN RAWLEIGH JACKSON

Partner with the Strupars in the Jamaica Courant.

The only Inventory traced was made 22 September 1847 for JRJ 'late of the Parish of Metcalfe Esq.' It may not be that of the JRJ son-in-law of Thomas Strupar (no.27) and partner of G. W. Strupar (no.35) but of a son. It contains no references to printing (with which all links were severed many years earlier) but includes a list of law books, valued at a mere £10 out of a total estate of

John Rawleigh Jackson continued

£335 18s.6d.; a list of some interest as showing the range of a Jamaican JP's working collection

4 vols Hawkins Pleas of the Crown	1 Petersdoff on Bail
4 do. Blackstone's Commentaries	2 Vols Peel's Acts
2 do. Phillips on Evidence	2 Archbold's Practice Common Pleas
2 Robinsons Formularies	1 Vol. Questions on Conveyancing
2 vols Selwyn's Law Nisi Prius	1 Vol. Archbold's Criminal Pleading
2 do. Starkie on Criminal Pleading	1 Archbold on pleading and evidence
2 do Leach's Crown Law	1 Roscoe's Digest
4 Blackstone's Commentaries	1 Vol.Fearne's Contingent Remainder
2 Vol. Archbold's Sessions Practice	1 do. do. Executing Devices
1 Vol. do. Committment	1 MacArthur on Courts Martial
1 Vol. Paley on Convictions	1 Jewil on the Office and Duty of Coroner
1 Gilbert on Uses by Sugden	4 Vols Williams' Justice

1 Magistrates Assistant

(Inventories liber 157 folio 107r).

47. EDWARD JORDON

Printer in partnership with Robert Osborn (no.49) in publication of The Watchman and later of the Morning Journal, fl.1828-69; died 1869.
Will dated 15 October 1850 and proved 16 April 1869, was concerned only with bequests to his family, and contains no references to the printing business.
No Inventory could be traced. (Wills liber 131 folio 25r).

48. MICHAEL DE CORDOVA

Printer in Kingston; younger brother of Raphael and son of Joshua (no.45). Took over control of The Gleaner in 1850. Died 1869.
Will proved 28 December 1869 left all his property to his widow and children, and contains no printing references. His brother Gabriel DeCordova (who continued to run the business) was named as one of the executors. No Inventory could be traced. (Wills liber 131 folio 80r).

49. ROBERT OSBORN

Printer of The Watchman and the Morning Journal in partnership with Edward Jordon (no.47); died 1878.
Will proved 25 April 1878 apart from a few minor bequests left his property between his own natural daughters June Gordon and Catherine Stewart and his grandchildren, the daughters of Joseph Smith, John Parry and his late son Robert Osborn junior. There were no references to printing. (Wills liber 133 page 467).
Inventory dated 18 November 1878 valued Osborn's total estate at £3,638 17s.5d. It included

Printing Office Water Lane Kingston
Sundry printing presses cases fixtures

Robert Osborn continued

types and other printing utensils			
valued at	145	-	-
Sundry pieces of furniture valued at	10	-	-
Sundry old type sold in New York for	10	4	3
Paper in bond valued at	19	12	1
An Order on the Treasury of this Island for			
payment for printing work	140	3	4

(Inventories liber 162 folio 172^v^).

============

INDEX OF PERSONS NAMED IN THE RECORDS

(Note that numbers in this index are to the numbered entries in the lists above, not to page numbers. Those entries which contain details of an individual's Will or Inventory are underlined. Slaves named in the documents are listed in a separate index at the end.)

INDEX OF SLAVES EMPLOYED IN THE PRINTING HOUSES

X
AN INVENTORY OF THE FIRST JAMAICAN PRINTING HOUSE

Jamaica was the first of the West Indian islands to which printing was introduced,[1] the first press being installed at the instance of the governor, Sir Nicholas Lawes, in 1718. No extensive study of the work of the first printer, Robert Baldwin, has been attempted.[2] His productions, very few of which survive, fall into a number of different categories: (1) A newspaper, *The Weekly Jamaica Courant*, which appears to have commenced publication on 28 May 1718. (2) Official publications such as *The Humble Address of the Assembly* to the Governor, together with the Governor's reply of 12 August 1718, and *The Tryals of Captain John Rackham and Other Pirates*, 1721. (3) Private ventures of Baldwin's, such as his edition of *Tobacco, a Poem* in 1719, or the *Jamaica Almanack for the Year 1719*, neither of which is known except from the advertisements which Baldwin included in *The Weekly Jamaica Courant*. (4) Proformas for bills of lading and similar jobbing work which like most such ephemera have disappeared completely.

As well as being a printer, Baldwin was a stationer, bookbinder, and bookseller, and from time to time advertised other even more miscellaneous goods than those handled by contemporary provincial printers in Britain, ranging from "very curious Pocket-Telliscopes," cordials against the gout, violins and flutes, to "painted paper for hangings." The exact date of Baldwin's death is not known, but it had occurred by 13 April 1722, on which date Letters of Administration of his estate were granted to his widow, Mary Baldwin.[3] Mrs.

1. Unless one gives credence to the statement of Moreau de St. Mery that a press was introduced into the Spanish part of Santo Domingo in the early Seventeenth Century (cf. Isaiah Thomas, *History of Printing in America*, 2nd. ed., Albany 1874, 1, p.8), or to the rumours that there was a press in Havana before the 1720s (cf. Jose Toribio Medina, *La imprenta en La Habana (1707-1810)*, Santiago de Chile, 1904; Lawrence S. Thompson, *Printing in Colonial Spanish America*, Hamden, Conn., 1962, p.94).

2. Cf. Frank Cundall, *A History of Printing in Jamaica from 1717 to 1834*, Kingston, 1935, which is corrected by Douglas McMurtrie, *The First Printing in Jamaica*, Evanston, 1942.

3. Jamaica Archives, Letters of Administration, Liber 2, fol.58.

Baldwin continued to run the business apparently with considerable success[4] until some time after 1734. By 1740 its direction was in the hands of Peter and Robert Baldwin who were (one presumes) her sons. Peter was dead before 5 February 1746;[5] and though there is no surviving evidence of the death of Robert Baldwin the younger, I suspect that he pre-deceased his brother. No Baldwin imprints after 1745 are known to exist.

The Letters of Administration granted to Mary Baldwin in 1722 required that an inventory of the estate of her husband be made, and it was entered on 16 February 1722/3. The transcript which survives in the Jamaica Archives at Spanish Town[6] is of particular interest as a record of the stock-in-trade of the first printer in the West Indies.

In some respects the inventory is a disappointment, giving no information on Baldwin's repertoire of types, nor of the range of books which he carried for sale. Examination of Baldwin's surviving printed work enables one to gather a fairly clear picture of his range of types; the only surviving early list of books[7] in Jamaica, those possessed by the Port Royal merchant Thomas Craddock in 1684, is of too early a date for speculation on the range of Baldwin's stock to be profitable.[8]

In *The Weekly Jamaica Courant* for 28 June 1721 Baldwin had advertised, as new stock just arrived from England, a collection of songbooks and instruction books for the violin, harpsicord, and flute, "likewise good Violins and Flutes." In the eighteen months before the inventory was drawn up, it would appear that these were sold out, unless Mrs. Baldwin failed to show the compilers of the inventory the complete range of her inherited stock. The absence of more binding equipment and materials (which Baldwin had advertised on 11 February 1718/19 and also on 15 April 1719) suggests that there were perhaps other appurtenances of her trade in the premises at Church Street, Kingston, of which the inventorists were not apprized. The wording of the inventory, with its misspellings of "Partridge" for Cartridge and "Marvil" for Marbled paper suggests that it was dictated to a clerk.

4. If one may accept the lines included by Samuel Keimer in *The Barbados Gazette* of 4 May 1734 (quoted by Thomas, v. 2, pp.189-90) as evidence:

E'en *Type* at *Jamaica*, our Island's reproach,
Is able to ride in her Chariot or Coach.

5. Jamaica Archives, Letters of Administration, liber 7, fol.30. Administration of the estate was granted on 5 Feb. 1746 to one John Cochrane, Practitioner in Physick. Although the grant required that an inventory be made and entered within six months, the latter has not survived.

6. Jamaica Archives, Inventories, liber 12, fol.131^{v}-132^{v}.

7. Jamaica Archives, Inventories, liber 2, pp.78-81.

8. Roderick Cave, "A West India Merchant's Stock; the Books of Thomas Craddock," forthcoming in the *Book Collector*.

In other respects, however, the inventory is very helpful, particularly for its detailed indication of the large stock of paper which Baldwin carried. Much of this was for his own printing and binding activities, but some of the paper, like the ink, quills etc. would have been to supply the stationery trade in Jamaica, for which Baldwin was well organized.[9]

An unusual feature of the inventory is perhaps to be found in the extent of Baldwin's trade debts. Jamaican merchants and tradesmen had to extend longer credit than was probably normal in Britain at the time, but later West Indian printers on occasion had great difficulty in collecting payment[10] and one feels that the figure of £100 for bad debt was cast too low.

Transcript of the Inventory

fol. 131^{v}-132^{v} Baldwin Robt Ent^{d} 18th ffeb.^{ry} 1722	An Invoice of Goods of Robert Baldwin's Lately Deceased

	A Printing Press with other Appurtenances belonging to it	£	10
17	Pair of Cases with Letters[11] in them and Twelve Chases		40

9. In an advertisement in *The Weekly Jamaica Courant* for 15 April 1721 Baldwin advertised a good range of stationery to be sold at his shop in Church Street "and likewise by Mr. Taylor on the Parade Spanish Town, and Mr. Fisher's at Port-Royal, who will then be supplied by him constantly, as may likewise other Shop-keepers in any other Parts of the Country."

10. In 1749 William Daniel petitioned for a grant from the Jamaican Assembly on the grounds that he had printed the Votes of the Assembly at an outlay of over £100, had received subscriptions to the value of £44 12s 6d, but had in fact been paid only £17 17s 3d (Frank Cundall, *The Press and Printers of Jamaica Prior to 1820*, Worcester, Mass., 1916, p.8).

11. Analysis of such surviving Baldwin Imprints as the present writer has seen shows that Robert Baldwin's repertoire of types were of the usual range of Dutch romans, and include the following sizes:

Four line Pica Initials = unidentified Dutch.
French Canon No. 3 = Rowe Mores, *Dissertation upon English Typographical Founders*, ed. Carter & Ricks (Oxford, 1961); Catalogue of the James Typefoundry, p.26 and p.117, note 96.
Two line Great Primer = Rowe Mores, p.28 and p.118, n.118; also shown in James Watson *The History of Printing* (Edinburgh, 1713), pp.xxviii-xxix.
Double Pica = Rowe Mores, p.32 and p.120, n.106.
Great Primer = Perhaps Tavernier's of 1580?
English = Perhaps Rowe Mores, p.38 and pp.121, 120, 121.
Pica = Unidentified.
Small Pica = Unidentified.
Plus a number of unidentified fleurons.
Baldwin's fonts were not large. In his most substantial surviving work, *The Tryals of Captain John Rackham and Other Pirates* (1721), he skillfully rang the changes between

2	Leaden Cistrons	1	10	
5	Frames	1		
A	Large Stone to Correct upon and Frame		15	
3	Reams of Demy Att 32/6 per Ream	4	17	6
40	Reams of London Arms[12] @ 15/ per D^{o}	30		
6	Ditto of ffine Post @ 27/6	8	5	
2	Reams of Medium att 40	4		
2	Reams of Royall @ 3/18	7	16	
2	Reams of Partridge[13] @ 22/6	2	5	
1	Ream of Imperiall	7	10	
1	Ream of Blew[14]	1	17	6
1	Ream of Brown Paper		7	6
4000	Dutch Quills[15]	9		
6	Standishes att 7/6 Each	2	5	
12	Pound of Wafers att 2^{s}/ a Pd	1	4	
12	Pound of Wax	1	16	
A	Parcel of Prints	3	18	
6	Dozen of Ink Powder	2		
6	Dozen of Pencils		15	
6	Dozen of Files	2	5	
1	Dozen of Folding Sticks[16]		12	
1	Ream of Marvil[17]	2	5	
4	Setts of Merchants Acco:^{t} Books	20		
36	Books[18]	9		
To	68 Printed Books	15		

his fonts of English, Pica, and Small Pica for most of the text, but there is some evidence of shortage of type in his substitution of italic for roman sorts in parts of this. Though small, his fonts were evidently sufficient for Jamaican needs, and there is no evidence of fresh type coming to the island before 1740.

12. Presumably Pot size, watermarked with the Arms of the City (Heawood 461, Gaskell, fig. 42).

13. I.e., cartridge paper.

14. On 15 April 1719 Baldwin had advertised an edition of Raphael Thorius' *Tobacco, a Poem in Two Books*, "Price 2s. 6d. stitch'd in Blew paper, and 6 Ryals Bound in Marble Paper." No copies are known to survive.

15. In the *Courant* for 11 Feb. 1718/19 Baldwin had advertised "All sorts of very good Parchment and Vellum Skins of all sizes, Writing Paper, Pencils, Penknives, Rulers, Standishes, Quils, VVax, VVafers, Sand, Black and Red Ink, Books for Accompts, Rul'd or Plain . . ." This and the following entries in the inventory indicate his stock as stationer.

16. Presumably these were folding rules.

17. I.e., marbled paper. See note 14 above.

18. Although the range of Baldwin's stock as bookseller/publisher is not known, this and the succeeding entry no doubt comprehend some of his own publications, and also some of the songbooks and "Very Neat and New Common-Prayer-Books" which he advertised in the *Courant* on 28 June 1721.

28 Reams of Holland Arms[19]	28	
A Standing Press[20]		15
A Parcell of old Books	15	
A Small Cutting Press, Iron Pin,[21] and 3 Pair of Boards		10
A Case with some Cutler's Ware in it	1	10
12 Reams of Printing Paper	5	10
15 Reams of Printing ffools Cap	4	10
A Parcel of WastPaper[22]		10
3 Reams of ffine Paper	2	5
6 Folio Books for Accounts	12	
4 Dozen Copy Books[23]	1	5
A Ream of small Quarto Guilt Paper		10
2 Reams of Octavo		15
2 Boys and 2 Women[24]	100	
2 Feather Beds and 2 Bolsters and 2 Bedsteads	15	
2 Cotts	1	10
A Mohogany Scruitore	6	
1 Ditto of Wainscoat	2	
10 Chairs	1	5
5 Silver Spoons	2	10
4 Tables	7	10
2 Looking Glasses	1	10
6 Pair of Sheets and 6 Pillowbers	4	10

19. Presumably foolscap-size paper with the Arms of Amsterdam (Heawood 342-438, Gaskell 34). Baldwin's printing of the *Speech of Sir Nicholas Lawes* on 1 Nov. 1718 (copy in the Institute of Jamaica) is on such paper.

20. This, and the next-but-one entry, are the only references in the inventory to binding equipment, yet on 15 April 1719 Baldwin had advertised in the *Courant* that he had "Workmen just arriv'd from England, who bind books neatly in Vellom and Parchment, and in all sorts of Leather, likewise Guild and Letter them on the Backs."

21. Presumably either a binder's lying press and plough are indicated (the "iron pin" being a bolt plough knife) or one of the adaptations of the lying press used by stationers, as described by J. A. Arnett, *Bibliopegia,* 1835, p.177.

22. This may indicate the spoiled copies of the *Courant* and other waste which Baldwin certainly used to make pasteboard for binding. Cf. the report by E. D. Burt on the discovery of two early issues of the *Courant* in rebinding the Vernon Papers in the British Museum (*British Museum Quarterly,* 11, no. 1, Oct. 1936, 20-21).

23. "N.B. School-Masters may be furnish'd with all sorts of Copy-Books for Children," Baldwin advertised in the *Courant* on 15 April 1719.

24. I.e. slaves. Later Mary Baldwin certainly used her slave Apollo to deliver the *Courant* in Kingston and Spanish Town, since on 25 March 1730 she advertised that he had absconded, and offered a reward for his return. There is some evidence from the late eighteenth century that Negroes (presumably slaves rather than freed men) were employed as pressmen, but it is improbable that Baldwin's two women and boys were used in the printing house. As Jamaican inventories of this period normally list white workers separately and distinctly from Negro slaves, it seems clear that Baldwin's binders and any other workmen he employed were free men.

	£	s	d
8 Table Cloths	3		
Two Desks and a Mohogany Counter	3		
4 Pewter Dishes		10	
18 Plates	1		
Cookroom Furniture	2	10	
The Amo:t of the Goods Appraised is	£ 414	18	6
Debts good is	£1170	11	10½
Bad Debt	100		
Totall of the whole	£1685	10	4½

In Obedience to a Warrant of Appraisement to us directed by Sir Nicholas Lawes wee have hereunto Annexed an Inventory of the Goods and Chattels Rights and Creditts of Robert Baldwin of Kingston Deced as to us shown by his Administratrix Mary Baldwin Amounting to Sixteen hundred Eighty ffive Pounds Ten Shillings and Four Pence Halfpenny Witness Our hands this 16th day of February 1722/3.

Exr

JOHN REEVES
SIDNEY MARRIOTT

XI

THOMAS CRADDOCK'S BOOKS
A WEST INDIA MERCHANT'S STOCK

TO ROGER ELLETSON of Liguanea, merchant, planter and crony of Sir Henry Morgan[1] the task of administering the estate of Thomas Craddock, a Port Royal merchant who died about the end of 1684, was probably neither welcome nor interesting. Port Royal, which rapidly became the centre of trade in Jamaica after the British conquest of the island from the Spanish in 1655, had by the 1680s grown into a bustling and substantially built town of some eight thousand souls. Although its heyday as the centre of buccaneering was past, Port Royal still had some claim to be regarded as the 'most wicked and sinful city in the world' when it was destroyed by earthquake in 1692.

Against this background, to examine the inventory[2] of Thomas Craddock's belongings suggests that he was probably rather different from other Port Royal merchants. Nothing is known of Craddock except for this inventory. From the furnishings of his dwelling-house he seems to have been well-to-do, but the inventory does little to suggest the extent of his business. Apart from two negro slaves Adam and Mingo valued at £60, 'a white man A. Cowper' valued at only £8 10*s* (presumably because the term of his indenture was drawing to a close), a few tarpaulins, barrels and coops on the wharf, and a considerable quantity of glass and glaziers' lead, there is little to indicate the scope of his trade. He may have been a glass merchant; he may have had goods on the high seas at the time of his death, which conjecturally would have figured in another inventory now lost.

[1] By whom, when the old pirate died in 1688, Elletson was left a horse of his own choosing plus Morgan's 'blue saddle and furniture thereunto belonging together with one case of pistols tipped with silver'.

[2] A copy of which is preserved in the Jamaica Archives at Spanish Town, Inventories, liber 2, pp. 78–81.

The slight extent of his affairs, allied to the fact that some of the books he owned were certainly published only a year or two earlier, suggests that Craddock may not have been long resident at Port Royal when he met his death. The English did not find it healthy there; as an early governor, Sir Thomas Modyford, put it, 'the Spaniards wondered much at the sickness of our people, until they knew of the strength of their drinks, but then they wondered more that they were not all dead'.

The interest of Craddock's inventory lies entirely in the careful and detailed list of books which it contains. The ties between bibliophily and Jamaica are strong—the Hibberts and Beckfords derived a substantial part of their fortunes from their Jamaican estates in the 18th century—and there are a few references to books in other 17th-century inventories,[3] but these are always couched in the vaguest terms. Craddock's list, in fact, is the earliest indication of what was owned and read in Jamaica.

From the inventory it seems that a number of Craddock's books were stock for sale to his fellow citizens at Port Royal: the Bibles (no. 42) and prayer books (43); the plays, pamphlets and songs (44); Flatman's *Poems* (68); Erasmus's *Colloquies* (72) and possibly one or two others. The rest were perhaps a personal library. A few were the sort of reference book that a merchant would find useful, such as Molloy's *De jure maritimo* (79) and Leybourne's *Arithmetick* (88). The choice of poetry is characteristic of the time: Herbert, Cowley and Cleveland but no Donne nor Marvell; Spenser and Du Bartas but no Milton. One would naturally expect some devotional works, but theologically the collection is very mixed, with Roman Catholic, Anglican and Quaker authors represented. One hesitates to draw conclusions from such evidence, but perhaps it reflects the unusual degree of religious toleration at Port Royal, where a synagogue, a Presbyterian church, a Roman Catholic chapel and a Quaker meeting-house all flourished in the shadow of the Anglican church, St Paul's.

[3] e.g. 'a pcele of old books' valued at '£3–0–0' in the inventory of Edmund Duck, 21 Nov. 1683; 'a saddle & a pcell of Bookes' valued at '£1–10–0' belonging to George North, 4 March 1684/5; 'sundry books vallued at 75/0' in Robert Forth's inventory, 2 January 1684/5.

The construction of the inventory is not without interest. Those who compiled it were apparently stumped by the Greek in two titles (7, 24); one suspects that binders' titles rather than title-pages were often the basis of their work. The list is nominally arranged by format, as one would expect in a list of that period, but (unless Craddock owned several editions unknown to bibliography) the books are very often of a different format from that indicated by the headings under which they were entered. One would scarcely expect much knowledge of formats from the clerks who compiled the list. Nor would one anticipate much knowledge of book prices, but the values set against the books do not in general seem unreasonable. To attempt to measure such appraisals against prices in the mother country is very hazardous of course, but there does seem to be some relationship. In one or two instances their valuation is higher than the book would have cost new in London (e.g. no. 65 valued at half a crown against the price of a shilling in the *Term Catalogues*), but in most instances it is lowered.

Did Thomas Craddock perhaps mark the price he had paid in his books?

In some other respects the list raises other questions which cannot be answered. Does the presence in it of some unbound books suggest that at this early date there were facilities for binding at Port Royal, or the reverse?

If any of Craddock's books survived the 1692 earthquake, they have since succumbed to the ravages of a tropical climate. The inventory remains as the sole memorial to Jamaica's first book collector and/or bookseller. In the list which follows I have attempted to name the books included, though the identification of edition is harder. All are conjectural of course; those of which I am less confident have a query beside them.

For assistance in this tentative identification I am indebted to Dr W. Cameron and Dr G. Garlock of London, Ontario, and to Professor T. A. Birrell of Nijmegen; for bringing the inventory to my attention my thanks are due to Dr David Buisseret of the University of the West Indies.

THE INVENTORY

In Pursuance of an Order from Hender Molesworth Esqr Lt Governo^{r} & Command^{r} in Chiefe of his Maties Island Jamaica &c directed to us whose names are underwritten & by vertue of the said Order being Authorised & Appointed sworn Appraisers of the Estate here after Mentioned have inventorised & Appraised the Goods & Chattles Rights & Creditts of Thomas Craddocke of Port Royal Merchant late Deceased as they were shewed unto us by Roger Elliston [*sic*] Esqr of Liguanea as Administrato^{r} to the Estate of the Aforesaid Thomas Craddock . . .

In the Closett up one p^{r} of Staires

BOOKS IN FOLIO

[1] S^{r}Richd Bakers Chronickle old 00:03:09
=Sir Richard Baker, *A chronicle of the kings of England*, London 1643, (Wing B501) or a later edition (Wing B502–509).

[2] Josephus Antiquity's of the Jews 00:07:06
=Flavius Josephus, *The famous and memorable works . . or Antiquities of the Jews*, tr. by Thomas Lodge, London 1602 (*STC* 14809) or one of the many 17th-century editions (*STC* 14810–14813a; Wing J1076–1079).

[3] Fox's Acts & Monuments 00:10:00
=John Foxe, *Actes and monuments*, London 1563, (*STC* 11222) or one of the many new editions (*STC* 11223–11228; Wing F2035–2036).

[4] Short view of the late troubles of Engl^{d} 00:08:09
=[Sir William Dugdale], *A short view of the late troubles in England*, Oxford 1681, (Wing D2492).

[5] Index in Sacra Biblia 00:07:06
?=*Index in Sacra Biblia locupletissimus, ex latina Imanuelis Tremellii et Francisci Junii versione*, Hanoviae, 1624, (BM 3109.ddd.8).

[6] Imperiall History 00:08:09
?=M. Baudier, *The History of the Imperial Estate of the grand seigneurs* 1635; or G. Laccary, *Historia imperatorum romanorum* 1671

[7] Scars . sighs etc of the church of England 00:06:03
=John Gauden, '*Ιερος δάκρυος, Ecclesiae Anglicanae suspiria, the tears, sighs complaints and prayers of the Church of England*, London 1659, (Wing G359).

[8] Curia Polititia much Damaged 00:01:03
Not identified.

[9] History of y^{e} duke of Espernon 00:07:06
=[Guillaume Girard], *The History of the life of the Duke of Espernon*, London 1670, (Wing G788).

[10] Bacons History of Henry ye 7th unbound 00:02:00
=Sir Francis Bacon, *The historie of the raigne of King Henry the seventh*, London 1622, (*STC* 1159) or a later edition (*STC* 1160–1161, Wing B298–300).

[11] Dto Bound 00:03:09

[12] Hookers Ecclesiastical Policy much damaged 00:05:00
=Richard Hooker, *Of the lawes of ecclesiasticall politie*, London 1594–7, (*STC* 13712) or a later edition (*STC* 13713–13720a, Wing H2635–2637).

[13] Bacons Naturall History 00:03:09
=Sir Francis Bacon, *Sylva sylvarum or a naturall history*, London 1627, (*STC* 1168) or a later edition (*STC* 1169–1173, Wing B327–334).

[14] Spencers Faiery Queen 00:05:00
=Edmund Spenser, *The faerie queene*, London 1590, (*STC* 23080) or a later edition (*STC* 23081–23085).

[15] 9th & 10th parts of Cleopatra 00:05:00
=Gautier de Coste, Seigneur de la Calprenede, *Hymen's præludia . . . 9th & 10th part*, London 1659, Wing L119).

[16] Plutarchs Lives Imperfect old Edition 00:05:00
=Plutarch, *The lives of the noble Grecians and Romans*, tr. by T. North, London 1579, (*STC* 20065) or one of the many later editions (*STC* 20066–20070, Wing P2633–2638).

[17] Cowley Poems 00:12:06
?=William King, *Poems of Mr Covvley and others*, Oxford 1668, (Wing K543) or perhaps *The works of Abraham Cowley*, London 1668 (Wing C6649) or a later edition (Wing C6650–6659).

[18] History of Richard the 2d by Buck 00:03:09
=Sir George Buck, *The history of the life and reigne of Richard the third*, London 1646; 2nd ed. 1647, (Wing B5306–5307).

[19] Gusman 00:10:00
?=[Carlos Garcia], *Guzman, Hinde and Hannam outstript, being a discovery of the whole art, mistery and antiquity of theeves and theeving*, London 1677, (Wing G211); or one of the many editions of Mabbe's translation of Aleman's *Guzman de Alfarache*.

[20] Cornelius Tacitus unbound & damaged 00:03:09
?=Publius Cornelius Tacitus, *Histories*, tr. Sir H. Savile, Oxford 1591, (*STC* 23642) or one of the later translations of his *Annals* (*STC* 23643–23648).

[21] Mystogogus Poeticus 00:02:00
=Alexander Ross, *Mystogogus poeticus, or the Muses interpreter*, London 1647, (Wing R1964) or a later edition (Wing R1965–1969).

[22] Hudibras ye 4 parts 00:05:00
=Samuel Butler, *Hudibras*, London 1663–78, (Wing B6296) or a later

edition (Wing B6297–6322); plus [Thomas D'Urfey], *Butler's ghost or Hudibras the fourth part*, London 1682, (Wing D2703).

[23] Sibbs bruised reed 00:01:00
=Richard Sibbes, *The bruised reed and smoaking flax*, London 1630, (*STC* 22479) or a later edition (*STC* 22480–22484; Wing S3732).

[24] The portraiture of Charles the 1st 00:01:00
=*Εἰκων βασίλικη, the pourtraicture of his Sacred Maiestie*, London 1648, (Wing E268) or one of the many other editions produced 1648–9 (Wing E269–311).

[25] Humane prudence 00:01:00
=William de Britaine, *Humane prudence*, London 1680, (Wing B4805).

[26] Epitome of the lives of the kings of France 00:01:06
=[Philippe de Comines], *An epitome of all the lives of the kings of France . . . tr. out of the French coppy by R.B. Esq.*, London 1639, (*STC* 5601=*STC* 11273=Wing C7322a).

[27] Mr Hobbs opinion considered by Philautus and Timothy 00:02:00
=[John Eachard], *Some opinions of Mr Hobbs considered in a second dialogue between Philautus and Timothy*, London 1673, (Wing E64).

[28] Herberts divine poems 00:02:00
? binder's title for George Herbert, *The temple*, Cambridge 1633 or a later edition, (*STC*13183–13188, Wing H1516–1523).

[29] State of England in Anno 70 00:01:03
=Edmund Chamberlayne, *Angliae Notitiae or the present state of England*, 4th ed. London 1670, (Wing C1822).

[30] An English Dictionary 00:01:06
?=H[enry] C[ockerham], *The English dictionarie*, London 1623, (*STC* 5461) or a later edition (*STC* 5462–5466, Wing C4864–4871).

[31] Mazarines Memoires 00:00:07½
=Hortense Mancini, duchesse de Mazarin, *The memoires* . . . London 1676, (Wing M1538).

[32] Anatomy of vegetables 00:01:06
=Nehemiah Grew, *The anatomy of vegetables begun*, London 1672, (Wing G1946).

[33] The Life of Fisher Bisshopp of Rochester 00:01:06
=Thomas Bayley, *The life and death of . . . John Fisher*, London 1655, (Wing B1513).

[34] Sandys Ovid Metamorphosis 00:02:00
=Publius Ovidius Naso, *Metamorphosis*, Englished by George Sandys, London 1626, (*STC* 18964) or one of the many later editions (*STC* 18965–18968, Wing 0684–688).

[35] Dialogues, French English & Latin 00:01:00
Not identified.

[36] Terence Comedies 00:00:06
?=Publius Terentius Afer, *Terences Comedies*, London 1667, (Wing T747).

[37] An English expositor 00:01:03
=J[ohn] B[ullokar], *An English expositor teaching the interpretation of the hardest words*, London 1616, (*STC* 4083) or a later edition (*STC* 4084, Wing B5429–5434).

[38] Via tuta 00:00:09
=Sir Humphrey Lynde, *Via tuta, the safe way leading all Christians to the true ancient and catholique faith*, London 1628, (*STC* 17097) or a later edition (*STC* 17098–17100A, Wing V290).

[39] Quarles Enchiridion 00:01:00
=Francis Quarles, *Enchyridion containing institutions divine and morall*, London 1640, (*STC* 20543) or a later edition (Wing Q86–97).

[40] Byfields Direction for reading of Scriptures 00:00:07½
=Nicholas Byfield, *Directions for the private reading of the scriptures*, London 1618, (*STC* 4214) or a later edition (*STC* 4215, Wing B 6383).

[41] Cluverius Geography 00:01:03
=Philip Clüver, *An introduction into geography*, Oxford 1657, (Wing C4640).

[42] 4 New gilt Bibles 01:00:00

[43] 6 New Common prayer
Books 3 with Psalmes
3 without } 00:12:00

[44] Thirty playes, Pamphlets, songs etc 01:10:00
Not identified.

[45] Howells Londinopolis 00:05:00
=James Howell, *Londinopolis, an historical discourse*, London 1657, (Wing H3090–3091).

[46] Craddocks Apostolicall history 00:07:06
=Samuel Craddock, *The apostolical history*, London 1672, (Wing C6744).

[47] Boccalius Parnassus 00:05:00
=Trajan Boccalini, *I ragguagli di Parnasso, or advertisements from Parnassus*, London 1656, (Wing B3380) or a later edition (Wing B3381–3384).

[48] Oates Exposition on St Jude 00:03:00
=Samuel Otes, *An explanation of the epistle of St Jude*, London 1633, (*STC* 18896).

[49] Jewells reply to Hardings answ[r] old unb[ound] 00:01:06
=John Jewel, *A replie unto M. Hardinges answeare* [to the sermon on 1 Cor.xi.23], London 1565, (*STC* 14606–14607).

[50] Dubartas 00:07:06
=Guillaume de Saluste du Bartas, *Divine weekes and workes*, tr. J.Sylvester, London 1641, (Wing D2405).

BOOKS IN QUARTO

[51] Riders Dictionary 00:03:00
=John Rider, *Dictionarie*, corr. & augm. by F. Holyoke, London 1606, (*STC* 21032) or a later edition (*STC* 21033–21036b, Wing R 1442–1443).

[52] Relacōn of ye sweating sicknes by Bacon 00:02:00
=Henry Stubbe, *The Lord Bacons relation of the sweating sickness examined*, London 1671, (Wing S6059).

[53] St George of Cappodocia 00:02:00
?=Peter Heylyn, *The historie of that famous Saint and Souldier of Christ Jesus, St George of Cappodocia*, London 1631, (*STC* 13272) or a later edition (*STC* 13273, Wing H2142).

[54] Patricks Pilgrimm 00:02:06
=Symon Patrick, *The parable of the pilgrim*, London 1665, (Wing P826) or a later edition (Wing P827–831).

[55] History of Independency 00:02:06
=Clement Walker, *The history of independency*, London 1648, (Wing W329) or a later edition (Wing W330–331); or the same author's *The compleat history of independency*, London 1661 (Wing W324).

[56] An Addresse to Protest.ts by Penn 00:01:03
=William Penn, *An address to protestants*, London 1678, 1679, (Wing P1247–1248).

[57] The Golden Fleece 00:02:00
?=W.S., *The Golden Fleece*, London 1656, (Wing S195); or J.F., *The Golden Fleece or old England restored*, London 1679, (Wing F37).

[58] A search made into matters of religion 00:02:06
=Francis Walsingham, *A search made into matters of religion*, St Omer 1609, 1615, (*STC* 25002–25003).

[59] Felthams resolves old Edition 00:03:00
=Owen Feltham, *Resolves divine, morall, political*, London 1623, (*STC* 10755) or a later edition (*STC* 10756–10761, Wing F 653–657).

[60] Pastor Fido 00:02:00
=Giovanni Battista Guarini, *Il pastor fido, the faithfull shepherd*, London 1647, (Wing G2174) or a later edition (Wing G2175–2177).

[61] Gregorii Posthuma 00:02:06
=John Gregory, *Gregorii posthuma*, London 1649, (Wing G1926) or a later edition (Wing G1927–1930).

[62] Immediate Revelation 00:02:00
=George Keith, *Immediate revelation*, Aberdeen 1668, (Wing K175) or a later edition (Wing K176–177) or rather less probably his *Divine immediate revelation*, London 1684–5, (Wing K157a, 158–159).

[63] A declaration of ye University of ye Churche 00:01:06
Not identified.

BOOKS IN OCTAVO

[64] Latine Bible vulgar Edition Imperfect 00:04:00
Presumably for vulgar one should read Vulgate.

[65] Grounds & Occasions of contempt of the clergy 00:02:06
=[John Eachard], *The grounds and occasions of the contempt of the church*, London 1670, (Wing E50) or a later edition (Wing E51–52).

[66] Reliquae sacrae Carolinae 00:03:00
=Charles I, *Reliquae sacrae Carolinae, the workes of that great Monarch collected and digested*, The Hague 1648, (Wing C2070) or a later edition (Wing C2071–2074).

[67] Contemplations Moral & Divine 00:02:00
=[Sir Matthew Hale], *Contemplations moral and divine*, London 1676, (Wing H225) or a later edition (Wing H225a–227).

[68] 2 New Flatmans Poems 00:04:00
=Thomas Flatman, *Poems and songs*, London 1674, (Wing F1151) or more probably the 1676 or 1683 edition (Wing F1152–1153).

[69] Causes of the decay of Christian piety 00:02:06
=[Richard Allestree], *Causes of the decay of Christian piety*, London 1668, (Wing A 1097) or a later edition (Wing A1098–1107).

[70] Contempt of the clergy 00:01:00
? Another copy of Eachard's book, no. 65 above?

[71] Want of Charity justly Charged on ye romanists 00:01:00
=Christopher Potter, *Want of charity justly charged on the Romanists*, Oxford 1633, London 1634, (*STC* 20135–20136).

[72] 2 Erasmus Colloquies 00:03:00
?=Desiderius Erasmus, *The colloquies* . . . London 1671, (Wing E3190).

[73] Flatmans poems old Edition 00:01:03
=Wing F1151?; see no. 68 above.

[74] Hugo Grotius annalls of ye Belgian warrs 00:03:00
=Hugo Grotius, *de rebus Belgicis, or the annals and history of the Low-Country wars* . . . , tr. by T. Manley, London 1655, (Wing G2097) or the 1665 edition (Wing G2098).

[75] Senecas Epistles & Naturall Questions 00:01:00
?=Lucius Annaeus Seneca, *The workes . . . both morall & naturall*, tr. Thomas Lodge, London 1614, (*STC* 22213) or a later edition (*STC* 22214, Wing S2514–2515a).

[76] Lively oracles given to us 00:01:06
=Richard Allestree, *The lively oracles given to us*, Oxford 1678, (Wing 6 A1149) or a later edition (Wing A1150–1153).

[77] Glanvilles blow at Sadducisme 00:01:03
=Joseph Glanvill, *A blow at modern Sadducism*, London 1668, (Wing G799) or a later edition (Wing G800).

[78] Freeholdrs grand Inquest 00:02:00
=Sir Robert Filmer, *The free-holders grand inquest*, London 1648, (Wing F912) or a later edition (Wing F913–916).

[79] De juro Maritimo 00:03:09
=[Charles Molloy], *De jure maritimo et navali, or a treatise* ... London, 1678, (Wing M2395) or a later edition (Wing M2396–2397).

[80] Tates Poems 00:01:06
=Nahum Tate, *Poems*, London 1677, (Wing T208), or less probably the 1684 edition (Wing T209).

[81] The learned man defended & reformed 00:02:00
Not identified.

[82] Paul Festeaus French Grammar 00:01:03
=Paul Festeau, *A grammar in French & English*, London 1675, (*Wing* F823–824).

[83] 5 Law books New 00:13:09

[84] Cleavelands Poems 00:01:00
=John Cleveland, *Poems*, London 1651, (Wing C4684) or a later edition (Wing C4685–4698).

[85] Whole duty of Man 00:02:00
=Richard Allestree, *The whole duty of man*, London 1658, (Wing A1169) or one of the many later editions (Wing A1170–1186).

[86] Discourse of Ecclesiastical policy 00:02:00
=[Samuel Parker], *A discourse of ecclesiastical politie*, London 1670, (Wing P459) or a later edition (Wing P460).

[87] The rule of Faith by Dr Tillotson 00:02:00
=John Tillotson, *The rule of faith*, London 1668, (Wing T1217) or the second edition, 1676 (Wing T1218).

[88] Leybornes Arithmetick 00:01:06
=William Leybourne, *Arithmetick, vulgar*, London 1657, (Wing L1891) or a later edition (Wing L1892–1894).

[89] Sr Francis Bacons Essayes 00:01:03
=Sir Francis Bacon, *Essays*, London 1597, (*STC* 1137) or a later edition (*STC* 1138–1151, Wing B283–288).

About the House [etc] [Signed] Alene Latrew **X**
Will: Haynes **X**

Note: The surviving copy of the inventory of Craddock's goods is undated. The two preceding it are dated 22 October 1684 and 14 January 1684/5 respectively; that following it: 16 February 1684/5. One can therefore presume that Craddock's inventory was completed some time in late January or early February 1685, and that Craddock died some weeks or months earlier.

XII
THE FIRST PRINTERS IN JAMAICA

Jamaica was conquered from the Spanish as part of Cromwell's 'western design' in 1655. Spanish guerilla resistance lasted for the next ten years, but the British hold on the island was confirmed by the Treaty of Madrid in 1670. Thereafter the development of the British colony was rapid, and particularly that of the old pirate lair Port Royal. "The wickedest city in the world", as it was called had a population of something like eight thousand souls, and two thousand or more substantial houses at the height of its prosperity before the great earthquake of 1692 caused it to disappear beneath the sea.

Mexico City had its first printer within twenty years of the first arrival of Cortes; Massachusetts a press twenty years after the *Mayflower*. That printing should not have been introduced to Jamaica until sixty years after the British conquest — or over two centuries after the first discovery by Columbus — suggests that the development of the 'noble art and mystery' was slow indeed.

Viewed in these terms printing in Jamaica seems of little importance. But it is a distorted view, and one which belies the real importance of the colony, as a centre of New World printing. Jamaica was the first of all the Caribbean islands into which printing was introduced[1], for *The Weekly Jamaica Courant* was the second regular newspaper to appear anywhere in the Americas[2], and the Island remained the natural centre for British printing in the western Caribbean until a very late date[3].

There is no doubt that Port Royal could have supported a printer in the 1680s. Though Sir Henry Morgan and his cronies were not, perhaps, the most promising of patrons for such a venture Port Royal boasted a theatre and some other evidences of cultural life[4], and there is little doubt an enterprising craftsman could have made his way.

The reasons why nobody attempted it are simple enough if one looks outside Jamaica at England and some of her North American colonies.

Throughout the second half of the seventeenth century control of the press was something which constantly exercised the minds of those in government, whether commonwealth or restored monarchy. Very much earlier restrictive legislation had limited printing to London and to the two university towns of Oxford and Cambridge. The number of master printers, the presses they could operate and the journeymen printers and apprentices they were allowed to employ, were all strictly regulated through the Stationers' Company. After the Restoration of King Charles II in 1660 some ingenious essays in fabricated history[5] purported to show that the original introduction of printing into England had been at the behest of the King, and that in consequence control of the press was within the royal prerogative. Most importantly under the Surveyor of Imprimery, Sir Roger L'Estrange, *all* printed work had to be licensed, and there was vigilant search and seizure of unlicensed books and printing equipment.

In those North American colonies which were most amenable to the royal wishes, the idea of printing did not receive much favour. Governor Berkeley of Virginia expressed the attitude of those in authority with admirable brevity:

"I thank God" he said in 1671, "that there are no free schools, nor printing; and I hope we shall not have these hundred years. For learning hath brought disobedience and heresy and sects into the world, and printing has divulged them and libels against the best of government. God keep us from both".

When some ten years later, a Jamestown merchant brought a printer into Virginia on his own initiative the Governor and Council took alarm and the printer was bound over to print nothing "until the signification of His Majesty's pleasure shall be known therein". When the signification came it was not encouraging, as it required that "no person be permitted to use any press for printing upon any occasion whatsoever". In turbulent and undisciplined Jamaica where the Governor was usually battling against a recalcitrant Assembly, it is unlikely any other policy would have been adopted.

The Licensing Acts, which for so long had restricted the number of printers and places they could work in England, finally lapsed in 1693. Within a few years printers had spread from London to all the principal towns. An important feature of this spread was in the development of local newspapers, such as *The Norwich Post* (1701), *The Bristol Post-Boy* (1702) or Sam Farley's *Exeter Postman* (1704). These papers provided a very useful service to the inhabitants of the districts surrounding the various market-towns in which they were published, and also formed the mainstay of the provincial printers' business.

The change in the climate of opinion in England, demonstrated by this growth of the provincial press, was not lost on Sir Nicholas Lawes, the key figure in the introduction of printing to Jamaica. Lawes had spent his early life in the island, rising to become its Attorney-General. In the early years of the eighteenth century he was living in England. Exposed to this expansion of the newspaper press in England he became aware of the advantages which would accrue were a printer to set up in Jamaica.

The need for a press was evidently felt in Jamaica, since in a message from the island's Council to the Assembly on 8 December 1715 it was stated that "they heartily wish that their house will join with them in establishing a printing press for publishing the Minutes of both bodies". Likewise, in *The Representation and Memorial of the Council of the Island of Jamaica* addressed to the Lords Commissioners for Trade and Plantations (and published in London in 1716) it was noted that "numberless lies and stories have been industriously spread about the country, which are not easily answer'd where there is no press".

No doubt Lawes (by that time Governor-Designate of Jamaica) was aware of this need which had been expressed by the Council, when he wrote to the Lords Commissioners on 1 October 1717:

> "I am of opinion if a printing press were set up in Jamaica it would be of great use, and benefit for publick intelligence, advertisements and many other things. But to prevent abuses, that might attend such a liberty, there should be but one, and that to be licensed to the Governor for the time being".[6]

Sir Nicholas did not limit his suggestion to this letter. At a meeting with the Commissioners on 10 October 1717 he again urged the value of a press in Jamaica, where it would be

> "a public convenience and advantage to commerce".[7]

Robert Baldwin

Evidently the new Governor's recommendation was approved by the Lords Commissioners, since we find that a printer named Robert Baldwin was established in Church Street, Kingston, very soon after Sir Nicholas Lawes's arrival at Port Royal in April 1718. It is possible that the printer sailed on the same vessel as the Governor to whom he was licensed, since it would not have taken him long to set up his printing equipment, and he did not start publication of his newspaper until the end of May in that year.

It is not possible to identify Baldwin with certainty. He *may* be the same as the Stationers' Company apprentice who was freed by patrimony on 6 February 1716[8], in which case one has straight away a connection with the Baldwin family who crop up in the printing trade in London throughout the eighteenth century. I think he was the same man, but there is no evidence. Nor is there any evidence surviving as to the contractual arrangements under which he came to the West Indies. One may conjecture (on the basis of the kind of work he was to produce, and by analogy from arrangements which were made in other colonies) that there was a tacit agreement that Baldwin would undertake such official printing as was needed in the colony, and would be paid for this like any other government contractor, and not as a salaried official. Quite clearly his official duties did not preclude him from undertaking other non-official printing on a regular commercial basis, nor curtail his right to branch out into other business fields.

It is interesting that although he was an official printer Baldwin settled in Kingston. This was instead of the capital city St. Jago de la Vega (Spanish Town) where the Governor resided and the Assembly met; and instead of Port Royal which, despite the earthquake of 1692 and subsequent devastation by fire and hurricane, remained the colony's principal port. It was a wise decision on Baldwin's part: in Kingston — which was rapidly growing as the island's commercial centre — he had ready access to both St. Jago and Port Royal, and his chance of developing his other business was far greater than it would have been in either of the other towns.

The equipment needed by a printer at that time was not extensive. The design of the wooden press had changed little since the fifteenth century, as indeed it was to undergo little alteration before it was superseded by cast-iron presses at the beginning of the nineteenth century. Detailed instructions on how to build a press had been given in Joseph Moxon's *Mechanick exercises on the whole art of printing* (London, 1683) and though it is probable that Baldwin brought his press with him, assembling it and repairs would not have been beyond the skill of local joiners, millwrights and blacksmiths.

Of course we cannot know what kind of press Baldwin had: whether the so-called Blaeu Press whose adoption Moxon had urged, or the older common press of which it was an improved version.

> "One new-fashion'd Dutch Press is worth a score of (the older presses)" wrote the Edinburgh printer James Watson in 1713. "I myself have known a Press of the new make brought hither from Holland, work near Twenty Years, and in all that time neither Smith nor Joiner call'd for to her; . . . I beseech you, as you are tender of your own interest, to bring home your Presses from Holland . . ."[9]

Baldin *was* "tender of his own interest" but whether he brought a Dutch press with him is uncertain. Surviving common presses used in the North American colonies are all of the "old fashion'd English" kind[10], which suggests Baldwin's press might have been of the same pattern.

About Baldwin's typefaces, however, there is no doubt. At the time he was gathering his equipment together, typefounding in England had not reached the high standard it was to achieve under William Caslon within ten or twelve years. Most English printers bought Dutch types, and comparison of the faces employed by Baldwin shows that his repertoire[11] was fairly typical. From an inventory of his goods made soon after his death[12] we know that he had seventeen cases of type: enough for all normal printing purposes, though examination of his work reveals that he sometimes ran short of individual letters. Brand-new when Baldwin went to Jamaica, these founts of type were still being used by his successors nearly a quarter of a century later.

Supplies of paper were another problem for the colonial printer. The inventory of his stock, already referred to, shows that Baldwin carried large stocks of paper of various sizes (e.g. "15 reams of Printing ffools Cap" etc.), some of which was obviously intended for his own printing business, but some of it for the stationery trade. Whether he made his own printing ink (as many European printers still did at that time) or imported in kegs, like some later Jamaican printers, we do not know: there is no reference to printing ink in his inventory.

Almost certainly the first publication from Baldwin's newly-established press in Church Street, Kingston was *A Pindarique Ode on the Arrival of His Excellency Sir Nicholas Lawes*, 1718. The anonymous verse no doubt pleased the Governor, but scarcely belongs with the ranks of great poetry as a short specimen will show:

> "Hark how the Voice of Joy breaks through the Air
> In pleasing Strains that captivate the Ear!
> Hark, 'tis great LAWES they sound!
> Eccho bears the Name around,
> And with the Great LAWES the vaulted Hills rebound, . . ."

Like all early West Indian printing, the four-page pamphlet is excessively rare. The only surviving copy[13], in Cheetham's Library, Manchester, is of the second edition, so the local demand must have been higher than Baldwin anticipated.

Publication of *The Weekly Jamaica Courant* seems to have started on 28 May 1718. According to Isaiah Thomas[14] writing in 1810 the paper continued until at least 1755, but pitifully few copies have survived, and none later than 1738. In the West Indies earthquake, hurricane, fire and termites have tidily removed all the evidence. The majority of copies which have survived have done so because they were sent by various governors with their despatches to the commissioners for Trade and Plantations in London, and are now in the Public Records Office. The two earliest known, the issues of 30 July and 5 August 1718, have survived because they were waste copies which Baldwin used to make pasteboard for binding a log-book for Admiral Vernon. These were discovered and restored when the British Museum was rebinding the Vernon papers in the 1930s.

These earliest issues of the *Courant* are of particular interest as not only do they contain the statement "published by authority" (as also do all the later surviving issues) but also an *Imprimatur*. There was no question of freedom of the press in Jamaica then!

Published at "one bit, or three-half-crowns a quarter" the *Courant* was a four-page demy publication, predictably similar in appearance to the earliest English provincial papers or those of the North American colonies. Its contents were those which were to become typical of West Indian newspapers[15] for a long time to come: European news culled from English papers (and therefore generally ten or twelve weeks late); government business (addresses to the Governor, official proclamations and the like); a little local news which included the prevailing prices of goods, and shipping intelligence. Although there were to be changes in the design and format of the *Courant* during the 1720s, the recipe for the contents remained unchanged: evidently it suited the needs of the merchants and planters who made up its readership.

The most important part of the paper — for its printer and his contemporary readers as well as ourselves — was in the advertisements which made up a substantial part of each issue. Examination of those in surviving issues of the *Courant* tell us a good deal more about its printer and his other business interests. On the *Courant*, two are of special interest:

> "This is to give Notice, to all the Gentlemen who live in the Parishes (of) St. Dorothy's, Clarendon and Vere[16], That they may be constantly supplied the Weekly Jamaica Courants, and all other things that have or may be list'd, at the Places following, and at such Times as is hereafter specified; that have or may subscribe for the Courants Quarterly, in the Parish of St. Dorothy's, may be supplied by Mr. Booth, Those in Clarendon by Mr. Hancock at the Cross, and those in Vere by Mr. Palfreeman, near the Church; whence a Negro will set out Wednesday Morning, and stop One Hour at the Cross; and likewise One Hour at Mr. Booth's, in order to take all Letters in his way from those Places to deliver them to Mr. Taylor on the Parade at Spanish Town, on Wednesday Evening; where he is to stay that Night, in

order to set out early the next Morning with the Newspapers, and Letters directed to the Places aforesaid, paying a Royal for each Letter, at either of the Parishes where they shall be left,

N.B. Those that are willing to have the Papers Quarterly are desired to send their Names to either of the aforesaid Places, where they will be constantly sent, by

Your Obliged Humble Servant
R.B."

(*Courant* no. 38, 11 Feb. 1718/19, p.3)

The suggestion implicit in the advertisement, that the circulation of the paper was well organised in the primitive conditions of the Jamaica of that time, is confirmed by a second advertisement. This appeared in the *Courant* long after Baldwin's death, when the business was being run by his widow Mary:

"Run away from *Mary Baldwin*, Printer in Kingston, a Negro Man named *Apollo*, who did deliver the News Papers at *Kingston* and *Spanish Town*. Whoever brings him to his Mistress aforesaid shall be well rewarded".

(*Courant* no. 675, 25 March 1730)

The fate of the wretched Apollo, precursor of the little boys who hawk the *Daily Gleaner* and the *Star* in Kingston's streets today, is unknown. Like many absconding slaves he might have been able to keep at liberty: Mrs. Baldwin was still advertising for his return at the end of June 1730.

Some of the other advertisements reveal the range of Robert Baldwin's business interests, which were as varied and miscellaneous as those of his contemporaries in provincial England. Readers of his issue of 30 July could purchase

"Very curious Pocket-Telliscopes, Reading Glasses and Machines to place in the Breast".

or might find comfort from his offer of

"A safe, Pleasant and Powerful Cordial against the GOUT, with Printed Directions how to use it".

On 11 February 1718/19 he was offering

"All sorts of very good Parchment and Vellum Skins of all sizes, Writing Papers, Pencils, Penknives, Rulers, Standishes, Quils, VVax, VVafers, Sand, Black and Red Ink, Books for Accompts, Rul'd or Plain, and Alphabets; Writings neatly Engross'd or Copeyed, Single or Double Bonds, and Bills of Lading . . ."

A little over a year later, on 17 April 1719, he was advertising

"Painted Paper for Hangings, Pocket-Books, Letter-Cases and Super-fine Cards, with all other Stationery-wares, sold

> at his Shops in Church-Street Kingston; and likewise by Mr. Taylor on the Parade Spanish Town, and Mr. Fisher's at Port Royal, who will then be supplied by him constantly . . ."

Evidently Baldwin had the island's wholesale and retail stationery trade pretty well sewn up.

Bookbinding was another substantial part of the Baldwin business, and was to remain so. Several of the advertisements deal with binding; one indicating that Baldwin had workmen just arrived from England

> "who bind Books neatly in Vellom and Parchment, and in all Sorts of Leather, likewise Guild and Letter them on the backs".

To printing, binding and stationery it was natural for Baldwin to add bookselling and publishing. Several advertisements refer to the availability of new Common-Prayer Books, Bibles, and copy-books for school-children; one is of special interest for the light it throws on the planters' amusements:

> "Just come from England, and to be sold at the Printer's, a choice Collection of the Newest Songs, with Notes, engrav'd on Copper Plates; Also Instruction-Books, with lessons for the Violin, Harpsichord and Flute; New Sets of Minuets, Rigadoons, and Country-Dances; likewise good Violins and Flutes".

(*Courant*, 28 June 1721)

As none of these items figures in the inventory of Baldwin's goods after his death within the year, it seems that this stock was quickly sold out.

Some of the books and pamphlets published from Baldwin's press were clearly the result of his official duties, and are discussed below. Others were equally certainly private ventures like that advertised 15 April 1719:

> "Lately Publish'd, TOBACCO, a Poem, in Two Books, Translated from the Latin of Raphael Thorius. JAMAICA: Reprinted by R. Baldwin in Church-Street, Kingston, Price **2s 6d**. Stitch'd in Blew Paper, and 6 Ryals Bound in Marble Paper".

No copy is known to survive of this book. Nor of another private venture

> "The Jamaica Almanack, for the year 1719. Calculated for this Meridian. By Nicholas Holst. Sold by R. Baldwin . . . Price 2 Ryals".

Forty years ago the Institute of Jamaica had a copy of a similar sheet almanac for 1734. Although it is now missing, from the description of it in Frank Cundall's *History of printing in Jamaica*

1717-1834 (Kingston 1935) I suspect that it was a regular annual publication from 1719 onwards which provided useful supplementary income for Baldwin and his heirs.

Mary Baldwin

Robert Baldwin had died by 13 April, 1722 on which date his widow Mary was granted Letters of Administration over his estate. These required that an inventory of his property be drawn up, and this was duly filed on 16 February 1723 —considerably over the six month period laid down by law, which perhaps suggests his affairs were in a confused state which it took his young widow some time to settle. The inventory[16] gives a very good picture of the extent of Baldwin's business and personal possessions. The total of £414-18s.6d. for the stock included "two boys and two women" valued at £100. These slaves were almost certainly domestic slaves; although there is considerable evidence[17] that slaves were employed as pressmen and binders later in the century, I doubt if that was the case with Baldwin —though the boys may have been used to deliver the papers.

The inventory also included a further £1170-11s.10½d. for 'debts good', and £100 for 'Bad Debt'. Kingston merchants and tradesmen always had to offer very long credit, and frequently accept payment in kind. No doubt a considerable part of these debts relate to Baldwin's official printing, for which his widow would — in time — have been paid, but one feels that setting bad debt at less than ten per cent was too optimistic on the appraisers' part.

Nevertheless, Mary Baldwin was sufficiently well-off to continue the business without apparent difficulty till such time as her sons were old enough to take over direction of the family concern. She may, in fact, have had a shrewder head for business than her husband. Certainly within twelve years she had apparently become very well-to-do. In 1734 Samuel Keimer, the second printer in Barbados, published a "sorrowful lamentation" which he addressed "to those wou'd be thought Gentlemen, who have long taken this paper, and never paid for it, and seem never to design to pay for it". In the verses — which were reprinted by Isaiah Thomas — he compared his own lamentable state with that of printers in Virginia, South Carolina and other colonies where printers were both honoured and prosperous. Of Mrs. Baldwin, he wrote

"E'en *Type* at Jamaica, our island's reproach,
Is able to ride in her Chariot or Coach".

Even allowing for a little poetic exaggeration, it would seem Mrs.

Baldwin's prosperity was known the other end of the Caribbean.

This prosperity came, no doubt, partly from the printing business, although so little of Mrs. Baldwin's output survives that it is impossible to say how much. The printing side of her business was managed for her (for a part of the time at any rate) by a printer named John Letts, who is probably to be identified with the John Letts who was apprenticed to Thomas Braddyll in London 1700-1707.

The advertisements in surviving issues of the *Courant* show that she was also branching out into new fields:

> "To be sold at the Printer's . . . these several sorts of Garden-Seeds, viz. Carrot, Spinage, Lettice, Cowcumber, Parsly, Asparagus, Cabbage, Red-Top Turnip; and very fresh Spaw-water, Cimmon, Dr. Steven's and Aqua Mirabilis, at reasonable Rates".

(*Courant*, 22 June 1722)

> "Spices of all sorts to be sold at the Printers very reasonable; likewise *Scots* snuff".

(*Courant*, 24 June 1730)

The real backbone of her business, however, I suspect to have been bookbinding, since all the planters needed a regular supply of account books. There was also a steady demand for binding and rebinding of printed books: Cundall has recorded an order to the Clerk of the Assembly to have books bound by Mrs. Baldwin if he could not get the work done in Spanish Town[18].

Peter and Robert Baldwin Jr.

After 1734, Mary Baldwin disappears into the mists of history. No record seems to survive in Jamaica of her remarriage or death or departure from the colony, and there is a gap in our knowledge of this first family of Jamaican printers till 1740. There *is* an issue of the *Courant* from 1738 among the Fulham papers in Lambeth Palace Library; tantalising since it is incomplete and one can't tell whether it was printed by Mary Baldwin or by her sons. But by 1740 the business was in their hands: on 30 September that year the island's Council ordered that £20-10s. should be paid to Peter and Robert Baldwin for printing proclamations and other official matter. Two pamphlets printed that year — *A letter from Don Blas de Lezo* and *A Letter from John Thomas Geraldino* (of which the only known copies are in the Library of the Institute of Jamaica) were printed for the Baldwin brothers by John Letts, in the self-same types which Robert Baldwin senior had brought to Jamaica in 1718.

Apart from these two pamphlets, and some ephemera which

one presumes to have come from their press, nothing else of their printing survives, save a single issue of *The Jamaica Gazette*, no. 96 of 14 December 1745 which was printed for them by Alexander Adamson, at two royals or 7s.6d. a quarter.

From this single issue — which seems complementary to the *Courant*, rather than a replacement for it — we learn that

> "The Office of Intelligence, is kept at the Printing Office in Kingston by Peter and Robert Baldwin. Where Money is Endeavour'd to be procur'd on good Security for Money, Ships and other Vessells charter'd and hired; Mortgages, Bonds & c. transacted, Houses Bought and Sold, Lett & Rented, Persons qualify'd in any Occupation may hear of Business, and Persons wanting such, may be informed of them: All kinds of Bargains whatsoever, in Commerce, or any other kind of Business, is carried on with the strictest Secrecy, the Principals only being brought together . . . The business of INSURANCE is carried on as usual".

The Baldwin brothers, then, had climbed from being merely printers and binders to a mixture of merchant bankers, realtors, insurance brokers and employment agency. In this more exalted sphere the mechanical trades were no doubt left to their employees. Apart from John Letts in 1740, and Adamson in 1745, we do not know who these employees were, though they may have included William Daniell, who had succeeded to the Baldwins' position as government printer by 1748.

There is no evidence surviving as to the success of the Baldwins' "Office of Intelligence", though to judge from the advertisements placed in their paper for "a young man qualify'd in Surgery and Pharmacy", for "Employment for an Overseer and Distiller" etc., it must have been well patronised. But however firmly established, it did not last long: Robert Baldwin the younger had (it seems) died or left Jamaica by the end of 1745, and within the month Peter Baldwin had succumbed to the disease rife in the island. On 5 February 1746 Letters of Administration of his estate were granted to one John Cochran, "Practitioner in Physick" in Kingston. The inventory ordered to be prepared within six months seems not to have survived, and there are no subsequent references to the Baldwins in Jamaican archives.

The publications of the first Jamaican printers

The surviving issues of the *Courant* are not only of interest for the evidence they contain about the printers of the newspaper. As H. P. Jacobs has shown[19], much of the content of the island's early newspapers is of very real value for historical studies.

Analysis of the advertisements in the fifteen issues which are known to survive of the *Courant*, for example, shows that advertisements for absconded slaves and indentured workers far outnumber those of any other categories. It seems (looking at the fifty or so advertisements of this nature) that many more white indentured workers than Negro slaves fled their employers, at any rate in relation to the numbers of each group. Does this reflect greater enterprise on the indentured workers' part? Or greater desperation with their abominable conditions? or merely that the chances of the white man making good his escape from the island were better?

Against the fifty advertisements of this kind, there were six for slave sales, six for strayed horses or cattle, eighteen for real estate, nine for property lost and found. We learn where we could hire a coach in Kingston, and on what conditions; where we could have watches and clocks mended; where we could attend a concert or buy furniture. Other advertisements offered the chance of buying coffee, or harness, or barrels of spoiled herrings.

Local news, as given in these issues of the paper, lacks the interest of the advertisements. But from time to time it adds substantially to our knowledge of the period. For example, the issue for 12 September 1722 is filled with accounts of the effect of the terrible hurricane which had struck the island on 28 August. One effect had been to prevent publication of the *Courant* for a week, but we can also read which vessels at Port Royal or the Kingston wharves had been wrecked, grounded or otherwise damaged. The effect at Port Royal had been particularly devastating, over 400 people having been killed and half the town destroyed; at Spanish Town (on the other hand) there had been no loss of life.

The *Courant* reported

> "It is remarkable that those Houses which were built by the Spaniards, sustain'd very little damage, tho' 'tis now 67 years since the conquest of the island. Consequently those Buildings are of much older date. From this we may reasonably conclude, that they had met with Accidents of the like nature, that put them upon that manner of building."

Despite this shrewd observation the style of building adopted in Jamaica remained different from (and inferior to) Spanish colonial architecture.

Other local items in the *Courant* seldom possess as much interest as this. Many of them contain the texts of proclamations or speeches by the Governor (which is of course the reason for the survival of these issues, sent by the Governors with their despatches to London). Sometimes, of course, these proclamations were printed separately: the speech of Sir Nicholas Lawes to the Council and Assembly on Thursday 6 November 1718[20] is an example of this kind of work. The Governor's rebuke, which is contained in this, is one which many later Governors of Jamaica would have wished to echo:

> "Gentlemen of the Council . . . You have hitherto spent your Time not so much in the true Service of the King, and your Country, as in gratifying your Passions and Resentments against each other, and enquiring into, and demanding Things of no other Consequence to the Publick, than to raise Heats, and beget Misunderstandings among you . . . Mr. Speaker and Gentlemen, I am sure the major part of you may lay your Hands upon your Hearts, and justly Confess, That you have left undone those Things that you ought to have Done, and that you have done those Things which you ought not to have done. WHEREFORE, by His Majesty's Authority . . . I do prorogue this Assembly . . ."

In a good many cases, no copies of the Baldwins' official printing have survived at all. Robert Baldwin was advertising in 1719 that

> "Gentlemen may be furnish'd with compleat sets of the Votes, Speeches and Addresses"

(of the House of Assembly), and there is some evidence that these were produced at any rate throughout his lifetime, but none are known to survive. Similarly we can compile a list of 'extra' Jamaican official publications from the *Courant* advertisements —such things as *An act for the more effectual suppressing of piracy* advertised for two royals in June 1722. Much of the printing, for private ventures as well as official use, would have been of ephemera most of which has vanished or is unidentifiable as from the Baldwins' press today. The Jamaica Archives' sets of the duplicate letters of administration of the 1730s and 1740s, for instance, are proformas printed in the same types and on the same papers as used in some of the Baldwins' other work, so we can assume that these forms were printed by them. The same is true, I think, of a certificate that the snow 'Greyhound' had been taken under naval control at Port Royal on 13th November 1740. This preprinted certificate form (with the details of vessel, date etc., filled in by hand) survives today in the John Carter Brown Library at Providence, R.I. But of the hundreds or thousands of bills of lading, letter of marque, ships articles and other proformas which would have been sold blank, we have no trace.

By far the most substantial of the separate publications of the

Baldwin period which have survived, official or unofficial, is the report of *The Tryals of Captain John Rackham and other pirates* printed in the spring of 1721[21]. The report is one of the best known of all piracy documents, since it describes two of the crew who turned out to be women, Anne Bonny and Mary Read. To produce this 44-page folio obviously stretched Baldwin's typographical resources very severely, but it was an example of book production of which he could justifiably have been proud. He was an accomplished craftsman, who set high standards for his successors as printers in Jamaica.

Notes

1. One William Simpson, an Edinburgh printer, had accompanied the crack-brained Scottish expedition to Darien in 1698, but nothing was produced by his press even if it was unloaded on arrival in America. Cf. John Prebble, *The Darien disaster*, (London, 1968).
2. *The Boston newsletter* first published by authority on 24 April 1704 was the first; an earlier unlicensed paper *Public occurances* having been suppressed after its issue in Boston 25 Sept. 1690.
3. Kingston printers supplied the needs of Belize (British Honduras) until the 1820s, and of the Cayman Islands until after World War 2.
4. Including, perhaps, a bookseller: Cf. Roderick Cave, 'The books of Thomas Craddock', *Book Collector*, Winter 1976, pp.
5. e.g. Richard Atkyns, *The original and growth of printing in England*, London 1664. Atkyns' account, based on a document he claimed to have seen in Lambeth Palace, was regarded with some suspicion by the more discerning of his contemporaries, but was not discredited for three quarters of a century.
6. Quoted by Frank Cundall, *A history of printing in Jamaica from 1717 to 1834* (Kingston, 1935) p.3.
7. *Journal of the Commissioners for Trade and Plantations March 1714/15 –October 1718* (London, 1924) p.277.
8. I am grateful to Prof. Donald McKenzie for this information.
9. James Watson, Preface to *The history of printing* (Edinburgh, 1713) p.xxii.
10. Lawrence C. Wroth, *The colonial printer*, 2nd ed. (Charlottesville, 1964) pp. 69-79.
11. Cf. Roderick Cave, 'An inventory of the first Jamaican printing house' *Papers of the Bibliographical Society of America*, v.69, 1975, pp. 560-565.
12. Jamaica Archives, Inventories, liber 12 fol. 131v-132v.
13. Reproduced by Douglas McMurtrie in his *The first printing in Jamaica* (Evanston, 1942).
14. In his *History of printing in America*.
15. Later papers often quoted local Caribbean and foreign news from one another, but this is the only feature they added to the Baldwin mixture.
16. Loc. cit.
17. Cf. Roderick Cave, 'The use of slave labour in West Indian printing houses' *The Library*, 5th series, v.30, 1975, pp. 241-243.
18. Frank Cundall, *The press and printers of Jamaica prior to 1820* (Worcester, Mass., 1916) p.8.
19. In his 'The Jamaican press 1789-1865', *Jamaica journal* September 1972.
20. The printed date is Wednesday 5 November, but this was changed in manuscript in the copy sent by Lawes to the Lords Commissioners in London.

21. The only surviving copies were sent by Lawes to the Lords Commissioners in June 1721, and are now in the Public Records Office.

XIII
TWO JAMAICAN PRINTERS

The early pattern of settlement in the English colony of Jamaica was uneven. The mountainous interior remained largely unsettled, inhabited only by the Maroons, escaped slaves who had made good their independence and whose descendants today still hold a privileged position. Some early settlements in the south-east, round Port Morant (mainly by settlers from St. Kitts) had declined: by the mid-1740s the population of some one hundred and fifty thousand, of whom all but ten to fifteen thousand were negro slaves, had its greatest concentration in the area around Kingston Harbour and to its west in the St. Catherine plains. Port Royal, the old pirate port at the mouth of Kingston harbour, had been devastated by earthquake in 1692 and 1744, and by fire and hurricanes in 1703, 1712, 1722 and 1744; only its importance as a naval station arrested its steady decline. St. Jago de la Vega (better known as Spanish Town) which was the old Spanish capital of the island in St. Catherine, retained its importance as the administrative centre of the colony, but was ill-situated for mercantile development. There were small but growing townships at Savanna-la-Mar in the south west, and at Montego Bay on the north coast. Yet all these were far outdistanced by Kingston, which had been founded after the Port Royal earthquake of 1692, and by the middle of the eighteenth century had achieved pre-eminence as the island's mercantile centre it has never since lost. It was with a shrewd business eye that Robert Baldwin had set up his Printing Office in Church Street, Kingston, in 1718.

Although some members of the plantocracy were cultured men with literary tastes — the Longs, the Beckfords, the Edwardses — the pattern into which the Baldwins' printing set was distinctly workaday. A weekly newspaper to serve the colony's mercantile needs and provide a vehicle for official proclamations; sheet almanacs, blank proformas for bills of lading, bonds, letter of marque and the like were to make up almost the total output of the Baldwins' printing business. The pattern was not peculiar to

Jamaica — in Barbados, in Antigua, in St. Kitts — indeed in Britain's southern American colonies, or even those in the East Indies — the type of work produced, and the style in which it was printed was to be remarkably similar.

It is against this background that the work of William Daniell and Curtis Brett must be judged. The typographic and other evidence is very slim, little of their output surviving, but in both cases there is enough to bring them some way out of the shadows surrounding the Jamaican press at mid-century.

When William Daniell arrived in Jamaica is not certain. He is probably to be identified with the William Daniel, son of Richard Daniel, farmer of Padworth, Berkshire, who on 2 July 1723 had been apprenticed to Abel Roper, bookseller of Westminster, for the usual period of seven years. It appears that he was established in Harbour Street, Kingston (the Fleet Street of Jamaican printers) by the summer of 1748, since the first issue of his newspaper, *The Jamaica Courant*, conjecturally appeared on 29 October that year[1].

Publication of a regular paper was an essential part of the business of almost every West Indian printer until well into the nineteenth century. In almost every British colony, from Antigua to Trinidad, from Belize to Guyana, one finds that the printer's first concern normally was to get his paper firmly established. Once that was done, the colony's jobbing and other printing work would come his way almost automatically. In most cases, in the smaller and poorer islands at any rate, the circulation of the papers was very small but the market for other printing work was smaller still, so that the difference between failure and success was dictated entirely by the extent of government advertising in it — a point that colonial Houses of Assembly, and Governors, were quick to recognize and use as a means of limiting press criticism[2].

Although Jamaica was the largest of the British sugar islands, and in the middle of the eighteenth century just entering upon its period of greatest prosperity, it is improbable that the *Jamaica Courant* circulated more than three or four hundred copies of each issue, if so many[3].

So few issues survive of the *Courant*[4] that one cannot judge whether Daniell's editorial matter ever put him at odds with authority, nor even say how much he charged for subscriptions or advertisements. All that one can say with confidence is that his paper accords closely with the pattern set by the Baldwins with the *Weekly Jamaica Courant*. It was a four-page crown folio paper in three columns, with pages one and four containing public announcements, a little overseas news culled from London or

North American papers, plus half a column or so of local news; with the two middle pages (and a good deal of the fourth) consisting entirely of advertisements.

These were for the return of absconded negro slaves and of indentured white labourers, for land and houses for sale, for provisions and dry goods recently imported by Kingston merchants. There was a selection of more personal matters: If Epaphroditus Houghton who had come to Jamaica in the late 1720s would communicate with such and such lawyers he would learn something to his advantage; Isaac DePass was informing the public that though the ship *Ruby* had been lost on the Florida coast, all the moneys she was carrying were saved, and so forth.

As well as the advertisements in his newspaper, William Daniell had another regular source of income from official sources: the *Votes of the House of Assembly*. Originally this had been a purely private venture, and a nearly disastrous one (which once more suggests that he was a newcomer to Jamaica) as his petition to the House of Assembly on 19 October 1749 claimed.

> that he, being authorised and enpowered by the honourable the Speaker, to print the votes of this honourable house, and hoping the expense of printing same would be defrayed by subscription, and not doubting but that a sufficient number of subscribers would be found to raise a fund for that purpose, he did . . . print the said votes from time to time, during the sitting of the last sessions but one:
>
> That the number of subscribers fell far short of his expectation, by which means he has not received a consideration adequate to the expense he has been at, and praying the house would give him such relief therein, as to the house should seem meet.

A small committee was set up to examine this petition. A week later they reported that since Daniell had printed the Votes of the House at an expense of £100 (5 at least — disregarding his own labour — and as he had received subscriptions amounting only to £44-2s-6d and one of this sum only £17-17s-3d had actually been paid to him, he "ought to have a reward equivalent to his expense and trouble"[6].

Daniell's failure to attract many subscribers, or to coax payment from those who had subscribed, was in fact very fortunate for him since his petition to the House of Assembly set a precedent for the payment from the public funds for such work. Not only did Daniell receive his £100 for the 1748 Votes, but as Printer to the Assembly he continued to receive similar annual payments for such work until his death. Later printers who succeeded to the title made a very handsome income from their official printing.

Two copies of the *Votes* as printed by Daniell survive in the library of the Massachusetts Historical Society[7]. Both are foolscap folios, the first covering the Assembly session from 18 September to 25 November 1753; the second the session 8 April to 19 May 1755. Despite the importance of this official business to Daniell, he took less care than one might have expected — the 1753 volume is headed VOTES OF THE HONOURAEBL ASSEMBLY . . .

As well as the *Votes*, Daniell printed some other official work, such as *The Speech of His Excellency Charles Knowles Esq.* the Governor *Tuesday, 8th April 1755* plus *The Addresses of the Honourable the Council and Assembly* which were made in reply[8].

On his own behalf Daniell published a number of other books and pamphlets, and in 1751 issued *The Merchants' Pocket Companion or an Almanack for the year of our Lord 1751*. Robert Baldwin had commenced publication of a sheet almanac in 1719, which seems to have been issued annually until well into the 1730s[9], but Daniell's was the first attempt at an almanac in book form: another type of publication which was to be a standard work for later Jamaican printers to issue. Only one copy of the 1751 *Merchant's Companion* survives[10], but one may conjecture that he continued production annually until his death in 1755.

Daniell's books included *An Essay on the Bilious or Yellow Fever of Jamaica* by John Williams, a well printed octavo pamphlet of 55 pages issued in 1750[11]. In July 1754 he published *The Justice of the Peace's Pocket Companion: or, the Office and Duty of a Justice epitomized . . . to which is added, the Office and Duty of a Coroner*. Priced at 7s6d, no copies of this useful sounding work are now known[12].

As well as his newspaper and other publishing ventures, Daniell was engaged in the miscellaneous trading activities typical of printers of the time. In the *Courant* he advertised in 1754 that at his shop[13]

> "may be had very reasonable, all the new Books and Pamphlets as published, in *London*, likewise all manner of Stationery".

Elsewhere in the same paper he was offering a *New and correct chart of the Windward Passage* plus *The New Mariner's Calendar* "just imported from London" and

> prospective [sic] views in Italy, France, Spain, England, Ireland &c. most beautifully coloured, with the Glasses for shewing them; Telescopes, Reading Glasses, Squire's Grand Elixir, Steven's Balsam of Life, Doctor James's pow-

der, Grenough's Tincture for the Teeth, famous British Oil &c. &c.

In all this he was very similar to the English provincial printers of the time, and to his predecessors in Jamaica, the Baldwin family. Where he differed from them was in his sources of supply for some of his materials.

The Baldwins had imported their presses, types, paper and other printing and bookbinding equipment and materials from England. Daniell did the same for press and types — Caslon Old Face was his main text type — but for paper and some other materials he negotiated for supplies from Benjamin Franklin in Philadelphia. In this, he was anticipating the changing trade in printers' supplies: whereas in 1750 it was a rarity for a West Indian printer to trade with North America, a century later it had become commonplace, while today only exceptionally will equipment or materials be procured from Europe.

Franklin had long before this had close connections with the printing trade in the West Indies. In Barbados his old acquaintances David Harry and Samuel Keimer had been the first printers in 1730, while in Antigua his protegé Thomas Smith (and after Smith's death, Franklin's nephew Benjamin Mecom) had the early monopoly of printing. That he should be interested in dealing with a Kingston printer was to be expected, but in this case the first move came from Daniell.

Among Franklin's papers in the American Philosophical Society four survive which bear on his dealings with the Kingston printer. The first is from Daniell:

> Sir, Kingston June 23rd June 1754
>
> In my Last of the 12th ultimo[14] I made proposial for dealing with you for paper which if Convenient should be glad you would be as Expeditious as possible in sending me the 50 Rms. of Demy Paper I wrote for alsoe a Sheet of Each sort of writing or printing paper you make with the prices per Rm. wrote on Each sheet as I am takeing some things in hand for the Press I shall take it a favour if you would Lett me know at onst the Lowest prices to save the Time a Second Letter will take to Come to your hand. I am Sir Your Most Obedient servant
>
> William Daniell
>
> P.S. Send me a Cask of 50 or 100 lb. of Pott ash and 50 lb. Brasileto pounded[15].
>
> To Benjamin Franklin Esqr. Philadelphia.

Evidently Daniell's letter crossed with one from Franklin which has not survived:

Kingston 29 June 1754

Gentlemen

Since my Last to you I received your Favour advising of not receiving my paper which I assure Is not oweing to any Neglect as I Never Fail Sending them and am very sorry they do not Come to your hands, for the Future shall Give more particular directions to the Captain that carries them, I am Gentlemen Your most Humble Servant

Will: Daniell

To Messrs. Franklan & Hall Phildelphia

Four months elapsed before Daniell received a partial fulfillment of his order with ten reams of demy paper, at 17s6d a ream, which were shipped to him on 28 September 1754[16].

Benjamin Franklane Esqr. Kingston 16th Novr. 1754

I Receiv'd 10 Rm. of Paper for which I am Greatly Oblig'd to you for as it Came very Opportunitely. I Beg you will be Kind Enough to Send per first Opportunity 50 Rm. More of the Like kind as Also (in persuance to my former Letters) a Sheet of Each Sort You Make, I beg leave to Remind You once More of Sending Me the Rest of my Order as I am Realy much in want, and Do Not Intend to apply anywhere Else. I am, Sir Your Most Obedient humble Servant

William Daniell

To Benjamin Franklin Esqr. Philadelphia

The only other reference to Daniell in the American Philosophical Society's collection is an undated note from Franklin to his wife:

Dame

Nota, bene. Send 50 Reams largest Demi to Mr Daniel, Printer at Jamaica.

Don't forget to enter it.

Send 3 Reams Do to Peter Timothy (etc)

Franklin was not to reap much advantage from his new business relationship with Daniell, since the latter was dead by the summer of 1755.

The exact date of his death is not known, but must have occurred in the period May-September of that year, since on 1 September 1755 an inventory of his estate was prepared in accordance with the law which required such to be made within six months of decease. Daniell evidently died intestate, since the

Inventory[17] names his widow Mary as *administratix* rather than *executrix*.

Unfortunately, the Inventory is far less full than that for Robert Baldwin[18] or some later members of the book trade in Jamaica whose Wills and Inventories tell us a good deal about their stock-in-trade[19]. The only items of booktrade interest in the Daniell inventory are

In the Stable			
Printing Office Materials &c	*£11-15s-0d*		
Sundries in Back Store	*2*	*0*	*0*
Book binding materials	*15*	*0*	*0*
In the Shop			
15 Reams of Printing Papter	*6*	*0*	*0*
4 boxes of damaged wafers		*2*	*6*
2 Mahogany counters	*1*	*15*	*0*
One writing desk	*1*	*3*	*9*
One large Mahogany Bookcase	*23*	*15*	*0*
Sundry Books	*25*	*0*	*0*
3 Reams Blue Paper	*1*	*3*	*9*

The other items in the inventory, mainly of household and personal effects, include some eight male and four female slaves. It is possible some of the male slaves were employed in the printing house as pressmen[20].

The total valuation set on Daniell's estate was £761-16s-3d *"excluding any book debts"* due to him at the time of death. Compared with the £414-18s-6d (excluding debts) that Robert Baldwin was worth in 1722, or the £164-8s-9d that the property of Daniell's contemporary and competitor, Alexander Davidson, was to be valued at in 1759, it is clear that Daniell was a relatively wealthy man who had done well from plying his trade as printer in the colony — the more so as there is some evidence that the inventory considerably undervalued his stock[21].

After his death, Daniell's business was carried on by his widow for a month or two at least. But the only surviving work from her press — the *Votes of the Assembly* for the period 23 September 1755-7 February 1756, bound in the Massachusetts Historical Society volume, shows that on 23 October 1755 the authorisation of the Speaker of the Assembly to print the Votes was transferred from Mrs. Daniell to Charles Somerset Woodham. Woodham completed the printing of the *Votes* for that session in the same types, having presumably taken charge of the business from the widow. But by 1757 official printing for the colony had passed into the hands of another printer, Curtis Brett.

Curtis Brett seems the most alive of all the rather shadowy and obscure figures in the early Jamaican book trade, for the very good reason that towards the end of his life he wrote a series of autobiographical letters addressed to his young son, in which he showed himself a stylist of no mean distinction, in the plain manner of the times. The account which follows is based in large part on these letters[22].

Curtis Brett was born in Dublin on 1 March 1720, the youngest son of a Dublin clothier who had (according to the family tradition) been compelled to take to trade because his own father's estate and fortune had been sequestrated in the Civil War. Curtis's father died young, but his son had already left home:

> A little before my father's death I had been put apprentice to a Bookseller who had also a printing apparatus in his house; of which latter I acquired some knowledge, being often in the printing office.

His master failing in business, Curtis's indentures were given up to him though he was still under age. Like many another young man, he went to London to seek his fortune.

> Hearing that Mr. Gardiner, a printer near Temple Bar, wanted a compositor, I ventured to offer him my services, with fear and trembling from a conscious deficiency in the knowledge of the (printing) art. Finding upon enquiry, I had not run away (which my young looks might well raise some suspicion of) he humanely employed me and gave me opportunity of improvement, of which I made good use, that in a little time I bought a new watch and had a convenient little purse. I was now ambitious of appearing well and keeping good company, which proved of great service to me as it made me carefully avoid all shabby, lazy, idle, disorderly fellows, and this recommended me to the notice of many persons of credit. I found myself in as happy a situation as anyone in my station of life.

From Mr. Gardner, Curtis Brett moved into the employment of William Strahan, in whose Printing Office in Wine Office Court he remained from 1743 to 1748. However, thinking of going into the plantations to seek his fortune, he was tempted by an offer from a gentleman going to Jamaica to join him as a storekeeper. Accordingly, in October 1748 he left London for the West Indies.

With his impressions of Jamaica, and his account of his early life there, we are not here concerned. Having lost everything in some unlucky business ventures, he became overseer on a sugar estate, but finding the work distasteful soon quit it. After some months clerking in Kingston, Brett moved to St. Jago, where he entered the counting house of Archibald Sinclair, a merchant of the town.

At that time, 1753-54, there was very considerable controversy over the future of St. Jago de la Vega as the island's capital. The captains of shipping arriving at Port Royal or at the Kingston wharves, the Kingston merchants and the planters in the east, all resented the need to make the hot and dusty journey across the St. Catherine plain to conduct their legal and administrative business in St. Jago. Under Governor Knowles an Act for the removal of the capital and the various public offices to Kingston was passed, despite bitter opposition from the St. Jago lobby. Petitions to England eventually resulted in the disallowance of the Act. But while the matter was in dispute in Jamaica, the St. Jago lobby was hampered severely by the fact that the only printers were in Kingston, and naturally supported the Kingston faction in their papers. Curtis Brett's presence in St. Jago at the right time was to make his fortune.

Impressed by Brett's appearance, and learning of his background as a printer, Judge Askew suggested to Brett that he should set up as a printer in St. Jago. Askew, Sir Charles Price and other Spanish Town gentlemen gave their support to the venture. In his new business Brett was assisted by Charles White, a former secretary in the government of the island (a creole, and not a trained printer).

The method adopted to enable Brett to acquire capital, and to obtain the necessary equipment, was very simple. Among the advertisements in Daniell's *Jamaica Courant* for 29 June 1754 were subscription proposals for a new edition of the *Laws of Jamaica*. This was to be priced at four pistoles[23] (two to be paid on subscription, the other two on delivery of the book) and would go to press as soon as two hundred subscriptions were filled. Price (who was organising the venture) had persuaded the Governor, the Council and the Assembly to support the work, and was guaranteeing the refund of subscriptions should the work not go ahead as planned. Brett and White, who were placed in charge of production, had to take no risks; a profitable return for their labour was guaranteed.

In June 1755 Brett embarked on a passage to London, taking the copy for the *Laws* with him, and using his time on board ship to get it ready for the press. On arrival in August 1755, he handed the work over to his old employer William Strahan, to have printed and bound. While this was being done, Brett himself was busy in collecting together all the equipment and supplier for his new printing office, and in seeking out capable journeymen printers willing to return with him to Jamaica.

At the beginning of March 1756, Brett sailed on his return trip to Jamaica, taking on board the *Rose* with him the completed edition of *The Laws of Jamaica* plus his newly purchased equipment. He evidently had this shipped in very good order, since within eight days of the vessel's docking on 30 April, he had transported his press, types and enough paper across to St. Jago to have the printing office set up and sufficiently organised to publish the first issue of a new paper, *The St. Jago Intelligencer*, on 8th May 1756.

As with Daniell's *Jamaica Courant* — which probably ceased publication on Daniell's death — there survive insufficient copies of the *St. Jago Intelligencer* for us to be able to discuss its editorial policies[24]. The only known surviving issue of this weekly paper as produced by Brett — no. 54 of Saturday, 15th May 1757 — is a folio on Pot paper, with three columns per page. The first page is devoted almost entirely to a cure for rabies taken from a pamphlet recently published in London; at the foot of page one and for a column and a half of page two, foreign and British news is given. Jamaican affairs then occupy half a column, and the rest of the paper is given over to advertisements for property, runaways, goods and services of exactly the same kind as found in Daniell's *Courant*.

The surviving issue is noticeably well printed and laid out, though in several of the advertisements one notices the use of italic capitals where the compositor had run short of roman sorts in the long primer text types — a typical stratagem to which most colonial printers had to resort. It includes several advertisements and announcements of interest: advertising, we learn, costs five shillings per week (or 15s per month) for advertisements "of a moderate length". Because some Kingston subscribers have complained that their advertisements have not been inserted in time

> This therefore is to give Notice, that to prevent miscarriages in future, a Boy will be sent down every Thursday morning to Mr. Forsyth[25] to receive such Advertisements as we shall be favoured with, and which shall be punctually inserted.

Elsewhere are details of subscription rates: 30s per annum in Spanish Town, and two pistoles post free to country subscribers. The country subscribers are reminded that payment has to be *in advance*, those who have not yet paid for the year ending June 1757 are requested to do so promptly, otherwise they can no longer be sent the paper. This latter advertisement is almost the same in every respect as those which were to appear from time to time in all West Indian papers until well into the nineteenth century.

This same issue of the *St. Jago Intelligencer* contains details of two other publications of Brett's. One was in his capacity as Printer to the Assembly (an office to which he had succeeded Daniell's executors in 1756): The *Articles of War* promulgated in consequence of the outbreak of the Seven Year's War. The other was described as

> In the press and shortly to be published, an address of some of the freeholders and inhabitants of the parich of St. A***, to P-p P-k, Esq; for the benefit of a poor author, who having nothing to subsist on but his honest labour and remarkable veracity, is in a starving condition, and therefore hopes the public will not grumble at the price of 6s3d each.

St. A*** was the Parish of St. Andrew, which Philip Pinnock represented in the Assembly. Whether the pamphlet was actually published (or the announcement was merely satirical) is uncertain; at this distance in time it is impossible to judge the who/what/why of the matter.

Very little of the printing done by Curtis Brett at Spanish Town survives. The Massachusetts Historical Society's volume of the *Votes of the Assembly* printed by Daniell includes one imperfect copy from the press of Curtis Brett & Co., for a session which started 27 September 1757. Brett almost certainly printed his own book almanac, *An almanack and register for Jamaica*, which was distributed by James Forsyth in Kingston: then as later a Kingston distributor for Spanish Town printing was a necessity[26]. Only one other work from Brett's press is known to have survived: *An Enquiry concerning the Trade, Commerce and Policy of Jamaica relative to the scarcity of Money . . . to which is added a Scheme for establishing a Public Bank* (1757). Apparently written by Brett's partner Charles White, it is a crown quarto of twelve sheets, well printed in the same mixture of Caslon and good Dutch romans that characterise the *St. Jago Intelligencer*[27].

Brett had good reason for the complacency with which he described his printing activities in his letters to his son:

> *The St. Jago Intelligencer* . . . was received with very good general applause and immediately a good number of gentlemen subscribed to it . . . so that our paper answered very well. Our volume of Laws went off pretty fast at a doubloon each . . . and from that time to this, I have never, thanks to the Almighty, been in want of money.

So successful, in fact was Brett that in 1761 "finding myself worth about £5000, and having had the marrow of the printing business" he decided to quit his old trade and turn merchant once more. His letters, though a fascinating account of his subsequent vicissitudes in Jamaica, in New York and in London before he finally retired to Chester, contain no further references to printing, nor any indication of how he disposed of his business in St. Jago. It is to be presumed that he was bought out by his old partner Charles White, since White was named Printer to the Assembly in Brett's place, together with one Matthew Moss. By 1768 the St. Jago printing office was in the hands of John Lowry and Robert Sherlock, who had evidently purchased White's share in the business[28]. They were both capable and expansionist businessmen: Sherlock in particular being associated with the spread of the business to Jamaica's third centre of printing, Montego Bay, where from 1773 onwards until the 1860s *The Cornwall Chronicle* was to be an important newspaper. In their capable hands printing continued to flourish at Spanish Town, while the *Intelligencer* (later renamed the *St. Jago de la Vega Gazette*) was to last into the 1840s.

William Daniell and Curtis Brett were not great printers. They introduced no advances in the art, nor did they print any work of lasting value or importance. Nevertheless, the publications for which they were responsible show them to have been good honest craftsmen, typical of the English provincial printers at a time when British workmanship was of very high quality. Translated from Britain to an exotic setting, their solid, no nonsense typography was to set a worthy standard for later Jamaican printers to emulate.

NOTES

1. The earliest issue traced (now in the Public Records Office) is no. 295 of Saturday, 29 June 1754. Although the relevant passage in Isaiah Thomas's History of Printing in America (2nd ed. Worcester, 1874) suggests that it was a continuation of the Baldwin's *Weekly Jamaica Courant* (founded 1718), I do not believe this to be the case. The latest extant issue (in the Fulham Papers in Lambeth Palace Library) of the *Weekly Jamaica Courant* is a damaged copy for 7 June 1738; by 1745 the Baldwin brothers were publishing *The Jamaica Gazette* which later passed into the control of Alexander Davidson, a competitor of Daniell's in Kingston.
2. Cf. Roderick Cave "The early printers of Grand Turk" *Papers of the Bibliographical Society of America*, v. 70, 1976, pp. 519-28.
3. In 1809, when the population of the island had doubled, the semi-official *St. Jago de la Vega Gazette* circulated 1000 copies of each issue. At the other end of the scale, however, many West Indian papers had less than one hundred subscribers.
4. Only those in the Jamaica despatches in the Public Records Office, London, have been traced.
5. Jamaican currency; £1 Jamaican equalled 13s4d sterling. (All figures quoted are in Jamaican currency).
6. Quoted by Frank Cundall, *The press and printers of Jamaica to 1820* (Worcester, 1916) pp. 8-9).

7. Shelfmark E.187-L.
8. The only known copies are in the John Carter Brown Library.
9. The only known copy is of the 1734 *Almanack*, formerly in the West India Reference Library of the Institute of Jamaica.
10. In the West India Reference Library, Institute of Jamaica.
11. Only known copy in the Library of the American Antiquarian Society.
12. Daniell advertised it in the *Courant* of 29 June 1754.
13. By that time he had moved from Harbour Street to new premises "in King Street, near the Post Office"..
14. Not found. The texts of these letters are quoted from *The Papers of Benjamin Franklin* ed. by Leonard Labaree *et al*, vol. 5 (New Haven, 1962).
15. Presumably the potash was required to make lye, and the braziletto wood for red writing ink, to serve Daniell's business as stationery.
16. George S. Eddy, *Account books kept by Benjamin Franklin: Ledger 'D'* 1739-1747 (New York, 1929) pp. 51-2 and 72.
17. Jamaica Archives, Inventories liber 35 fol. 204 r-v.
18. Jamaica Archives, Inventories liber 12 fol. 131 v. Relevant portions have been published; *Papers of the Bibliographical Society of America*, v. 69, 1975, pp. 560-565.
19. Roderick Cave, *A Digest of Wills and Inventories of Members of the Jamaican Book Trade*; preliminary draft text. Mona, 1976 (Working Papers on West Indian Printing, no. 18).
20. Cf. Roderick Cave, "The use of slave labour in West Indian Printing Houses", *The Library*, 5th series v. 30 no. 3, 1975, pp. 241-3.
21. The paper shipped by Franklin to Daniell at 17s6d a ream is valued at only 8s0d a ream in the inventory. Similarly the 3 reams of blue paper at £1-3s-9d in Daniell's inventory is to be compared with the 1 ream at £1-17s-6d in that of Baldwin; while Daniell's "Printing Office Materials &c" at £11-15s-0d is remarkably low beside the £42-10s-0d which was fetched by Alexander Davidson's 'Printing press and materials sold at public vendue' in Kingston in 1759.
22. The West India Reference Library, Institute of Jamaica MSTIO is a modern transcription (and in part summary) of the letters, presented some years ago by one of Brett's descendants, Mrs. Helen Brett Lloyd of Toronto. Despite her help (which it is my pleasure to acknowledge) I have been unable to trace the present whereabouts of the original letters from which the transcription was made.
23. One pistole was at that time worth 25s0d (Jamaican currency). Four pistoles made one doubloon.
24. Apart from no. 54 (now in the West India Reference Library, Institute of Jamaica) the only issue traced is that for 16 April 1768, in the Library of the American Antiquarian Society.
25. James Forsyth was a Kingston bookseller of the period.
26. The only surviving copy known is the issue for 1760, now in the John Carter Brown Library. The printer's name is not given, but the typographical evidence suggests that it was from Brett's press.
27. The surviving copy is now in the West India Reference Library, Institute of Jamaica.
28. White's inventory (Jamaica Archives, Inventories liber 55, folio 107 r) of 8 October 1774 includes details of bonds for £284 issued by Lowry & Sherlock, and payable to White. Lowry's inventory also contained references to White.

XIV
THE PLANTOCRACY'S PASSION FOR *PORCUPINE*

ALTHOUGH previous writers[1] on William Cobbett have noted that *Porcupine's works* (London, 1801) includes a number of subscribers in Jamaica in the list of names prefixed to volume one, there has been no attempt to explain why the sales were so large there. Admittedly, the island was at the height of its prosperity at the turn of the eighteenth and nineteenth centuries. Yet for a colony with some thirty thousand white inhabitants to subscribe to 170[2] copies of a book of which only 202 were subscribed in Britain shows that the popularity of *Porcupine* with the planters was very considerable.

The purpose of this note is to describe how the planter's latent interest was serviced, rather than to explore why *Porcupine* appealed. Much more research on the reading trends of the planter class is necessary before speculation is profitable. The immediate simple explanation, that Cobbett's aggressive Englishness was likely to be popular in British America, is clearly inadequate since subscriptions from Canada, New Brunswick, and Nova Scotia were only forty-eight in number, and there were only two[3] from the eastern Caribbean.

While he was still in the United States, Cobbett had established business relations with the Kingston firm of Stevenson Aikman & Smith.[4] Several issues of their newspaper *The Diary and Kingston daily advertiser*[5] for June 1799 included Cobbett's subscription proposals for 'a new, entire and neat edition of Porcupine's Works' dated from Philadelphia 1 May 1799. I suspect that this advertisement, like most similar subscription proposals at the time, would also have appeared in the three weekly county papers of Jamaica:

[1] Cf. M. L. Pearl, *William Cobbett; a bibliographical account of his life and times*, Oxford 1953, and Pierce W. Gaines, *William Cobbett and the United States 1792–1835; a bibliography*, Worcester, Mass., 1971.

[2] In fact 172 copies were subscribed through the Jamaican booksellers, but two were for other islands.

[3] Sir John Alleyne, Bt. in Barbados, and Charles Grant in Martinique.

[4] Thomas Stevenson had been manager of William Aikman's book and stationery store in Kingston in 1784; by 1795 he was in partnership with Andrew Aikman who edited their paper *The diary and Kingston daily advertiser* till 1802, when ill health compelled him to leave Jamaica. Robert Smith, who had joined the partnership in the late 1790s, thereafter continued with Stevenson as Stevenson & Smith till 1808 when Stevenson retired and the style of the firm became Smith & Kinnear.

[5] Set in the West India Reference Library, Institute of Jamaica.

Alexander Aikman's Kingston *Royal gazette*, Lewis and Lunan's *St. Jago de la Vega gazette*, and the *Cornwall chronicle* published by James Fannin at Montego Bay (see above pp. 194, 195).

Cobbett's advertisement was for the American edition of his works, due for publication in the United States in August 1799, and about December in Britain, at a price (to subscribers) of $20 and four and a half guineas respectively. Of the five agents named to receive subscriptions, only Stevenson Aikman & Smith were outside the British Isles. No price in Jamaican currency was quoted, nor a date of delivery, though intending subscribers no doubt presumed there would be a local mark-up and that their copies would come directly from Philadelphia rather than Britain.

As a result of Dr. Benjamin Rush's legal action against Cobbett, the American edition was seized and never reached the subscribers. No doubt the Rush–Cobbett controversy increased Jamaican interest: Cobbett's Account Book 1796–1800[6] has, at folio 18, a statement of his sales to the island:

1800 Stevenson Aikman & Smith Jamaica

March 15	To 25 Suvarow's Campaigns[7] @ 2·50	62·50	
	100 Rush Lights No. 1	25·00	
	100 Rush Lights No. 2	25·00	
31	100 Rush Lights No. 3	25·00	
April 16	100 Rush Lights No. 4[8]	25·00	
		162·50	
	Commission 25 per cent	40·62½	
			121·87½

By February 1802, the Kingston booksellers had received their copies of the London edition of *Porcupine's works*, and were advertising the twelve volumes at £9. 6*s*. 8*d*. in boards or £12 bound and gilt.[9] The lists of subscribers in volume one includes 111 names for Jamaica. Headed by the Earl of Balcarres, the Lieutenant-Governor, and by Admiral Sir Hyde Parker (the Commander-in-Chief, Jamaica station), the list is virtually a roll-call of the members of the House of Assembly and the other important planters in the island. Only two subscribed for more than single copies, apart from the booksellers. Stevenson Aikman & Smith took forty-five copies and Meyer & Schutze[10] four copies; the single copy subscribed by James Fannin was probably for himself.

[6] Now in the American Antiquarian Society Library. My thanks are due to the society for a Fred Harris Daniels Fellowship which enabled me to consult this and other West Indiana in their collections.

[7] Gaines no. 50.

[8] These four issues are Gaines no. 51a, 52a, 53a, and 54a respectively.

[9] Jamaican currency, the sterling equivalents being approximately £6. 5*s*. and £8 respectively.

[10] Active as booksellers in King Street, Kingston, *c*. 1798–*c*. 1802. Henry Meyer was in business alone in 1796; by August 1804 S. W. Schutze was advertising as a bookbinder in Church Street, Kingston.

Unfortunately, little use can be made of the list of Jamaican subscribers as published, since it is incomplete. In what should have been (and was not) an apologetic advertisement in the *Royal gazette*, 6 February 1802, Stevenson Aikman & Smith announced the arrival of *Porcupine* and added 'subscribers thereto are requested to come forward early, and claim their copies. As we have mislaid the subscription List, for the present, we are unable to deliver the Books with that correctness we would wish.'

Perhaps the long delay in publication had caused Jamaican interest to wane. Whether all the subscribers on this supplementary list came forward to claim their copies is uncertain. But the valuation of £4 attached to the set bought by Jonathan Nevett Sherlock, in an inventory[11] which does not otherwise seem to undervalue his estate, suggests that by the Spring of 1803 there was no great demand for *Porcupine*.

[11] Jamaica Archives, Inventories, liber 99, fol. 111r, the inventory is dated 20 March 1803. Sherlock had been printer of the *Royal gazette* for Alexander Aikman before his death about 20 October 1802.

XV
GOOD NEWS FROM ROMANS

Having come across "Romans Charts of the Gulph and Passage" frequently in the advertisements and stock records of booksellers in the West Indies of the 1780s[1] an announcement signed by Bernard Romans in the Montego Bay newspaper *The Cornwall Chronicle* of 27 March 1784 [2] naturally caught my eye. That the surveyor and hydrographer – of whom I knew very little – had been resident in Jamaica came as a surprise; a surprise deepened by reference to *DNB*. According to the account of his life given there, he was never in Jamaica: having abandoned his post as Botanist of West Florida to join the American revolutionary forces in 1775, and subsequently taking part in the capture of Ticonderoga and later serving as a military engineer, *DNB* stated that in 1779 he was captured (probably at Stoney Point on the Hudson), taken as a prisoner to England, and when peace came worked there as an engineer until 1784 when he embarked on a vessel bound for New York, taking a large sum of money with him. No more is heard of him, and he was presumed to have been murdered while on board.

Turning to *DAB* I found a very different account, based in part upon a petition for a pension [3] made by his widow (Elizabeth Whiting, to whom Romans had originally been introduced by Washington) as late as 1846. By this account – prepared sixty years after the event and "according to her best recollection" – in 1780, about eighteen months after their marriage Romans had been ordered to join the Southern Continental Army in South Carolina, and had taken passage from New London or New Haven. The vessel being captured, he was taken prisoner to Montego Bay in Jamaica and held there until 1783. Mrs Romans's statement [4] went on that the British authorities had refused to include him in an exchange of prisoners of war "on account of his . . . ability to do so much injury to the British interests" and continued

> her said husband, as she was informed and believes, was shipped by the British authorities under the pretext of sending him thence to some port in the United States, and he was said to have died on his passage, though from circumstances attending his demise his friends had good reason to believe him to have been wilfully murdered.

This whetted my interest. Subsequent investigation of Romans's own works[5] and of biographical and bibliographical studies[6] have not turned up any more information on Romans in Jamaica, and suggest that his announcement in *The Cornwall Chronicle* remains unknown.

E. Lee Philips described Romans as

> a universal genius . . . a botanist, engineer, mathematician, artist, surveyor, engraver, writer, cartographer, linguist, soldier, seaman, and he possessed many other talents, any one of which would have given distinction.[7]

Though pitching it strongly, this was not untrue as a description of the various skills this remarkable man possessed. Nevertheless, as a later writer observed, the available records also show that

> he was quarrelsome, impatient, and quick to take offence; almost without exception, he had difficulty in getting along with others. Perhaps because of this or possibly impelled by an insatiable wanderlust he went from one job to another, ever heeding the beat of distant drums. Yet, throughout, he demonstrated a singleness of purpose . . . His maps, books, and other publications . . . remain a monument to his abilities and determination.[8]

Some of these characteristics are evident in his *Cornwall Chronicle* piece. We may never know whether it was on his voyage from Montego Bay in May 1784 that he died in suspicious circumstances, but two months earlier he was alive, writing in his characteristic acerbic style, and making plans for the future.

Montego Bay, March 27, 1784

I intend to leave this island in May next. B. Romans.[9]

To the Public

> I propose to visit Europe soon, where I shall republish all my geographical works, particularly my large hydrographic surveys from the East end of Hispaniola to the West of Mississippi.[10]
>
> It is now more than ten years ago when I thought I had silenced the tongue of Malice, with respect to this performance, the merit of which was then, by the true spirit of Envy, given to others. During my having the work at press every possible method was used to hurt the sale; pamphlets were printed that were stiled "Surveys of the Coast." Even Mrs Woolhead's press,[11] in Kingston, brought forth an essay of this kind, ascribed to a person who was never on the coast until two or three years after I was there last, and even he has disclaimed all knowledge of it.[12] Since its first journey abroad, it shews itself in spurious and mutilated editions; erroneous enough; additions that have no existence, and alterations that are "All in the Wrong". The intended publication will be extremely neat, and present itself with so many, and such great additions, now lying unpublished, as will make the most sceptical head, or the most detracting heart, acknowledge that none but he that was in its execution could produce it. It is a darling work of mine; and if Heaven saves my life, I will establish it. I am so confident of its truth and value, that I hesitate not to foretell positively, that it will never mislead anyone who follows it with scrupulous attention, nor do I doubt that future friends of true nautical

science will acknowledge it, "opus nec ignis, nec poterit ferum, nec edax abolere vetustas" it will remain a goodly part of my "monumentum – Ære perennius."

Those gentlemen who wish to possess themselves of this new edition, will do me a favour in acquainting me with their intentions by letter, post paid, or verbally, that I may be enabled to judge how many may be wanted in this island.[13] I do not mean this to promote a subscription, much less a bait hove out for advances.[14]

I know not how it happens, but Detraction takes great pains in persecuting me, and that with matters of which the babe of a day is not more innocent than I am. A man frequently exposes himself to become the sport of fools whom his heart despises; but a recent affair thrust upon me, with the most indecent abuse, will not suffer me to remain silent under the abominable falsehoods that have been propagated: were the libels true, I would consider myself guilty of the most atrocious felony.

Two reports, and, thank Heaven, the license of invention has not coined a greater number! have been industriously propagated. I hear very often, "that I have obtained, and continue to receive, a pension from his Britannic Majesty." The case is thus, in 1774 an allowance was granted me by his Majesty on the following terms, as far as I can recollect: "Fifty pounds, as an allowance to B. R. for his useful discoveries in botany and physic." The letter of notice, under the hands of Edmund Rush Wegg, Esq. Attorney General for West Florida, lies now with Mrs Romans, among other papers of value. This did not come to hand till near two years were due; and knowing that, in consequence, 100 £ must necessarily issue from the Treasury, before my sincere thanks and disinterested resignation could reach England, I drew for the sum, imagining it was well for me to enjoy that benefit, as to let it lay in other hands, because I doubted much its return to the spring from whence it flowed; but with my bill handsomely apologized, and declined all further receipt, the complexion of the times convincing me that I could no longer receive it, consonant to the feelings of an honest mind; yet 50 £ sterling per ann. makes a man lead a life of great comfort in the country where I resided, and with such an introduction as this, I might have aspired at very honourable or lucrative employments at the beginning of the war. Let the records of Britain speak for me! Let my most inveterate envier lay his hand to his heart, and recollect whether he was ever capable of so candid a conduct in his life![15]

But an obscure person, lately arrived, has told a tale I have just heard, for the first time, i.e. "the Marine Society has employed me to MAKE DRAUGHTS," as it is elegantly expressed; "I received their money, and gave my labours to others." Was I a man fond of ridicule, I would here find a noble field for exertion. Truly that excellent institution would do themselves much honour by paying a man, with 50 £ New-York currency, for a dozen years hard labour, deep study, exposure of constitution of the severest kind, with some other et ceteras! The truth is, that, on my first arrival at New-York, I presented the Society with my manuscript;[16] an examining Committee was appointed, to whom I produced my field work and journals; it happened to meet their approbation so much, that a resolve passed for giving me 50 £ out of their Treasury, for which I gave my bond, with condition, that, if I really published the work, the bond should be returned. This favour had large subscriptions and advances joined to it, and I was unanimously elected an honorary member of the Society. The publication took place, and I received my indemnification, near ten years ago, from Mr Anthony Griffiths, Secretary to the Society; it remaining with the letter above mentioned prevents my bringing it in proof; but to my comfort, all the world knows the publication, and the father of that useful society is now here; he was kind enough to charge himself with copies for two men of first character in Europe; if any person of worth chuse they may hear him vouch it. This gentleman may not recollect the matter of the money, but he well knows the first birth of the production: without him the useful corporation here mentioned, would not have been a promoter of science, nor shone foremost as a most illustrious dispensor of charity; it would not have adorned its front with so many brilliant names, nor would it have enjoyed any funds, but have remained an obscure mean club; and by the bye, I would wish my reporter to examine his mind whether he cannot bring to memory a set of beings who have had cunning enough to abuse, even this respectable institution, by meanly contriving to filch a living out of it, and yet wish to have it believed, that they are of consequence enough to be known by the frequenters of every polite circle – To explain why I did not oppose sudden mean abuse, with violence, would subject me to be ridiculed for sheltering myself behind stale precepts of morality. My heart is conscious that those who know me well, in several parts of the world, need no testimony of my readiness when the public calls for my service – I hope I will meet indulgence from the unprejudiced for this length of words. I know not that I have ever wilfully hurt any one in any respect: if there be any who have heard, or found, that I have fallen into any sallies of indiscretion, and are hurt by it, I crave their pardon.

NOTES

1. e.g. "Roman's Draughts of the Gulph & Windward Passage, with books of directions," advertised by William Aikman in the *Supplement to the* [Jamaica] *Royal Gazette* 5 April 1783; "7 Romans Charts of the Gulph and Passage" listed in the Inventory of Aikman's estate, valued at 19s. 6d. each (Jamaica Archives, Inventories, liber 69 ff. 9–22); "Roman's Gulf & Windward Passage, with Directions" offered for sale by John Wells of Nassau (*Bahama Gazette*, 30 July 1785).
2. Set in Avon County Reference Library, Bristol. I am indebted to Michael Gibson for photocopies of Romans's Announcement in this issue, and that of 10 April 1784.
3. Made under the Act of Congress passed in 1832, which granted pensions to widows of Revolutionary soldiers and officers. Her claim was rejected on the grounds that Romans's service though meritorious had not been military in nature.
4. It is printed in full in P. Lee Phillips, *Notes on the Life and Work of Bernard Romans* (Deland, 1924) pp. 68–70.
5. Particularly his *A Concise Natural History of East and West Florida* (New York, the Author, 1775) which contains 'by Way of Appendix' those directions to navigators for the coast of Florida and for the Gulf and Windward passages to which Romans refers in his advertisment.
6. P. Lee Phillips, *op. cit.*, and the facsimile reprint of the 1924 edition edited with an introduction by John D. Ware (Gainesville, 1975).
7. P. Lee Phillips, *op. cit.*, p. 71.
8. John D. Ware, in the 1975 reprint of Phillips, pp. lxxxvi–lxxxvii.
9. This was a formal advertisement required of all those leaving Jamaica, to forewarn creditors and others who might have claims on persons leaving.

10. i.e. the work issued to the public 'by Way of Appendix' to his *Concise Natural History of East and West Florida* (1775).
11. Ann Woolhead succeeded to the printing business of her husband Thomas Woolhead (active as a printer in Kingston from about 1756) on the latter's death in 1778, running it until her own death in 1782 when it passed to John Thomas William Bennett. No trace has been found of her "essay of this kind" which is unknown to Jamaican bibliographers.
12. Unless this reference is to George Gauld, who had also been employed in surveying the Florida coasts, and with whom Romans had a squabble about priority of work, I cannot identify the surveyor who is meant.
13. There had been only one Jamaican subscriber (Richard Martin of Rio Bueno) out of the 392 taking copies of his *Concise Natural History* . . . in 1775, but in view of the circumstances of the American Revolution it is not surprising that there should have been no more.
14. A good many subscription proposals were published in the last quarter of the seventeenth century in Jamaica (cf. Appendix 2 to my 'Printing in Eighteenth Century Jamaica' elsewhere in this volume – pp. 117–24). From the number of proposals for books which seem never to have been published, I suspect that some of these were indeed 'bait hove out for advances'.
    The text of Romans's notice, as reprinted in the *Cornwall Chronicle* of 10 April 1784 ends at this point. Whether Romans was persuaded by friends that the later sections were superfluous or he was unwilling to pay the printer's charges for so long an advertisment, or the printer himself needed the space for more pressing matter I cannot judge.
15. Governor Chester of West Florida had recommended Romans's appointment as provincial botanist in 1772, and this was approved by the Secretary of State, Lord Dartmouth, in December of that year. For the fiscal year 1773–4, the allowance of £50 was included in the budget, but as he stated Romans had already left West Florida by that time. Although he was himself satisfied by his conduct, this was by no means the view taken in Whitehall; cf. Ware's Introduction to Phillips, *op. cit.*, p. lv.
16. i.e. *A Concise Natural History* . . . Romans was admitted to membership of the Marine Society of New York on 2 August 1773.

XVI
EARLY CIRCULATING LIBRARIES IN JAMAICA

"In the West-Indies, every gentleman almost takes out his own library with him; and what books may be wanted are generally sold in the stores of merchants, who import them from England with other goods, although the capital of each of the islands has one person who calls himself a bookseller, keeps a small reading-Library, binds, deals in stationery, and keeps a few books, such as he judges are most in demand, which he sells at an advance of 70 1. and 100 1. *per cent.*"

In these few lines, appended to Henry Lemoine's article on 'Printing and bookselling in America' which he contributed to the November 1796 issue of the *Gentleman's Magazine,*[1] the West Indian book trade and West Indian libraries are dismissed in a characteristic way. The economic decline of the sugar colonies from the 1830s until well into the present century, and the social changes which came about with the decline of the planter class in the islands, have tended to conceal the importance that the Caribbean colonies once had as a market for English publishing.[2] Yet, as Giles Barber has shown in his elegant analysis of the Customs House records,[3] between 1701 and 1780 the West Indian colonies imported books to a value of 53,580 pounds from Britain.

Of this total, Jamaica received books valued at 22,849 pounds, a figure which should be compared with the imports into the colonies of New York (24,986 pounds) and Pennsylvania (18,611 pounds) during the same period. Viewed differently, on the basis of the Customs House valuation of books at 4 pounds per hundredweight, over two hundred and eighty five tons were taken to Jamaica – which in the immortal phrase of V. S. Naipaul's *The Mystic Masseur,* is a lot of book.

We cannot tell what proportion of these books was purchased by local booksellers for stock or taken on consignment, how much was of books printed in London for the Jamaican market (like the edition of *The Laws of Jamaica* which the Spanish town printer-stationer Curtis Brett had printed for him by William Strahan in 1756), how much was of gentlemen taking out their own libraries with them, or whether any of the books found their way into circulating libraries. Surviving documentation both in Britain and Jamaica is very scanty: apart from the fact that there had been a parish library in Port Royal before 1721,[4] and that another parochial library was sent out to the island in 1724,[5] there appears to be no extant information on Jamaican libraries before the last twenty years of the eighteenth century. The fate of these two hundred and eighty five tons is likely to remain a mystery.

For the period from 1779 onwards, however, more information is available, and a valuable pioneering study by Hazel Bennett[6] chronicled the development of private and subscription libraries in the island for the century to 1879 when the Institute of Jamaica was founded, and a new phase in library development in Jamaica began.

Though printing was introduced into the colony as early as 1718, very few issues of the island's newspapers before 1779 now survive, and those which survive are widely dispersed. Even for the nineteenth century earthquake, hurricane, fire, termites and neglect have taken such a toll that several newspapers are known only from contemporary references, and many more survive in a few scattered issues. In the course of work on printing in Jamaica the present writer has scanned almost all surviving papers he could trace,[7] and the notes which follow on circulating libraries will serve to amplify Mrs Bennett's account.

The clientele of the libraries which existed in Jamaica for the sixty-year period from 1779 onwards was infinitely more different from the users of the Jamaica Library Service today, than the difference between the public for libraries in Philadelphia or Plymouth in 1779 and two hundred years later. Jamaica society of the kind which existed then – the plantocracy – was to disappear completely together with the economy of sugar and slavery which supported it. The users of the early Jamaican libraries were the planters and their families; the merchants, lawyers, doctors and tradesmen who plied their libing in Kingston and half-a dozen smaller towns in the island. Most of them, like the military and naval personnel based in the colony, would – even if born in Jamaica – have regarded themselves as English,[8] retaining an expatriate mentality, and considering their sojourn in Jamaica as temporary. It was a shifting, restless society, and the unhealthiness of the island for the European-born made it still more transient. Those who could afford it left the colony; for those lower in the scale – the shopmen, clerks, plantation overseers – there was no such solution. The majority of these were Scots; sometimes men of considerable culture and education, and one may speculate that they formed part of the clientele of the libraries insofar as their humble earnings permitted; and their part in forming the respect of the emerging *Jamaican* society for education and books was not slight. In the early years of the nineteenth century without doubt specifically Jamaican elements appeared as users of libraries; the free men of colour and the numerically small but significant Jewish population of the island.

The structure of Jamaican society – a plantation economy based on sugar and coffee – produced difficulties for the merchant, which affected the bookseller and circulating library proprietor as severely as other tradesmen. Quite apart from the chronic shortage of coin in the island, the nature of the planting business demanded that merchants should give long credit. The prosperous owner of the semi-official *Royal Gazette* could in 1821 mention that some who took his paper were two, three, even four years in arrears, and mildly say subscribers 'are once more reminded of the propriety of liquidating' their debts,[9] but for many tradesmen such a burden of unsettled accounts was disastrous. One suspects several of the circulating libraries listed below failed to survive for this reason.

Though not the capital of the colony, Kingston was the mercantile centre and by far the most populous town in the island. Its position, convenient for access both to the capital of St. Jago de la Vega (Spanish Town) and the naval base of Port Royal, had made it the natural choice for the Caribbean's first printer to set up shop there in 1718. For similar reasons what was probably the first circulating library in Jamaica was established there in 1779. Its proprietor, William Aikman (a Scot from Bo'ness who had previously been a bookseller and binder in Annapolis, Maryland) had moved to Jamaica in 1775, setting up as a bookseller and stationer in fashionable King Street.

The first reference to his circulating library appears in *The Jamaica Mercury* 26 June 1779,[10] in which he advertised that

> a catalogue of the additions he has made to his *Circulating Library* will be delivered to his subscribers on Monday the 12th of July.

No doubt Aikman had started his library before he commenced publication of *The Jamaica Mercury* on 1 May 1779, but it was not to prove a successful adjunct to his thriving business as the island's chief bookseller and stationer. In the *Mercury* supplement of 26 February 1780 appeared the following:

> To the Friends of Polite Literature.
> William Aikman, from the small number of subscribers to his Circulating Library, finds, that the income arising from it, is not adequate to the necessary expense of importing such a number of NEW BOOKS, as to keep the LIBRARY on a respectable footing, is sorry he shall be under the necessity of depriving such Ladies and Gentlemen, as would wish to peruse the best *English* Authors at a moderate expense, of that satisfac-

> tion, by dropping the Library and disposing of the books early in 1781; – till which time it will be open, for the accommodation of those Gentlemen and Ladies who wish to avail themselves of the convenience of reading upon easy terms.

Although this advertisement was repeated in the *Mercury* several times during 1780, there were insufficient 'Friends of Polite Literature' (or insufficiently convinced of the easiness of the terms) to persuade Aikman to change his plans, and the stock of his library was eventually dispersed by auction on 6th and 7th November 1781.

A second venture followed rapidly at the chief settlement on the island's north shore at Montego Bay. The town's printer and bookseller, James Fannin, was in the 1780s one of the island's more enterprising and adventurous tradesmen, publishing (for example) his own editions of *Yorick's Letters to Eliza* and of Goethe's *The Sorrows of Young Werther,* pirated from London editions. By June 1784 he had established the 'St. James's Circulating Library', and in his newspaper *The Cornwall Chronicle* of 18 June of that year[11] he advised subscribers of revised conditions of membership:

1. Every subscriber to pay two guineas[12] per annum in advance, to have two books at a time, which they may change once a day.
2. Subscribers to give in their names and places of abode, and if required, the value of the books they take away; and not to lend any of the books, on penalty of forfeiting their subscription.
3. As there will be at all times many books in circulation subscribers to prevent disappointment or delay, are to send a list of ten or twelve numbers of such books as they want, thus: 1, 30, 57, 612, 721
4. No subscriber to have more than one book beyond a fortnight, on their being obliged to keep and pay for the same; if belonging to a set, to pay for the whole.
5. If any book is wrote in, or the leaf of a book is torn or damaged, while in the custody of a subscriber, that book, or if it should belong to a set, the set of books to be paid for.
6. Subscribers residing at a distance from the Bay, or in the parishes of Trelawny and Hanover, may be supplied with a large quantity of books, on paying *five pounds,* they sending for, and returning the books to the LIBRARY.

Catalogues five shillings each.

> N.B. The LIBRARY will be open from eight in the morning, till six in the evening.

Like William Aikman before him, Fannin found that there was little or no profit in his circulating library, and on 4 June 1785 (the year's subscription period being complete) he advertised that he was selling off the stock. He continued a successful printing bookselling and stationery business in Montego Bay into the nineteenth century, but neither he nor his successors in the *Cornwall Chronicle* office seem to have dabbled in the circulating library business again.

Only slight evidence survives for later ventures in this field at Montego Bay: a single advertisement in the *Cornwall Chronicle* of 23 February 1816[13] reveals that Asa W. Wilder was augmenting his circulating library with

> over 700 volumes of the latest publications, consisting of Novels, Romances, Sporting Magazines & c.

Twenty years later, Montego Bay lacked not only a circulating library, but also any bookseller or stationer from whom reading matter could be purchased. Sensing opportunity in this dearth, David Wauchope advertised, in the *Jamaica Standard* of 30 January 1839[14] that he was setting up a Public Library and Reading Room. Having had many years' experience 'in one of the first houses in London' he was confident that his venture would give satisfaction. Its stock was to consist of the daily and weekly newspapers published in London and Edinburgh, plus those of the island, and would contain

> all the best historical works, most amusing biographies, voyages and travels, novels and romances.

A week later Wauchope announced his terms: for a doubloon[15] per annum subscribers would have first choice of new additions to the library and could borrow two sets (three sets for country subscribers). Those paying a lower subscription had a more limited choice, and would be allowed to borrow only a single set at a time. The fact that on 13 July 1839 he advertised that non-subscribers would soon be allowed to borrow for a daily charge is perhaps an indication that he too was finding the circulating library less profitable than he had hoped, though his business was still in existence in 1841.

In Kingston, the failure of Aikman's circulating library did not dissuade others from venturing into the same field. Another library was certainly active by 1788, as on 5 May that year David Bower advertised in the *Jamaica Gazette*[16] for the return of overdue books, previous advertisements having produced little result.

Bower, despite his difficulties with overdues, felt that the prospects for his 'Kingston Circulating Library' were good. In 2 July 1788 he announced that he was going to London to augment its stock:

> The collection which the subscriber intends to form in London, will consist of about *three thousand* volumes of the most esteemed *ancient* and *modern authors,* viz. *Natural and Moral Philosophy, History, Memoirs, Lives, Voyages,* and *Travels, Poetry* and *Dramatic Works, Miscellanies,* with a great variety of the *best Novels* and *Periodical Publications.* – And this number shall be constantly kept up by regular and early supplies from the most eminent booksellers in London, with whom he means to establish a regular correspondence.
> For the amusement of such Gentlemen as may be inclined to pass an hour in the Library, the subscriber intends collecting a variety of the most curious and entertaining pamphlets.

The advertisement concluded by soliciting subscriptions to his venture, and by asking for subscribers' suggestions for books to be bought. A further advertisement, on 17 September 1788, again solicited subscribers to come forward before he sailed on 15 October.

The files of Jamaican newspapers of this period are too incomplete for us to learn when Bower returned to Jamaica. His library still continued successful, and the Kingston *Daily Advertiser* of 21 January 1790[17] contained an announcement of some additions received for its stock. On 27 February 1790 he made a further announcement of fresh accessions to his Library.

From these lists we may conclude that much of Bower's stock was of light ephemeral reading, and of recent publications:

> Mammuth, or human nature displayed ... 2 vols., Maddon's Female Ruin 2 vols., Fair Circassian 1 vol., European Magazine for 1782–8, Ladies Magazine for 1788

and other titles of a similar nature. However, by no means all his acquisitions were lightweight, or by any means new. They included such books as

> Ward's Lives of the Professors of Gresham College, 1740; Original Works of Mr Abraham Cowley in a neat folio ... published in 1674; Robertson's History of Greece 1 vol. 8 vo.

Meanwhile, he was planning an interesting extension to his business. Though Kingston was the mercantile centre of Jamaica, much of the island's administrative and legal business was normally transacted in the capital St. Jago de la Vega, some miles away to the west across the St. Catherine plains. On 29 January 1790 Bower advertised his intention of setting up a Law Library, and stated that he would be waiting on gentlemen of the profession for their advice on what should be purchased for it. For the five-guinea charge, subscribers would be permitted use of his other circulating library as well as the law library. On 24 February he informed subscribers that during the Assizes in St. Jago the stock of the law library would be made available in premises he had taken there.

This promising venture, however, came to nothing. In the spring of that year Bower fell victim to one or other of the diseases then the scourge of Jamaica. On 9 March he was compelled to advertise asking his debtors to settle their accounts promptly, his

> indisposition increasing obliging him to leave the island sooner than he intended.

The affairs of the Kington Circulating Library, and of the abortive Law Library were wound up. An auction of Bower's stock was publicised in the *Daily Advertiser* of 14 March 1791.[18]

No later attempts at providing circulating library facilities in St. Jago have been discovered. No doubt its relative proximity to Kingston, and the availability of the House of Assembly Library in St. Jago, at least from 1806 onwards, are the reasons since the town clearly had a relatively large and wealthy population.

Bower's Kingston Circulating Library was not the only one active in the town in the late 1780s. Before Bower had sailed to London to obtain additional stock for his venture, another local tradesman was planning his own circulating library which was to have a much longer life. This was Thomas Stevenson.

Stevenson had been settled in Jamaica for some time, and been manager of William Aikman's shop in King Street. When Aikman dies in 1784, he bequeathed a half-share in the bookselling and stationery business to Stevenson; the other half being left to his brother John Aikman, who was then under age.[19] The bookselling and stationery business prospered, and on 12 September 1788 – in rivalry to Bower's advertisements – Stevenson issued his own proposals[20] for a circulating library. Its stock, of some three to four thousand volumes initially, was to be purchased in Britain by John Aikman (who seems to have remained there, no doubt acting as purchasing agent for the partnership thereafter). Subscriptions were set at two guineas and three pounds five shillings; town members were to be allowed one set, of up to three volumes, for a maximum of fifteen days; country members were allowed three weeks for their reading. A printed catalogue of the collection was to be supplied to subscribers free of charge.

In the *Kingston Chronicle* of 19 August 1789[21] Stevenson announced that the books had been received from Britain, and would soon be available to subscribers. A week later, in the *Kingston Chronicle* of 26 August[22] subscribers were informed that the library was now ready for use, but that production of the catalogue was not yet complete. It is to be regretted that no copies of this catalogue, nor of those produced by the other circulating libraries in Jamaica, are now known to exist. Although we can form a reasonably accurate picture of what the Kingston, St. Jago and Montego Bay booksellers expected their customers to buy (from their advertisements of new importations of stock), hard fact is scarce on the reading tastes of the plantocracy. As far as Stevenson's Circulating Library was concerned, we can get some indication of what he expected to appeal from sources such as his list of new publications received, in the *Daily Advertiser* of 13 January 1790:[23] *Zeluco,* Piozzi's *Travels through France, Letters from Barbary,* a *History of Antigua* are representative. Usually Stevenson's advertisements are less informative on specific titles: in the *Daily Advertiser* of 12 January 1791,[24] for instance, he merely announced the receipt of a further fifteen hundred volumes from Britain.

One may presume that Stevenson's Circulating Library continued to flourish – or at least to exist – throughout the period of the 1790s and 1800s. It was only one of his several business undertakings: not only was he Kingston's principal bookseller and stationer, from 1788 onwards he was publisher of *The New Jamaica Almanack and Register,* and from 1796 joint proprietor of *The Diary and Kingston Daily Advertiser* which lasted until 1803, when its editor Andrew Aikman was compelled for reasons of health to quit Jamaica. From 1804 until Stevenson retired in 1808, he was in partnership with Robert Smith, a native of Berwick-on-Tweed who had come to Jamaica some time before 1799. Jamaican newspapers of this period are particularly scarce, and I have found no references to the Circulating Library during this period, or indeed until 1819. There is a passing reference to a commercial library in a book published in 1808[25]; no doubt this is the same as that run by Stevenson & Smith.

From 1808 onwards the firm continued under the style of Smith & Kinnear. That its activities still included the circulating library is clear from their announcement of a considerable addition to its stock, in the *Royal Gazette* 22 June 1819.[26] A further advertisement for a variety of new publications received for the library, appeared in the same paper on 1 May 1820. Six months later, on 2 December 1820, Smith & Kinnear once more advertised in the *Royal Gazette,* offering the Circulating Library for sale as a going concern with upwards of twelve thousand volumes.

It was not to pass into other hands, however. In a further *Royal Gazette* advertisement on 30 December, Smith informed readers that the partnership was being dissolved, and that he would be continuing the business alone. All subscribers two years or more in arrears, he warned, would have their names struck off unless they paid promptly. Printed catalogues of the library, recently much augmented, were in active preparation and would soon be ready.

By 1825, Robert Smith was in a fresh partnership, and had revamped his library. The advertisement, which appeared in several of the island's newspapers,[27] gives a good picture of an institution intended to appeal to the Jamaican public:

> Smith & Clark   Kingston, January 1, 1825
>
> The proprietors of the Circulating Library, having for some time past found it impossible to conduct their establishment with ease to themselves, or satisfaction to their subscribers, for want of room, have removed from their old store to that a few doors higher, and opposite Lewis's Repository in King Street, where they have a considerable expence, fitted up a cool and spacious Apartment as a LIBRARY and READING ROOM where they hope to give accommodation to their subscribers as also to Gentlemen from the Country, who may think proper to resort to it as a place of retirement and amusement.
>
> Files of the ISLAND PAPERS will be kept on the table, and it is intended to augment the number of ENGLISH and SCOTCH PERIODICALS, exclusively for the use of the Room, by each packet.
>
> They have always on hand, a general assortment of stationery and a large collection of books, catalogues of which may had on application.
>
> Bookbinding executed with neatness and despatch.

Smith & Clark were in business as late as 1838, and in August of that year advertised[28] for sale several hundred surplus volumes from the Library. I have found no later references to the firm or its Circulating Library, but suspect that later that year, or early in 1839 it must have been taken over by Bravo & Co. From an advertisement in the *Morning Journal,* 2 May 1839[29] we learn that subscribers then paid five pounds a year, non-subscribers 5d. per volume plus 10d, a day, and that the Library had shrunk to something over seven thousands volumes. Bravo's Library was still in existence in 1841, when the firm acted as subscription agent for Edward Grimley's *The Convict, a tale of Venice,*[30] but I have found no other references to it.

In expanding their libraries to provide reading room facilities, Smith & Clark in Kingston, or David Wauchope in Montego Bay, were following an old pattern. One suspects that the 'gentlemen from the country' visiting the libraries must have been able to obtain refreshment for the body as well as the mind.

The role of the Coffee House in Britain has been well described by Paul Kaufman.[31] The only reference to a Coffee House of this kind in the West Indies that I have found, was run in Kingston in the early 1790s. In the *Daily Advertiser* 28 January 1790[32] is an advertisement for a new coffee house, inserted by one Ebenezer Edie. In expatiating on the comfort and convenience of his establishments, Edie informed readers that it would include a

> room furnished with all Newspapers and Prices Current, for the entertainment and information of the subscribers.

Though entry to other parts of the coffee house was open to all comers, it appears that this room was restricted to members paying a subscription. That it was closer to the English type of coffee-house library than to the various other "Commercial Rooms" or "Marine Intelligence Rooms" that existed at a later period in Jamaica[33] seems clear from the fact that Edie's name was included as an agent in the subscription proposals for several Jamaican publications at this time. His Subscriber's Room no doubt contained a similar selection of "curious and entertaining pamphlets" to that advertised by David Bower in the previous year.

In the 1830s there was an attempt at a rather specialised circulating library in Kingston. Then (as now) Jamaica had a special love of music and dance, and most booksellers and stationers carried some instruments, instruction books and sheet music as a normal part of their stock, while in Kingston there were several shopmen whose main business was in this field. One of the most enterprising was Francis Egan, who not only dealt in imported music, but published in his own right at 53 Harbour Street. Such works as his Creole "Apprentice" tunes (the St. Mary's Sha Sha, Massa Tommy etc.) for piano, flute and violin, or the Belmore and Sligo quadrilles arranged for piano, flute, violin or guitar sound particularly attractive.[34]

In August 1834, Egan advertised[35] that he was starting a circulating library, on moderate terms, and that he had made arrangements to receive the latest works from London. Subscribers to his library, he emphasised, would be able to borrow elementary, scientific or practical works on vocal and instrumental music, *bound.* A catalogue of the library would be ready on 1

September. It was a brave effort, but even with its specialised stock it could not compete with the much larger and old-established library of Smith & Clark, and on 26 April 1836 the whole of Egan's private and circulating library – some 948 volumes in all – was dispersed at auction.[36]

Kingston, St. Jago de la Vega and Montego Bay were not the only towns in Jamaica in which one might have expected to find some commercial attempts at library provision. Savanna-la-Mar at the southwestern end of the island supported a newspaper in the late 1780s and early 1790s; on the north coast Falmouth had a newspaper (and for a considerable period two or more) from 1790 onwards. Both had the potential market for a circulating library, but I have found no evidence to suggest that any attempt was made to set one up. The only other attempts at a commercial undertaking that have been traced were both based at Morant Bay, in the Parish of St. Thomas-in-the-East at the southeastern end of the island. At the beginning of 1819, D. Wilson & Co. announced[37] the establishment of the 'Morant Bay Circulating Library and Reading Room'. To be open from seven in the morning until eight at night, it provided both stabling and a postchaise, and was to be furnished with books, periodicals and newspapers from London, Liverpool, Bristol, Edinburgh, Glasgow and Cork, plus those published in Jamaica. The subscription was set at a doubloon; masters of vessels could join for eight dollars (i.e. half the normal subscription) while those resident more than twenty miles from Morant Bay could use the facilities if introduced by a subscriber.

It appears that Wilson's attempt did not last very long. In July 1822 an advertisement by James Scott[38] informed the public that he was setting up a 'Circulating Library and Commercial Rooms' to serve Morant Bay. His Library, he claimed, already had an excellent assortment of books, of which a printed catalogue was in preparation for subscribers. Arrangements had been made with a London bookseller, he stated, to send out new publications for the Library. As before, subscriptions were set at one doubloon per annum. No other references to Scott's Library have been found, and one must suspect that it too had only a short life.

In the other districts of Jamaica, commercial circulating libraries were not attempted. Instead, the reading public in each parish banded together to form book clubs or subscription libraries. Their potential readership was not large; Hazel Bennett has drawn attention[39] to the St. George's Library Society, at Buff Bay, which was active from 1824 onwards. In 1838 it had seventy-nine members who had paid a doubloon entrance fee, and an annual subscription of £2-6s.8d. So small a membership, in what was undoubtedly the most lively of these societies in early Victorian Jamaica, was however merely a reflection of the small white population of the parish. The 1844 census records the population of St. George's as 8,800, of whom Mrs Bennett estimated not more than 400 were white. Even if one allows that some of the free coloured population (though not, of course, the recently-emancipated ex-slaves) were potential members of the Library Society, its actual membership was a not insignificant proportion of the whole.

The St. George's Library Society was not, however, the first such undertaking in the island, as Mrs Bennett's sources led her to believe. The *Royal Gazette* of 24 March 1819 contained the announcement of a meeting of the St. Elizabeth's Book Club at Black River, called to divide the books and settle the accounts. Probably this body is to be identified with the Black River Book Club, the name of which appears in the list of the 281 subscribers to the *Jamaica Quarterly Journal and Literary Gazette,* which commenced publication in July 1818.[40]

Another such hitherto unknown group was the St. Mary's Circulating Library, whose members were called to a meeting at the Court-House, Manning's Town, on 15 August 1834. From the wording of this advertisement[41] it seems probable that despite its name this was in fact a book club and without permanent premises of its own. A further similar meeting was called in 1836.[42] Maybe there were other such societies which had a brief existence in the Jamaica of the late eighteenth or early nineteenth centuries; the dearth of contemporary newspaper files or other documentary evidence makes it a matter of speculation.

NOTES

1. Lemoine's article, which was based largely and without acknowledgement on Leman Thomas Rede's 'Introductory Discourse' to his *Bibliotheca Americana* (London, 1789), was reprinted in George L. Gomme, *The Gentleman's Magazine Library* (London, 1888).
2. For the eighteenth and early nineteenth centuries, this means books and pamphlets published in Britain and Ireland. Though not insignificant in influence, books from North American publishers represented only a very small proportion of the trade before the 1840s, although American papers circulated widely to the islands.
3. Giles Barber, 'Books from the old world and for the new: the British international trade in books in the eighteenth century' *Studies on Voltaire and the eighteenth century,* CLI – CLV, 1976, 185–224.
4. Lambeth Palace, Fulham Papers, xvii, ff. 215–6.
5. Lambeth Palace, Fulham Papers, xvii, ff. 175–9.
6. Hazel Bennett, 'Private and subscription libraries in Jamaica before 1879'. *Journal of Library History,* 3, 1968, 242–9.
7. All those traced of the eighteenth century and the first forty years of the nineteenth century which were available in Britain, the United States and Jamaica. The fragile state of the Institute of Jamaica's files of newspapers of the Victorian period prevented scanning for the later period. Research for this work was made possible by grants from the American Antiquarian Society and the British Academy, to whom my thanks are due.
8. Or Welsh, Scottish, or Irish.

9. *Royal Gazette* 17 March 1821. Set in the Public Record Office, London (C.O. 141/17).
10. Set in the British Library Newspaper Room, Colindale.
11. Set in Bristol Reference Library.
12. Probably not Jamaican currency but sterling; at that time £1 currency was worth approximately 14s.3d. sterling, so that the subscription would have been nearly £3 currency.
13. Set in the West India Reference Library, Institute of Jamaica.
14. Set in the British Library Newspaper Room, Colindale.
15. i.e. £5-6s.8d. currency.
16. Set in the Royal Commonwealth Society Library, London.
17. Set in the British Library Newspaper Room.
18. Set in the American Antiquarian Society, Worcester, Mass.
19. Jamaica Archives, Wills, liber 50 f. 180 v.
20. *Jamaica Gazette* 20 September 1788; set in the Royal Commonwealth Society Library.
21. Copy in Boston Public Library, Mass.
22. Copy in the British Library Newspaper Room.
23. Set in the British Library Newspaper Room.
24. Set in the American Antiquarian Society.
25. (John Stewart) *An Account of Jamaica and its inhabitants by a gentleman long resident in the West Indies* (London, 1808) p. 171.
26. Set in the Public Record Office (C.O. 141/11).
27. e.g. *Royal Gazette* (set in the Public Record Office, C.O. 141/22); *Kingston Chronicle* (set in the West India Reference Library, Institute of Jamaica).
28. *Royal Gazette and Jamaica Times,* 14 August 1838, set in the Public Record Office (C.O. 141/32).
29. Copy in the West India Reference Library, Institute of Jamaica.
30. *Cornwall Chronicle* 16 January 1841; copy in the West India Reference Library.
31. Paul Kaufman, 'Coffee Houses as Reading Centres', in his *Libraries and their users* (London, 1969) pp. 115–27.
32. Set in the British Library Newspaper Room.
33. e.g. The Commercial Rooms owned by James Mitchell when he died in 1829 (Jamaica Archives, Wills, liber 110 f. 160 v.).
34. These were advertised by Egan in the *Royal Gazette* from 19 December 1835 (set in the Public Record Office, C.O. 141/29). The titles of Egan's pieces refer to the partial abolition of slavery the previous year (by which the slaves had become apprentices) and to Lords Belmore and Sligo, Governors of Jamaica.
35. *Jamaica Herald,* 8 August 1834. Set in the Library of Congress, Washington D.C.
36. *Kingston Chronicle,* 22 April 1836. Set in the Public Record Office (C.O. 142/3).
37. *Royal Gazette* 2 January 1819. Set in the Public Record Office (C.O. 141/13).
38. *Royal Gazette* 10 July 1822. Set in the Public Record Office (C.O. 141/19).
39. Vide supra, reference 6.
40. Set in Rhodes House Library, Oxford.
41. *Jamaica Herald* 7 August 1834. Set in the Library of Congress.
42. *Royal Gazette* 10 May 1836 (C.O. 141/30).

XVII
THE FIRST JAMAICAN PRIVATE PRESS

THE Reverend George Wilson Bridges, though better remembered than most of his fellow churchmen of the 1820s, is not highly esteemed in Jamaica. In a society still rather self-consciously post colonial, in which collective folk-memories of slavery are assiduously fostered by some of those in the island's political life, and in which there is an aura of enthusiastic evangelism about all Churches of whatever creed—in such a society an Anglican clergyman of the old style, whose political beliefs tended to make him support the slave owners, and who disliked the island, has little chance of finding friends. Even his reputation as author of one of the more important books on the history of the island, *Annals of Jamaica* (published in London in 1828), is tainted. In style deliberately modelled upon Gibbon's *Decline and Fall*, it is not without power. Yet modern Jamaican historians whose opinion one must respect have suggested that in some instances Bridges followed his model so closely that he permitted the style to mould his matter; a serious charge.

There would be no point in inflicting this rather recondite information on readers of *The Private Library*, were this all that could be said about Bridges. But as a book collector, connoisseur of fine typography and (I suspect) owner of the first private press in the island, at a time when colonial collectors and typophiles were rare indeed, he perhaps merits a short note.

Nearly all the information we have about Bridges' life is contained in his own *Voice from Jamaica* (London, 1823), and his *Outline and notes of twenty-nine years 1834–1862* (London? privately printed, 1862) or in references to him in the memoirs of the Baptist and Wesleyan missionaries in Jamaica, such as Bleby's *Death struggles of slavery* (3rd edition, 1868), or John Clarke's *Memorials of Baptist missionaries in Jamaica* (London, 1869). As Bridges had come to represent to them all that was wrong in the established Church, their highly-coloured accounts are scarcely to be relied upon, while the very sad account Bridges gave of his own life also needs to be used with caution.

Born (perhaps at Ilford) in the late 1780s Bridges was educated at Trinity College Oxford and at the University of Utrecht. In 1814 he persuaded a girl from Cheltenham to elope with him to Scotland. Before this he had held various curacies in Essex, Norfolk, Hampshire and London, so he tells us in his *Voice from Jamaica.* His elopement came at an unlucky moment, coinciding with his father's loss of most of his fortune, so that he was deprived of the allowance of £200 per year he had previously received; and he was at the same time compelled to part with his reversionary interests in the family estates and, it seems, in the family living in Leicestershire in order to settle his college debts. One imagines his elopement cannot have helped his chances of preferment in the Church, and that it was in an attempt to retrieve his fortunes that he went to Jamaica the following year.

In Jamaica he fell on his feet, the Governor (the Duke of Manchester) giving him the rectorship of the newly formed parish of Manchester in 1817. He remained Rector of Manchester, based in the pleasant upland town of Mandeville, for six years, and in 1823 was translated to the much richer parish of St. Ann's on the north side of the island. His situation for some ten or eleven years was easy: he built up a 'rare and well chosen' library of some seven or eight thousand volumes, wrote his *Annals of Jamaica* and had an active if not altogether well-chosen life in defending the plantocracy against the more extreme propaganda of the anti-slavery-movement and in resisting the encroachments of the dissenters upon what he regarded as the proper concern of the established Church. Living, in other words, as many a Tory divine in England chose to live. But in 1834 the first of several blows struck him: his wife of twenty years suddenly left him and returned to England, leaving him to care for his young family alone. His eldest son was already at school in England; and then in 1837 he had the horror of seeing his four daughters drowned before his eyes in a boating accident in St. Ann's Bay. Crazed with grief, the following year he abandoned Jamaica and with his one remaining son went to the backwoods of Canada 'at a moment when if I had not gone wild, I should doubtless have gone mad.' After a few years in Canada he returned to Europe, to a curacy in Gloucestershire, then subsequently to Malta where he lived some years, and apparently dabbled in photography. A clergyman writing in the 1890s recalled that some views of the Holy Land which Bridges had taken made him a favourite at evening parties in the island. He eventually settled in Beachley, Hampshire, where he was vicar at the time of his death in 1863.

Of his library, which was presumably dispersed at the time he left Jamaica so precipitately in 1838, no trace remains. One may doubt whether it was as extensive as his memory of it, but from the evidence of his own writings it is clear that he was very widely read. In the Jamaica of that time, there was no public library of any description. Bridges did indeed make use of the resources of the library of Alexander Aikman Sr., King's Printer in Jamaica, but he would have been compelled to build up his own resources as well. One may guess that it was a scholar's working collection rather than a cabinet of choice things, though the passage of time has made some of the things he quoted, and probably possessed, very rare indeed. That it has disappeared completely is not surprising in an island subject to earthquake, hurricane and the ravages of termites: Aikman's library, referred to above, was brought by the House of Assembly on his death in 1838, and subsequently the House's library passed into the possession of the Institute of Jamaica, established in 1876. Such was the rate of attrition that forty years later the Institute's librarian was unable to identify any book in its stock as having been Aikman's.

The present writer came upon Bridges indirectly, while exploring the history of printing in Jamaica. After the introduction of printing in 1718, the craft gradually developed so that by the end of the century there were printers not only in Spanish Town (the old capital of the colony) and Kingston but also in Savanna-la-Mar, Montego Bay and Falmouth. Nearly all the printers made their livings from the production of a daily or weekly newspaper combined with some jobbing work—the occasional pamphlet on tropical diseases, agricultural topics, and so forth. In investigating the careers of some of these printers, and trying to establish precisely what *were* the relationships between different firms, I found in the Institute of Jamaica's excellent West India Reference Library two imprints which appeared odd. Both were on works by Bridges.

The first is *The Statistical history of the Parish of Manchester, in the island of Jamaica*, by the *Reverend Georges Bridges*. . . 'Jamaica, Printed by the Author, at the Wakefield Press, 1824'. This little octavo pamphlet of fourteen leaves, side-stitched, is an undistinguished piece of printing on wove paper, without signatures. Jamaican printers were not used to bookwork, and their make-ready was often very bad, but the pamphlet does not look as though it had been produced by a commercial printer. The margins are slightly odd, and there is a typographical unity about the pamphlet which is highly unlike other Jamaican printing of the time: text and title-page both being in but two sizes of the same rather undistinguished Scotch Roman face. Odd for a commercial printer, but just what one would expect from an amateur with a limited range of types. The imprint too is suggestive: Wakefield was the name of the property near St. Ann's Bay which Bridges occupied for the first few years after his move to the north coast, and there was no commercial printer in St. Ann's Bay for another forty or fifty years. The *Statistical history* bears the half-title 'Notes pour servir a l'histoire de la Jamaique. Division 13. Chapter 22', and the pamphlet was in fact a trial for what later developed into *The Annals of Jamaica.*

The second of Bridges' Jamaican publications may not, by the purists, be regarded as truly a private press production, but it is still more interesting. Entitled *A Service for the Parochial Church of St. Ann, Jamaica, arranged and engraved by the Rector*, it was 'Printed at the Pontine Press, 1827' and was sold for the benefit of the choir, price 10*s.* (Jamaican currency).

This pamphlet contains, as well as the title-leaf, three leaves of letterpress printed (rather badly, on one side only) in what seems to be the same face as the *Statistical history.* These leaves are followed by ten leaves of music, printed by lithography. The first of them bears at the foot the legend 'Geo. W. Bridges. lithogr. 1827' and the words for the music are recognisably in his hand. Presumably Bridges had purchased one of the small lithographic presses of the kind marketed by Ruthven or Taylor & Martineau from the early 1820s onwards and taught himself the craft. This is the earliest example of lithographic printing in Jamaica known to me, although lithography was introduced into Belize (British Honduras) and Bermuda at about this time, and was practised commercially in Kingston within the next two or three years.

Unfortunately neither of these pamphlets is in sufficiently good condition to reproduce satisfactorily, and the copies in the Institute of Jamaica are the only ones I have been able to trace. There are none in the British Museum, Bodley or the *National Union Catalog* of American research libraries.

There is no other evidence for Bridges as a private printer that I have been able to find, but as almost all his publications with Jamaican imprints are known only from one or two copies, he may well have produced more which have not survived.

One presumes that after the death of his daughters, and his abrupt departure from Jamaica, Bridges dabbled no more in printing. The references to his Palestinian photography are suggestive: many a late Victorian amateur printer abandoned the black art for the easier successes of photography—though whether one could describe photography as 'easy' in the days before the development of the dry plate is another matter, and in the 1840s Bridges was obviously an early practitioner of the craft.

Though he may have done no more printing, it is clear that he had not lost interest in typography. This is confirmed by his pamphlet *Outline and notes of twenty-nine years*, which he had printed for him in 1862 to clear his 'guileless but deluded' wife's memory of 'the most foul and unfounded charges against her'. He was able to do this as a result of information which had only very recently come into his hands, he tells us, but the account tells of such extraordinary malevolence and injustice on the part of his wife's and his own family that one can scarcely credit it. That is perhaps by the way; what *is* pertinent is that this old, sick and grieving clergyman (who for years had his £40 per annum from Beachley as his only income and for years had not left Beachley) chose to have his little quarto pamphlet printed in Caslon Old Face, using the long s and its ligatures, and in two colours. To be sure by 1862 the Caslon revival was more than fifteen years old, but one would scarcely expect its use in the antique style unless by the author's express wish.

XVIII
THE ST. JAMES PRINTERY
Montego Bay

Readers of Wright and White's *Exploring Jamaica* (London, Deutsch, 1969) may recall their recommendation of the St. James Printery among the tourist sights of Montego Bay.

For those at all interested in printing, the St. James Printery has more to offer than any other printing house in Jamaica, and in entering its doors, one is immediately reminded of the way in which, until recently, all Jamaican printing was undertaken.

True, the St. James Printery as it now stands is only fifty-five years old, but in its arrangement (and the fact that all the work printed there is from handset type) it could be almost as old as its oldest equipment, which takes us back to the middle of the nineteenth century.

According to Wright & White, the present firm took over the business of D.A. Corinaldi, for some time publisher of a newspaper called *The Nineteenth Century and St. James's Gazette*, which appears to have started publication in 1882. Corinaldi had in turn been successor to Sidney Levien, proprietor and editor of a weekly paper, *The County Union.*[1] At the time of the Morant Bay Rebellion, Levien was imprisoned for seditious libel for a pamphlet he had printed criticising Governor Eyre's handling of the affair. More importantly—for the subject of this note—Levien had the previous year, 1864, incorporated into his paper *The Cornwall Chronicle*, a paper which with some changes of subtitle, and of course proprietor, had been appearing since 1773. In other words, the St. James Printery has an uninterrupted line of descent from the first printing house set up on the north side of the island.

At the far end of the St. James Printery, after one has penetrated beyond the composing area, is a very interesting press. Known locally as Levien's Press, it is a very handsome example of the iron handpress named the Columbian Press.

Invented about 1812 by George Clymer (1754–1834) of Philadelphia, the Columbian Press is probably the most memorable of all nineteenth century presses.[2] The comment by T.C. Hansard in his *Typographia* (London, 1825), is worth repeating:

> If the merits of a machine were to be appreciated wholly by its ornamental appearance, certainly no other press could enter into competition with "The Columbian". No British-made machinery was every so lavishly embellished.

We have a somewhat high-sounding title to begin with; and then, which way soever our eyes are turned from head to foot or foot to head, some extraordinary features present themselves—on each pillar of the staple a caduceus of the universal messenger, Hermes—alligators, and other draconic serpents emblematise, on the levers, the power of wisdom—then, for *the balance of power* (we rude barbarians of the old world make mere cast-iron *lumps* serve to inforce our notions of the *balance of power*) we see, surmounting the Columbian press, the American eagle with extended wings, and grasping in his talons Jove's thunderbolts, combined with the olive branch of Peace, and cornucopia of Plenty, all handsomely bronzed and gilt, *resisting and bearing down* ALL OTHER POWER!

Hansard, however justifiable his annoyance at the aggressive Americanism of the Columbian's design, had missed the point. Clymer's design, with all the extravagant embellishments, was merely good business. Nobody who saw a Columbian press could mistake it for anything else, and the commercial advantages of this scarcely need to be pointed out.

In other ways, too, Clymer showed himself an excellent advertising man, by presenting examples of his press to various reigning monarchs. Expensive, but it paid off: not only did the Czar of Russia present him with a gift of six thousand roubles, and the King of the Netherlands bestow on him a gold medal, but Clymer was also able to use their letters in further advertising.

However skillfully conducted an advertising campaign might be, it won't lead to much if the product itself is no good. The Columbian Press was a good press, an extremely good one, which rapidly gained a wide appeal in the printing trade.

This popularity—probably due to the fact that it was slightly less arduous to operate than its two rivals, the English 'Stanhope' and 'Albion' presses, as well as to its advertising—is easily illustrated in several ways. Columbian presses were made by firms in England, Scotland, France, Holland and Germany, and continued to be manufactured with little change right down until the First World War. Surviving examples—and there are well over sixty Columbians still in existence—turn up in not only Europe and North America, but also in India, South Africa, Australia and New Zealand; ample evidence of the high regard felt by colonial printers for this machine.

Though it is difficult to do more than guess at the extent of the popularity of the Columbian in the West Indies, I think it is significant that the three early nineteenth century presses which have survived, are all Columbians—one in the Royal Victoria Institute, Port of Spain (formerly owned by Yuille's Printery), one in the Museum in Georgetown, Guyana (formerly owned by the *Argosy*), and the one in Montego Bay. Only the last is still in everyday use, but a century and a quarter ago no doubt many of the region's newspapers—the *Gleaner*, the *Port of Spain Gazette*—were printed on these trouble-free and nearly indestructable presses.

George Clymer went to London and set up in business building his presses there in 1817. In 1830 he entered into partnership with one Dixon, and after his death in 1834 the firm Clymer & Dixon continued to build the Columbian.

The St. James Printery's Columbian was not, however, built by this firm, though one would never guess it from the handsome engraved brassplate on the press, which reads 'Columbian Press Invented by George Clymer Manufactory, 120 Aldersgate Street, London 1842'.

This plate was used by another firm, Wood & Sharwoods, who had rapidly cashed in on the expiry of Clymer's patents but were still happy to use his name. The price they charged for the press (of Double Crown size, 33 x 22 ¾ inches) was £70. Even with freight to Jamaica added, the purchaser[3] —and his successors in business—got a bargain!

There is nothing else in the St. James Printery of equal interest, although it does possess four platen presses of some age. The platen press was developed in America in the 1850s.[4] Operated by treadle (later often by power instead), these presses were particularly suited to small jobbing work—letterheads, small hand-bills and the like—and rapidly became the mainstay of many a small printer's business. A very large number of different machines were marketed—at least 123 in the United States alone in the period to 1940. The St. James Printery has two presses made by the Kelsey Company of Meriden, Connecticut: a 'Union' press (which were made from 1898 until 1939), and a 'Star' press, first made in 1901 and which continued in production as recently as 1953. There is one press made by John Haddon & Co. (an English firm) and one which bears no indication of its maker.

The wood type (used for posters) owned by the Printery is disappointing. A little of it is stamped 'Hamilton Two Rivers Wisconsin', and may date from the late 19th century; the rest is rather run of the mill twentieth century type. I suspect that it, like most of the metal type, came from the English firm of Stephenson Blake in Sheffield.

NOTES

1 Corinaldi's *The nineteenth century* is, surprisingly, not mentioned by George F. Judah in his article on "The newspaper history of Jamaica" (*Jamaica Times*, 14 January 1899 & 21 January 1899); and Levien's *County Union* is mentioned only in passing. The West Indian Reference Library has only one issue (16 January 1883) of *The nineteenth century* and none of Levien's paper, but a few copies of it survive in the British Museum.

2 Cf. Jacob Kainen, *George Clymer and the Columbian Press*, New York/San Francisco 1950, and James Moran, 'The Columbian Press' *Journal of the Printing Historical Society,* No. 5, 1969, pp. 1–23. The details on prices etc. are drawn from these two sources.

3 Perhaps Levien, or possibly Alexander Holmes, from 1826 to 1862 the printer/publisher of *The Cornwall Chronicle*.

4 Ralph Green, *A history of the platen jobber*, Chicago 1953.

XIX
A PROPOSAL FOR A PAPERMILL IN JAMAICA. 1824

The West Indian book trade, like so many other trades carried on in the sugar islands, was entirely dependent on importations. Presses, types, ink, paper all had to be imported; although negro slaves were often used as pressmen in the eighteeth and early nineteenth centuries (1), even compositors often had to be drawn from outside the island until the latter part of the nineteenth century.

Although local markets were far too small to make local production of printing equipment practicable, papermaking was a different matter. In the early years of the nineteenth century when the use of new fibres for papermaking was being investigated (2), the islands' economic state was still sufficiently buoyant for a small papermill to be worth considering. An article in the north coast newspaper *The Cornwall Gazette* (3) reprinted in *The Jamaica Journal and Kingston Chronicle* (4), 11 December 1824, put forward proposals for such a mill. Like many such suggestions it fell on deaf ears. No mill was built on the Martha Brae or any other Jamaican river, and the island's printers remained dependent on imported supplies of paper. Of the various fibres which the anonymous author (5) suggested could be used, only one, cannabis, has been turned to economic advantage in Jamaica–and that not for papermaking! Although in the present century attention has from time to time been turned to the possibility of papermaking using bagasse (6), the cane-waste left after sugar production, Jamaica is still to add papermaking to its industries.

Every man, say Addison, Johnson, Chesterfield, and Watt
can speak best on his own profession, and being
so connected with that of

PAPER MANUFACTURING,

We beg to suggest to the country what benefit would result to the Island of Jamaica from the manufacture of this article alone. A ream of printing paper consists of 472 sheets, and take the average value at £ 1 sterling, or, deducting drawback and including every thing in the shape of expence, £ 2 currency.– Since the establishment of several additional newspapers here, the consumption of printing paper is materially increased, and by a rough calculation must amount to at least 3000 reams, including books, pamphlets, jobs, &c. &c. per annum.– Thus, on this alone, £ 6000 would be gained to, and spent in the country. – Stationery, cards, fancy papers, and pasteboards, and wrapping paper would nearly double this amount, say, however £ 8000 ! here is £ 14,000 sent out of the country, while almost every material of which it is made grows in the country, or in the shape of linen rags thrown in sport on the wings of the wind. However, the Kingston merchant need only insert in his Prices Current the price of *rags* here, and colonies and colonists that never descended to their last *shift* of human economy, will now turn its fragments into a staple of export for the Paper Mills of Jamaica ! If, therefore, we take their very rags from them, they surely will not refuse good printing or writing paper in exchange. Besides old linen, cotton or calico, is used in the manufacture of paper. A variety both of exotic and indigenous plants of this country could be converted into it. We shall mention a few; – the Penguin (7), the Dagger Plant (8), Chinese hemp *(cannabis)* (9) introduced here by Mr Wallen in 1773, which would grow luxuriantly. The lace tree, inner bark, also, is of an admirable texture for the formation of the pulp of paper (10). – "Thus far we go before the wind," and thus far all is practicable. Let us inquire if the rest be not also practicable. A Company, protected, or chartered by the Legislature, could easily, with the help of the Martha Brae, or any other river put the mills in motion. A capital of £ 5000 would more than establish a Mill large enough for this country. – Say £ 6000, which would yield to the capitalist about 23 per cent. per annum. – A superintendant, or foreman might be obtained from the Kentish or the Scotch Mills at an easy rate, as wages go at present. Negro boys, or women could perform the rest. Then the country must give its support to the Company, and the Honourable House have recourse to more 'sanitary' policy than that of sending the journals to be printed out of the country (11), depriving a number of deserving and intelligent labourers of a portion of their yearly income, by which they contribute their humble mites to support the country.

NOTES

1. Roderick Cave, 'The Use of Slave Labour in West Indian Printing Houses' *The Library*, 5th series, v.5 no. 3, September 1975, pp.241-3.

2. cf. John Murray, *Practical Remarks on Modern Paper* (Edinburgh, Blackwood, 1829) chapter 3 pp.69-98, or his *An Account of the Phormium Tenax, or New-Zealand Flax* (London, H. Renshaw, 1836).

3. Published by Dobie & Hoole at Falmouth, Jamaica from June 1823 as a biweekly under the editorship of Alexander Holmes (former editor and proprieter of *The Bermudian*) until 25 January 1825, when as a result of a dispute between Holmes and Hoole the former left to start his *West-India Gazette* and Hoole took over editorship of the *Cornwall Gazette* himself. Very few copies survive of this paper, the only extensive set I have seen (in the West India Reference Library, Institute of Jamaica) ceases with the issue for 11 January 1825. I have not seen the issue with the papermaking proposal reprinted here.

4. Published weekly in Kingstom from 1823 as the Sunday edition of *The Kingston Chronicle and Jamaica Journal.* The set used was that in the American Antiquarian Society.

5. Probably Edward Hoole, the editor of *The Cornwall Gazette.* Other copy which was also reprinted from the *Gazette* suggests that it was from the editor's hand.

6. I have seen good quality bagasse paper made experimentally at the Imperial College of Tropical Agriculture, Trinidad, in the early 1960s, and have been informed that it is made in Cuba today.

7. *Bromelia pinguin,* pinguin or 'pingwing' a plant not unlike the pineapple (though its small acidic fruit is normally eaten only by children); sometimes used as a live fence in Jamaica.

8. Unless this is also a reference to *cannabis sativa* 'dagga', not identified. One of the sharp-spiked agaves such as the 'curato' or 'maypole' may be meant. *Agave sisalane,* sisal hemp, is an important commercial souce of fibre for cordage in Yucatan and East Africa.

9. *Cannabis sativa*, 'grass', 'cabbage', 'ganja', which grows prolifically in Jamaica. The attribution of its introduction to Matthew Wallen is of interest: according to C. Dennis Adams, *The Blue Mahoe and Other Bush* (Kingston, Sangsters, 1971) Chapter XVII, 'The Weed', the first reference to the presence of cannabis in the island was in Grisebach's *Flora of the British West Indian Islands,* (1860), in which it was simply recorded as an earlier introduction to Jamaica.

10. *Lagetta lagetto (Lagetta lineata).* As Sir Hans Sloane wrote in 1725

> what is most strange in this Tree is, that the inward Bark is made up of about twelve Coats, Layers, or Tunicles, appearing white and solid, which if cut off for some Length, cleared of its outward Cuticula, or Bark, and extended by the Fingers, the Filaments or Threads thereof ... form a Web not unlike Gause, Lace, or thin Muslin.

I do not know of any experiments made with this for papermaking, but the rather similar New Zealand lacebark, *Plagianthus betulinus*, has been found to have qualities like some of the Japanese *gampi* and *kozo* fibres, and is well-suited for high quality papers.

11. A reference to the economy measure adopted by the Assembly, which had found it was cheaper to have its Journals printed in Britain than in Jamaica, where the Aikmans had usually been the contractors for the work. The competition for the lucrative contracts for printing the Assembly's work was very strong in the 1820s.

American goods into the British islands, but the progress of the war was to prevent this.

In the succeeding decade St Bartholomew was to provide the United States with access to traditional markets denied them by the British Navigation Acts. At one time, St Bartholomew was the only West Indian island freely open to American shipping; at another only Swedish vessels were permitted to trade with independent Haiti. Later, when peace between England and France had followed the final defeat of Napoleon, Gustavia was one of the ports used by privateers (or pirates) sailing under South American colours in the wars of independence against Spain – or so it was claimed in St Kitts, although the St Bartholomew paper denied that it was so. It *was* true of St Eustatius, and it is improbable that the Swedish authorities in Gustavia would have been able to prevent their merchants from such activity. The merchants were usually of British, American, French or Dutch origin and though they had taken the precaution of taking out Swedish citizenship their true allegiance was to their own personal fortunes.

The rôle of St Bartholomew in Caribbean history of the early nineteenth century has no doubt been neglected because historians have hitherto been unaware of the valuable source material surviving in the colony's newspaper.

The present writer's examination of the American Antiquarian Society's set of *The Report of St Bartholomew* was made during a study of its West Indian imprints which was made possible by a Fred Harris Daniels fellowship in the summer of 1976. The paper was of enough interest to follow up by enquiry in Sweden: through the courtesy of the Royal Library in Stockholm I have been provided with a microfilm of a complete file of *The Report,* made up from the Royal Library's own copies plus some filmed from those in The Royal Archives and in Uppsala University Library. This microfilm has now been deposited in the American Antiquarian Society's library in Worcester, Massachusetts.

In nearly every West Indian colony printing was introduced before the end of the eighteenth century. *The Report* of 28 August 1804 contains a suggestion that Gustavia may have had a press as early as March 1799[1] – a press set up for reasons rather different from those which obtained in other islands[2] – but the earliest surviving evidence for the colony's press is an 1804 *Avertissement* now in Jämtlands bibliotek, Ostersund[3], indicating that a press was starting under the direction of Andrew Berstedt.

Bergstedt, *Justiciarius* of the colony, was obviously the controlling figure in the publication of *The Report of St Bartholomew,* of which the first issue was published on Monday April 2nd, 1804, although his name does not appear in the paper.

The first issue of the paper set a pattern for its physical production which was to change little. Set in the rather debased roman types typical of German type foundries of the period (types which had presumably been shipped out from Sweden), it contained four pages approximately $7^1/_2 \times 11$ inches, set in two columns. Pages 1 and 2 contain an entertaining 'Dialogue between one of the *Editors* and a *Reader* to serve as Prospectus.' A neat device, avoiding the pomposity of most papers' prospectuses, and not without a rather ponderous wit, the Dialogue was to describe the future contents of the paper fairly clearly:

> '*Editor.* – Shortly my Report will contain all matters within my reach consistent with Laws, Morals, and Decorum, and for the rest usefull or amusing.
> *Reader.* Aye, aye! We will hear of Balls, Marooning Parties, Cavalcades, Lectures on Heads, Pantomines breaking the Ears of the Spectators, Run aways and so forth.
> *Editor.* Pray! What else do You read in the best papers of Europe?
> *Reader.* And the important ————
> *Editor.* "Accounts, You mean, of Ministerial and Military differences, Extra ordinary accidents, cases of law, Matters of Police" oh! my Report shall mind all these matters: J'll tell You for instance, How Sweden is at war and at Peace again with the Belligerent Powers twice a day; How St Martins has been taken and retaken in one day by Capitulation and Recapitulation between no parties at all . . .'

The literary style of the Dialogue suggests it was written by one whose mother tongue was English, but one or two typographical features of its setting (such as the use of J for I, and a few peculiarities of spelling) are perhaps indicative that the compositor was Swedish. The rest of the newspaper, both editorial and advertising matter, was also mostly English: save for a few advertisements and proclamations in French (and the vary rare advertisement in Dutch) no other language was used at any time in *The Report.*

At the end of the last page of the first issue was the advertisement

> The editors have the honour of Acquainting the Public, that *The Report of St Bartholomew* will in case of success continue and one Sheet thereof be published very Monday (Holy Days excepted) – Subscribers pay $8 a year and others 3 bitts per Number on application to *Mr Kindberg,* who is generally to be found at the Court Office; He will also receive any Advertisements or other writings, to be inserted in this periodical paper.

Beneath this was the imprint "Gustavia at the College Print." St Bartholomew's press, then, was in the school set up (in the early years of Swedish rule in the island) by public subscription.

Later issues of *The Report* follow the same basic pattern. The first page generally included proclamations issued by the Governor or his officers, with mercantile matters (Swedish–British treaties on free trade, reports of Swedish vessels running the British blockade of Martinique and Guadeloupe and so forth) forming a considerable proportion of most issues. The pitifully small amount of advertising (as compared with contemporary newspapers from the British islands) was generally less than a column on the last page. It consisted of the usual mixture of estates for sale, lost and found property, runaway slaves and so forth – occasionally for property in St Martin where the paper seems also to have circulated. The cost of advertising was $1 for three insertions.

Occasionally *the Report* was to contain matter of some special literary or historical interest. Number 7, of May 14th 1804 contained the text of a "Song on His Majesty's High Birthday, composed by Sammuel Augustus Mathews, sung in St Bartholomew's Government House November 1st 1798." Mathews was an interesting character who made a close study of the slave population: in 1793 he had been resident in St Eustatius where he wrote (and set a considerable amount of the type for) *The Lying Hero, or an answer to J. B. Moreton's Manners and Customs in the West Indies* (Eustatius, Edward L. Low for the Author).[4] He later moved to Gustavia, took out citizenship and as an important merchant became a member of the island's governing Council. Later, in number 52 of *The Report,* Saturday, May 18th 1805, the texts of four slave songs in 'West India Negro English' were submitted by him "to give distant Readers an idea of the common language of the English Negroes." A few issues earlier, on May 5th 1805, the editors had reprinted *Thoughts expressed at the Burial of Miss Sophia Fahlberg the 1st December 1804* by John Eric Forsström, Rector of the Swedish Church in Gustavia, on the grounds that this was the first piece of literature from the hand of a Swede to have been printed in the colony.

An idea of the content of other issues of *The Report* has already been given in the historical note on the colony above. In the early numbers of *The Report* attempts at 'Swedification' – by a series of articles on the history and geography of Sweden, by explanations of Swedish law and so forth – were much in evidence. Very much later, from number 131 of June 1st 1811 onwards until the end of that year, *The Report* contained a series of "Extracts from Sketches of a Political and Commercial Review of the Island of St Bartholomew from the cession of it by Lewis the 16th to Gustavus the 3rd of Sweden. By a Member of the Court of Justice." This series is of very considerable

value, particularly amplified by the ordinances, lists of shipping and other administrative and mercantile matters which were regularly published throughout the newspaper's career.

The course of *The Report* did not run smoothly. From number 13 of Thursday, June 28th 1804 onwards, publication was intended every Thursday (instead of Mondays as before) but by mid-August of that year the Editors felt compelled to apologise for "the unwarrantable neglect of one of our printers" which had caused several numbers to be late and to contain errors. The situation was to worsen, with later issues in 1805 and 1806 sometimes having two or three weeks' interval between publication of successive numbers. Things came to a head in June/July 1806, when the editors dismissed their (sole) printer and suspended publication completely. However, in August 1806 they were persuaded to revive *The Report*

> "if not weekly, at least so as to give a regular course to those matters, where insertion in our paper has of late become indispensible for the Colony; and as we for such purpose provisionally shall have to act the printer's part, we will more than ever stand in need of the indulgence of our readers."

The Editorial Staff of the paper continued in this way until number 104 (and the second volume) was completed on July 4th 1807. However, having failed to secure a printer, they had decided to suspend production completely, though promising the publication of some supplements to complete articles in progress. Only one such supplement seems to have been produced: on September 12th 1807 an index of royal proclamations and treaties, ordinances, etc., which had appeared in *The Report* was distributed gratis to subscribers by Andrew Bergstedt.

For thirty months the Swedish colony was to be without any paper of its own. During this period, reliance on the newspapers of St Kitts, which already enjoyed some circulation in Gustavia (and were frequently the source of news items included in *The Report*) became greater, towards the end of 1809 someone with training as a printer turned up in Gustavia. Although the demands on Bergstedt's time as Justiciarius and as a merchant had been intensified by his appointment as commandant of the island's newly-formed militia, he decided to resume his editorial task and resumed publication of *The Report* with number 105 on Wednesday January 10th 1810. The terms of subscription laid down in the prospectus included an undertaking by the subscriber not to withdraw from the subscription list "because the paper may innocently and undesignedly happen to hit the subscriber in any point." This time the imprint was simply "Gustavia, Printed by Andrew Bergstedt."

Only four months later, on April 19th 1810, Bergstedt was apologising for the delay in publication of number 118 "because the Printer (unfortunately for the Editor) had just turned Merchant." But before the year was out Bergstedt had other troubles on his mind. His power in the island seems to have gone to his head, and an enquiry into his conduct was ordered in October.[5]

Shortly afterwards, and confusing the situation still more, Samuel Fahlberg, who held the offices of Colonial Secretary, Chief Engineer, Director in Geometry and King's Physician in the colony – evidently a man of many parts – fled the island for Barbados. The constitutional crisis in Sweden (in which the incompetent King Gustavus IV had been deposed in 1809, and the former Regent was elected King as Charles XIII) had its repercussions in Gustavia when the news that the French General Bernardotte had been chosen as Crown Prince reached the island. Fahlberg, having failed to persuade the Governor of St Bartholomew to hold the colony for the deposed King Gustavus tried unsuccessfully to persuade the British authorities in Barbados to seize the island, according to an extraordinary issue of *The Report* of Monday May 6th 1811.

This event followed a brief pamphlet war in the colony, in which papers by 'Fair Play,' 'Ignoramus,' and 'Philo-Ignoramus' circulated round the town. Although Bergstedt's role in the affair is not clear, he seems to have lost control of *The Report* for a period. Between February 14th and 5th May 1811 no issue of the paper were published, and the latter (number 127) was printed by Nicolas Pedersen.[6] Though Bergstedt's name appears again in the imprints of numbers 131 and 132 of June 1st and 8th, he had himself found it prudent to leave the colony. When he returned from Boston in the schooner *Pilgrim* toward the end of the month, the Governor refused him permission to land on the grounds that his safety could not be guaranteed.[7] Instead, Bergstedt had to proceed to St Eustatius, and returned to Sweden shortly afterwards, although his wife remained in Gustavia to settle his affairs.

A further seven issues of *The Report,* with no indication of printer or publisher, appeared up to August 10th 1810. The paper then ceased publication as a result of the death of its printer/compositor.

However, publication was resumed on 23 November 1811 by one John Allan as its printer/editor. Allan had arrived only recently in Gustavia, and in a formal editorial stated that he trembled for the fate of his first essay in a country where he was not known. Furthermore, he continued more firmly, he knew "nothing of the sins of his Editorial progenitors; or if they had any was not prepared to have them visited on him . . ."

Under Allan's competent direction *The Report* continued for three months. But with the conclusion of his first quarter, in number 154 of Febru-

ary 17th 1812, he ceased publication having in that issue warned that he would be obliged to do so unless the number of subscriptions increased.

Over two years later he tried again, recommencing with volume 4, number 155 on Saturday July 23rd 1814. His editorial held out no great promises, and once more after three months' issues he stated that "it will be perceived that we have not been oppressed by favour and obligation." In *The Report* number 167 of October 22nd 1814, he gave a unique record of a colonial newspaper's financing:

> Forty-three names constitute the whole number of our subscribers.[8] These at 2 dollars per quarter give 86 dollars. Eight Public Summons (an unusual number for the time) interspersed through and three times inserted in *The Report* at 3 dollars each make 24 dollars. And a few private notices and advertisements, including those of the Vice Fiscal, amounting in the last quarter to about 16 dollars more, added to 25 which Government allows for a quarter's insertion of its orders and ordinances, will make when all is collected an aggregate of 151 dollars.
>
> For our own labour as Compositor and Printer, we receive 6 dollars for each paper, at which rate 13 numbers will require 73 dollars. The owner[9] of the Office and of the Press and materials, is satisfied with 4 dollars weekly, making 52 dollars per quarter. For paper, oil, soap and other contingencies we distribute each week a dollar and a half making in 13 weeks 19 dollars and 50 cents. All these items summed up . . . will leave a surplus for us as Editor, of one dollar and fifty cents per quarter . . .

Nevertheless, Allan continued publication more or less regularly. By June 1817, when the island's economy was at a low ebb, he reported that the number of subscribers had dropped to 26. The peace in Europe had made foreign news (and the demand for *The Report*) of less importance, and to increase the value of the paper Allan started reprinting all public ordinances and royal edicts since 1785 which were still in force. In this way he carried on until number 361 of May 17th 1819.

There was then a three month lapse in publication, explained by his "ill state of health" after which publication was resumed until October 28th 1819. This issue, number 368, was very badly printed, and bears the imprint "printed for John Allan," unlike the "printed by John Allan" and superior presswork on preceding issues. Number 368 bears no indication that the paper was ceasing publication, but it is the latest to survive.

Whether there was any later printing in St Bartholomew remains a mystery. None is known in Stockholm or Uppsala, but in 1827 a St Kitts newspaper

gave the *St Bartholomew Chronicle* as the byline for a local news report, and it seems probable that John Allan or another enterprising printer continued work in the Swedish colony, despite the competition from the St Kitts newspapers and their printers.

APPENDIX

Overseas Newspapers quoted in The Report of St Bartholomew

The purpose of this list is to indicate the range of newspapers quoted by the editors of the Swedish colony's paper. It is not comprehensive: since much of the news in *The Report* was lifted from the columns of the *New York Spectator,* the London *Star,* and the various St Kitts' papers, not every byline from such papers has been listed. Often sources were quoted only vaguely: "Reports from France," "a New York paper" etc., and such non-specific bylines have been excluded. The lack of reporting direct from Sweden is very marked.

Bylines have been cited as given; in several instances no doubt the newspapers' formal titles were different from the form given.

1804 St Christopher Advertiser
(St Christopher) Charribbean Courier
Philadelphia Gazette
(London) Star
American Citizen
St Christopher Courier
St Christopher Chronicle
1805 Bridgetown Gazette
St Christopher Advertiser
Barbados Mercury
Antigua Journal
New York Spectator
Dominica Journal
New York Mercantile Advertiser
Gazette de la Martinique
Philadelphia Political and Commercial Register
New York Evening Post

1806	Lancaster Gazette
	True American Commercial Advertiser
	London Sun
	Antigua Gazette
1807	(London) Times
	Norfolk Portsmouth Herald
	Poulson's American Daily Advertiser
1810	Bell's Weekly Messenger
	Baltimore Evening Post
	New York Salmagundi
1811	St Thomas Gazette
	True American Commercial Advertiser
	Philadelphia Gazette
	Boston Repertory
	Barbados Mercury
1812	(Cadiz) Semanario Patriotico
	St Croix Gazette
1814	Amsterdam Courant
1815	Barbados Times
	Antigua Gazette
	Antigua Weekly Register
	Curaçao Gazette
	Barbados Mercury
	Bermuda Gazette
	Philadelphia Gazette
	Baltimore Telegraph
	Northern Whig
1816	National Intelligencer
1817	New York Gazette and General Advertiser
	Boston Patriot
	Havanna Diary
	National Intelligencer
	St Vincent Gazette
	Martinique Gazette
1818	St Vincent Register
	Grenada Royal Gazette
	New York Commercial Advertiser
1819	Dominica Chronicle
	Richmond Enquirer
	Barbados Globe
	Antigua Register

NOTES

1. In an account of the College Institution in Gustavia, reporting that on 15 March 1799 the Free Builders Lodge issued a publication *which was afterwards printed and distributed round the town,* stating that the institution had been sanctioned by the King.
2. cf. Roderick Cave 'Aspects of early printing and the book trade in the West Indies' forthcoming in *Library Quarterly,* April 1978.
3. Item 47 in *S. Barthélemy, en Svensk koloni 1784–1878.* Katalog utarbetad av Heribert Seitz (Stockholm, 1934).
4. There is a copy of Mathew's book in Boston Public Library; Shelf mark *XH.714D.M42L.
5. A report of this (which I have not seen) apparently appeared in the *St Christopher Courier* October 10th, 1810.
6. The Uppsala copy of this issue, apparently the only one to survive, is very badly printed and the imprint cannot be made out very clearly.
7. *Report of St Bartholomew* no. 134, June 22nd 1811. It was natural that the St Bartholomew merchants should have anticipated disaster for themselves and the colony if Bernardotte's policies brought about alliance with France (as was confidently expected, not least by the French).
8. Though a low number of subscribers, a good many other papers in Antigua St Kitts and Tobago for example never achieved a three-figure circulation. And not all subscribers paid promptly, if at all.
9. Presumably still Bergstedt, whose wife did not leave the island until March 1815.

PRINTING IN TRINIDAD

XXI
THE HISTORY OF PRINTING IN TRINIDAD
Some Preliminary Notes

INTRODUCTION

Unlike such other West Indian islands as Barbados, Guadeloupe and Jamaica, whose printing history has been studied in some depth by writers on printing history who were also familiar with the general history of the territory, the place of printing and the book trade in Trinidad has received little attention. In view of the importance the colony gained in the nineteenth century, and the relative wealth of material still available for study in Trinidad, this neglect is unfortunate. Although some Trinidadian imprints are of course recorded in Ragatz's classic *Guide to the Study of British Caribbean History 1763-1834* (Washington, 1932) the lack of a comprehensive record of Trinidadian publications, like that in Jerome Handler's *Guide to Source Materials for the Study of Barbados History 1627-1834* (Carbondale, 1971) throws the student back on a very limited number of studies or his own original research.

Those studies which have been made are essentially of two kinds. On the one hand are those written by bibliographers and typographic historians; notably the Chilean José Toribio Medina and the American Douglas C. McMurtrie. Toribio Medina was concerned with printing in Spain's overseas dominions, of which (in bibliographical terms) Trinidad formed only a very insignificant part. McMurtrie, in his *Notes on the Beginning of Printing on the Island of Trinidad* (Fort Worth, 1943) put together a useful summary of what was then known, written with the expert knowledge of one who had made studies of printing in some of the other West Indian islands as well as North America. Nevertheless, the value of his *Notes* was diminished by the fact that he had to rely on information communicated to him rather than handling many of the publications himself, and he was unfamiliar with Trinidadian history.

The second group consists of works written by Trinidadians. Edward W. David's *Note on the Introduction of Printing into Trinidad de Barlovento* which was circulated in typescript (Port-of-Spain? 1950?) was a useful secondary work, but flawed by errors in some of the sources on which David relied. Lionel Fraser's *History of Trinidad* (Port-of-Spain, 1891-6) included some valuable information on the early newspapers published in the island; the centenary issue of *The Port of Spain Gazette* (21 September 1925) also contained some very useful material, though not without errors. More recent books, such as Errol Hill's *The Trinidad Carnival* (Austin, 1972) contain some interesting sidelights on the nineteenth

century press. The best example is V. S. Naipaul's *The Loss of El Dorado*, a superbly readable history which (in the Penguin edition, 1972; earlier British and American hard-back editions are much less full) contains much of value of the Trinidad press under the early British governors. But to write the history of printing in Trinidad was not Naipaul's purpose, of course; *The Loss of El Dorado* like these other Trinidadian books lacks the specialist typographical approach.

One honourable exception is to be found in a history of the Trinidad Government Printing Office written by the Government Printer, Leslie O. Weekes. His *1st Hundred Years 1873-1973* presents the history of an important institution, written by one who is both Trinidadian and printing historian, and will serve as a model for the other studies of individual printing and book trade firms and institutions in the West Indies for which we wait.

The notes which follow are based on consultation of the sources mentioned above, on discussions with Mr Weekes and with Mr Enos Sewlal (Government Archivist) and on a quick examination of files of some of the early Trinidad newspapers preserved in the Trinidad Archives and the Trinidad Public Library which I was able to undertake in an all-too-brief return to Trinidad in 1974. I have supplemented this with such other information on Trinidad as has turned up during my research (in the Public Record Office and the American Antiquarian Society in particular) on printing in other West Indian islands.

Much work remains to be done, particularly through systematic examination of the Trinidad files in the Colonial Office papers in the Public Record Office (the C.O. 295 series in particular) and in Trinidad itself, on the wealth of local publications deposited in the Registrar-General's Office in the Red House, Port-of-Spain.

In the narrow limits of historical bibliography, such work is essential as a step for the preparation of a comprehensive retrospective national bibliography that one hopes independent Trinidad & Tobago will produce before too long. In the wider field of Trinidad's history, the attitudes adopted by the various newspaper proprietors and editors (and by their readers) to the social and political questions of their day – towards Carnival, or East Indian immigration, for instance – are of real importance in understanding modern Trinidadian society. Studies of this kind are difficult indeed until a proper bibliographical foundation has been laid. *The Port of Spain Gazette,* for instance, is often regarded as the mouthpiece of the old plantocracy; when I lived in Trinidad in the early 1960s it had ceased publication, but was still spoken of in the way an Englishman might perhaps recall the *Morning Post.* No doubt it was totally out of touch with progressive thought in post-1945 Trinidad, but 'mouthpiece of the old plantocracy' is an over-simplification as even cursory examination of the paper's history shows. At different times during its long life, and in the hands of different editors, its stance (and its role) changed very considerably. That it should have survived so long, when the life of most Trinidad newspapers was so brief, was not due only to luck. A detailed study of this newspaper alone would be of great value.

XX
PRINTING IN THE SWEDISH WEST INDIES

Among the many West Indian newspapers of great rarity and importance in the collections of the American Antiquarian Society is a short run of *The Report of St Bartholomew.* Acquired since Waldo Lincoln compiled his 'List of Newspapers of the West Indies and Bermuda in the Library of the Society' which was included in the April 1926 issue of the Society's *Proceedings,* the very existence of the newspaper was unknown to Lowell Ragatz when he compiled his *Guide for the study of British Caribbean History 1763–1834* (Washington, 1932). The Society's set of *The Report,* in fact, appears to be the only surviving examplar outside Sweden of printing in the Swedish West Indies.

That there ever was a Swedish colony in the Caribbean comes as a surprise. Nevertheless, from 1784, when King Gustav III of Sweden purchased the island of St Bartholomew from Louis XVI of France, until 1878 (when the colony was ceded back to France) the Swedes had a small West Indian presence in competition with the Danes, the Dutch, the English, French and Spanish.

St Bartholomew is a small island at the northern end of the Leeward Islands, its closest neighbours of any importance being the British colony of St. Kitts, Dutch St Eustatius, and St Martin (which was split between the Dutch and French), with the Danish islands of St Thomas and St Croix to the west. Now a complete backwater, for a short period in the early nineteenth century it enjoyed intervals of considerable prosperity, with its capital Gustavia supporting a population of 4,000 or more, and its roadsteads crowded with shipping of many nations.

The colony's prosperity came entirely from its unique political position throughout the period of the Napoleonic wars. Being neutral, and protected (however imperfectly) by Swedish–British treaties of friendship, Gustavia was the perfect trans-shipment port, and vessels under the Swedish flag could trade with a freedom denied to all others by one or other of the belligerent powers. In the 1780s and 1790 the Danish merchants of St Thomas and the Dutch in St Eustatius had been the main channel for the importation of

PRINTING IN ST. BARTHOLOMEW

THE INTRODUCTION OF PRINTING

Until the closing decades of Spanish rule, Trinidad was too unimportant, too little developed, for printing to be introduced. Not until Governor Chacon's administration was a press set up in the island.

The earliest Trinidadian publication known is a twelve-page folio pamphlet cited by Toribio Medina as in the Archivo de las Indias: Ordenanza publicada en el Puerto de Espana, el 11 de Agosto 1786, on which the imprint is Del Puerto de Espana, De la Imprenta de Don Juan Cassan.

Cassan may safely be identified as the French printer Jean Cassan, who in 1779 had been printer of the *Gazette Royale de la Grenade* at Fort Royal (St George's) Grenada. Grenada's closeness to Trinidad was to continue to encourage members of the book trade in one to move to the other, as will be seen below.

The only other publication from Spanish Trinidad known to me, and the only one I have examined, is a proclamation in Spanish, French and English issued by Governor Chacon in August 1791 and now in the Public Record Office (C.O.71/21). This was printed (in very poor, worn types) by Pedro Ginet. It is almost certain that this was the same Ginet who turns up as 'Imprimeur de la Republique' in Guadeloupe, who in 1804 was printing the *Journal Officiel de la Guadeloupe et Dependances* there.

We may catch a very faint glimpse of one of the more unusual and demanding commissions of Governor Chacon, in a brief description of the 1790 carnival which was written by one of the recent immigrants to Trinidad in a letter to a correspondent in Antigua, and reprinted in John Wells's *Bahama Gazette* of 30 April 1790:

> At the Governour's entertainment (which was very grand) there sat down to supper above 200 people. We had every good thing that could be procured; on the table was set a large cake, with an image on the top, representing the King, and stuck round, as full as ever it could hold, with little silk flags, on which was printed "Long live King Charles the Fourth" in Spanish, French, and English, one of which was given by the Governour to each person in their own language, which they wore in their hat and bosoms the remainder of the night ....

It is amusing to think of the republican Ginet labouring away to print these flags!

It is clear that in the late 1780s an official *Gaceta* was being published in Port-of-Spain. 'The Trinidad Gazette' appears as a by-line on a news report reprinted in John Wells's *Bahama Gazette* on 17 January 1789; in another document in the Archivo de las Indias which is cited by Toribio Medina, Governor Chacon reported to the King of Spain (27 January 1790) that he had ordered a certain Juan Viloux, editor of the weekly *Gaceta* to leave the island

> for having reprinted in it, without my approval, various articles from the foreign newspapers about the present revolution in France, in which were published items calculated to spread dissension, corrupt the true faith, and disturb the good order of our rule.

Chacon's action was approved by royal order on 25 May 1790.

'Juan Viloux' is a disguise under which the real editor concerned has remained hidden for too long: he was the interesting F. J. Willox de Douay. After his expulsion from Trinidad, Willox soon turns up elsewhere in the Caribbean, as partner with Sextius Buffardin d'Aix in production of *Le Furet Colonial et Reviseur Universel* which started publication at Charlotteville (Roseau), Dominica, in April 1791. In *Le Furet Colonial* of 25 September 1791 Willox printed an *Avis* which included

> le soussigné, ci-devant Redacteur du *Courrier de la Trinité Espagnole,* de celui *de la Martinique & des Petites Antilles,* & aujourd'hui cooperateur associé au *Furet Colonial,* prie ses sousscripteurs debiteurs des dites feuilles de prendres en consideration les disagremens que lui ont fait eprouver sa loyauté et ses principés sous des gouvernements arbitraires, & d'acquitter au plutôt entre les mains des ses receveurs le montant de leur sous-scriptions. Il engage encore plusieurs particuliers de Port d'Espagne, ses reliquataires de quelques sommes, a être de meilleure foi & à remplir au plutôt la promesse qu'ils lui ont fait lors de son depart.

Willox turned up again as 'Imprimeur du Gouvernement' in St Pierre, Martinique, in 1793. What happened to him afterwards I do not know.

PRINTING UNDER THE BRITISH

It has been suggested that Matthew Gallagher, the first printer to work in Port-of-Spain after Governor Chacon had surrendered to General Abercrombie in February 1797, was already at work there before that date. There were a good many Irish Catholics among the immigrants to Trinidad after the island was opened to Catholic colonisation in 1776, and it is quite possible that Gallagher could have gone there in the last years of Spanish rule. In 1791, when Willox de Douay was working on *Le Furet Colonial* in Dominica, Gallagher was also in the island as printer of another French newspaper, *Le Censeur Impartial ou l'Aristocrate Devoilé.* By February 1794 he was printing the *Weekly Courant and Charibbean Advertiser* in St George's, Grenada.

Although Gallagher then disappears from view for five years, and Fedon's insurrection in 1795 made Grenada an unattractive place to remain, I think it more probable that Gallagher did not move to Port-of-Spain until after the British invasion. He was certainly in Trinidad by June 1799, and on 21st of that month advertised (in the Grenada *St George's Chronicle*) for a compositor who was needed in Port-of-Spain. Bibliographical examination of Picton's 1797 Proclamation (cited by Naipaul, p. 149) might establish whether it came from Gallagher's shop. By 1800 it is clear that his business in Port-of-Spain was well established, and in that year he started publication of the *Trinidad Weekly Courant.*

By Naipaul's account, the *Courant* was a well-edited paper, and Gallagher was a printer of some taste and competence. For some years he seems to have had a monopoly of printing in Trinidad, most of his work apart from the *Courant* being jobbing printing, and such official work as was required. In the period of government by the Commissioners (Fullarton, Hood and Picton) this cannot always have been easy.

In 1808, at the instance of Governor Hislop, who had been asked by the authorities in Venezuela for help in setting up a press, Gallagher went to Caracas taking with him an old wooden press from Grenada (no doubt that which he had used earlier for the *Weekly Courant and Charibbean Advertiser)*. Publication of the *Gaceta de Caracas* was started there by the firm of Gallagher y Lamb; one of their employees was later to introduce printing into Curaçao. It seems that after the *Gaceta* was well-established, Gallagher left the running of the Caracas venture to his partner, as he soon returned himself to Port-of-Spain.

Despite Governor Hislop's patronage, in 1810 Gallagher ran afoul of George Smith, the island's one-man Royal Audiencia. The British settlers in Trinidad were anxious for the introduction of British law and a British constitution (that is, an elected Assembly) for the new colony. For printing their petition and supporting letters, against Smith's instructions, Gallagher received a three-month gaol sentence which Hislop was without power to commute. Smith's action highlighted the conflict of powers between the Governor and the Royal Audiencia, and provided a demonstration of the ease with which officials could muzzle the press in Trinidad. Gallagher's own *Letters and Documents relative to the Emprisonment and Discharge of the Author* was published in 1810.

At this time, Gallagher's *Courant* was challenged by another paper, the *Trinidad Independant Gazette* printed by John Johnston. A study of this newspaper (of which some copies survive in the Public Record Office, C. O. 295/24) is a desideratum. Gallagher and his paper survived the competition, and in 1813 his paper became a biweekly under the style *Trinidad Courant and Commercial Gazette* which lasted until at least 1817, and I suspect until 1819 (in which year a government order was printed by Gallagher's executors) but I have not seen any copies from this period. Nor is the disposal of his equipment by his executors clear.

GOVERNMENT PRINTING

Until the establishment of the Government Printing Office in 1873, official printing was farmed out among various printers in the colony. On more than one occasion, printers were disciplined by the government by the withdrawal (or threat of withdrawal) of official printing.

Printers engaged on official work at different times included

Matthew Gallagher 1800, 1813, 1814, 1815, 1817; executors 1819
C. Lloyd 1813, 1824, 1825, 1828
Charles Rollin Beach 1815
William Lewer 1820, 1821, 1822, 1824
J. Holman & Co 1824
James Ramsay 1829, 1833
F. C. Bowen 1839
H.J. Mills, 1845, 1847-59, 1869
Otto Wenkstern 1869
T. W. Carr 1870

Most of these men appear elsewhere in the Trinidad printing or book trade as well. Charles Rollin Beach, an American, soon moved elsewhere: in 1816 marrying Sarah Stockdale of Bermuda and thereby aquiring title to the *Bermuda Gazette* which had been started by her father Joseph Stockdale in 1784. C. Lloyd I cannot identify unless he is the same man as the Lloyd who was Organist of Holy Trinity Church in 1828, when he advertised (in the *Trinidad Guardian* of 13 February 1829) that he taught music and was a music-seller in Port-of-Spain.

LATER NEWSPAPERS

The Trinidad Gazette

Between 9 September 1820 and the summer of 1825, the *Trinidad Gazette* was issued biweekly by William Lewer from 28 Queen Street, at a price of £ 5 per annum, payable in advance. In French and English, Lewer's paper was well produced and competently edited; it bears comparison with other West Indian papers of the time very well.

In its columns, from time to time Lewer advertised other publications from his own press, such as the *Trinidad Book Almanac* and the *Trinidad Sheet Almanac*, both advertised 2 January 1822. No doubt publication of both was an annual event, though I have not seen any copies. In the same issue, 2 January 1822, he advertised *The Common Place Book* 'ruled throughout for every day in the year', and on 21 December 1822 he offered Blank Muster Rolls and Company's Returns – both obviously intended for officers in the local militia. Other publications noted include *The Plantation Record Book of Punishments Inflicted on Slaves*, and 'a French translation of His Majesty's Order in Council of the 10th March 1824', both advertised on 7 July 1824.

Several of Lewer's advertisments refer to his stocks of stationery, his moderate charges for jobbing printing, that he can meet needs for bookbinding in all its branches, has received a supply of London almanacs and so forth – the typical range of stock and services of an enterprising printer of the time. Of rather more interest was his advertisment of 2 February 1825 of 'a few copies of a letter addressed to Charles Rose Ellis Esq. M.P. (on sugar duties) by Samuel Turner Esq. FRS – Published lately at Antigua by Loving and Hill – Price six shillings currency.' West Indian newspaper proprietors of course had regular exchanges with their contemporaries in other islands, indeed they depended very heavily on these for their newsgathering, but such evidence as this of additional trade contacts are rather uncommon.

In March 1825 Lewer lost his position as government printer, and in no. 523 of his *Gazette* (14 September 1825) announced that he was bringing it to a close, and would himself be leaving the colony to return to London where he would be setting up as a periodical subscription agent for the colonies. I have not been able to establish whether he was successful in this venture.

To fill the gap left by the closure of Lewer's *Trinidad Gazette*, two new papers were started in Port-of-Spain, the *Port of Spain Gazette* which started publication from Lewer's old address in Queen Street on 21 September 1825, and the *Trinidad Guardian* started by J. W. Irwin from 10 Frederick Street on 21 October 1825. The history of Irwin's paper is outlined in another paper of mine ('The first *Trinidad Guardian*') and is therefore not dealt with further here.

The *Port of Spain Gazette*

Although this newspaper (hereafter called *PoSG*) was to have a long and not undistinguished place in West Indian journalism – of which the fullest account is given in its centenary issue of 21 September 1925 – in its earliest days it was very far from certain to survive, particularly while it was battling with the *Trinidad Guardian* in a market really too small to support both papers. Only the most important points in the early history of *PoSG* are given below.

From 21 September 1825 until September 1829 its proprietors were named in the paper as John Holman & Co., for whom the paper was printed by Holman. On 30 September 1829 the style of the proprietors was changed to Belk & Holman, with Holman continuing as printer. The new partnership was not a success, however: on 7 November 1829 an advertisment announced the dissolution of the partnership, and in that issue William Belk was named as proprietor; no printer was named at all.

One week later, in no. 433 (14 November 1829) Belk announced the paper would be ceasing publication:

> We are painfully necessitated to take leave of our subscribers and the Public in general, assuring them that our utmost endeavours have been exerted to continue the publication of the Port of Spain Gazette, but circumstances of a peculiar nature have compelled us to relinquish its further publication.

It is evident that there had been a battle for control between Belk and Holman, and that although the first skirmish had gone in Belk's favour, in the end Holman – having found a new partner – had emerged the victor. After a week without publication of *PoSG*, on 21 November no. 434 was published with this announcement:

> The publication of the Port of Spain Gazette having been partially suspended, and commencing as it were a new paper, the present proprietors beg leave most respectfully to announce to the Public that the Gazette will continue to be published as usual, on Wednesdays and Saturdays–Unforeseen circumstances rendered the omission of last Wednesday's Gazette unavoidable; and the new Proprietors will make speedy arrangements to ensure a correct and early delivery of the paper.
>
> Mr Holman takes this opportunity of returning his most grateful acknowledgements to his Friends and the Public, for the Patronage which they have afforded the Gazette since its establishment, and trusts that his future exertions in the profession, will ensure a continuance of that kindness which they have so conspicuously evinced–assuring the Patrons of the Gazette that no exertion on his part or that of his associate, will be wanting, to ensure Public favor.

Subscriptions to the paper were being charged from that issue onwards, at £ 10 per annum, payable in advance. The imprint revealed the identity of Holman's new associate: H. J. Mills, a bookseller who came originally from Thetford in Norfolk, who had been in business in Frederick Street since 1826 or earlier. His bookselling and stationery business was brought into the partnership and thereafter traded as Holman & Mills, Stationers. The printing house remained for a while at 28 Queen Street, but in December 1829 was removed to 14 Frederick Street.

Belk advertised his printing equipment for sale on 2 December 1829. For the next few years, apart from the rivalry with the now-failing *Trinidad Guardian*, the affairs of the *PoSG* progressed uneventfully. In the winter of 1829-30 its columns were filled with lists advertising the books being added to Holman & Mills' newly formed Subscription Library; a separate catalogue of its stock of more than 3,000 volumes was also published. The *PoSG* frequently carried advertisments for some of the other venture of Holman & Mills: *The Trinidad Almanac*, an edition of *Adele, or the Dubious Widow,* a lithographic view of the Eastern Promenade in King Street, and so on.

In 1832 Holman died, and Mills entered a new partnership with a Mr Stewart who acted as editor: according to Fraser (*History of Trinidad*, vol.2 p.333) however, the real owner of the paper was a Mr Drinan, 'a merchant of some standing'. By this time, feeling betweeen the old party of merchants and planters on the one hand and the anti-slavery group dubbed 'The Saints' was running very high. The *PoSG* was bitter in its attacks on Chief Justice Scotland, who had made himself very unpopular with the planter party by his evident leaning towards the Saints. At first, as a response to these attacks the Chief Justice contented himself with depriving the *PoSG* of the valuable Court advertising – perhaps part of the reason that the paper had to increase its subscription from £ 5 to £ 6 from 1 January 1833.

Then the *PoSG* overreached itself in its attacks on Scotland, and its continued existence was threatened by a successful libel action which he brought against it. Mills & Stewart, required to pay damages of £ 1,200 plus costs of £ 300, were sold up: their printing equipment and circulating library (which they had valued at £ 3,500) were sold for £ 162, and as they did not realize enough to cover the judgment, the hapless printers were incarcerated in the Royal Gaol as well. Scotland's rather contemptible victory was less than he had hoped: Mills and Stewart had enough supporters after the case had made them into martyrs to weather this, and for some months afterwards *PoSG* editorials were dated from No. 1, Clarence Street (the address of the Royal Gaol). In this period, too, they published E. L. Joseph's satire on the militia laws, *Martial Law in Trinidad, a Musical Farce in Two Acts* issued at 10s. in July 1833.

On their release from gaol in January 1834, Stewart had had enough, and the partnership was dissolved. Publication of the *PoSG* was continued by Mills alone, until his death at the age of 65 in May 1870. Mills was also responsible for publishing several other books important in Trinidadian society, such as E. L. Joseph's *History of Trinidad* (1838), and in his riper years he was frequently the contractor for government printing.

On Mills's death, ownership of the paper passed to his son Frederick Losh Mills. He had little taste for newspaper work in the competitive scene of the 1870s, and in issue no. 4,667 of 30 July 1870 issued a farewell from the paper his father had run for so long. However, after more than forty years' life the *PoSG* had become an institution too well liked to be allowed to die, and it was therefore revived by others, with a new series being started on Saturday 10 September 1870, under the direction of Henry James Clark. Published from 9 Chacon Street, the new series was priced at $10 per year.

Under Clark's able direction the paper prospered. But in 1873 Clark was successful in his application for the new post of Government Printer. This salaried official post was not compatible with his publication of a newspaper which was often critical of government policy, and Clark was therefore obliged to dispose of *PoSG*. For a few weeks after his appointment as Government Printer took effect in October 1873, before he had been able to make more suitable long-term arrangements, he dealt with the problem by issuing *PoSG* with no editorial matter. Then from 1 November the paper appeared under the imprint of George H. Clark (no doubt a relative, perhaps a son, who had newly arrived from England). George Clark had no previous experience of newspaper work, and ran the *PoSG* for only three months.

From 1 February 1874 the paper's plant and goodwill were taken over by Martial Antoine, who had been foreman since H. J. Clark had started the new series of the *PoSG* in September 1870. At an earlier stage in his career, Antoine had been printer of the *St Lucia Palladium* (1847) and I suspect that he was a St Lucian himself. Antoine started another new series of the *PoSG*, once more from the old editorial address at 14 Frederick Street. His regime lasted for only eighteen months, however: perhaps the reason for his departure was the paper's libel on L. M. Fraser in 1875, for which it had to publish a retraction and apology. From 24 August 1875 the *PoSG* was published from the same address by T.R.N. Laughlin.

Laughlin was subsequently to move to various addresses in Chacon Street, in 1893 being back in H. J. Clark's premises at number 9. In the late 1880s the paper became a daily. Though Laughlin remained connected with the *PoSG* until his death in 1921, in November 1900 he sold the paper to Louis F. Ambard, and Joseph de la Sauvagère became editor. When the latter died in February 1910, editorship was taken over by the proprietor's son André Ambard. With the paper's subsequent history until it was discontinued in the 1950s I have not been concerned.

The Royal Gazette

According to Fraser (*History of Trinidad* v.2 pp.265-6) another paper, the *Royal Gazette* was started in 1832 as a counterweight to the *PoSG*; a paper which 'was looked upon as the organ of the "Saints".' It was edited by a Port-of-Spain grocer of advanced views, Young Anderson. Far from being the mouthpiece of Whitehall policy, however closely it coincided with the Colonial Office in its anti-slavery views, it soon became associated with the group of British settlers who were seeking control of local affairs. I have not seen this paper, which in 1833 had been retitled *The Colonial Observer*, but there are several references to it in the Trinidad indexes prepared in the Colonial Office, and I suspect some copies may survive in the C. O. 295 series in the Public Record Office. Ragatz confuses this paper with the *Trinidad Royal Gazette by Authority* which started publication late in 1833. The earliest issue of this I have seen is no. 148 of 2 January 1835.

The *Trinidad Royal Gazette* existed only to publish official notices and advertisments, and was produced under contract by whichever printer had tendered successfully for government printing. From the Trinidad Public Library's incomplete run, it is clear that from January 1835 until September 1838 it was printed by James Ramsay, up till 1837 from 10 St Vincent Street, but in 1839 from the corner of St Vincent and King Streets.

The last issue with Ramsay's imprint is vol. 7 no. 584 of Friday 6 September 1839. The next published, on Wednesday 18 September, was 'Printed and Published by F. C. Bowen, Government Printer, Office No – [sic] St Vincent Street.' Previously published bi-weekly, on 20 September 1839 Bowen announced that in future it would appear only weekly, at $3 per annum, with advertising charged at only half the rates of other Port-of-Spain papers.

As I have not seen issues for the year 1840 I do not know when Bowen lost the contract, but the issues for 1841 bear the imprint 'George Scotland jr, Government Printer, Office no – [sic] St Vincent Street.' George Scotland junior was no printer; he was in fact the son of the Chief Justice, and the *PoSG*'s libel on him in 1833 had alleged that Chief Justice Scotland had bent the law by having his son appointed Escribano of the Supreme Court while the latter was still below the age set for this appointment. Whether political jobbery had enabled the young Scotland to secure the lucrative government printing contract would be good to know.

Issues of the *Trinidad Royal Gazette* for 1842 are also missing from the files I was able to examine, but by 'volume 4 number 3' of 19 April 1843 the government printing contract was firmly in the hands of Henry James Mills (owner of the *PoSG*) and the *Gazette* continued to be printed by him throughout the 1840s.

Although from its nature, the *Trinidad Royal Gazette* contained little which tells us about the state of the printing trade in the island, its publication of lists of Assessors [jurors] in the Court for the Trial of Criminal Prosecutions sometimes gave the occupations of those who were as householders qualified for this duty. Thus in February 1835 five printers were named:

W. Robertson living in	Upper Princes Street
H.J. Mills	Edward Street
Edward Miller	Hanover Street
P.Westmoreland	Hanover Street
John E. Lynch	Hanover Street

In 1837 I have found only the names of Robertson and Mills (now in Frederick Street); in 1839 Mills, Frederick C. Bowen (Henry Street) and James Ramsay (Abercrombie Street). In the 1845 list the only name found was that of John E. Lynch (Queen Street).

The Trinidad Standard & West India Journal

Published biweekly on Tuesdays and Fridays, apparently from January 1838 (first issue seen is no. 105 of 1 January 1839) by F. C. Bowen, Trinidad Standard Printing Office, Frederick Street, price $12 p.a. From 4 October 1840 (no. 271) the imprint was Bowen & Treacher; from 1 July 1841 (no. 365) Treacher & Co. This issue contains a farewell from Bowen, thanking readers in his native colony &c. &c. Bowen had been an energetic man, rivalling Mills at the *PoSG* with his range of other printing, jobbing work and so forth. The only issues I have seen later than 1841 are those for 1846 (in the American Antiquarian Society Library) by which time the paper was being printed and published by John McSwiney. McSwiney also issued a monthly supplement or shipping news, prices current, advertisments etc. I believe publication of the *Standard* ceased in 1847.

The Trinidad Spectator, and Port of Spain and San Fernando Advertiser

A biweekly evening paper, published from Wednesday 4 June 1845 by Charles S. Legge at 34 King Street, price $10 p.a. Legge was evidently new to newspaper work, and in his third issue apologised for the number of typographical errors in the previous numbers, having in his inexperience, he said, been unaware of the need for vigilant proofreading!

The Trinidad Public Library's set closes with the issues for May 1847, the last produced by Legge. He announced that the paper was being continued by C. Y. Jardine; Jardine presumably did so as the Registrar-General's set (not seen) is reported to cover the period 1845-8.

The Trinidadian

Published weekly by George Numa des Sources, from 1 and 2a Henry Street, price $10 p. a. From the Trinidad Public Library's very fragile and incomplete run (from v.2 no.52, 24 November 1849 - v.4 no.66, 31 January 1853) the paper seems to have started in 1848. It seems to have ceased publication sometime in 1853.

The San Fernando Gazette

Publication of this interesting little newspaper, the first to be produced outside Port-of-Spain, is discussed in the separate article 'Early Printing in Southern Trinidad' elsewhere in this volume.

The Trinidad Free Press

Not seen. The Registrar-General's Office is reported to have a set for 1851-53. The paper seems to have ceased publication in 1853, as in 1854 the *Trinidad Palladium* claimed to be continuing its aims.

The Herald

So far as I can tell, there was no connection between Charles Henry Mills, the printer of this paper at the General Printing Office, 1 Brunswick Square, and H.J. Mills of the *PoSG. The Herald* seems to have started as a biweekly in 1852; from v.3 no.1 of 6 January 1854 (the earliest issue I have seen) it was published weekly at $6 p. a. The paper claimed to be non-sectarian; Wesleyan advertisments appear in its columns. The last issue in the Trinidad Archives is that of 9 June 1854. It contains no hint that publication was ceasing, but – as Mills started another paper in December 1854 – I suspect that it had ceased publication before then.

The Trinidad Palladium. A Political and Literary Journal

Published weekly, price $6 p. a., by George Somerall at 4 St Vincent Street from 5 April 1854. Intended to continue the same policies as the *Trinidad Free Press,* it seems not to have lasted beyond its twenty-first number, 26 August 1854.

The Trinidad Examiner

Started as a biweekly price $10 p. a. by Charles Henry Mills (formerly publisher of *The Herald*) from 1 December 1854. Mills stated that the paper was being started because of general dissatisfaction with the tone of the *PoSG* whose editor was nothing but a government lackey.

Though there was a place for an effective opposition paper, Mills lacked the financial resources to fill it. The last issue in the Trinidad Archives set, no.64 of 28 August 1855, contained this heartcry:

> Circumstances over which we had no control, has [sic] caused the issue of the present number to be delayed. In plain words we say the pecuniary embarrassed circumstances of the Proprietor has been the cause, and if friends of the *Examiner* would but come forward with the 'tin' that is due (especially the Country Subscribers) no such drawbacks would occur in future .... We also beg to inform those subscribers who have not paid that they will be indiscriminately sued.

The Trinidad Reporter, and Agricultural and Commercial Journal

Published weekly in 1854 by William Charles McDaniel from 17 Frederick Street at $8 p. a. The Trinidad Archives' file is for 1854 only, but the paper may have lasted into the following year.

The Trinidad Sentinel

A weekly, published at $ 8 p. a. on Thursdays by Alexander Murray (formerly of the *San Fernando Gazette*) from 3 Abercrombie Street. Publication probably started at the beginning of 1856, though the earliest issue seen is v.3 no.4, whole no.158, 4 February 1858. The Trinidad Archives' set closes with no. 204, 30 December 1858, but the Registrar-General's holdings are reported to cover the years 1856-63. As Murray did not return to San Fernando to revive his *Gazette* there until 1865, I suspect that his *Sentinel* may have continued beyond 1863.

The Trinidad Press and Advocate of the People

An evening paper, published biweekly on Wednesdays and Saturdays from 4 May 1859 by a Barbadian, William Herbert of 13 Frederick Street. Priced at $ 10 p.a., Herbert's paper was apparently in the Roman Catholic interest, his other publications including *Two Lectures* by Archbishop Spaccapietra, written in answer to three sermons by the Anglican Rector of Holy Trinity in 1860. Although the last issue filed in the Trinidad Public Library's set is no.80 of 4 Feruary 1860, as Herbert was advertising in it his large range of new display faces which would allow him to do even better jobbing work in the future, it seems unlikely this was the last to be published.

The Trinidad Colonist

A biweekly published on Tuesdays and Fridays by William Herbert from the same address, from October 1861. Its editorial tone was strong: 'The Trinidad Colonist claims British Institutions as their right. Away with an obsolete form of government. Taxation without representation is tyranny and robbery.' The last issue I have seen is no.123 of 19 December 1862 (Trinidad Public Library).

The Star of the West

I have not seen this paper, of which the Registrar-General's office is reported to have a file for the years 1862 to 1874. The paper was edited by one Gawthorne, and his editorial rivalry with William Herbert was bitter and acrimonious.

The Trinidad Chronicle

Publication of this important biweekly paper seems to have started in the autumn of 1864; by the first issue I have seen (no.120 of 2 January 1866) it was being published from 4a Abercrombie Street. Its editorial direction was in the able hands of Otto Wenkstern, a Prussian who had formerly been on the editorial staff of *The Times* in London. Wenkstern died in the yellow fever outbreak of 1869/70; but the paper continued until about 1885. In 1872 it was being published by T.W. Carr of 13 Frederick Street.

The New Era

Printed and published by the partnership of Samuel Carter and Joseph Lewis at 3 Abercrombie Street, appearing on Monday evenings from November 1869. price $ 8 p. a. In 1874 Carter left to purchase the *San Fernando Gazette* from Alexander Murray's heirs, and *The New Era* was continued by Lewis alone. The last issue I have seen – still published from the same address – is no. 711 of 12 April 1886, but from the evidence of the Trinidad Blue Books, publication seems to have continued as late as 1892.

The Echo of Trinidad

Published on Wednesdays, apparently from some time in 1871. By the time of publication of volume 6 new series no. 288, 5 January 1876 (the earliest I have seen) it was being printed and published by Ajax Voisinage at 71 Queen Street, price $ 10 p. a. The Trinidad Archives' brief file closes with no. 320 of 16 August 1876; the paper was certainly defunct by October of that year. Martial Antoine's *Trinidad Palladium* seems to have been its successor.

The Trinidad Monthly

A literary journal published sporadically in 1871/2 under the editorship of J.J. Thomas, author of *Froudacity* and *The Creole Grammar.* I have not seen it; according to Donald Wood (in his Introduction to the New Beacon edition of *Froudacity)* the journal died for lack of contributors and subscribers; not by any means the first West Indian literary magazine to succumb for these reasons.

The Telegraph

I have not seen this newspaper, of which the Registrar-General's Office is reported to have a set for 1871-75.

Le Petit Farceur

Another of the thorns in the side of government placed by William Herbert; this one a comic illustrated paper apparently of the *Punch* style. I have not seen any copies; the Registrar-General's Office is said to have a set for 1872 but as the *Trinidad Chronicle* of 1 October 1872 referred to it in the past tense I suspect that it had already ceased publication by then.

Fair Play. A Weekly Newspaper of Politics, Agriculture, Literature, Science and Art.

Started as a weekly on 9 October 1874 by Henry Schuller Billouin at 4a Abercrombie Street. By no. 14 of 7 January 1875 it claimed to have the largest circulation of any newspaper in Trinidad, though in the same issue it complained of readers who while warning the editor of 'the risk of being *bought*' did not pay their own subscriptions without repeated application.

At the end of its first year of life, *Fair Play* claimed that it had as many subscribers as any three of its four contemporaries in Port-of-Spain. It announced that from volume two it would appear under the title *Fair Play. And Trinidad and Venezuelan News*, as it was incorporating the equipment of the late *Trinidad News,* a newspaper I have not come across otherwise. From the start of 1876 it appeared in larger format; the address was changed to 1B Lower Chacon Street in October of that year. The Registrar-General's set closes with no.534 of 21 August 1884, but internal evidence suggests the paper continued beyond that date.

The Trinidad Palladium

Although the title had been used before (by George Somersall in 1854) this was the name chosen for a weekly paper started by Martial Antoine (formerly of the *PoSG*) on 28 October 1876. It was published from 71 Queen Street; Antoine appears to have taken over the plant from Ajax Voisinage, and his paper is almost identical with Voisinage's *Echo of Trinidad* in design. Antoine's opposition to the *PoSG* which is strongly expressed in this paper was no doubt due to the circumstances in which he left the paper (see above).

Volume 7 no.339, 30 June 1883, contained the following announcement:

> With the present issue will cease the publication of *The Palladium.* This is caused by the recent illness of the Proprietor and Publisher who cannot, at present, devote the attention and energy which the *Palladium* requires .... In returning thanks to subscribers ... the Proprietor deems it becoming to say that the paper has been honestly employed as an organ for advocating liberal measures which, in this community, has been rendered necessary by the force of previous circumstances, while conservatism on essential principles has not been wanting.

Antoine reported the sale of the plant but not the names of the purchasers. In November 1884 'Pixy's Jobbing Office' was working from the same address.

The Trinidad Recorder

A weekly paper issued on Wednesdays by the partnership of Allers and Blondel. The earliest issue I have seen in vol. 2 no.30 of 2 January 1884, for which the editorial office was at 3 Abercrombie Street, the address also of *The New Era* (see above) which may account for a reference to the paper in the *San Fernando Gazette* which stated that Allers and Blondel had previously been publishers of the *Advertiser*, a paper I have not seen.

The *Recorder* was not a success. Apart from a delay of two weeks between publication of no.37 (5 March) and number 38 (19 March 1884) for which the reason given was the familiar one of financial difficulties caused by subscribers who did not pay up, there was then a further three weeks gap before no.39, which appeared in a larger format from 36 Queen Street to which the printing office had been removed. Even for nineteenth century Trinidad there was unusual casualness in the attitude of the publishers, tellingly revealed by the note which appeared in the last issue of 18 June 1884:

> The Publishers of the 'Recorder' beg to be excused for issuing the paper without the first and fourth pages. Upon going to press the forme burst, and both pages went to pi.
> They also take this opportunity of thanking their many friends for past patronage, and to inform them that it being impossible to continue under existing circumstances, the present issue closes the career of the 'Trinidad Recorder'.

Trinidad Review

According to Donald Woods' note in his edition of *Froudacity*, this paper was being edited by J. J. Thomas when it ceased publication in November 1884. I have not seen it.

Pixy

A very interesting satirical paper, printed and published fortnightly from 8 March 1884 by Anthony Charles Blondel (probably one of the partners in the earlier *Advertiser* and *Trinidad Recorder*). Issued initially from 2a Abercrombie Street, in November 1884 Blondell removed to Pixy's Jobbing Office at 71 Queen Street, where as well as jobbing printing he advertised a full binding service, lettering, gilding and marbling.

Pixy is valuable for its social comment. Most issues have a full-page wood-engraved cartoon, showing that Port-of-Spain had craftsmen competent in this medium. The last issue I have seen (in the Trinidad Archives) is no.27 of 20 December 1884; it contains no hint that the paper was ceasing publication and *Pixy* may have continued into 1885.

Public Opinion

The earliest issue I have seen of this important biweekly is no.676 of Tuesday 5 January 1892, when it was being published by Joseph de la Sauvagère (later with the *PoSG*) from 41 Queen Street. Publication seems to have started in 1885.

From 20 June 1892 it was incorporated into the *Trinidad Daily News*. Selling at 3 cents a copy, it was continued from the same address (under the title *Daily News, an Independent Newspaper*) by William Lockhart. I have not seen any copies later than 30 June 1893, but publication seems to have continued to 1896.

El Venezolano

Several of the Port-of-Spain papers included some matter in Spanish as well as the more usual English and French (e.g. *Fair Play*). The Registrar-General's Office is reported to have a set of this paper for the period 1886-88. I have not seen it, but from its title assume it was a Spanish-language paper produced for one of the Venezuelan groups in Port-of-Spain.

Catholic News

Started as an official weekly organ of the church on 6 May 1892, 'to give Catholic information in the first place, and on all occasions to explain and if needs be, to defend the doctrines and practices of the Catholic Church.'
Although church matters predominate, it was not exclusively a Church newspaper. The first issues were 'printed and published for the Proprietor by Charles Joseph Williams, 33 St Ann's Road'. Williams was succeeded by Jean Arnaud at the end of 1894; three years later his name in the imprint was replaced by that of George V. Sutherland, O. P. The editorial office was removed to 31 Marine Square in December 1906 when Henry Casey took over control. It seems fairly certain all these men were clergy and only in a legal sense the printers of the paper.

The paper was very successful (3,000 copies being sold of the first issue) and although there were few advertisers in the early numbers, its wide circulation to such other islands as Grenada, St Vincent and St Lucia as well as in Trinidad soon made it attractive to the mercantile community, and by the end of June 1892 nearly half the space was taken up by advertisments. The paper lasted at least into the 1930s.

The Mirror

Most Port-of-Spain papers at the end of the nineteenth century were of four pages, with a fairly large sheet size. *The Mirror* which started publication as a daily on 28 January 1898 was by contrast an eight-page tabloid, sold at the low price of 2 cents a copy and aimed at a popular market. Published by Richard Richardson Mole from 3 Abercrombie Street, it continued until 1917.

PERSONNEL AND EQUIPMENT OF THE TRINIDAD PRINTERS

The early printers and proprietors were largely men from Britain or from other West Indian colonies (e. g. Lewer, Mills, Herbert, Antoine). By mid-century, some of those in charge were undoubtedly Trinidad-born, as one would except from the number of times that the early printers advertised for intelligent boys to serve as apprentices to the printing business. From their names, one would guess that some (such as Voisinage, Blondel or de la Sauvagere) were from the French creole element in the colony.

In some other West Indian islands such as Jamaica and Antigua, slaves were used as pressmen or even compositors in some printing houses of the eighteenth and early nineteenth centuries. I have found no evidence for the use of slaves in the Trinidad printing trade. I have, on the other hand, been told on reliable evidence that female compositors were employed in Port-of-Spain in the years before World War I. It would be interesting to know when, and under what circumstances, women entered the printing trade.

The first printers in the island used the old wooden common-press which had survived with little change since its invention in the fifteenth century. By the time such men as William Lewer came to Trinidad, cast-iron hand-presses of the Stanhope, Columbian and Albion kinds were well-known. Although not specially cheap at the start of the nineteenth century, the iron press had the great advantage of being termite-proof. Without doubt the 'patent press' which William Belk advertised for sale in the *PoSG* in December 1829, or the "Royal Printing Press" offered by Holman & Co. in December 1826, were iron presses. The only one to have survived in Trinidad is the Columbian now in the Museum, presented many years ago by Yuille's Printerie. When enquiring at Yuille's in the early 1960s about such presses – once the backbone of newspaper production in the island – I was told that several such had been sold to jobbing printers in the smaller islands of the eastern Caribbean.

Most of the typefaces used in the early nineteenth century seem to have come from British typefounders, though of course in founts equipped with all the accented sorts needed for printing in French. Some of the display faces used by such printers as Martial Antoine have a French look to them, but more typographical research would be needed to determine whether they were French types.

American penetration of the Trinidad market can probably be dated from the middle of the nineteenth century. I very much doubt whether Alexander Murray of the *San Fernando Gazette* was the only printer in Trinidad to reprint the advertisment of the Bruce Typefoundry, New York, in 1851, and thereby get (free of charge) types fo five times the value of the advertisment. Unfortunately, the statistics of imports published in the Trinidad Blue Books are much less detailed than those of some other colonies, and it is not possible to determine from them the sources and values of imports of printing equipment.

XXII
THE FIRST *TRINIDAD GUARDIAN*

In 1825 the British colony of Trinidad, which had been conquered from the Spanish in 1797, had a single paper, the bi-weekly *Trinidad Gazette.* Its printer was an Englishman, William Lewer, and although in the young colony the commercial prospects for a printer were not brilliant, his monopoly no doubt seemed to have assured him of the contract for official advertisements which provided a substantial part of most colonial printers' incomes.

As an Englishman, catering to a considerable extent to the other British planters and tradesmen who had come to the island since its conquest—rather than to the Spanish/French creole planters already there—Lewer espoused the political standpoint of these British subjects. British planters in neighbouring Barbados and in other Caribbean colonies had a considerable degree of self-government through their elective Houses of Assembly; why should the British subjects in Trinidad not have similar powers in place of the antiquated and imperfectly-understood Spanish colonial system which still prevailed in the island?

No doubt Lewer was relying in his criticisms of the system, on the fact that the Governor, Sir Ralph Woodford was an English gentleman with an Englishman's ideas about freedom of the press. He was wrong. Sir Ralph Woodford *was* an English gentleman, but he had also been invested by London with all the powers of the court of Royal Audience in Caracas, so that he was at one and the same time Dean, *Oidor, Fiscal, Escribano, Relator.* He was also Intendant of the Royal Domain and *corregidor* of the *cabildo.*[1] And he took himself and his powers seriously, as Lewer learned to his cost.

The *Trinidad Gazette* of 30 March 1825 contained (as an official advertisement) the text of two letters it can have given Lewer no pleasure to print:

> Government House, 24th March 1825
>
> Sir, I have received the commands of His Excellency the Governor to acquaint you that from the tenor of the language with which your Paper has been lately filled, His Excellency has resolved to cancel your appointment as Government Printer. You will therefore be pleased to insert the enclosed notification in your *Gazette.*
>
> I am, Sir, your obedient servant,
>
> Frederick Hammett Acting Secretary
>
> Government House 24th March 1825
>
> His Excellency the Governor has been pleased to cancel the appointment of Mr. W. Lewer to be Government Printer.
>
> By Command, Frederick Hammett,
> Acting Secretary.

Lewer was not the first, nor the last of West Indian newspaper proprietors to be disciplined in this way. Usually it brought the desired change in editorial tone quite quickly, or the proprietor could comfort himself with the thought that a change in the composition of the House of Assembly would once more favour a newspaper of his standpoint. But not in Trinidad, and certainly not under Governor Woodford. By the summer of 1825 it was clear to Lewer that the government contract would not be restored to him, and that without it he would continue to lose money on each issue of the *Trinidad Gazette* he published. He decided therefore to bring it to a close, and in the last issue (vol. 5 no. 523) of 14 September 1825 announced that he was quitting the colony and returning to London where he would be setting up as a periodicals subscription agent for the colonies.

To fill the vacuum left by the death of Trinidad's only newspaper, two would-be successors were announced in the last issue of Lewer's *Gazette*. The first was the *Port of Spain Gazette* to be published by John Holman and Company from Lewer's old address at 28 Queen Street. The first few issues of the *Port of Spain Gazette* (which started publication on 21 September 1825) announced that they had by purchase acquired Lewer's copyright etc., in the *Trinidad Gazette* which was incorporated in their journal. What was *not* stated—but was far more important—was that the transaction disposed neatly of the Governor's ill will toward Lewer: the *Port of Spain Gazette* carried official advertising from the start, and it was certainly the greater financial stability this gave the business which in the long term helped the *Port of Spain Gazette* to survive into the second half of the twentieth century.

Although hindsight shows that the officially supported *Port of Spain Gazette* was to succeed, it was by no means clear at the time. Lewer, in fact, seems to have sold the goodwill in his paper to Holman at the same time that he sold equipment to another:

> The subscriber begs leave to inform his friends and the Public, that he has been induced, at the earnest commendation of the most respectable Inhabitants of the Colony, to purchase a Printing Press and Materials, from Mr. Lewer, and intends to publish a Newspaper as soon as the necessary arrangements can be made—He has the pleasure to announce that his Paper will be supported by the same able talent that has rendered the *Trinidad Gazette* so deservedly popular in all the Colonies; and he confidently hopes, by proper attention, to render it worthy of Public Patronage.
>
> J. W. Irwin,
>
> No. 10 Frederick Street, September 14th.[2]

The most respectable inhabitants of the Colony; the same able talent: the British protestant faction opposed to the Governor's policies, and the same leader writers who had offended Sir Ralph Woodford before. Not a combination likely to be successful in winning over official Trinidad, and it was no doubt this fact (rather than the month's delay in the appearance of Irwin's first issue) which was to enable Holman and his *Port of Spain Gazette* to secure the government contract. But this was the mid-1820's, at a time when planters in all the sugar colonies were becoming alarmed, and a little shrill, at the success the emancipation lobby was having in Britain. A reactionary journal opposed to emancipation of the slaves, and supporting the interests of the planters against the more liberal attitudes which prevailed in Whitehall (and Whitehall's appointees to colonial offices) and which was financially independent from official pressure would have seemed even more important in Trinidad than in the other islands where the Houses of Assembly were still firmly under planter control.

Irwin's newspaper, *The Trinidad Guardian*, was first published on Friday 21 October 1825. The subscription rate for the weekly journal of four folio pages was set at £4, or £5 for subscribers in other West Indian colonies. How many subscribers the paper gained is not recorded, but there was sufficient public interest for the 500 copies printed of the early issues to have been brought up within five months of the paper's first appearance. On 17 March 1827 Irwin advertised that:

> In consequence of the repeated demands for regular files of the *Guardian* by new subscribers in this Colony, the neighbouring islands and in Europe . . . the proprietor will feel infinitely obliged to any of his friends who may be inclined to part with them, for numbers 1, 2, 3, 4 and 12. Or he will give a liberal price for any of the above numbers separately.

However, this early success was not to assure Irwin of a prosperous future. There were no government advertisements in the *Guardian*, and the number of non-official advertisements, though comparable in number with those of other West Indian papers of the time, would not have swelled his profits very much. Nevertheless by 26 May 1826 Irwin felt it safe to advertise that from June onward the paper would be published twice a week, and at the same time the printing house would move to more commodious quarters at 48 King Street.

Three months later, in September 1826, Irwin advertised the opening of his St. Vincent Street Reading Room, and invited subscribers at £8 per annum to town members, and half that for those in the country. Members would have access to files of ten British, three French and three American papers, plus a further twenty four West Indian, and the usual reference books and services attached to commercial rooms of this kind. As soon as there were enough subscribers, Irwin advertised, he would add more reference works, periodical publications and start a circulating library.

Irwin was by now over-extended: the circulating library never materialized, and the *Guardian* was running into difficulties. To judge from the surviving copies in the Public Record Office, London[3] he was without funds to purchase fresh stocks of paper from mid-November 1826 onwards. These copies are printed on blue papers of various smaller sizes which have been made up to the size of the normal *Guardian* sheets (approx. 26 x 20) by pasting strips on to them. (The joins are skilfully enough done, but the effect of the double thickness on the presswork can be imagined!). Not until March 1827 was paper of the right size to be used again.[4]

It is not certain whether Irwin tried to dispose of his printing business to escape from his financial embarrassments at the end of 1826, but such an attempt would explain an advertisement which appeared in both English and French versions in both the *Port of Spain Gazette* and the *Guardian* in mid-December 1826:

> To be disposed of. An assortment of Printing Types and Materials, together with an excellent Royal Printing Press, forming a complete Establishment necessary to carry on a Newspaper of large dimension, in either the English, French or Spanish Languages.
>
> The above articles are perfectly new, and of the best quality, having been selected by a person experienced in the Printing Business.
>
> For terms &c. apply at the Office of the Paper.

If the advertisement was from Irwin it met no immediate response, but on 1 June 1827 financial control of the *Guardian* passed out of Irwin's hands:

> *Trinidad Guardian* office. Mr. John Shoel having been this day admitted a

> Partner in this Printing Office, the business will in future be carried on under the Firm of John Shoel and Company. J. W. Irwin, King Street, 1 June 1827.

Under this new imprint the *Trinidad Guardian* continued to appear through 1828 and into 1829 without apparent production difficulties. But from the early months of 1829 the old difficulties over supply of paper emerged once more. In February and March several issues were on paper with strips pasted on vertically to make a larger sheet; in July the paper had strips pasted horizontally at the foot; in August the *Guardian* was once more printed on blue paper; by October supplies were so short that strips had to be pasted on both the first and second leaves of each issue to make up a sheet of the right size. With difficulties like these, it is little wonder that the standard of presswork was—shall we say—uneven?

Though the *Guardian* appeared to be on its last legs, the *Port of Spain Gazette* was also in difficulties. On 30 September 1829, Holman was compelled to enter into a partnership with one William Belk, for much the same reasons that Irwin had been taken over by Shoel. The partnership of Belk & Holman lasted only one month, then Belk alone issued the paper for two issues following the dissolution of the partnership. On 14 November 1829 Belk announced:

> We are painfully necessitated to take leave of our subscribers and the Public in general, assuring them that our utmost endeavours have been exerted to continue the publication of the *Port of Spain Gazette*, but circumstances of a peculiar nature have compelled us to relinquish its further publication.

The *Port of Spain Gazette* was dead! exulted Irwin in the editorial columns of the *Guardian*. He was too soon: the *Gazette* was *not* dead. The battle between Holman and Belk for its control, which seemed to have been won by Belk when their partnership was dissolved was settled within another week. Holman, who had entered into another partnership with one H. J. Mills (a bookbinder from Thetford in Norfolk, whose advertisements for binding and copperplate printing had appeared in the *Guardian* as early as 7 April 1826) was able to resume publication on 21 November 1829.

The first issue of the new series of the *Gazette*, 'commencing as it were a new paper' contained an editorial announcement of the usual sort, in which the new proprietors Holman & Mills thanked their friends for past patronage, assured them of their best exertions for the future, and so forth. Evidently the new partnership was better founded than that of Belk & Holman[5], and Holman was in good shape to take Irwin's competition on. 'My dear Gardy—you are in error—the Port of Spain Gazette is still alive' he triumphantly noted at the end of his editorial announcement of 21 November; one of the very few occasions on which the *Gazette* condescended to notice the existence of the *Guardian* at all.

Before the uncertainty over the future of the *Gazette* had developed, the *Guardian* had from 4 August 1829 carried an advertisement offering for sale the copyright in the *Guardian*, plus the presses, types, etc. for carrying the paper on. The new owner, it was advertised, would take possession from 1 December 1829: evidently the partnership between Shoel and Irwin was to be brought to an end two and a half years after Shoel had entered the business. As it transpired, however, ownership of the paper remained with Shoel & Company as before: it seems that Shoel provided more capital against the security of Irwin's plant.

The surviving set of the *Trinidad Guardian* for 1830 lacks many issues, and the numbering of surviving issues is erratic[6] so that it is impossible to say whether Irwin was again compelled to resort to made-up sheets of paper on which to print the newspaper. On 4 February 1831 he was sanguine enough about the future of his business to advertise his need for two compositors. He was seeking a steady white married man who was perfectly master of his trade, he announced: preference would be given to one who had 'a son of sufficient age to be bound an apprentice to the business.'

Despite this, the end was in sight. Almost immediately issues on patched-up paper appear once more, and the number of advertisements included in the paper goes into a marked decline from March 1831 onwards. Shoel had had enough, and from the first issue to be published in July of that year the paper once more advertised the copyright, goodwill and equipment of the *Guardian* for sale, at a price reduced by one-third from that which had been asked in 1829. Possession would be given on 1 December 1831; if not disposed of, the plant would be sold by public auction.

Within another six weeks, no prospective purchaser of the paper having appeared, the *Guardian* (from 19 August onwards) carried another advertisement from H. Graham, Deputy Vendue Master in Port of Spain. On Thursday 8 December 1831, Graham announced, he would be selling the *Guardian* copyright and equipment plus 'the few articles of household furniture belonging to J. W. Irwin'. From then on, the paper had the mark of death on it, with no advertising save that of the auctioneer and of a few shopmen who were Irwin's neighbours. The last issue filed is number '709' of Friday 25 November, after which the *Guardian* (and its unfortunate printer) disappear from sight.

For a while, the *Port of Spain Gazette* was without competitors. But for a short while only: although it had managed to steer an editorial course sufficiently acceptable to the government of Trinidad to retain the official printing contracts, its pro-planter bias was displeasing to Whitehall and official Port of Spain. No doubt it was only the fact that the *Guardian* was (from the government's point of view) even worse that kept the contracts with Holman & Mills. In 1832, however, a new weekly newspaper called the *Royal Gazette* was started in the interests of the antislavery party and with official encouragement as a counterbalance to the *Port of Spain Gazette.* Edited by Young Anderson, a Port of Spain grocer who was a leading figure in the party of the 'saints', the paper by 1833 had been re-named the *Colonial Observer and Trinidad Gazette*[7]. It is ironic that it was probably printed on the equipment of the defunct *Guardian.*

Apart from its production difficulties, the *Trinidad Guardian* was a competently produced newspaper, by no means inferior to other West Indian papers of the time. Its news was culled from the usual range of British and American papers, with colonial news being taken from sister papers like the *Barbados Globe*, the Jamaica *Royal Gazette*, the *Montego Bay Gazette*, the *Honduras Gazette*, the *Grenada Free Press* and so forth. As the organ of the slave owning planters, its editorial columns poured scorn on the news as given in 'the Official' as it termed the *Port of Spain Gazette*, although the tone of its attacks was restrained indeed as compared with that of some other West Indian papers. Its columns were filled with news likely to be of comfort to the slave owners: of the attempts being made to persuade James

McQueen, the able editor of the pro-slavery *Glasgow Courier* to start a London paper to protect the interests of the West Indian proprietors against the abolitionist lobby which had an almost complete monopoly of support among the London papers. McQueen was shrewd enough not to take this on: the days of slavery were drawing rapidly to a close, and even in the West Indies a newspaper which adopted too extreme a pro-slavery position was to be in difficulties, as Irwin's case proved.

Nearly ninety years later, in 1917, a new *Trinidad Guardian* was to be founded in Port of Spain. Once more in opposition to the *Port of Spain Gazette*, the 'official' newspaper of the colony; in this sense at least Irwin's paper had not been entirely forgotten in Trinidad.

NOTES

1 V. S. Naipaul, *The Loss of El Dorado*, rev. ed. (Harmondsworth 1972) pp. 366–367.

2 *Trinidad Gazette* 14 Sept. 1825.

3 No other files of the *Trinidad Guardian* are known.

4 Because of their remoteness from suppliers, West Indian newspaper proprietors (particularly in small and poor colonies) quite often had to resort to paper of different colour, texture or size, when their stocks ran out. During the Napoleonic wars (and again in World War II) this was quite common, and usually the papers' editorial notices would explain the change. However, it is improbable that Irwin's difficulties can be accounted for in this way, since they occurred in a time of peace and prosperity in one of the larger colonies, none of whose other printers seem to have had any problems in obtaining paper stocks.

5 Holman & Mills continued in partnership till May 1832; Mills continued as proprietor of the paper till his death in May 1870.

6 No. 469 of Friday 20 August 1830 is followed by no. '500' of 24 August; later, no. '701' of 28 October 1831 follows no. '619' of 21 October.

7 The *Royal Gazette*'s production is mentioned by L. M. Frazer in his *History of Trinidad* (Port of Spain 1891–1896); no surviving copies have been traced.

XXIII
EARLY PRINTING IN SOUTHERN TRINIDAD

Printing was late to come to Trinidad. Under the Spanish, and for the first half-century of British rule, the craft was concentrated in the capital Port-of-Spain as one would expect in a young and underpopulated colony.

During the early years of Victoria's reign the rich lands in the south of the island, around Naparima Hill and the little town of San Fernando, were being opened to agriculture. Though communication by land was painfully slow, by sea the passage from Port-of-Spain to San Fernando was very easy – philatelists will recall the special issue of 'Lady McLeod' stamps for letters carried this way – and the capital's newspapers circulated quickly to the southern settlements. At least one of them, *The Trinidad Spectator* (1845-8) claimed in its subtitle to be the 'Port of Spain and San Fernando Advertiser.'

Despite the ease with which Port-of-Spain papers could reach the south, by mid-century when San Fernando had a population of about three thousand, with perhaps another seventeen thousand in its hinterland, it was sufficiently populous to surpass many other pioneering colonial settlements which had their own newspaper and jobbing office at which an ambitious printer could hope to make a satisfactory living.

The man tempted by San Fernando's promise was one Alexander Murray. By his own account he had previously been the printer and publisher of the *Carriacou Observer.* [1] Carriacou, a small island some thirteen square miles in the Grenadines (the chain of islands between St. Vincent and Grenada) one would imagine to be one of the most unpromising places for a newspaper to flourish. In the early nineteenth century it had received many immigrants from the land-clearances in Scotland; whether the printer was a Scot (as his name suggests) or a creole I have been unable to establish.

In San Fernando Murray set up office at No. 14 High Street, and on 6 February 1850 published the first number of *The San Fernando Gazette and Naparima Agricultural and Commercial Advertiser.* [2] Planned to be published twice a week, on Wednesdays and Saturdays, its subscription was set at $ 6 when paid quarterly in advance, or $ 8 paid in arrears; indiviual copies cost 10 ¢ each. Number 1 carried Murray's prospectus, which was reprinted in the second issue also. It contained large claims and promises which are usual in such pieces – Murray trusting his reputation as conductor of the *Carriacou Observer* would serve as sufficient guarantee of his impartiality and so forth.

Consisting of four pages measuring approximately 15 by 10 inches, the paper was set in three columns, and carried the usual mixture of advertisements, local news and foreign reports lifted from the *Gazette*'s British, American and other West Indian contemporaries which characterised the Caribbean press of the mid-nineteenth century. Like most of its Trinidadian contemporaries, it included matter in both French and English. Very wisely, Murray paid particular attention to agricultural topics and matter of local importance – the need for improved postal services in the south of the island, and for local courts with increased jurisdiction, so that more actions could be heard locally thus avoiding the difficulty and expense of hearings in Port-of-Spain. Careful attention of this sort no doubt attracted a few more subscribers; more importantly (from Murray's point of view) it persuaded the San Fernando Borough Council that the *Gazette* was the right organ to publish full accounts of its business, and for this the Council paid Murray a subsidy.

At first, one suggests, Murray was working on a very tight budget. There was a wide variety from one issue to another in the paper used (a very common sign of financial stringency among West Indian printers) and in August and September 1850 he was compelled to print some issues on a flimsy blue-green paper. Ironically enough, this has survived the ravages of time and the Trinidad climate far better than the stock of paper he normally used. Publication twice a week would have called for a small staff of compositors and pressmen, soon augmented by an apprentice, 'a young lad who is acquainted with the English and French languages' for whom Murray had advertised in his first issues.

With the issue for 22 March 1851 (n. 118) Murray enlarged the format of the paper, to a page-size of approximately 20 by 12 inches, set in four columns. In this same issue for the first time he specified his charges for advertising: 1 $ minimum for up to ten lines, thereafter 10 ¢ per line. As usual, advertisements which were kept standing for three or more insertions were charged a lower rate.

In May 1851, Murray reprinted an advertisement from Bruce's Typefoundry in New York. By the terms of this, all newspaper proprietors who printed it before 31 August 1851 could claim type to the value of five times the normal cost of the advertisement from the Bruce Foundry. This is the earliest certain evidence I have found of American penetration into the Trinidadian printing trade.

Despite the jobbing work, and other publications which Murray produced, such as *The Naparima Almanac for the Year 1851,*[3] the market for a printer in San Fernando was too limited to satisfy Murray's ambitions. In 1853 he left Trinidad for St. George's, Grenada, where he established the weekly *Grenada Observer*[4] in May of that year. The *San Fernando Gazette* was presumably left in the hands of his employees who lacked Murray's own drive; it gradually ran down until publication was discontinued in late 1854 or early 1855.[5]

Murray may have continued to own a jobbing printing business in San Fernando for the next few years, but I have found no evidence. He himself had returned from Grenada to Port-of-Spain by 1856. From 1856 until 1863 or 1864 he was running the *Trinidad Sentinel* from 3 Abercrombie Street in the capital. But by December 1865 he had determined to try again in the south of Trinidad, and on Wednesday 20 December he issued volume 1 number 1 of the *San Fernando Gazette,* new series.

Working now from no. 1 High Street in San Fernando, Murray put out the first two numbers of his paper free of charge, though from January 1866 it was sold at a subscription set at $ 6 per annum. Now published as a weekly, and in a slightly smaller format (approximately 18 by 12 inches, three columns), the revived paper was sufficiently successful for Murray to continue it until his death in August 1874. Production was not entirely without problems: the issues for 6 and 13 January 1866 were execrably printed, and Murray apologetically explained that 'one of the principal levers' on his press had broken, and attempts to repair the press had not yet been effectual.

After Murray's death, his executors sold the *Gazette* and the plant to Samuel Carter, who resumed publication with a New Series of the paper on 12 September 1874. Carter (1837-95) was another 'small islander' who had come to Trinidad: born in Scarborough, Tobago, the son of the medical officer at the Tobago garrison, Carter had at the age of eleven been bound apprentice to Angus Melvill, a Scottish printer who was then printer of the *Tobago Chronicle*.[6] Having completed his apprenticeship, Carter moved to Port-of-Spain in 1856, and worked for some time for the Barbadian William Herbert on his *Trinidad Press*. He subsequently moved to the highly regarded *Trinidad Chronicle* (then ably edited by Otto Wenkstern) where he had charge of the printing department. After Wenkstern's death in 1869 Carter joined forces with Joseph Lewis in publication of the *New Era*, leaving this partnership in 1874 when he purchased the *San Fernando Gazette* from Murray's executors.

Carter was thoroughly experienced in the Trinidad newspaper trade, and made a good job of running the *Gazette*. Nevertheless, he was not able to avoid one of the commonest problems – not only in Trinidad, or even the West Indies, but throughout the colonial world – of getting his subscribers actually to pay for their papers:

> Until arrangements are made to put the paper on a better footing [he wrote in the last issue for 1877] the publication of the *San Fernando Gazette* will be suspended from 1st January 1878. We have no desire of discontinuing the publication of the paper, but we find it impossible to carry on under existing circumstances. For the last two years we have not been able to collect as much money, in the shape of subscriptions, as would pay for the paper and ink used for printing the *Gazette*, and we have no wish of getting further in debt . . . We shall be glad if subscribers in arrears will come forward and pay up, and thus enable us to recommence the publication of the paper at an early date. Job printing will still be carried on at the office.

Carter was more fortunate than many another similarly-circumstanced newspaper printer. Enough subscribers came forward and paid up for him to recommence publication of the *Gazette* from 6 April 1878. Thereafter he seems to have prospered; in July 1882 enlarging the format to a 24 by 18 page of six columns, and publishing twice a week under the modified title *San Fernando Gazette and Trinidad News*. Initially priced at $ 8 per annum, the subscription was first reduced to $ 5 and then by the time of Carter's death in October 1895, to $ 2 a year. The lowered cost was no doubt partly due to the increased advertising that the paper now carried, but also (I believe) represents a response to the lowered prices of the Port-of-Spain papers which could now circulate easily in the south of Trinidad.

After Carter's death, the *Gazette* was continued by his sons, with Ethelbert Nicholson Carter as manager. He lacked the sound business sense of his father, and from Monday 2 December 1895 started a *Daily Bulletin* priced at $ 6 a year to replace the old *Gazette*. This attempt to resist the inroads of the Port-of-Spain papers was as ill-judged as it was under-capitalized. To a correspondent, who in the issue of 9 December 1895 asked whether the townspeople of San Fernando could 'afford the luxury of maintaining a daily newspaper' as only one hundred and fifty copies of the Port-of-Spain dailies circulated in the town, Carter retorted that the evidence of his print order, having increased from 800 to 1100 copies after three issues, showed clearly that it could. Somewhat disingenuously, he then confessed that he was cutting to three issues a week, giving as reason the fact that as the *Gazette* office had no cylinder press, production problems were too great for daily publication!

Even three issues a week could be managed only until the end of the month; from January 1896 without any further announcement in the *Gazette*'s columns, publication was reduced again to two issues a week. Throughout that year the situation deteriorated still further. On 28 November 1896, in an editorial commenting on the closure of the Port-of-Spain *Trinidad Daily News*, Carter indicated that unless business improved he would have to cut back to issuing the *Gazette* only weekly, or indeed close the newspaper altogether. No copies of the *San Fernando Gazette* later than 22 December 1896 have been found, and I conclude that the paper did not live into 1897. Not until the short-lived *San Fernando Star* [7] appeared in June 1906 was southern Trinidad again to have its own newspaper.

NOTES

1. No copies of this newspaper have been traced. Its title appears as a by-line in several other West Indian newspapers in the late 1840s: *The Dominica Colonist* 21 August 1847 (soon after Murray's establishment of the paper); the *Antigua Herald* 30 November 1847; *Antigua Observer* 4 April 1848.
2. Incomplete sets are held in the Trinidad Archives, and in the Trinidad Public Library; microfilm copies of the latter's set were made by the University of Florida Libraries and are available through Bell & Howell.
3. Advertised, price 40 ¢, in the *Gazette* of 28 December 1850. No copy traced.
4. Known to me only from a mutilated copy of no. 34, 27 December 1853, now in the American Antiquarian Society Library.
5. The Trinidad Archives' set closes with the issue for 22 December 1854, but that issue bears no indication of impending closure.
6. I am indebted to Edwina Peters-Roberts for identifying Melvill and his newspaper for me.
7. Published by Richard Edward Simmonds from 17 June 1906; discontinued 31 March 1907, revived as *The Star* 8 June–28 November 1907 (no. 82). The next issue, number 83, was dated 15 February 1907 [i.e. 1908] and is perhaps the worst printed West Indian newspaper I have seen. I suspect that it was, as it deserved to be, the last issue of *The Star*.

PRINTING IN THE TURKS AND CAICOS ISLANDS

XXIV
THE EARLY PRINTERS OF GRAND TURK

The Turks and Caicos Islands are a British dependency in the Caribbean about ninety miles north of Hispaniola and at the extreme southeastern end of the Bahamas archipelago, of which geographically they form a part. Though discovered about 1512 by Ponce de Leon they were never settled by the Spanish. Well suited for salt-raking (but for little else) Grand Turk and Salt Cay were gradually settled from Bermuda by the British, and after the American revolution the population was increased by a number of Loyalists and their slaves from the southern colonies.

In the first part of the nineteenth century the settlements were ruled from the Bahamas, and no doubt any printing needs they had were met either from Nassau (into which John Wells, a Loyalist refugee from South Carolina, had introduced printing in 1783) or from Bermuda, where J. Stockdale had set up a press in 1784.

On 19 February 1845 one Samuel Nelmes issued a prospectus for a weekly newspaper, the *Turks Islands Gazette and Commercial Reporter* dated from Grand Cay (= Grand Turk):

The undersigned proposes to publish at the time and place above mentioned, a Weekly Newspaper, in Folio; and respectfully solicits the attention of the Inhabitants of the

Colony generally, and of Turks Islands particularly, to this intimation of his design: he hopes that in accordance with their literary taste and intellectual pursuits, they will favourably receive this project and tender that promise of support which will encourage him to carry it into execution.

In offering this Journal to the Public, it is not the intention of the undersigned to trumpet its praise, but it is nevertheless requisite as an introduction, that a few notes in conjunction with its principal and leading features should be sounded—it will be liberal in its religious and political character—it will endeavour to foster the best qualities of social life—it will reject all communications that may not be of a moral or beneficial nature; it will be the channel of Commercial News, and the organ of Local Improvement—it will encourage a temperate though firm discussion of what are emphatically termed the grievances of The Turks Islanders; it will show that union is strength, and incite a confidential reliance on the Mother Country in matters touching the rights and privileges of all classes of Her Majesty's subjects.

As natural consequence of such a course, the undersigned would further expect, as he most sincerely hopes to witness, a general diminution of what may be styled the opposite sentiments existing in the minds of the Inhabitants of different portions of the Colony. With these benevolent objects in view thus declared by way of Prospectus, the undersigned . . . does not appeal to Turks Islands alone, but to the Colony at large, and from all he courteously solicits Patronage.

In the Editorial in the first issue, of 5 March 1845, Nelmes wrote in much the same strain, with further reference to the virtues of a free press as a guardian against oppression or abuses. In this, as in his prospectus, there is little that is highly individual and which could not have appeared with very little change in many new colonial papers. Nevertheless in publishing the *Turks Islands Gazette* Nelmes was in a slightly different position from most small-town editors, as witness his advertisement "To shipmasters" which he included in the first issue:

The editor of this Paper, is desirous of making known to masters of vessels passing through Turks Islands Passage, that, should they wish to be reported, by their Standing in close to Grand Cay, so as to enable the Pilots to board and receive their report, as well as such Newspapers as may be spared, he will feel a pleasure in making mention of them in his Marine List. Having no regular Line of Packets running to this place, we are chiefly indebted to and dependent on Masters of Vessels, for Foreign News. He would be happy to supply Masters of Vessels, in Port, with Papers, if they will call at the Printing Office, before their departure.

This reliance on the good will of the passing shipping for overseas news was to last until connection with the Direct West Indian Cable in 1898, and until then the Turks Islands printers had frequently to report "no news" as they had received no foreign papers since the previous issue. When foreign news was received, it was culled from many sources. English and American papers of the eastern seaboard preponderate, but those of Jamaica, Barbados, Bermuda, Guiana, and other West Indian colonies are frequently quoted, and on occasion reports came from much further afield, such as *The New Era* of Sierra Leone. At the time Nelmes started his paper, the total population of the Turks Islands was under three thousand, and his commercial prospects were not bright. Priced at $7 per annum, payable quarterly in advance, his paper would have been beyond the means of many of the islanders, and though the paper may possibly have circulated to Great Inagua and other of the southern Bahama Islands, on the whole his appeal not to the Turks Islanders alone "but to the Colony at large" fell on deaf ears. In vol. 1 no. 8, he commented rather tartly that although two months had elapsed since the first appearance of the *Turks Islands Gazette*, the Nassau press had yet to notice its existence.

Apart from subscriptions, Nelmes had some income from advertising, for which he charged at the rate: "Advertisements not exceeding half a square, will be inserted for Three Shillings, and for each time continued One Shilling and Sixpence; for a square, Five Shillings and for each insertion after, Two Shillings and Sixpence: larger advts. charged accordingly. A great reduction made to Subscribers advertising by the year." Early issues seldom have more than eight or nine advertisements, about a column, and though the number slowly rose the printer's income from this source must have been small. He supplemented it by selling stationery, schoolbooks, etc. (advertised 18 June 1845) and by bookbinding (advertised 21 April 1846); no doubt by a certain amount of jobbing printing ("Orders for printing in its various branches, will be thankfully received and promptly attended to" he advertised in every issue). Some independent publications were also attempted: on 2 December 1845 he announced: "In The Press and will shortly be published, The Constitution of The Dominican Republic, In The Island of Saint Domingo. A 12mo pamphlet, containing about 32 pages, and translated from the Spanish Language, by Sydney Cross Esq." On 13 January 1846 he announced this as just published, and also advertised the *Turks Islands Sheet Almanack* as just published and ready for sale, price 1s.6d.[1]

By March 1847 the *Turks Islands Gazette* had passed into the ownership of Horatio Stubbs, a Grand Turk merchant under whose direction the newspaper was continued until 1849. Its last issue, vol. 5 no. 36 of 22 August 1849, was however published under the imprint of George A. Lee.

1. The only copy of Cross's translation of the Constitution I have traced in the United States is that in the New York Public Library (NUC ND 0323659). It is not in the British Library. No copies of the *Sheet Almanack* have been traced.

Although Nelmes had merely aimed at "a temperate though firm discussion of . . . the grievances of The Turks Islanders" the newspaper had in fact become the vehicle for the Separatist movement among the Turks Islanders. Unlike the sugar colonies, in the 1840s and 1850s the Turks were enjoying a relative prosperity and in 1848 the movement was successful in having the Islands removed from the colony of the Bahamas and created a presidency with their own legislative assembly. It was as a result of this political change that Lee discontinued the *Turks Island Gazette*, replacing it from 29 August 1849 by *The Royal Gazette and Turks Islands Commercial, Literary and Political Journal.*

The subscription to the *Royal Gazette* was set at the same rate as for its predecessor, with the rates for advertising similarly calculated. Yet for the first time its printer had the chance of augmenting his income from another source, since in an "independent" colony there was official printing to be undertaken, and the only printer in the colony could look forward to a small but assured payment from public funds.

By 16 November 1850 (and possibly earlier) ownership of the *Royal Gazette* had passed from Lee to Richard Darrel, a member of an old Turks Islands family, and for some years he enjoyed the undisputed production of a newspaper for the colony. But by the end of 1853 his editorial espousal of the party of opposition to the government of President Forth had opened the way for a rival newspaper of different political complexion.

On 14 January 1854 was published the first issue of the *Royal Standard and Gazette of the Turks & Caicos Islands*. Edited by Joseph F. Hutchings (1826-90) who had recently come to Grand Turk from his native Bermuda, it was published on Saturdays instead of Wednesdays (as was the *Royal Gazette*), had a larger page size than its rival, and was priced at only $5 per year.

The present writer has been unable to locate copies of the *Royal Gazette* for 1854, or of the prospectus or the first two issues of its new competitor. It is clear, however, that the *Gazette*'s attacks upon the *Royal Standard* were bitter, describing it as being "upheld by rumsellers" and so forth. Hutchings, however, at first adopted a lofty tone:

> To Correspondents. Enquirer. Your communication is inadmissible. It is greatly to be regretted that in the expression of opinions through The Royal Gazette writers have been permitted to indulge in personalities and low invectives, to a degree which, to say the least, has placed them without the sphere of gentlemanly consideration. The practice of admitting such communications to the columns of The Royal Gazette alone excuses the attempt of Enquirer to get his communication into the columns of The Standard. . . . (*Royal Standard* 28 Jan 1854)

At first the competition between the two papers went all in the *Royal Standard*'s favor, since on 19 February 1854 the following Government Notice was published,

It is hereby notified for general information that the publication of all 'GOVERNMENT NOTICES' is transferred from the '*Turks Islands Royal Gazette*' to the Columns of the '*Royal Standard*', and that all Government Notices appearing in the last named Paper—and such only—are henceforth to be deemed and acted upon as authentic and official Communications.

It is hereby further notified, that the transfer above alluded to, has been deemed necessary in consequence of certain errors made in the publication in the Turks Islands *Royal Gazette of the 18th January last*, of the Proclamation for proroguing the Legislative Council of these Islands. . . .

Which *Several Errors*—having been committed in Publication—the Editor of The Gazette was repeatedly called upon by the Executive Government to explain; and failing to do so, satisfactorily, as will more conspicuously appear on reference being made to an 'Editorial' or leading article published in the *Royal Gazette of the 8th Instant*—His Honor the President, after taking the advice and opinion of the Members of the Executive Council thereon, has deemed it requisite that the 'Editor' who is also the 'Printer' of the *Royal Gazette* should no longer be intrusted with the Printing of Government Notices.

By His Honor's Command
J. J. McIntosh
Colonial Secretary.

Deprived of the monopoly of government printing for the moment, the *Gazette*'s adherents tried other methods of defeating Hutchings. A trumped-up action for libel, brought against him in February 1854 by the only two legal practitioners in the colony's Supreme Court, caused him some inconvenience until it was eventually dismissed when tried on 15 May 1854. Other petty forms of legal harassment were more successful, until in the issue of 25 November 1854 Hutchings struck out at his chief tormenter, who was one of the leader writers in the *Royal Gazette:* "The impertinence of Mr. Francis Ellis, Queens Advocate, is beyond endurance. Pigmy and ill-shapen as he is, both physically and mentally, he seems to be never so happy as when using his venomous tongue in scandalising us, and that too on the most public occasions. . . ." Though presented with an undoubted libel, Ellis failed to respond to this, and thereafter was noticeably less willing to abuse Hutchings in public. Perhaps he regarded the *Royal Standard* as a spent force, for in June 1854 public printing had been removed from the *Standard* and restored to the *Royal Gazette* as a result of Hutchings' publication of a letter from John L. Nelson, the U. S. Consul in Grand Turk, which the administration regarded as libelous. In addition, President Forth had left the Colony, and his successor President Inglis in aiming for a policy of reconciliation between the differing political groups had encouraged the anti-Forth elements for whom the *Royal Gazette* had been the mouthpiece. Hutchings' financial state was very precarious.

By the beginning of 1855, the pro-*Standard* elements in the Legislative Assembly had rallied enough to ensure that Hutchings' tender for public printing was accepted for the year, in place of Darrel's bid, although the *Gazette* supporters opposed this change. The fact that Hutchings' bid was so much lower than his rival's made the matter a foregone conclusion, the two bids being as follows:

Darrel; *Gazette* Office

Weekly Government Notices	3d. per line, first insertion half price subsequent insertions
Blank forms etc.	6s.3d. per quire
Ordinances	6s.3d. per page

Hutchings; *Standard* Office

Weekly Government Notices	1d. per line
Blank forms etc.	3s.10d. per quire
Ordinances	4s.0d. per foolscap page.

Having regained the contract for official printing, Hutchings and the *Royal Standard* never thereafter lost it. In cash terms it was not great (for the half year July-December 1854 the cost was £62 2s. 6d.) but it probably made the difference between bankruptcy and a modest living. Darrel struggled on with the *Royal Gazette* at least until the end of 1857, but thereafter it disappeared from view. Possibly the successful action for libel which President Inglis brought in September 1857 against David Basden, a *Royal Gazette* writer (who was fined £50 and imprisoned for a year) was the final reason for the paper's closure.

For the rest of his life Joseph Hutchings continued to issue the *Royal Standard* weekly. In it he followed the familiar pattern which Samuel Nelmes had first adopted with the *Turks Islands Gazette:* page 1 of each issue containing poetry and prose, culled from English and American magazines; pages 2 and 3 containing the editorial matter, official reports, news of shipping, the salt crop and other local affairs,[2] plus some foreign news and advertisements; and page 4

2. There was considerable interest in Grand Turk in the affairs of their nearest neighbor, the Dominican Republic. From February 1878 the reports were generally drawn from the pages of the Puerto Plata *Journal of Commerce*, a weekly newspaper in English printed by Henry A. Taylor, a Bahamian. I have not been able to trace this paper: it is not in Charno: *Latin American Newspapers in United States Libraries: a Union List* (Austin, 1968).

advertisements and other literary matter. On occasion—during the Crimean war, the Indian mutiny—he would issue a broadside supplement. As time wore on, the number of advertisements from overseas (for Holloway's Pills, for Dr. J. Collis Browne's Chlorodyne, for both of which Hutchings was local agent) increased.

Though the 1840s had been a time of relative prosperity for the Turks Islands, by the late 1860s the salt industry was in decline, and in 1874 the Turks and Caicos lost their independent status, being attached as a dependency of Jamaica (resuming their "independent" colonial status only in 1959 when Jamaica achieved full internal self-government). The decline in the settlement's fortunes hit Hutchings; from an income of £150 for public printing in 1868 he dropped to £100 and then to a low of £75 per annum in 1881 and 1882; the figure thereafter being £100 per annum once more. Several times in his end-of-year editorials Hutchings referred to the difficulty of continuing; for example at the end of 1879 printing a letter from the Commissio..er (who had replaced the President as chief executive with the attachment to Jamaica):

Sir, As the sum of £100 voted annually for Public Printing expires with the Appropriation Ordinance on the 31st of the month, there is, strictly speaking after that date no authority for me to pay you. But as it would be unfair to you to stop so suddenly the verbal arrangement now existing with the Government, which is understood to be equally binding on both sides, I presume you will continue to carry on the work for three months longer at the existing rate of £8 6s. 8d. per month. After that date, I am not in a position at present, to make any arrangement for the Public Printing of this settlement.

I have & c.
R. B. Llewelyn, *Commissioner*
23 December 1879.

But by this time the *Royal Standard* had become an institution and Hutchings enough of an establishment figure in Grand Turk for this difficulty to be smoothed over.

During the early 1880s the appearance of the *Royal Standard* steadily deteriorated, until in 1887 the paper was revamped. The issue of 1 January 1887 has the following editorial:

The present issue of the *Standard* commences its *thirty-fourth* year and we have much pleasure in presenting to our patrons the first number of 1887 in an entirely new dress. Type, like the human frame and all else mutable, will wear out and thirty three years constant but careful use of the type with which this paper has been printed, compels us to abandon it for something newer and more showey. Financially this extra outlay is rather an expensive one, but, as we have ever endeavoured, in the interest of this little settlement, to keep pace with the times, *in appearance at least*, we trust our effort, in this direction, will be appreciated.

The new types were text types only; for display in advertisements Hutchings continued to use his existing repertoire. I have been unable to identify the source of Hutchings' new types: as most of the trade of the Turks Islands was with New York they probably came from American type foundries rather than British suppliers.

On 19 November 1890 Joseph Hutchings died. In so small a settlement the newspaper editor was a substantial and well-liked figure, regarded very differently from the disreputable publisher of a Negro paper that he had first been considered. He was the settlement's senior justice of the peace (an office he had held nearly thirty years), had been a pilot's commissioner and Dominican consul for twenty years, and a member of the Legislative Board for the last two years of his life; in recognition of all these services he was given the equivalent of a state funeral.

The *Royal Standard* was continued by Hugh H. Hutchings, one of his two sons, who had previously directed the paper while his father was abroad on business in 1888. At first he made few changes in the newspaper apart from increasing the amount of advertising it contained, by means of a one-page supplement which became more or less a regular feature. When a challenge to his monopoly of printing in Grand Turk came after two years, he was confident enough of his position to accord it a friendlier reception than the *Gazette* had given his father a generation earlier:

"Welcome, little stranger,
Into this world of danger."

On Wednesday morning last appeared the *Weekly Record*, Vol. 1, No. 1. From a prospectus issued some weeks ago we had understood this publication was to have been named the *Pelican*; we compliment the proprietors on this change for the better. Since the appearance of the *Record*, we have been puzzled to know under what particular category to place the publication of the paper. For the establishment of a newspaper there are generally two reasons: 1st, as a commercial or speculative undertaking; 2nd., to put forward, advocate and support some particular cause. The latter does not appear from the first issue; and, as for the former, had the proprietors asked the advice of any one familiar with newspaper work in Turks Islands, we are sure they would have had very discouraging answers. The rewards and emoluments of the editor of *The Royal Standard* have been *kicks* (figuratively so far as boots are concerned, of course, but most substantial and satisfying in the matter of abuse) *and half pence*—and the former in the greater proportion. If the *Record* has been started as a commercial undertaking, as a money-making concern, we have no hesitation in saying from our own experience, and from that of our honoured predecessor, that it will end in failure. Upwards of a quarter of a century ago the *Turks Islands Gazette* died of starvation; at that time, when these Islands were in a much more prosperous condition than they are today, it was generally admitted that the community was not large enough to support two newspapers. Today the community is smaller and poorer. Probably the out-put of the *Record* will not involve any heavy expenditure, as it is barely more than one half the size of *The Royal Standard*, and the cost of labour, paper and other supplies will be very much less, yet we cannot but fear that the responsibility, worry and trouble necessary for the careful and proper editing of this little journal, will have but little thanks and poorer remuneration at the hands of the public. Yet we say: go on and prosper.

(*Royal Standard* 10 Sept. 1892)

Subsequently Hutchings' tone got a little sharper, when a writer in the *Weekly Record* gave vent to "a contemptuous expression as to the so-called youth and inexperience of the Editor of the *Royal Standard*," but he was in little danger from the rival. No copies of the *Weekly Record* appear to have survived, and after about eighteen months it ceased publication: "Since the beginning of the year the *St. Christopher Gazette*, the *Nassau Times*, the *Grenada People* and the Turks Island *Colonial Record* have dropped out of existence" (*Royal Standard* 5 May 1894).

By the end of January 1898 the isolation of the Turks Islands was no more, as the connection with the outside world by the lines of the Direct West India Cable Company, mooted for many years, had become an established fact. Reliance on news from the outside, through papers left by passing ships, was a thing of the past. The first use of the Cable Company for foreign news came with the *Maine* incident, and the outbreak of the Spanish-American war; thereafter all foreign news appeared under the credit line "By Direct West India Cable."

At the same time, the interest of the *Royal Standard* declined. Hugh Hutchings was primarily a merchant, having in 1891 purchased a general store "Under the Awning" and a haberdashers "The Millinery." To an increasing extent the columns of the *Royal Standard* became a vehicle for advertising his stock in these two enterprises. From January 1896 the paper was published in a larger format, with a five-column page of 24″ x 15″ approx., instead of the three-column 19″ x 12″ size formerly used:

OUR NEW PRINT. In entering on the forty third year of a not uneventful life, the *Royal Standard* appears in a slightly changed form: Our slender space has been increased, the rates of subscriptions and advertising have been reduced, and every effort will be made to ensure the increased usefulness and popularity of the paper. All of this costs money, and we have placed the price at a figure as low as we possibly can, our *free list* has been blotted out, and subscriptions will for the future be billed quarterly. Attention is directed to the fact that a special discount of 25 per cent will be allowed on all yearly subscriptions paid in advance.

Our policy in the past has, we hope, earned the confidence of our readers. We trust our venture will meet with the approval and increased patronage of the public.

(*Royal Standard*, 4 Jan 1896)

In its new form, the subscription was $4 per year, with advertisements charged at 6d per column inch, and tradesmen's notices, 2½" x 2½" weekly at £1 15s. per year. Though becoming more and more the advertising sheet for Hutchings' commercial ventures with a little news added, the paper continued successfully until the spring of 1907. But in that year, changes were introduced into the administration of Turks Islands affairs which sufficiently explain why the Institute of Jamaica's holdings of the paper (formerly Hutchings' own file copies) cease with the last issue for June 1907. Following the pattern of most of the other British colonial territories in the Caribbean, in which during the second half of the nineteenth century contract printing of official work by commercial printers had been replaced by the establishment of a Government Printing Office, in 1907 an official Printing Office was set up on Grand Turk.

On 19 April 1907 (and thereafter until the end of June) the *Royal Standard* included an advertisement asking all persons indebted to Hutchings to settle with him immediately. On 1 May a public notice appeared, stating that the Governor in Chief (i.e. of Jamaica) had appointed "H. Houston Hutchings Esq. J.P. to be Clerk to the Commissioners, Inspector of Schools and Superintendant of the Printing Office." Thereafter the statement in the *Royal Standard* imprint, that Hugh H. Hutchings was "contractor for Government Printing," ceased to appear. Without the government business to sustain the paper, it would have lost money,[3] and as soon as possible after Hutchings' official appointment had been confirmed by the Colonial Office in London (on 20 June 1907) he brought the paper to a close.[4]

3. In his comments on the *Weekly Record* Hutchings had observed that the *Royal Gazette* had died of starvation, and in many of the poorer British Caribbean colonies deprivation of government advertising or other support brought about the immediate closure of the paper. Cf. Henry Breen, *St. Lucia: Historical, Statistical and Descriptive* (London, 1844) in which (pp.265-67) he describes how a similar measure in that colony in 1831 had "the untoward effect of stifling the voice of the press . . . for a period of nearly five years. . . ."

4. These notes are based on examination of the files of the various Turks Islands newspapers now in the West India Reference Library, Institute of Jamaica. Their copies were formerly those possessed by Hugh H. Hutchings, and contain a bookplate stating they were loaned by him to the Victoria Public Library and Free Reading Room in Grand

INDEX